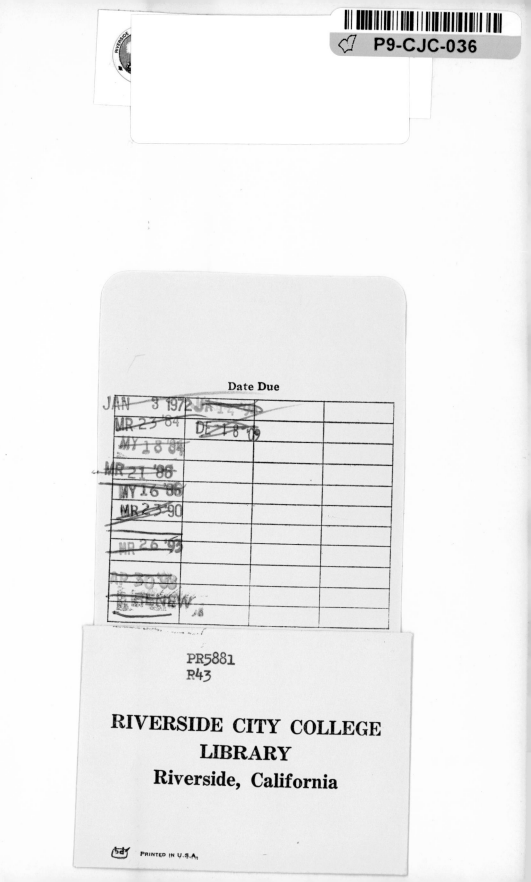

WORDSWORTH

The Chronology of the Early Years

1770–1799

Wordsworth

The Chronology of the Early Years

1770–1799

MARK L. REED

HARVARD UNIVERSITY PRESS

CAMBRIDGE, MASSACHUSETTS

1967

© Copyright 1967 by the President and Fellows of Harvard College

n by Oxford University Press, London

Publication of this book has been aided by a
grant from the Hyder Edward Rollins Fund

Library of Congress Catalog Card Number: 66–21344

Printed in the United States of America

for

Frederick A. Pottle

Preface

THE project of which the present volume represents the first step is not a new one. It was born over two decades ago in the mind of Frederick A. Pottle. Basic groundwork was laid in the early 1940's by graduate students of Professor Pottle's (several now distinguished as scholars in various fields of literature, including Wordsworth), who prepared under his direction a series of short chronologies covering Wordsworth's entire life by periods of a few years (a major exception was the unified treatment of the years 1770–1789). The original studies covering the years dealt with in the present volume were compiled by J. R. Baird (1770–1789), Selby Hanssen (1790–1794), and Lawrence Willson (1795–1799). When James Boswell put an end to hopes of Professor Pottle's completing the project, the work passed to Robert Daniel, who began the process of bringing the materials on Wordsworth's first thirty years into accordance with recent scholarship, but was then in turn prevented from continuing. I have had the honor to be allowed by Professors Pottle and Daniel to take over from that point. My own efforts have been simply to supplement their aims: to note the relevant implications of the most modern texts of Wordsworth's writings, to take into account useful discoveries of recent research, and to include whatever information of possible value I have been able to add through my own studies, especially of manuscript materials.

The extent and diversity of my debts for information and aid over many years from friends, scholars, and institutions can hardly be suggested, much less adequately represented, by either my notes or the following remarks. Professor Pottle, who kindly and tolerantly directed my first efforts, undertaken as a Scholar of the House at Yale College, at extended discussion of Wordsworth, has not only allowed me to carry on the present project but has given much time for valuable comment, correction, and encouragement. I owe warm thanks to Professor Daniel. Herschel C. Baker and Walter Jackson Bate directed

vii

the compilation of an early portion of the present volume, covering the years 1770–1791, in the form of a doctoral dissertation for Harvard University. Their assistance in that project is a minor part of the debts I owe both, and Professor Baker's patience in discussing the stylistic problems that the work has posed is responsible for much of whatever order and clarity the book now possesses. It would be difficult to express my gratitude adequately for the unsparing contribution of time, care, information, suggestion, and every other description of help I have had from Miss Carol Landon, C. Y. Lang, David Perkins, and Jonathan Wordsworth.

Research abroad has centered on the valuable resources of the Dove Cottage Library, to the Trustees of which I am most grateful for permission to make use of the unpublished materials there. For many personal as well as scholarly and official favors I owe very special thanks to the Chairman of the Dove Cottage Trustees, Basil Willey, and the Secretary, Mrs. Mary Moorman. The loss to my work, and to scholarship in general, in the deaths in early 1961 of Miss Helen Darbishire and Mrs. J. P. Hogan, both so generous of advice and attention, is irreplaceable. To Mr. J. P. Hogan, who allowed me to make further use of his late wife's notes and other scholarly materials after her death, I am more grateful than I can say. Mrs. Hogan showed me writings and information from T. W. Thompson that incorporated several items of chronological interest used below; I am indebted to Mr. Thompson's general permission to Mrs. Hogan to convey such information to others at her discretion, and regret having been unable to establish contact with him personally.

I wish it were possible to thank, with the completeness each deserves, the following institutions and their staffs: Archives Nationales, Paris; Archives de la Préfecture de la Police, Paris; Assay Master and Assay Office, Birmingham; Bibliothèque Nationale, Paris; Birmingham Public Library; Bristol University Library; British Museum; Cambridge University Library; Cornell University Library, especially the Cornell Wordsworth Collection; Dr. Williams Library; Duke University Library; Fitzwilliam Museum Library; Harvard University Library; Hatfield College, University of Durham; Keele University Library; Pembroke College Library; Pierpont Morgan Library; Princeton University Library; St. John's College Library; Trinity College

Preface

Library; Tullie House Library, Carlisle, especially for permission to examine and use information from the Diary of James Losh; University of North Carolina Library; Victoria and Albert Museum; Wedgwood Museum, Barlaston; Yale University Library.

For varied and extensive favors, scholarly and personal, I owe great thanks to: Lord Abinger; Mrs. Walter Baker; the Reverend J. S. Boys Smith; Herbert Cahoon; Miss Nesta Clutterbuck, librarian of the Dove Cottage Library; Miss Margaret Crum; Mrs. Dorothy Wordsworth Dickson; Lawrence G. Evans; John Finch; Albert Friedman; Major David Gibson-Watt; E. L. Griggs; E. R. Hardy; George Mills Harper; A. H. Healey; C. Roy Hudleston; Bishop C. Hunt; the Reverend John Jackson; Miss Phoebe Johnson, former librarian of the Dove Cottage Library; B. C. Jones; Mrs. C. Y. Lang; the Reverend John E. Lee; J. R. MacGillivray; Mrs. Basil Marsden-Smedley; J. B. Meriwether; the Venerable W. E. A. Pugh; Eric Robinson; John Rothney; Ben Ross Schneider; Chester L. Shaver; Floyd Stoddard; Mr. and Mrs. Robert Townsend; W. Tynemouth; Robert Voitle; George Watson; Mrs. Siegfried Wenzel; John Wilson of the Halifax Antiquarian Society; Miss Jane Wisely; R. S. Woof.

Essential assistance toward the completion of the first volume of this study and pursuit of research for the later volumes has been provided by a Fulbright scholarship, a Frank Knox Memorial fellowship, a grant from the American Philosophical Society, a grant from the University of North Carolina–Duke Cooperative Program in the Humanities, and grants from the University of North Carolina Research Council. I hope that what follows can in some measure justify such kindness and generosity.

In the late stages of preparation of this volume I was kindly allowed by Chester L. Shaver and The Clarendon Press to examine page proofs of Professor Shaver's forthcoming revision of the De Selincourt *Early Letters*. Information taken from this source is designated by the abbreviation *EY* and the page number indicated by the proof.

Last and best thanks to my wife Martha, who gave the most help (as well as the most kinds of help) of all.

M.R.

ix

Contents

I like to be particular in dates,
Not only of the age, and year, but moon;
    They are a sort of post-house, where the Fates
Change horses, making history change its tune,
    Then spur away o'er empires and o'er states,
Leaving at last not much besides chronology.
                    Don Juan, I, 818–823

Introduction

IF A full-scale chronology is desirable for any English author, Wordsworth's claim to such treatment is disproportionately large. The greatness of his stature in absolute terms abides no question, and the fact that his development took place in a pattern definable in chronological terms is an assumption of every major critical study since Legouis' *La Jeunesse de Wordsworth*. The most compelling aspect of the claim is the enduring excitement, complexity, and suggestiveness of the relationships between the facts of Wordsworth's personal experience and the character of its treatment in his poetry. For the subject matter of his poems reflects his personal experience, or says that it does (the distinction must be kept clear), in degree unparalleled in any English poet of similar importance. That chronologies are in fact desirable for other writers should not, however, require lengthy argument. A list of dates may in instances be, as *Don Juan* implies, only the last trace of the gallop of the Fates across the achievement of man, but where the achievement still survives, it can plainly be something of greater worth.

Each scholarly or critical approach to literature has its own degree of dependence on other approaches and on information not directly literary at all. Some kinds of literary studies clearly need no chronological assistance. In commonly accepted terms of modern criticism, to take an obvious instance, the reading of a work of literature *as* itself depends only on the work of literature. Information not contained or referred to there serves the function, in analysis, of ornament or analogue, although the critic's original response to the work may have involved, and have been assisted and enlarged by, recollections of many kinds from his past life and reading. The symbolic function of Spenser's variously rephrased refrain "That all the woods shal answer and theyr eccho ring" is amply defined by the interrelationships of the personal, the physical, the spiritual, and the musical elsewhere in the *Epithalamion*, even if knowledge of other Spenserian woods—like those inhabited by the monster Error and those that sheltered Una's rescuers,

I

the good-natured and educable satyrs, in Book I of *The Faerie Queene*—enables readier apprehension of the line's full force. Proper use of modes of criticism that explain or evaluate literature in terms of external standards or bodies of thought may, likewise, in some instances depend on outside information—chronological or otherwise—and in some instances not. A play of Shakespeare may be evaluated apart from any historical considerations as philosophically consistent or inconsistent, successful or unsuccessful, by standards of Marxist doctrine; large areas of Blake may be illuminated by the use of Freudian terminology and frames of reference. Alternatively, serious attempts to explain certain aspects of *Hamlet* as the result of Shakespeare's reading of *Das Kapital* or certain aspects of *Jerusalem* as the result of Blake's reading of the *Introductory Lectures* would not be scholarship but foolishness.

Mature scholarship of any sort must be based on accurate awareness of the attainable facts concerning the subject being examined. Chances of reaching the goal, nevertheless, seem to be diminishing rapidly in the field of English literature. Direct consideration of a work on its own terms and a number of other types of analysis or evaluation independent of temporal relationships have attained levels of sophistication where a reader not already committed exclusively to the approach in question seldom dare aspire. Any kind of study or critical mode to which use of dates, biography, or relative order of events or writings is integral must face troubles created not only by dearth of knowledge but abundance of attempts to provide it. The quantity of research presently in published form about almost any great English or American writer forbids even the biographer to attempt presentation and consideration of all immediately relevant known facts; most of the information he does present cannot—and ordinarily should not—be in settled methodical form. The potential helpfulness of a systematically chronological collection of primary information toward more rapid and efficient establishment of facts, dates, and order of events must be, in these circumstances, abundantly clear. It is safe to suggest that a need for such studies is likely to be felt increasingly. It may, indeed, not be purely fanciful to hope for a time when the student of any major English author will have available to him a detailed chronology for an aid of day-to-day usefulness as fundamental as that of authoritative texts, a bibliography describing the works and relevant scholarship and criticism, and a biography presenting a broad factual, philosophical, psychological, and aesthetic history of the author's life and production.

The problem remains, as far as method is concerned, that even a chronologist cannot avoid engaging to some degree in a process of selection of his information. The truth is, as Algernon Moncrieff remarked, rarely pure and never simple, and the significance and importance of facts will vary with the needs and interests of the beholder; almost any fact may prove valuable. But every sight the writer under study must have seen, every book or newspaper he read, every thought and every feeling he probably had, can hardly be reported or speculated upon. Likewise, concerning every author the amount and kinds of information differ, as do the reliability of the information and the amount of conjecture possible or required. Format and handling of contents must adapt themselves to the needs of the individual subject. A Chaucer chronology that confined all speculation to footnotes would consist of little else but footnotes; a chronology of Yeats that placed all definitely established facts and personal speculation alike in the main text would swell to vast length. Neither would be very convenient.

The primary criterion employed in the present study as a guideline for the selection of the contents of the main entries from the welter of information and tenable speculation that could be considered germane to Wordsworth's life and work is that of whether the facts in question are documented, one way or another, as having a direct connection with the poet or, where relevant, his near relations. When documentation of this kind exists, the materials are included (if I know of them), usually in the main text, occasionally in notes or appendices; when it does not exist, they ordinarily are not. Some exceptions are made in the case of various major political events or major landmarks in the life of Coleridge. Many times documentation has been indirect and has consisted simply of evidence sufficient to indicate the practical certainty or substantial probability of an event.

In all but a few peripheral cases effort has been made to indicate the earliest surviving sources for the information reported, and I have largely avoided listing subsequent repetition of that information on what seems ultimately the authority of the earlier source or sources cited. For the most part little appeared to be gained by extensive citation

3

of previous scholarly errors on a given point; exceptions are commonly instances when an apparent error occurs in a study that is likely to be regarded as particularly authoritative on whatever question is under consideration. Where there seems to be room for more than one opinion, or where no solution seems adequate, I have tried to put matters as straight as possible (even though the results may at times unhappily produce as much frustration as enlightenment). Frequent mention of important secondary materials, especially recent biographical discussion of an event or period, has appeared useful, particularly where the discussion provides extensive background information (this type of reference will most frequently take the reader to Mrs. Moorman's *William Wordsworth: A Biography*). Another object has been to note significant references in Wordsworth's writings to the occasion or period cited.

The main text is regularly given over to brief notations of events—as best their nature and duration can be determined—together with references to the sources of the evidence for them and appropriate cross references, including occasional allusion to secondary materials of special interest. Where discussion is called for, it is placed in the notes or, in a few especially long instances, in appendices. Some types of information are not normally placed in the text at all. With a few exceptions writings of Wordsworth not capable of being dated so specifically as within a given year are omitted, although all writings of appreciable length of which I know (excluding a few juvenile fragments) appear in the general chronological list of the poet's works that precedes the main body of the text. And two important areas within Wordsworth's life (in addition to the materials cited above) have not received systematic treatment: no methodical effort is made at listing Wordsworth's friends at a given time except where they share a part in a specific event; or at listing Wordsworth's reading except where the reading has a specific bearing on the solution of some other problem. Systematic speculation concerning letters that do not survive has seemed justified only occasionally.

So far as the chronology has a model, it is the *Chronologie critique de la vie et des œuvres de Rousseau* by L. J. Courtois (*Annales de la Société J.-J. Rousseau*, 1923). The present work follows Courtois mainly in presenting only basic factual information (or whatever approximation of it is attainable) in the text and placing discussion and peripheral comment in footnotes. Major departures from Courtois are the use of either abbreviated titles or full references in the description of sources instead of numbers corresponding to a complete listing of sources; the general chronological list of the writer's works; and the extensive use of appendices for long discussions.

The stylistic conventions employed throughout will cause little confusion after brief acquaintance, but the following brief remarks may be of assistance.

1. Square brackets. Square brackets enclose materials which have their origin in, or seem largely to depend on, editorial interpretation, regardless of the degree of probability for the date or event which the relevant evidence suggests. They also enclose materials which have undergone a large amount of editorial organization or involve extended editorial comment; see, for example, entries 1783:10 or 1795:9. And they are used, often with additional qualification, when the accuracy of the source for the materials enclosed seems somehow (perhaps only because of the compiler's own ignorance of the original source) open to question on the basis of other relevant considerations; see, for example, 1779:5 or 1790:100. Square brackets are not used when the information given is simply taken from—not interpreted or inferred from—the source, and when no evidence points to inaccuracy in the source. (It is obvious that some cases will exist where absence of proof of inaccuracy constitutes no guarantee of accuracy.) Where dates have been precisely defined in the main text, I have not hesitated at times to dispense with some square brackets in citation of dates in notes or appendices if it seemed that doing so would increase ease of reading.

2. Expression of degrees of probability. The number of degrees of probability in matters of dates and events recorded has necessitated a flexible approach in this regard, and no limited set of conventions has sufficed for all needs. The primary rule has been to aim at clarity in the individual entries while maintaining as much stylistic consistency as reasonably possible. The phrases most commonly used for expression of degrees of probability are "probably," "perhaps," and "possibly." The words as just listed represent a descending order of probability, with "probably" indicating greatest likelihood. Other phrases, as a rule self-explanatory, have been used as need has suggested. Most

instances in which probability rather than certainty is involved will have been based on some kind of editorial assumption, and hence appear in square brackets.

3. Descriptions of periods of time. A dash between two dates indicates that the period bounded by the two dates will be discussed. A date followed by a parenthetically enclosed dash and date indicates that a specific date is to be dealt with first, then next, within the same entry, a larger period beginning with that date. See, for example, 1786:4. Any other parenthetical material will be explained by the text or notes. For a day or other limited period not definable otherwise than as falling between two other dates a "between——and——" style is employed.

It should be added that throughout capitalization of titles of works has been standardized, and superscript letters in quotations have been brought down to the line.

Short Forms of Citation

Alfoxden Nb	Notebook used at Alfoxden, Dove Cottage Papers MS Verse 19
Alger	J. G. Alger, *Englishmen in the French Revolution* (London, 1889)
AM	*The Ancient Mariner*
App crit	*Apparatus criticus*
Autobiog Mem	Autobiographical Memoranda dictated by Wordsworth, Nov 1847. Pub. *Mem* I, 1–17
AV	Emile Legouis, *William Wordsworth and Annette Vallon* (London, 1922)
AW	Ann Wordsworth, mother of Wordsworth
Aza P	Azariah Pinney
Bateson	F. W. Bateson, *Wordsworth. A Reinterpretation* (London, 1956)
Beatty *RP*	*Wordsworth. Representative Poems*, ed. Arthur Beatty (Garden City, 1937)
BL	*Biographia Literaria.* Unless otherwise noted, the reference is to the edition of J. Shawcross (Oxford, 1958)
Blanshard	Frances Blanshard, *Portraits of Wordsworth* (Ithaca, 1959)
BM	British Museum
BNYPL	*Bulletin of The New York Public Library*
CCC	Christopher Crackanthorpe Cookson (1745–1799), from 1792 surnamed Crackanthorpe, uncle of W[1]
Christabel Nb	Christabel Notebook, Dove Cottage Papers MS Verse 18
Cornell	*The Cornell Wordsworth Collection*, comp. G. H. Healey (Ithaca, 1957)
Cottle *Recollections*	Joseph Cottle, *Early Recollections; Chiefly Relating to the Late Samuel Taylor Coleridge* (London, 1837)

---

[1] The spelling "Crackanthorpe," as used by Burke's *Landed Gentry*, is regularly employed throughout, although various records drop the final "e."

Cottle *Reminiscences*	Joseph Cottle, *Reminiscences of Samuel Taylor Coleridge and Robert Southey* (London, 1848)
CRH	C. Roy Hudleston. Where used alone, or with reference not explained elsewhere, indicates transcriptions made by Mr. Hudleston of Wordsworth family records and materials in custody of Messrs. Bleaymire and Shepherd, Penrith
CRH *Transactions*	C. Roy Hudleston, "Ann Crackanthorpe: Wordsworth's Great-aunt," *Transactions of the Cumberland and Westmorland Antiquarian and Archaeological Society* N.S. LX (1960), 135–55
CW	Christopher Wordsworth, brother of Wordsworth
CWAA Soc	Cumberland and Westmorland Antiquarian and Archaeological Society
CWAA Soc *Transactions*	*Transactions of the Cumberland and Westmorland Antiquarian and Archaeological Society*
Daniel *MLR*	R. W. Daniel, "The Publication of 'Lyrical Ballads,'" *Modern Language Review* XXXIII (1938), 406–10
DC; DCP	Dove Cottage; Dove Cottage Papers
DNB	*Dictionary of National Biography*
DS	*Descriptive Sketches*
DW	Dorothy Wordsworth, sister of Wordsworth
DWJ	*Journals of Dorothy Wordsworth*, ed. Ernest de Selincourt (London, 1959). 2 vols
Eagleston	A. J. Eagleston, "Wordsworth, Coleridge, and the Spy," *Coleridge, Studies by Several Hands*, ed. Edmund Blunden and E. L. Griggs (London, 1934), 73–87
EdS	Ernest de Selincourt
EdS *DW*	Ernest de Selincourt, *Dorothy Wordsworth, A Biography* (Oxford, 1933)
EKC	E. K. Chambers, *Samuel Taylor Coleridge* (Oxford, 1938)
EKC *RES*	E. K. Chambers, "The Date of Coleridge's *Kubla Khan*," *Review of English Studies* XI (1935), 78–80
EL	*Early Letters of William and Dorothy Wordsworth*, ed. Ernest de Selincourt (Oxford, 1935). Unless otherwise stated, numbers immediately following this abbreviation refer to page numbers (not to numbers of the letters)

Evans and Pinney	Bergen Evans and Hester Pinney, "Racedown and the Wordsworths," *Review of English Studies* VIII (1932), 1–18
EW	*An Evening Walk*
EY	See page ix
Fink	Z. S. Fink, *The Early Wordsworthian Milieu* (Oxford, 1958)
First Acquaintance	William Hazlitt, *My First Acquaintance with Poets*, in *The Complete Works of William Hazlitt*, ed. P. P. Howe (London, 1930–34), XVII, 106–22
FV	*The Female Vagrant*
G&S	*Guilt and Sorrow*
GCL	General Chronological List of Writings, below
GGW	Gordon G. Wordsworth, grandson of the poet
GGW *Cornhill*	Gordon G. Wordsworth, "The Boyhood of Wordsworth," *Cornhill Magazine* CXXI (1920), 410–20
GGW *Some Notes*	Gordon G. Wordsworth, *Some Notes on the Wordsworths of Peniston and Their Aumbry* (Ambleside, 1929)
GGW *TLS*	Gordon G. Wordsworth in the *Times Literary Supplement* XXV (22 July 1926), 496
Gill Diary	Diary of Joseph Gill, caretaker at Racedown, in Papers of the Pinney family, on deposit in the Bristol University Library
Godwin Diary	Diary of William Godwin, Microfilms of Abinger Collection, Duke University Library
Grosart	*The Prose Works of William Wordsworth*, ed. A. B. Grosart (London, 1876). 3 vols
Hale White	*A Description of the Wordsworth and Coleridge Manuscripts in the Possession of Mr. T. Norton Longman*, ed. W. Hale White (London, 1897)
Hanson	Lawrence Hanson, *The Life of S. T. Coleridge: the Early Years* (London, 1938)
Hardy	Charles Hardy, *A Register of Ships Employed in the Service of the East India Company*, rev. H. C. Hardy (London, 1811)
Harper	G. M. Harper, *William Wordsworth, His Life, Work, and Influence* (New York, 1916). 2 vols
Harper (R)	G. M. Harper, the same, revised (New York, 1929). 1 vol

HCR	Henry Crabb Robinson
HCR *Diary*	*Diary, Reminiscences, and Correspondence of Henry Crabb Robinson*, ed. Thomas Sadler (London, 1869). 3 vols
HCR & W Circle	*The Correspondence of Henry Crabb Robinson with the Wordsworth Circle*, ed. E. J. Morley (Oxford, 1927). 2 vols
HUL	Harvard University Library
IF; IF notes	Isabella Fenwick; notes dictated to her by Wordsworth
JEGP	*Journal of English and Germanic Philology*
JFP Sr.; JFP Jr.	John Frederick Pinney Sr.; John Frederick Pinney Jr.
Joyce	Herbert Joyce, *History of the British Post Office* (London, 1893)
JP, JPM	Jane Pollard, later (1795) Jane Pollard Marshall, friend of Dorothy Wordsworth
JRM	James R. MacGillivray. Where used alone refers to JRM's unpublished Harvard University doctoral dissertation, "Wordsworth and His Revolutionary Acquaintances," 1930
JRM *RES*	James R. MacGillivray, "An Early Poem and Letter by Wordsworth," *Review of English Studies* N.S. V (1954), 62–65
JW; JW Sr.	John Wordsworth, brother of Wordsworth; John Wordsworth Sr., father of Wordsworth
Lamb *Letters*	*The Letters of Charles Lamb, to Which Are Added Those of His Sister Mary Lamb*, ed. E. V. Lucas (London, 1935). 3 vols
Landon *BNYPL*	Carol Landon, "Wordsworth's Racedown Period: Some Uncertainties Resolved," *Bulletin of the New York Public Library* LXVIII (1964), 100–09
Landon *RES*	Carol Landon, "Wordsworth, Coleridge, and the *Morning Post*: An Early Version of 'The Seven Sisters,'" *Review of English Studies* N.S. XI (1960), 392–402
LB	*Lyrical Ballads*
LB 1798	*Lyrical Ballads, with a Few Other Poems*, 1798. Unless otherwise stated, the issue referred to is that of J. and A. Arch, London
LB 1800	*Lyrical Ballads, with Other Poems* (London, 1800). 2 vols

LB 1802	*Lyrical Ballads, with Pastoral and Other Poems* (London, 1802). 2 vols
Litchfield	R. B. Litchfield, *Tom Wedgwood* (London, 1903)
Lloyd	D. Myrddin Lloyd, "Wordsworth and Wales," *National Library of Wales Journal* VI (1950), 338–50
LLSYT	*Lines Left upon a Seat in a Yew-tree*
Losh Diary	Diary of James Losh, in Tullie House Library, Carlisle
LY	*The Letters of William and Dorothy Wordsworth, The Later Years,* ed. Ernest de Selincourt (Oxford, 1939). 3 vols
Margoliouth	H. M. Margoliouth, *Wordsworth and Coleridge* (Oxford, 1953)
Margoliouth *N&Q*	H. M. Margoliouth, "Wordsworth and Coleridge: Dates in May and June, 1798," *Notes and Queries* CXCVIII (1953), 352–54
MC	*The Morning Chronicle* (London)
Mem	Christopher Wordsworth, *Memoirs of William Wordsworth* (London, 1851). 2 vols
Mem (R)	The same, ed. Henry Reed (Boston, 1851). 2 vols. This edition is cited only when its readings or pagination differ from *Mem*
MH	Mary Hutchinson, later (1802) Mary Wordsworth, wife of Wordsworth
MLN	*Modern Language Notes*
MLR	*Modern Language Review*
Moorman I	Mary Moorman, *William Wordsworth, A Biography, The Early Years, 1770–1803* (Oxford, 1957; reprinted from corrected sheets, 1965)
Moorman *Transactions*	Mary Moorman, "Ann Tyson's Ledger: An Eighteenth-Century Account-book," *Transactions of the Cumberland and Westmorland Antiquarian and Archaeological Society* N.S. L (1950), 152–63
MP	*The Morning Post* (London)
MS	Manuscript. Any manuscript not otherwise described is in the Dove Cottage Papers
MW	Mary Wordsworth (formerly Mary Hutchinson), wife of Wordsworth
MW *Letters*	*The Letters of Mary Wordsworth 1800–1855,* ed. Mary E. Burton (Oxford, 1958)

MY	*The Letters of William and Dorothy Wordsworth, The Middle Years*, ed. Ernest de Selincourt (Oxford, 1937). 2 vols
Nb	Notebook. Any notebook not otherwise described is in the Dove Cottage Papers
Nb 18A	Dove Cottage Papers MS Verse 18A
N&Q	*Notes and Queries*
OCB	*The Old Cumberland Beggar*
OMT	*Old Man Travelling. Animal Tranquillity and Decay*
Paterson	Paterson's *Roads* (London), 1799
PB	*Peter Bell*
Peek	K. M. Peek, *Wordsworth in England* (Bryn Mawr, 1943)
Penrith	*The Parish Registers of St. Andrew's, Penrith*, comp. J. F. Haswell (*Cumberland and Westmorland Antiquarian and Archaeological Society*, 1938——). 5 vols pub
PMLA	*Publications of the Modern Language Association*
Poems 1815	*Poems by William Wordsworth* (London, 1815). 2 vols
Poole *B and B*	[Thomas Poole,] "John Walford," *Bristol and Bath Magazine* II (1833), 168–79
PP	Papers of the Pinney family, on deposit in the Bristol University Library
PR	Parish Register
Prel	*The Prelude*, ed. Ernest de Selincourt, revised by Helen Darbishire (Oxford, 1959)
Prel	*The Prelude*, version of 1805, text of Prel
Prel$_2$	*The Prelude*, version of 1850, text of Prel
Prel (EdS)	*The Prelude*, ed. Ernest de Selincourt (Oxford, 1950)
PW	*Poetical Works*. Where used alone, refers to *The Poetical Works of William Wordsworth*, ed. Ernest de Selincourt and Helen Darbishire (Oxford, 1940–49). 5 vols
PW (Dowden)	*The Poetical Works of William Wordsworth*, ed. Edward Dowden (London, 1892–93). 7 vols
PW (Knight, 1882–89)	*The Poetical Works of William Wordsworth*, ed. William Knight (Edinburgh, 1882–89). 11 vols
PW (Knight, 1896)	*The Poetical Works of William Wordsworth*, ed. William Knight (London, 1896). 8 vols
PW (Oxford)	*The Poetical Works of Wordsworth*, ed. Thomas

	Hutchinson, revised by Ernest de Selincourt (Oxford, 1936). Oxford Standard Authors edition
PW (Smith)	*The Poems of William Wordsworth*, ed. N. C. Smith (London, 1908). 3 vols
Racedown Nb	Notebook used at Racedown, Dove Cottage Papers MS Verse 12
RC	*The Ruined Cottage*
Reed *UTQ*	Mark L. Reed, "Wordsworth, Coleridge, and the 'Plan' of the *Lyrical Ballads*," *University of Toronto Quarterly* XXXIV (1964–65), 238–53
RES	*Review of English Studies*
Robertson	Eric Robertson, *Wordsworthshire* (London, 1911)
RW; RW of Branthwaite; RW of Whitehaven	Richard Wordsworth, brother of Wordsworth; Richard Wordsworth of Branthwaite (1752–1816), first cousin; Richard Wordsworth of Whitehaven (1733–1794), uncle
Sandford	Mrs. Henry Sandford, *Thomas Poole and His Friends* (London, 1888). 2 vols
Sara C	Sara Coleridge, wife of Samuel Taylor Coleridge
Schneider	Ben Ross Schneider, *Wordsworth's Cambridge Education* (Cambridge, England, 1957)
Scott *Admissions*	Sir R. F. Scott, *Admissions to the College of St. John the Evangelist* (Cambridge, England, 1893–1931). 4 vols
Shaver *RES*	Chester L. Shaver, "Wordsworth's Vaudracour and Wilkinson's Wanderer," *Review of English Studies* N.S. XII (1961), 55–57
Shaver *Transactions*	Chester L. Shaver, "The Griffith Family: Wordsworth's Kinsmen," *Transactions of the Cumberland and Westmorland Antiquarian and Archaeological Society* N.S. LXIII (1963), 199–230
Smith	Elsie Smith, *An Estimate of Wordsworth by His Contemporaries* (Oxford, 1932)
Smyser *PMLA*	Jane W. Smyser, "Coleridge's Use of Wordsworth's Juvenilia," *PMLA* LXV (1950), 419–26
Some Letters	*Some Letters of the Wordsworth Family*, ed. L. N. Broughton (Ithaca, 1942)
SP	*Salisbury Plain*
STC	Samuel Taylor Coleridge
STCL	*Collected Letters of Samuel Taylor Coleridge*, ed. E. L. Griggs (Oxford, 1956——). 4 vols pub

STCNB	*The Notebooks of Samuel Taylor Coleridge*, ed. Kathleen Coburn (New York, 1957——). 2 vols (each in 2 parts) pub
STCPW	*The Complete Poetical Works of Samuel Taylor Coleridge*, ed. E. H. Coleridge (Oxford, 1912). 2 vols
STCPW 1893	*The Poetical Works of Samuel Taylor Coleridge*, ed. J. D. Campbell (London, 1893)
Stud Phil	*Studies in Philology*
TA	*Lines Composed a Few Miles above Tintern Abbey*
TLS	London *Times Literary Supplement*
TWT	T. W. Thompson of Windermere, formerly of Hawkshead
TWT *Hawkshead Church*	T. W. Thompson, *Hawkshead Church, Chapelry and Parish* (Hawkshead, 1959)
TWT *W's Hawkshead*	T. W. Thompson, *Wordsworth's Hawkshead*, dialect play presented at Wordsworth Centenary at Hawkshead, 1950 (mimeographed copy)
V of E	*The Vale of Esthwaite*
Venn	J. A. Venn, *Alumni Cantabrigiensis* (Cambridge, England, 1922–54). Unless otherwise stated, information from this source is taken from the article on the person being discussed
W	Wordsworth. When used alone, refers to William Wordsworth
W at Cambridge	*Wordsworth at Cambridge*, a Record of the Commemoration held at St. John's College, April, 1950 (Cambridge, England, 1950)
WFD	G. M. Harper, *Wordsworth's French Daughter* (Princeton, 1921)
Woof	R. S. Woof. Where used without qualification refers to Woof's unpublished University of Toronto doctoral dissertation, "The Literary Relations of Wordsworth and Coleridge," 1959
Woof *SB*	R. S. Woof, "Wordsworth's Poetry and Stuart's Newspapers: 1797–1803," *Studies in Bibliography* XV (1962), 149–89
Woof *UTQ*	R. S. Woof, "Coleridge and Thomasina Dennis," *University of Toronto Quarterly* XXXII (1962–63), 36–54
W Soc *Transactions*	*Transactions of the Wordsworth Society* (1882–c 1886)

General Chronological List of Wordsworth's Writings with Their First Published Appearances

1. Verses on the subject of The Summer Vacation (in response to school assignment by William Taylor; not surviving)
   [Probably composed after 20 Sept, perhaps in early Oct, 1784. (See Appendix III.)]

2. Fragments: Drafts, mostly or all for a poem on a heroic theme, quoted Fink 76, 80, 86, 88, 95
   [Possibly written as early as 1784 (probably after 20 Sept)–1785; probably written 1787 or 1788. (See Appendix V.)]

3. Verses on the subject of the arrest of the Castlehows (composition uncertain; possibly never existed)
   [Possibly composed autumn 1784, or an indeterminate time after. (See Appendix III.)]

4. Verses on the subject of The Return to School, perhaps entitled *The Pleasure of Change* (not surviving)
   [Perhaps composed between c 20 Dec 1784 and c 20 Jan 1785. (See Appendix III; 1784:16.)]

5. *Lines Written as a School Exercise at Hawkshead*
   [Probably composed in or shortly before June 1785. Almost certainly composed by that month. (See 1785:4.)] Pub. *Mem.*

6. *Septimius and Acme*
   [Probably composed between 1786 and 1791 inclusive, very likely among the earlier of these years. A remote chance may exist that the poem was written during the Racedown period (26 Sept 1795—probably 2 July 1797). (See Appendix IV.)] Pub. *PW.*

7. *From the Greek*
   [Probably composed between 1786 and 1791 inclusive, very likely

15

close to 1786. Almost certainly composed by 23 May 1794. (See Appendix IV.)] Pub. *MP* 13 Feb 1798. (See Woof *SB* 165.)

8. Fragments:
   a. "Derwent Again I Hear Thy Evening Call" (unpublished sonnet fragment apparently entitled *On Returning to a Cottage, a Favorite Residence* [? *of the Author,*] *after a Long Absence*)
   b. Drafts concerning the death of a woman, resembling *Address to the Ocean* (unpublished)
   [Possibly written during late school years (1786–1787), college years (1787–1791), or the Racedown period (26 Sept 1795–probably 2 July 1797). A remote chance may exist that at least *a* was written in early 1794; *b* almost certainly written before 21 Nov 1796 (see 1796:70).][1]

9. Fragment: *To Melpomene* (unpublished)
   [Probably written 1786 or 1787.][2]

10. *The Death of a Starling*
    Lesbia
    [*Beauty and Moonlight, an Ode,*] *Fragment*
    [Perhaps composed 1786.][3] *The Death of a Starling* pub. *PW*. *Lesbia* pub.

[1] These fragments appear in MS Verse 4. Miss Landon has provided the title of *a* (I have silently corrected W's punctuation). While the subject is uncertain, W's reference is probably to a visit to Windy Brow or Cockermouth, and before early 1794 he had had no opportunity to return to either place "after a long absence." Verse 4, however, is not known to have been in use in early 1794, or between then and the Racedown period. W may have imaginatively protracted a relatively short absence into a "long" for poetic purposes or have been envisioning a future return. The date of *b* is based simply on known times of main use of Verse 4.

[2] This brief fragment of an ode, in iambic tetrameter couplets, appears toward the end of Nb Verse 4. Style and autograph suggest that it is schoolboy work of the same general period as *V of E* and other early efforts in this verse pattern.

[3] *The Death of a Starling* is found in a fair MS copy in Verse 4 following the part of *Anacreon* that appears on the first surviving pages. It appears to have been copied into the Nb about the same time as *Anacreon*. Since the latter, in the form in which it was originally copied into the Nb, was surely composed not later than 7 Aug, and since no real indication exists even that *The Starling* was composed after *Anacreon*, there seems no reason to disagree with EdS's conjecture of 1786 as the date for the poem (*PW* I, 367, and Moorman I, 58, also give this date).

Woof *SB* 169 and Miss Landon note that *Lesbia* (dated by EdS 1795–1797 from its appearance in the Racedown Nb) must also have been among the fair copies at the

MP 11 Apr 1798. (See Woof *SB* 169.) [*Beauty and Moonlight*] pub. after revision (by STC) as *Lewti MP* 13 Apr 1798. (See Woof *SB* 170.)

11. *Anacreon*
[Probably composed on or shortly before 7 Aug 1786. Almost certainly composed by that date. (See 1786:14.)] Pub. *PW*.

12. *The Dog. An Idyllium*
[Perhaps written late 1786; probably in existence by end of 1787.][4] Pub. *PW*.

---

[4] *The Dog. An Idyllium* is the next fair copy in Verse 4 after [*Beauty and Moonlight*], as indicated *PW* I, 367 (see GCL 10n). The next fair copy in the Nb, the first version of *Dirge*, probably dates from 1787. *The Dog* was probably composed before the end of 1787; yet one can only conjecture that it postdates *Anacreon*. The autograph resembles that of the preceding fair copies, although the end of the poem (from "If while I gazed") appears to have been copied in at another time from the lines preceding it. Drafts of other materials for the poem appear toward the end of the Nb. Work on *The Dog* might have extended over some time; one hesitates to give it a more specific date than that suggested above. (Moorman I, 65–66, suggests that the subject of these verses may have drowned not long before W left Hawkshead, but happily *Prel* IV.84–120 and *Prel*$_2$ IV.93–130 indicate that "the Dog" was enjoying a cheerful old age when the poet returned to Hawkshead in the summer of 1788.)

---

beginning of Verse 4. Only two lines remain, at the top of one of the early pages; the three preceding pages have been torn out. The autograph and spacing of the lines leave little doubt that some version of the poem was copied into the Nb near the time of the (originally) fair copies immediately preceding and following it (*The Starling* and [*Beauty and Moonlight*]). The same conclusions that were reached about the date of *The Starling* apply in this case.

[*Beauty and Moonlight*] is given a similar date for the same reasons. The MS appears directly after that of *The Starling* and *Lesbia* in Verse 4, and seems to have been copied in about the same time. I do not, however, think there is any reason for supposing with EdS (*PW* I, 367) that W is particularly likely to have written the poem after returning to school from the summer holidays. The poem could be based on memories of MH, as EdS suggests (on other "Marys" W may have known, or known of, during the Hawkshead years see Bateson 65–67 and note on *A Ballad*, Appendix II, C5), but W hardly need have been parted from her to feel—or imagine he felt—the sentiments he expresses.

17

13. *The Vale of Esthwaite*
    Extract from the Conclusion of a Poem, Composed in Anticipation of Leaving School (a version is composed as part of *V of E*)
    [Parts of *V of E* perhaps composed in 1786. Bulk of composition probably spring–summer 1787. *V of E* version of *Extract* probably composed spring or summer 1787. Some composition probably continued into early 1788.][5] *V of E* pub. *PW*. *Extract* pub. *Poems* 1815.

[5] The only indication given by EdS directly useful in dating the composition of the longest of W's early poems is the quotation (*PW* I, 368) of the title which W places before a number of extracts from the work copied into Nb Verse 4: "*Various Extracts from the Vale of Esthwaite, A Poem, Written at Hawkshead in the Spring and Summer 1787.*" Fink 19 assumes that such was the date of composition; EdS in *The Early Wordsworth* (London, 1936) 27n and Bateson 212 make the same assumption. Moorman I, 60, places the work "during his last two years at school." Further consideration and a comparison of the three Nb's in which passages of the poem appear in MS (see *PW* I, 368) suggest that certain refinements are possible in this regard.

The lines on the death of W's father and related events (418–37) could not, of course, have been written before early 1787; those on his sister (528–35) almost surely not before summer 1787. Both appear in EdS's MS A (DCP MS Verse 3). That W was hard at work on the poem "spring and summer 1787" admits no doubt. But very few of the "extracts" could have been copied before at least late summer or fall 1787. The possibility that they were copied during the winter of 1787–88 cannot be excluded as they follow after the main drafts and copies of *Dirge* in Verse 4. And work on *Dirge* did not cease before early 1788. The autograph and general appearance of the excerpts, however, suggest that *V of E* was copied in at much the same time as *The Death of a Starling*, *Lesbia*, and the like, while the *Dirge* is written in a clearly different autograph. Wherever there is any basis for the establishment of relationship in time between EdS's MS A and MS B (in Nb Verse 4) by comparison of parallel passages, the readings of B are later. The only work in the Nb containing *V of E* MS A for which a date can be suggested from internal evidence is the prose fragment in which W takes leave of Helvellyn; that subject suggests composition about the time of W's departure for Cambridge. EdS's MS C (MS Verse 5), where passages in it are parallel to passages in A or B, is clearly later than either A or B. Both around and after the "extracts" in B, furthermore, appear great numbers of corrections and drafts which must have been added after the original excerpts made not before late summer or fall 1787. C, as implied, is later than A or B, and is the MS noted by EdS (*PW* I, 369) as having "1000" (obviously referring to the line number) beside what now stands as line 241 of the printed version; the figure is indicative of the great length the poem had attained by the time of MS C, and MS C itself is heavily corrected. That MS seems to be the latest one surviving. Moorman I, 86, appears to imply that most of this copying took place at Hawkshead in late summer 1787, but it looks hardly possible that W had ceased to copy and correct C before the year 1788 was begun, and his work on the

14. Fragments:
    a. *On the Death of an Unfortunate Lady* (unpublished)
    b. *A Winter's Evening—Fragment of an Ode to Winter* (unpublished)
    c. Prose fragment concerning dreamlike shapes seen by W while lying in bed (unpublished; cf PREL 533)
    [Probably written 1787.][6]

15. Fragment: *A Tale* (prose; unpublished)
    [Possibly written summer 1787; probably written c summer 1788, 1789, or later. (See Appendix VI.)]

16. *Sonnet, on Seeing Miss Helen Maria Williams Weep at a Tale of Distress*
    [Probably composed in, certainly completed by, early 1787, before c Mar. (See 1787:7; 1787:4.)] Pub. [probably c 1 Apr 1787] in *European Magazine* for Mar 1787. (See 1787:7.)

17. *Sonnet Written by Mr. ___ Immediately after the Death of His Wife*
    [Probably composed on or shortly before 2 Mar 1787. Almost certainly composed by that date. (See 1787:4.)] Pub. *PW.*

[6] *On the Death of an Unfortunate Lady* consists of nine lines written on a quarto sheet similar to those containing *Anacreon* and *Sonnet Written by Mr. ___* (see GCL 11, 17). The autograph and ink are quite alike in all these verses, and it may be that both poems dealt with the same subject. *A Winter's Evening* appears on another similar quarto sheet and both in autograph and ink resembles *On the Death of an Unfortunate Lady* and *Sonnet Written by Mr. ___*. The other side of this sheet contains a fair copy of the last three stanzas of *A Ballad* dated 23, 24 Mar 1787.

The brief but interesting prose fragment on the dreamlike shapes that W saw while lying in bed appears in a small Nb, DCP Verse 3, occupied mostly by MS A of *V of E*. As MS A is probably entirely or almost entirely work of 1787 (see 1787:5), and as the Farewell to Helvellyn (GCL 19), the only other important entry in the Nb, appears to belong to 1787, this fragment can be conjectured to belong to that year also.

poem may well have continued into the early part of that year (see Appendix V). Some desultory composition eventually used in the poem may have taken place in 1786 (W was certainly working in iambic tetrameter couplets by 7 Aug 1786; see 1786:14); but W's "Spring and Summer 1787" may be taken as adequate indication that intensive work on the poem did not take place until then.

The thoughts forming the basis of *Extract* could perhaps have arisen in W's mind as early as late summer 1783 (see 1783:8), and he possibly made some poetic formulation of them before 1787. W dates the poem itself 1786 in his IF note to it. Both MSS A and B of *V of E*, however, contain work on these verses; in the latter MS the lines stand among the "Extracts" said to have been composed "Spring and Summer 1787." The *Extract* in something like its present form possibly dates, then, as early as 1786, but spring or summer 1787 would appear a safer guess.

18. *A Ballad*
[Probably composed on or shortly before 23, 24 Mar 1787. Almost certainly composed by those dates. (See 1787:6.)] Pub. *PW*.

19. A Farewell to Helvellyn, "What is it that tells my soul the sun is setting[?]" (Ossianic prose; unpublished)
[Perhaps composed c 23 Oct 1787. (See 1787:22.)]

20. *Lines Left upon a Seat in a Yew-tree*
[A few lines eventually used in this poem perhaps composed as early as mid-1787. Bulk of composition probably early 1797, perhaps after 8 Feb, and by July. (See 1797:3.)] [7] Pub. *LB* 1798.

21. *Dirge, Sung by a Minstrel*
    a. First version, for a boy. [Probably written late 1787. (See 1787:26.)]
    b. Second version, for a "maid." Written Jan 1788 [and possibly shortly after]. (See 1788:7.) Pub. *PW*.

22. Fragments:
    a. Drafts, developed into blank verse, of an elaborate description of a storm, comparing the storm to an eagle or condor (unpublished)
    b. Drafts describing someone's madness as the "shipwreck of a soul" (unpublished)
    [Probably written in early and/or summer 1788. (See Appendix V.)]

23. Various translations from Vergil, esp. *Georgics* (including passage cited Schneider 165, and part of *Moschus*), in heroic couplets and blank verse (in large part unpublished)

---

[7] The IF note to *Lines Left upon a Seat in a Yew-tree* states that that poem was "composed in part at school at Hawkshead." My dating is partly, thus, in deference to W, for there is only his own word to suggest that any composition took place so early. W's comment in the same note that the scene of the yew tree was a favorite walk of his "during the latter part of his school time," would imply that any attempt to write about the scene probably did not take place much, if at all, before 1786 or 1787.

EdS remarks (*PW* I, 329) that W's statement that part of *Lines Left upon a Seat in a Yew-tree* was composed "at Hawkshead" does not necessarily imply that W wrote it while still at school, for he visited Hawkshead in both 1788 and 1789. This conclusion is probably forced. W says "at school at Hawkshead," and the phrase "at school" normally indicates "while attending school as a student."

[Couplets probably written early 1788—possibly as late as summer. Blank verse probably written summer and/or autumn 1788, with some composition possibly slightly later. (See Appendix V.)]

24. *Orpheus and Eurydice* (translation from Vergil, *Georgics* IV.464–77, 485–527)
    Short prose draft forming basis for *EW* 37–42 (unpublished; see Moorman I, 115n)
    Fragment: Simile describing the terror of a shepherd (unpublished)
    [Probably written early 1788, perhaps by late spring. (See Appendix V.)] *Orpheus and Eurydice* pub. *PW*.

25. Two prose epitaphs, in MS Verse 4 (unpublished, but see *DWJ* I, 103)
    [Possibly written c early 1788, but date uncertain. (See Appendix VI.)]

26. Fragment: Blank verse toward a poem on Milton (*PW* V, 362)
    [Perhaps written c early 1788.] [8]

27. Fragment: *Cambridge to Hawkshead* (prose; see Moorman I, 105)
    [Probably written 8 June 1788. (See 1788:17.)]

28. *An Evening Walk* (see also GCL 24)
    a. Development of conception of, and early work on, *EW*
    b. Development, from blank verse to heroic couplets, of a passage describing a female vagrant freezing with her two children; the passage forms the basis for *EW* 257–300
    c. Development into heroic couplets of a description of pity, *V of E* 125–30, 139–52; the passage forms the basis of *EW* 379–88
    [Probably c summer and autumn 1788, with some composition possibly slightly later. (See Appendix V.)]
    d. Draft of lines forming basis for *EW* 125–38 (including lines on the cock based on Rosset). [Perhaps late summer or autumn 1788; possibly later, any time up to late Jan 1793. (See Appendix V; 1793:4.)]
    e. Bulk of composition. [Probably largely late 1788 and 1789, esp. summer 1789. Some composition perhaps took place later. (See Appendix V.)]

[8] This conjecture, such as it is, is made only on the basis of the probable dates of other heavily Miltonic blank verse that W wrote at Cambridge, including *The Horse*, *Moschus*, and the fragments of natural description in Verse 4. (See Appendix V.)

f. Early postpublication revisions and additions (not published by W). [Probably written between early Apr and late in the year 1794. (See 1794:7.)]

Pub. 29 Jan 1793. (See *MC* of that date.)

29. *In Part from Moschus—Lament for Bion*
[Probably written c summer and autumn 1788, with some composition possibly slightly later. (See GCL 23; Appendix V.)] Pub. *PW*.

30. Fragment: Heroic description of a warrior moving (apparently) to battle (prose; unpublished)
Description of a castle, in blank verse; the passage forms the basis of *Gothic Tale* 17–23 (unpublished)
Several fragments of natural description, in blank verse (unpublished)
[Probably written c summer 1788. (See Appendix V.)]

31. *The Horse* (translation of Vergil, *Georgics* III.75–94)
Ode to Apollo
Draft of a few lines mentioning a figure whose eyes glow as he gazes into the chasm of the "Infant Rhine" (unpublished)
[Probably written late summer or autumn 1788, but possibly slightly later. The unpublished draft less certainly of this date. (See Appendix V.)] *The Horse* and *Ode to Apollo* pub. *PW*.

32. *Written in Very Early Youth*
a. Copy, partially draft, of early version of this poem (Racedown Nb; unpublished). [Perhaps written between c late 1788 and 1791 inclusive, but possibly later—any time up to probably 2 July 1797. (See Appendix IV.)]
b. Final version. [Perhaps composed any time between c late 1788 and shortly before publication. (See Appendix IV.)]
Pub. *MP* 13 Feb 1802. (See Woof *SB* 182–83.)

33. *Lines Written while Sailing in a Boat at Evening*
Remembrance of Collins
a. Draft of sonnet forming basis of both poems (earliest version of either poem; unpublished). [Possibly written as early as between c late 1788 and 1791 inclusive, but perhaps later—any time up to shortly before 29 Mar 1797. (See Appendix IV; 1797:17.)]
b. *Written on the Thames near Richmond* (earliest surviving complete version; see Cornell opp. p. 400). [Probably composed early 1797; certainly composed by 29 Mar 1797. (See Appendix IV; 1797:17.)]

c. Final version, two poems with titles as above. [Probably composed between 29 Mar 1797 and 30 May 1798. (See 1797:17; 1798:138.)]

Pub. (final version) *LB* 1798.

34. Fragment: Stanza of translation from Ariosto (Racedown Nb; unpublished)

Composition possibly later contributive to *The Old Man of the Alps* (Racedown Nb; surviving in stubs only)

[Possibly written sometime between c late 1788 and probably 2 July 1797. (See Appendix IV.)] [9]

35. "When Slow from Pensive Twilight's Latest Gleams" (unpublished sonnet; see Bateson 212)

[Perhaps composed between c late 1788 and 1791 inclusive; part or all possibly later, esp. Racedown period (26 Sept 1795–probably 2 July 1797). (See Appendix VI.)]

36. "If Grief Dismiss Me Not to Them That Rest"

[Probably translated from the Italian between c late 1788 and 1791 inclusive. (See Appendix IV; Woof *SB* 166–67.)] Pub. *MP* 13 Feb 1798. (See Woof *SB* 166.)

37. "Sweet Was the Walk along the Narrow Lane"

[Probably composed between June 1789 and Apr 1792.] [10] Pub. *PW* (Knight, 1882–89) IX.

---

[9] W and DW read Ariosto for an indefinite period following 20 Mar 1796 (see *EL* 156); Appendix IV mentions W's established acquaintance with Ariosto in 1790 and the possibility of his having used the Racedown Nb then. No work in the Nb is known to date after mid-1797.

Miss Landon has pointed out to me that a few stub readings of work torn from the Racedown Nb seem to bear more than a chance resemblance to *The Old Man of the Alps*, but further conclusions, including conjecture about the dates (beyond what can be concluded about the dates of the use of the Nb as a whole), appear impossible.

[10] The sonnet possibly combines feelings associated with W's visit to Forncett in June (and perhaps part of July) 1789 and his visit of Dec–Jan 1790–91 (see *EL* 46, 72–73, 93) but the season pictured in the poem is spring or summer. The poem could have been written any time between June of 1789 and the time DW quotes the poem on 8 May 1792 (allowing slightly more than a week for travel of a letter from W in France). Like the drafts for *Written in Very Early Youth*, *Written on the Thames near Richmond*, and "When Slow from Pensive Twilight's Latest Gleams," these verses possibly show the influence of Bowles's *Fourteen Sonnets*, which W read during Christmas holidays 1789–90, but see Appendix IV.

38. *Septimi Gades*

Fragment: Description of effects of the sun in melting snow and ice among high mountains, illustrated by an anecdote of a personal adventure in the Alps (prose; unpublished)

[Perhaps written late 1790 or shortly after. *Septimi Gades* probably completed by late 1791. (Appendix IV.) The fragment probably written by 23 May 1794.][11] *Septimi Gades* pub. *PW*.

39. *Descriptive Sketches*

[Some composition possibly in late 1790 and 1791. Bulk of composition probably between 6 Dec 1791 and perhaps late Nov or early Dec 1792, esp. after mid-May 1792. Some composition possibly up to shortly before publication. Some additions and corrections made possibly not long after publication. (See 1791:37; Appendix V; *PW* I, 42–89 *app crit*.)] Pub. 29 Jan 1793. (See *MC* of that date; also Shaver *RES* 57n.)

40. *The Female Vagrant*

[Possibly composed in some form by c 1791; earliest surviving version incorporated in *Salisbury Plain*. (See GCL 45.)] Pub. *LB* 1798.

41. *The Birth of Love*

[Probably adapted from the French between 1792 and 23 May 1794.] Pub. *MC* 21 Aug 1795.[12]

[11] While the date of the incident described in the fragment is determinable (see 1790:81), all that is clear about the time of the composition of the passage (in Nb Verse 4) is that it must have followed the 1790 walking trip (W could not have had the large Nb along with him on the tour; see, for example, *Mem* I, 14). One might guess that it was written not long after the trip, but no certainty can exist in the matter. As noted in Woof, the fragment contributes to a stanza (no. 51) in *SP* MS 1; hence it was in any case quite likely written by 23 May 1794 (see GCL 45).

[12] The note, plainly by Wrangham, that introduces the poem on its first publication speaks of it as "done lately." A copy of the poem, however, appears in the Windy Brow Nb, where it is obviously copied in from another source; so the poem was probably completed before the conclusion of the 1794 visit at Windy Brow. Southey, who had good reason to know, said the poem was college work—see F. Christiansen, "The Date of Wordsworth's 'The Birth of Love,'" *MLN* LIII (1938), 282, and JRM in "The Date of Composition of *The Borderers*," *MLN* XLIX (1934), 104–11. I have not succeeded in determining where W discovered the French original, "L'Education de l'Amour," by the Vicompte de Ségur (see *La Lyre française*, ed. G. Masson, London, 1892); but the poem appears anonymously in the *Almanach des Muses, ou Choix Poesies fugitives de 1792, Annee 1793*, and hence most likely first appeared in 1792. There are some variants in the French version both as quoted by the

42. *A Letter to the Bishop of Llandaff*
    [Probably composed June 1793 or shortly after. (See 1793:12.)] Pub.
    Grosart.

43. Fragment: "How Sweet to Walk along the Woody Steep" (*PW* I,
307–08)
    [Probably written between perhaps late June, more likely early July and
    late July or early August 1793. (See 1793:18; Appendix IV.)]

44. "In Vain Did Time and Nature Toil To Throw" (unpublished sonnet)
    "The Western Clouds a Deepening Gloom Display" (unpublished
elegaic quatrains)
    [Probably composed between late July and Sept 1793, before W's
    departure for France. (See 1793:21.)]

45. *Salisbury Plain* (original version of *Guilt and Sorrow*)
    a. MS 1. [Bulk of composition probably between late July and Sept
1793, before W's departure for France (see 1793:21). Almost certainly
composed by 23 May 1794. (See Appendix XII.)]
    b. Addition of the sailor and his story. [Probably composed mostly or
entirely between 26 Sept and 20 Nov 1795. (See 1795:36; Appendix XII.)]
    c. MS 2. [Probably written between very late Apr 1799 and c 5 June
1800. (See Appendix XII.)]
    (W probably did no further work on this poem until he prepared it for
    its publication in 1842 as *Guilt and Sorrow*.)

46. *Inscription for a Seat by the Pathway Side Ascending to Windy Brow*
    [Probably composed between early Apr and mid-May 1794. Almost
    certainly composed by 23 May. (See 1794:8.)] Pub. *PW*.

47. *Juvenal*
    a. Translation of Juvenal VIII.1–86. (This work, probably composed
with Wrangham, does not survive, unless *Juvenal* 163–73 represents a
revision of efforts made at this time on 85–86.) [Perhaps composed between
late Feb and 21 Aug 1795. (See Appendix XIV.)]

MC and by Wrangham's *Poems*, where W's verses appeared next, which correspond
to the 1805 reading of Ségur's poem quoted by Masson; so that W's source was
probably not the *Almanach*—the readings in which, incidentally, look earlier than the
other versions.

b. *Juvenal* 1–28 and imitation of VIII.87–124 (not surviving). [Probably composed between 15 Aug and 26 Sept 1795. (See Appendix XIV.)]

c. *Juvenal* 29–162 (imitating VIII.163–230, 254–75), 163–73 (imitating VIII.85–86). [Probably composed between 7 Mar and Apr 1796. (See Appendix XIV.)]

Pub. *PW*.

48. "The Hour Bell Sounds"
[Translated from the French probably in early 1796, after 2 Jan. (Landon *BNYPL*; 1796:5; Appendix XVI.)] Pub. *MP* 10 May 1798. (See Landon *RES* 392n; Woof *SB* 170–72.)

49. *XVI a, b* (*PW* I, 292–95)
The Convict
Fragment of a Gothic Tale
[Perhaps written early 1796, more probably between 21 Mar and early Oct 1796. (See Landon *BNYPL*; Appendices XII, XVI; 1796:2.)] *XVI a, b* pub. *PW*. *The Convict* pub. *MP* 14 Dec 1797. (See Woof *SB* 160–64.) *Fragment of a Gothic Tale* pub. *PW*.

50. *Address to the Ocean*
[Probably composed between mid-Apr and mid-Nov 1796. Certainly completed by 21 Nov 1796. Some chance may exist of earlier composition. (See Appendix XVI.)] Pub. *Weekly Entertainer* 21 Nov 1796. (See JRM *RES*.)

51. Fragment: *Argument for Suicide*
[Probably written between the latter half of 1796 and early 1797; possibly written as late as summer 1797. (See GCL 52a; Appendix XVII.)] Pub. *PW*.

52. *The Borderers* and Prefatory Essay
a. First version of play, and MS A (which contains fragments from two early stages of the play, most probably antedating completion of the first version). [Bulk of composition probably between the latter half, probably late, 1796 and late Feb 1797. Some composition possibly extended into summer 1797. (See Appendix X; *PW* I, 342–49.)]
b. Prefatory Essay. [Probably composed at the same time as the first version of the play. (See Appendix X.)]
c. Stage revision (the extent to which the first version of the play was altered here is not clear). [Probably between c Sept and 12 Nov 1797 and between 20 Nov and 8 Dec 1797. (See Appendix X.)]

d. MS B. [Probably written between very late Apr 1799 and c 5 June 1800. (See Appendix X.)]

The Borderers pub. after final revision 1842. Prefatory Essay pub. *PW*.

53. *The Old Cumberland Beggar*
   Old Man Travelling. Animal Tranquillity and Decay
   a. *Description of a Beggar* (earliest version of either poem)
      Old Man Travelling (probably composed as part of *Description of a Beggar*)
   [Probably composed between the latter half of 1796 and early June 1797. (See Appendix XV.)]
   b. *The Old Cumberland Beggar* (first version as independent poem). [Probably composed between 25 Jan and 5 Mar 1798. (See Appendix XV.)]
   c. *OCB*, published version. [Probably composed between very late Apr 1799 and 10 Oct 1800. (See Appendix XV.)]
   OCB pub. *LB* 1800. *OMT* pub. *LB* 1798.

54. Fragment: "Yet Once Again" (*PW* V, 340)
   [Probably composed between the latter half of 1796 and early June 1797. (See Appendix XVII.)]

55. Fragment: The Baker's Cart (*PW* I, 315–16)
   [Written between probably the latter half of, even more probably late, 1796 and c Mar 1797. (See Appendices XIII, XVII.)]

56. *Inscription for a Seat by a Road Side, Half Way up a Steep Hill, Facing the South*
   Stanzas, probably toward the poem which eventually developed into *The Three Graves* (incomplete; unpublished)
   The Three Graves, Part II
   [Probably composed between c 28 Nov 1796 and 4 June 1797. (See 1796:72.)] *Inscription* pub. *MP* 21 Oct 1800. (See Woof *SB* 178–80.) Most of *The Three Graves*, Part II, pub. *STCPW* 1893.

57. *The Ruined Cottage* (original version of *Excursion* I; see also GCL 64)
   a. *Excursion* I.871–916. [Probably composed c Mar–Apr 1797. (See Appendix XIII; 1797:9.)]

b. Early unified version of *RC* probably including or based on materials represented by *Excursion* I.871–916

Fragments in Racedown Nb

RC MS A

[Probably composed between c Mar and 4–7 June 1797. Additional work on unified version possible between 4–7 June and 7–14 July or even later 1797. (See Appendix XIII.)]

c. Entries in Christabel Nb, including passages corresponding to MS B (*PW* V) 318–21, 338–41, 322–25, 342–56, 359–61, 353–58 (and see *app crit*), 681–93, and stubs on which probably appeared lines 697–728. [Possibly written between c Mar and early summer 1797. Almost certainly written by, and probably written in, early 1798. (See Appendices IX, XIII.)]

d. Entries in Alfoxden Nb, including passages corresponding to MS B 457–60, 467–70, 461–62, 459–92, and 31–32, some fragments quoted *PW* V, 413, and lines on the Pedlar (including materials used *Prel* II.321–41) quotations from which appear *PW* V, 413; also, as indicated by stubs, drafts for [?633–?643, ?656–665, ?667–?673, ?30–61, ?301–?309, 333–?343]. [Probably composed between 25 Jan and 5 Mar 1798, at least mainly after the materials in Christabel. The lines on the Pedlar probably written between 25 Jan and 19 Mar 1798. (See Appendices IX, XIII.)]

e. MS B. [Probably written between 25 Jan and 5 Mar 1798 (and after the work of Alfoxden and Christabel), with some revisions (see esp. *f* below) shortly after. (See Appendices IX, XIII.)]

f. Conclusions, including "Addendum," to MS B (*PW* V, 400–04), corresponding to *Excursion* IV.958–68, 1207–75. [Perhaps composed between 25 Jan and 5 Mar 1798, more probably shortly after 5 Mar, esp. between 6 Mar and c 10 Mar. (See Appendix XIII.)]

g. MS B$_2$ (later, abbreviated version of MS B). Written 5, [6] Mar [1798]. (See 1798:59.)

h. Drafts toward lines on Pedlar *PW* V, 405–08, lines 5–82 (see 406n), omitting lines parallel to 25–38 and 56–78. [Probably written between 6 Oct 1798 and early 1802. (See Appendix IX.)]

i. Lines quoted *PW* V, 414 from *PB* MS 2. [Probably written between 6 Oct 1798 and c 5 June 1800. (See GCL 72n.)]

j. MS D (in Nb 18A). [Probably written between possibly c 14–21 Mar, more certainly very late Apr, 1799 and perhaps c 5 June, fairly certainly c July, 1800. (See Appendices IX, XIII.)]

Pub. in form of *Excursion* I 1814.

58. Fragment: *Incipient Madness*
[Probably written between c Mar and 4–7 June 1797. (See Appendix XIII.)] Pub. *PW*.

59. *A Somersetshire Tragedy* (only a few lines survive)
[Perhaps composed c Apr–May, fairly certainly between 29 Mar and autumn, 1797. (See 1797:19; Bateson 130–32.)]
a. Eight lines describing Robert's wife's negligence of her household duties (in Nb 18A). [Perhaps written 1800, by late Oct. (See Appendix IX.)]
b. Couplet (and some related drafts) in *PB* MS 2. [Probably written between 6 Oct 1798 and c 5 June 1800. (See GCL 72n.)]

60. *The Farmer of Tilsbury Vale*
The Reverie of Poor Susan
A Character
[Probably composed after 29 Mar 1797. *Farmer* composed between probably 30 Mar 1797 and 18 July 1800. *Reverie* composed between probably 30 Mar 1797 and 13 Aug 1800. *A Character* composed between probably 30 Mar 1797 and 15 Oct 1800, and probably completed in present form between 15 Sept and 15 Oct 1800. (See Appendix IX.)] *Farmer* pub. *MP* 21 July 1800. (See Woof *SB* 173.) *Reverie, A Character* pub. *LB* 1800.

61. *A Night-Piece*
[Bulk of composition probably 25 Jan 1798. Certainly composed in *PW* "MS" form by late Oct 1800. (See 1798:13; Appendix IX.)] Pub. *Poems* 1815.

62. *Prospectus to The Recluse*
[Some composition possibly between c 25 Jan and 5 Mar 1798, more certainly between c 25 Jan 1798 and early 1800. MS 1 probably not earlier than 1800. (See PREL xlv–vi; *PW* V, 363–64, 372.)][13] Pub. *Excursion* 1814.

63. *The Prelude*
a. The Discharged Soldier (*Prel* IV.363–504, *Prel*₂ IV.370–469). [Basic materials probably written between 25 Jan and 5 Mar 1798. (See esp. *Prel*

---

[13] The notebook in which MS 1 appears was used extensively in 1808 (see *PW* IV, 372), and gives no indication of having been in use, in any case, before W's residence at Grasmere. It resembles the notebooks of *Prel* MSS W, X, Y (see PREL xxix–xxxii) and DCP MS Verse 58 (see *PW* V, 371).

IV.450–67, Alfoxden variants; PREL 536–37). Composed in *Prel* form (with Nb 18A variants) by late Oct 1800. (See 1798:14; Appendix IX; 1798:18.)]

    b. Materials, including lines on the Pedlar, contributive esp. to *Prel* II.321–41, *Prel*₂ II.302–22. These materials are made up of Alfoxden Nb fragments quoted *PW* V, 340–42, esp. 340, *II, i*, and *PW* V, 413. [Probably written between 25 Jan and 19 Mar 1798. (See Appendix IX; GCL 64.)]

    c. Materials contributive to *Prel* II.416–34, *Prel* III.124–67 in *RC* MS B. [Probably written between 25 Jan and 5 Mar 1798. (See GCL 57e.)]

    d. MS JJ (PREL 633–42) (the first substantial work toward an auto-biographical poem resembling *The Prelude*; includes drafts used in the Preamble). [Probably entirely written between 6 Oct 1798 and 23 Feb 1799; written in part, at least, before late Dec 1798. (See 1798:201.)]

        1. The Stolen Boat (*Prel* I.372–427, *Prel*₂ I.357–400), growing out of materials in JJ
        At least lines 25–63 of *The Influence of Natural Objects* (*Prel* I.452–89, *Prel*₂ I.425–63)
        [Probably composed between 6 Oct and possibly 14 Dec, probably 21 or 28 Dec, 1798. (See 1798:203.)] *Influence* pub. *The Friend* 28 Dec 1809.
        2. "There Was a Boy" (*Prel* V.389–422, *Prel*₂ V.364–97. [Probably composed between 6 Oct and late Nov or early Dec 1798. (See 1798:204; 1798:208.)]
        3. Preamble (*Prel* I.1–54; *Prel*₂ I.1–45). [Perhaps composed between 6 Oct 1798 and early 1800, with main composition possibly between 17 Nov 1799 and early 1800.][14]

    e. Materials contributive to *Prel* XII.194–201, *Prel*₂ XIII.195–202 (see *PW* V, 344–45)

[14] John Finch, in an unpublished article on the composition of the Preamble, advances arguments for supposing the passage composed in 1799, and suggests that the emotions that form its subject are W's feelings on his return to Grasmere after parting from STC in the Lakes in Nov 1799. The content of the lines forbids serious entertainment of the idea that W is referring in them mainly to his departure from Goslar, but I incline to think that if they were composed any time near the end of 1799 they must look forward to the moment of W's and DW's settlement at Grasmere or reflect emotions associated with the journey thither. The passage cannot be established, on present evidence, as composed in its present form before W's residence at Grasmere. (See 1795:34.)

Materials forming basis of *Prel* XI.15–22, *Prel*₂ XII.24–31 and *Prel*
XI.214–21, *Prel*₂ XII.165–71
[Probably written between 6 Oct 1798 and late Oct 1800. (See Appendices
IX, XI.)]
   f. Formation of definite plan for an autobiographical poem addressed
to Samuel Taylor Coleridge. [Perhaps c early 1799, by c 14–21 Mar or 20
or 21 Apr; probably between 20 or 21 Apr and Sept 1799. (W had earlier
commenced work on an autobiographical poem—which was to become
The Prelude—without this plan fully in mind.) (See 1799:4; Appendix
XII.)]
    g. *The Prelude* I, II
        1. Early version of what is now *Prel* I (including at least lines 271–304,
           310–14, and—from Nb stubs—331–45, 407–11, 419–27, 485–88,
           567–70), in Christabel Nb. [Probably written between 6 Oct 1798
           and c 5 June 1800, but after MS JJ. (See Appendix IX.)]
        2. Early version of at least a concluding part of what is now *Prel* I
           and an abortive start on *Prel* II, in Nb 18A (see Prel xxvii).
           [Probably written between 6 Oct 1798 and c 5 June 1800, after
           MS JJ and perhaps after Christabel Nb MS; the abortive start on
           Prel II probably composed between possibly c 14–21 Mar, prob-
           ably 20 or 21 Apr, 1799 and c 5 June 1800. (See Appendices IX,
           XII.)]
        3. Lines toward *Prel* II quoted Prel 525; other fragments possibly
           intended for *Prel* I or II in *PB* MS 2 (see esp. Prel 533). [Probably
           written between 6 Oct 1798 and c 5 June 1800. (See GCL 72n.)]
        4. Earliest MSS of *Prel* II (excluding lines mentioned above, *g*2),
           MSS RV, U, V (see Prel xxviii–ix), MSS U and V including
           Prel I and II (as described Prel), MS RV including *Prel* II alone.
           These materials also include lines on which are based *Prel* V.450–72,
           *Prel*₂ V.426–50, *Prel*₂ VIII.458–75, *Prel* XI.258–316, 343–89, *Prel*₂
           XII.208–61, 286–332. [Probably written between possibly c 14–21
           Mar, probably 20 or 21 Apr, 1799 and c 5 June 1800, the drafts in
           PB MS 2 (see above, *g*3) preceding MS RV, and MS RV preceding
           the other two MSS. (See Appendix XII.)]
   h. *The Simplon Pass* (*Prel* VI.553–72, *Prel*₂ VI.621–40). [Perhaps composed 1799, probably 1804. (See 1799:2.)]

64. Fragments: *PW* V, 340–41, *II, i, ii, iii, iv* [perhaps intended for *RC*]
   [Probably written between 25 Jan and 19 Mar 1798. (See Appendix
IX.)]

65. *To My Sister*
[Probably composed between 1 and 9 Mar 1798, most probably on 6, 8, or 9 Mar. (See 1798:53.)] Pub. *LB* 1798.

66. *Goody Blake and Harry Gill*
[Probably composed between early Mar (after 6 Mar) and c 16 May 1798. (See 1798:62n; 1798:131; 1798:138.)] Pub. *LB* 1798.

67. *Complaint of a Forsaken Indian Woman*
"Her Eyes Are Wild"
The Idiot Boy
The Last of the Flock
We Are Seven
Simon Lee
[Probably composed between early Mar and c 16 May 1798. (See 1798:51; Reed *UTQ* 245.)] Pub. *LB* 1798.

68. *"A Whirl-blast from behind the Hill"*
[Probably composed 19 Mar 1798. (See 1798:76; 1798:78.)] Pub. *LB* 1800.

69. *The Thorn*
[At least the first two stanzas probably composed 19 Mar 1798; the remainder of the poem probably composed very shortly after, almost certainly by c 16 May 1798. (See 1798:78; 1798:112.)] Pub. *LB* 1800.

70. Fragments: *PW* V, 341, *II, v, vii*
[Probably written between 19 Mar and c 16 May 1798. (See Appendix IX.)]

71. *Lines Written in Early Spring*
Anecdote for Fathers
[Composed between possibly early Mar, probably early Apr, and c 16 May 1798. (See 1798:52; Reed *UTQ* 245.)] Pub. *LB* 1798.

72. *Peter Bell.* First version, and MS 1 (if the two are not the same)
[Probably composed between 20 Apr and c 16 May 1798. (See 1798:113.)][15]

[15] As observed by Floyd Stoddard, in his doctoral dissertation now in progress at Cornell University, the 20 Apr comment of *DWJ*, "Began Peter Bell today," is a curious manner of referring to any poem except one that already has a fairly sub-

Andrew Jones
"I Love upon a Stormy Night" (*PW* II, 464)
[Probably composed between 20 Apr 1798 and c 5 June 1800 as part
of *PB*. *Andrew Jones* certainly in existence as a separate poem by 13 Aug
1800. (See Appendix IX; *PW* II, 531; Hale White 11.)] *PB* pub. 1819.
Andrew Jones pub. *LB* 1800.

73. "Away, Away, It Is the Air" (*PW* IV, 357–58)
Fragments: *PW* V, 341, *vi*, *viii*; 341–42, *ix*; 342, *III*, 1–11 (a draft)
[Perhaps written between 20 Apr and c 16 May 1798 or shortly after.
(See Appendix IX.)]

74. *Expostulation and Reply*
The Tables Turned
[Probably composed 23 May 1798 or very shortly after. Almost certainly
composed by 12 June 1798. (See 1798:137; 1798:142.)] Pub. *LB* 1798.

75. *Lines Composed a Few Miles above Tintern Abbey*
[Begun possibly 10 July, probably 11 July, completed 13 July 1798.
(See 1798:157–160.)] Pub. *LB* 1798.

---

stantial existence; possibly DW is speaking of the commencement of a copy. On the
other hand, DW at times wrote up her journal entries late (see, for example, *DWJ* I,
12) and could be looking back. Also, she speaks of the moon's being crescent that day;
she would probably be more likely to make a mental juxtaposition of the crescent
moon and the beginning of the poem than the crescent moon and the beginning of a
copy of the poem (see the poem's Prologue).

MSS 2 and 3 of *PB* clearly date from about the same time (see *PW* II, 528). Inasmuch
as stubs and surviving lines toward *The Brothers* and a note for *Joanna* are among the
materials written in MS 2 between—and esp. in the case of *The Brothers* almost
certainly before—parts II and III of *PB*, the likelihood is that neither MS can date
before the beginning of 1800. The Nb in which MS 2 is found, however, is identical
with other Nbs (MSS Journal 3, 4, 5) in DCP surely obtained in Germany, and the
fragments toward *RC* and *Prel* grouped here (the *Prel* materials include a version of
II.216–24 preceding that of MS RV) between parts II and III of *PB* may be dated
between the arrival at Goslar and c 5 June 1800. A couplet (with related drafts)
probably for *A Somersetshire Tragedy* adjoins the fragments, "Her face bespoke a weak
and witless soul/Which none could think worthwhile to teach or to [?controul]"; it
can be given the same date. Stubs following the couplet suggest that Spenserian
stanzas once stood next; they possibly contained other work on the *Tragedy* (see also
Appendix IX).

33

76. Record of conversations with Klopstock, in MS Journal 5
[Probably written 26 Sept 1798 or shortly after. (See 1798:188.)] Pub.
The Friend 21 Dec 1809.

77. Fragment of a Moral Essay, in MS Journal 5 (see Bateson 185)
[Probably written between 26 Sept 1798 and 23 Feb 1799.][16]

78. Fragment: *PW* V, 344–45, *ix* (see also GCL 63e)
[Probably written between 6 Oct 1798 and late Oct 1800. (See Appendix IX.)]

79. *The Danish Boy*
Ruth
To a Sexton
The Matthew Poems:
a. *Matthew*
b. *The Fountain*
c. *The Two April Mornings*
   1. *Die Zwey Aprilmorgens* (German translation of *The Two April Mornings*; translator unknown. Unpublished.)
d. "Could I the Priest's Consent Have Gained" (*PW* IV, 452–53)
e. "Remembering How Thou Didst Beguile" (*PW* IV, 453–55)
f. *Address to the Scholars of the Village School of* ——
[All except *c*1 probably composed between 6 Oct 1798 and 23 Feb 1799; almost certainly composed between 6 Oct 1798 and late Apr 1799. (See 1798:200.) *Die Zwey Aprilmorgens* probably composed between 6 Oct 1798 and early 1802. (See Appendix IX.)] "Could I," "Remembering" pub. *PW*. *Address* pub. 1842. All others (except *c*1) pub. *LB* 1800.

80. *Lucy Gray*
Written in Germany on One of the Coldest Days of the Century
A Poet's Epitaph
Ellen Irwin
[Probably composed between 6 Oct 1798 and 23 Feb 1799. *Ellen Irwin* possibly composed any time between 6 Oct 1798 and 29 July 1800. Some chance may exist that *Written in Germany* was composed 25 Dec 1798. (See 1798:201; Hale White 6–9.)] Pub. *LB* 1800.

[16] The only known time of the use of the Nb is during the German visit before the Wordsworths' departure from Goslar. The fragment appears in the Nb after GCL 76 and before *Prel* MS JJ.

81. "How Sweet When Crimson Colours Dart" (*PW* II, 465)
"One Day the Darling of My Heart" (not surviving; see *EL* 222)
"A Slumber Did My Spirit Seal"
[Probably composed between 6 Oct and Dec 1798, possibly Jan 1799.
(See 1798:202.)] "How Sweet" pub., possibly after revision (by STC),
as *Alcaeus to Sappho, MP* 24 Nov 1800. (See Landon *RES* 395; Woof
SB 180.) "A Slumber" pub. *LB* 1800.

82. "She Dwelt among the Untrodden Ways"
"Strange Fits of Passion I Have Known"
[First versions probably composed between 6 Oct and possibly 14 Dec
probably 21 or 28 Dec, 1798. (See 1798:203.)] Pub. *LB* 1800.

83. *Nutting*
a. The poem as finally published. [Probably composed between 6 Oct
and possibly 14 Dec, probably 21 or 28 Dec, 1798. (See Appendix XI.)]
b. Long version, including "I would not strike a flower" (see PREL
612–14) and *Ode to Lycoris, Sequel* 42–45. [Composed between 6 Oct 1798
and c 5 June 1800. *Ode to Lycoris, Sequel* lines perhaps composed between
possibly 14 Dec, probably 21 or 28 Dec, 1798 and c 5 June 1800. (See
Appendix XI.)]
Pub. *LB* 1800.

84. *The Excursion* (see also GCL 57, 62, 63)
a. *Excursion* IX.1–26, 124–52 (1–152 with 18A variants). [Lines 128–40
probably written between 6 Oct 1798 and late Oct 1800; the other lines
probably written between early 1799 and late Oct 1800. (See Appendix IX.
Cf *PW* V, 471.)]
b. Lines corresponding to *Excursion* VIII.276–334 ("There is a law
severe"). [Probably written between early 1799 and late Oct 1800. (See
Appendix IX.)]

85. Fragment: *Redundance* (*PW* V, 346)
[Probably composed between early 1799 and late Oct 1800. (See
Appendix IX.)]

86. "Three Years She Grew in Sun and Shower"
[Probably composed between 23 and 27 Feb 1799. (See 1799:13.)] Pub.
LB 1800.

87. *The Brothers*
[Begun probably shortly before, certainly by, 24 Dec 1799; completed probably early 1800. (See 1799:96.)] Pub. *LB* 1800.

88. *To M.H.*
[Composed on or shortly before 28 Dec 1799. Certainly composed between 20 and 28 Dec 1799. (See 1799:101.)] Pub. *LB* 1800.

Chronology, 1741—1799

1741

1. Nov 27

John Wordsworth (d. 1783), second son of Richard Wordsworth (1690–1760) of Westmorland and Mary Robinson Wordsworth (1700–1773) of Appleby, Westmorland, [born on this date or shortly before and] baptized at Sockbridge, Westmorland, near Penrith. (*Mem* I, 30; GGW *Cornhill* 411–12; GGW *Some Notes* 24; *EL* 565; Moorman I, 8n; *Registers of the Parish Church of Barton, Westmorland*, comp. Henry Brierley, CWAA Soc, 1917.)[1]

1748

1. Jan 20

Ann Cookson (d. 1778), daughter of William Cookson (1711–1787) and Dorothy Crackanthorpe Cookson (1720–1792) [born on this date or shortly before and] baptized at Penrith. (GGW *Cornhill* 412; GGW *Some Notes* 24; *EL* 567.)[1]

[1] The Barton PR states simply that JW Sr. was baptized this day. GGW *Some Notes* 24 states, however—claiming the authority of the PR—that JW was both born and baptized on 27 Nov. Richard W, law-agent of the Westmorland properties of the Lowther family, receiver-general for the County of Cumberland, and clerk of the peace, owned a farm estate at Sockbridge (see Moorman I, 8).

[1] *Mem* I, 30, records the year as 1747. It is probable that *Mem* has confused Old Style dating with New Style, and that the sources cited in the text are correct in terms of the modern calendar. GGW states only (from the Penrith PR) that Ann Cookson was baptized 20 Jan. She was probably born on that day or shortly before. William Cookson was a mercer of Penrith, and Dorothy Crackanthorpe Cookson was the sister and heiress of James Crackanthorpe of Newbiggin Hall, near Penrith (see references cited in text).

1764

1. [By Dec]

[JW Sr., now attorney-at-law, moves to Cockermouth, Cumberland, as law-agent to Sir James Lowther. (GGW *Cornhill* 411.)][1]

1766

1. Feb 5

JW Sr. marries Ann Cookson at Penrith. (W Family Bibles in the possession of Mrs. Dickson and DCP.)

2. June 22

· Marie-Anne Vallon (d. 10 Jan 1841), later commonly called Annette Vallon, sixth child and third daughter of Jean-Léonard and Françoise-Yvon Vallon, born at Blois. (*AV* 8, 110–11.)

1768

1. Feb 9

John Hutchinson (1736–1785) marries Mary Monkhouse (1745–1783) at Penrith. (Robertson 154; *EL* 566.)

2. Aug 19

Richard Wordsworth (d. 19 May 1816), first son of JW Sr. and AW, born at Cockermouth at 11:30 PM. (W Family Bibles in the possession of Mrs. Dickson and DCP.)[1]

[1] JW Sr.'s duties included those of bailiff and recording officer of the Borough of Cockermouth, and, probably in 1774 and after, coroner of the Siegniory of Millom (GGW *Cornhill* 411–12; Moorman I, 6). Moorman I, 7, implies that JW Sr. began to work for Lowther in 1765, but there is no reason to doubt GGW. JW Sr. served his employer for at least nineteen years, through Dec 1783.

[1] The statement of *PW* (Knight, 1882–89) IX, 11, and *PW* (Oxford) xxv (the latter perhaps based on the former) that RW was born 19 May must be the result of confusion with the date of his death.

3. Aug 29

RW baptized at Cockermouth. (W Family Bibles in the possession of Mrs. Dickson and DCP.)[2]

1770

1. Apr 7

William Wordsworth (d. 23 Apr 1850), second son of JW Sr. and AW, born at Cockermouth at 10 PM. (W Family Bibles in the possession of Mrs. Dickson and DCP.)[1]

2. [Apr 7 ff]

[References in W's own writings to the years before he entered Hawkshead School (see 1779:1) which are capable of relatively specific dating are noted below. On this period generally see esp. Moorman I, 1–21. References capable of only imprecise dating have seemed too numerous for inclusion in the text at this point. For these passages, many of them important, see Appendix I.]

3. Apr 13

W baptized at Cockermouth. (W Family Bibles in the possession of Mrs. Dickson and DCP.)[1]

---

[2] Although Robertson 26 correctly states that the PR gives a date of 29 Sept for this event, the Family Bibles must be taken as final authority. *Mem* I, 31, perhaps drawing on one or both Bibles, also gives a date of 29 Aug.

[1] Some confusion has been created by apparent disagreement between *Mem* I, 29, 31, which give a date of 13 Apr for W's baptism (see also Charles Wordsworth, *Annals of My Early Life*, London, 1891, 2), and the Cockermouth PR:

> 1772
> [Baptized:] William, Son of Mr John Wordsworth
> Attorney at Law Aged 1 year 9 months & 11 days
> Dorothy, His daughter, Aged 3 Weeks & 2 Days
>
> 18th Jan'ry.

The conflict is clarified, but only to a point, by the W Family Bibles, which state that W was baptized 13 Apr at Cockermouth and christened 18 Jan 1772. The Bibles also

4. Aug 16

Mary Hutchinson (d. 17 Jan 1859), first daughter of John and Mary Hutchinson, born at Penrith. (GGW *TLS*; GGW *Some Notes* 24.)[2]

1771

1. Dec 25

Dorothy Wordsworth (d. 25 Jan 1855), only daughter of JW Sr. and AW, born at Cockermouth at 10 PM. (W Family Bibles in the possession of Mrs. Dickson and DCP.)[1]

1772

1. Jan 18

DW baptized and christened, W christened at Cockermouth. (W Family Bibles in the possession of Mrs. Dickson and DCP; Cockermouth PR. See 1770:3n.)

---

[2] Penrith does not mention MH's birth or baptism.

[1] The statement of the Cockermouth PR (see 1770:3n) that DW was baptized "Aged 3 Weeks & 2 Days" suggests a birth date of 26 Dec, but the Family Bibles are surely correct. DW herself never doubted that she was born 25 Dec (see, for example, *EL* 13, 19, 555, 559; *MY* 803).

---

state that DW was baptized and christened on 18 Jan. I am indebted to E. R. Hardy of the Berkeley Divinity School for an explanation of the unusual distinction made by the Bibles between the commonly synonymous terms "baptize" and "christen": In late medieval and early modern England many children (probably more in some parts of the country than others) were, because of the high incidence of infant mortality, baptized immediately after birth; but so that the fact might be publicly known, and the child received into the fellowship of the Church, a service of reception would follow at a later date, and previously omitted ceremonies would then take place. The eighteenth-century usage was evidently to term this ceremony (which is given no title in the Prayer Book) "christening," as it publicly declared the child a Christian. (See the English Prayer Book of 1662.) Professor Pottle has brought to my attention a letter from Bennet Langton to James Boswell, 10 Aug 1776, in which Langton notes Dr. Johnson's approval of this form of reception, in the absence of which "the *publick* Proof is wanting that the Christening has been performed at all."

2. Dec 4

John Wordsworth (d. 5 Feb 1805), third son of JW Sr. and AW, born at Cockermouth at 4 AM. (W Family Bibles in the possession of Mrs. Dickson and DCP.)

1773

1. Jan 6

JW baptized at Cockermouth. (Cockermouth PR.)[1]

2. [c the year beginning 1773 May 15]

[W and other members of his family probably live with W's grandparents at Penrith. W perhaps attends the infant school of Dame Ann Birkett—or Birkhead; 1715–1790 (Penrith; CRH)—with MH. (JW Sr.'s Accounts, DCP; *Mem* I, 8; GGW, Notes on the Family Accounts, DCP; GGW *Cornhill* 414–15; *PW*, Knight, 1882–89, X, 421–22.)][2]

---

[1] Robertson 26–27 incorrectly states that JW's baptism is not recorded in the PR. The PR itself errs in giving JW's age as "one Month and five days."

[2] In *Mem* I, 8 (Autobiog Mem), W states that the time "of [his] infancy and early boyhood was passed partly at Cockermouth and partly with [his] mother's parents at Penrith." As remarked in GGW *Cornhill* 414–15, a "careful study of the [family] accounts gives ground for the conjecture that lengthy visits of the whole family to the grandparents at Penrith, as Wordsworth himself has hinted, were by no means infrequent." GGW's Notes on the Family Accounts comment that the family maidservant Amy, who was with the W's 1771–77, received no payment for the half year beginning Whitsuntide 1775 or for the winter of 1776–77. In point of fact, JW Sr.'s accounts show that she received no payment for the full years from Whitsuntide 1773 to Whitsuntide 1774, and from Whitsuntide 1775 to Whitsuntide 1776, as well as none from Martinmas 1776 to Whitsuntide 1777. (JW Sr. employs the term "Whitsuntide" in the legal sense of 15 May rather than in reference to the religious feast.) GGW's inference that the gaps in payment may well indicate times at which most of the W's removed to Penrith seems reasonable. (A weekly payment of –/2/6 to a nurse through the year of 1773–74 implies that someone—probably at least AW, who is noted in the accounts as making part of the payments—remained at Cockermouth, and it is doubtful that JW Sr. with his business commitments could have passed any extended visits at Penrith. He addresses a business letter from Cockermouth 7 Feb 1777—Cornell 2583.) One must suppose that W paid other, shorter visits to Penrith from time to time through his childhood, but the periods suggested by the accounts would altogether justify W's comment above (see also 1777:1). There is no evidence

1774

1. [During this year]

Sir James Lowther obtains control of the Seigniory of Millom, between Duddon Sands and Whitehaven. [Probably during this year] JW Sr. is made coroner of Millom. (Moorman I, 6.)[1]

2. [Probably Apr (–1776 Oct)]

[RW enters the Rev. Mr. Gilbank's grammar school at Cockermouth. (He remains there until at least Oct 1776.) (JW Sr.'s Accounts, DCP.)][2]

---

[1] JW Sr.'s obligations in Millom were eventually to be the indirect cause of his death (see 1783:10).

[2] The following are the accounts of JW Sr. concerning W's and RW's attendance at Gilbanks' school:

1774 13° Octr 2 Qrs due this day for Dicky at ye Gramr School	0/15/0
1774 Novr 10th Sent per Dicky	/15/0
13° Apl 1775 2 Qrs due this day	/15/0
1775 May 25° Sent per Dicky	/15/0
1776 13° Octr Richard 1 year	1/10/0
22d Octr William half a year	/15/0
1776 22° Octr paid Mr Gilbanks	2/ 5/0

On the possibility of later study under Gilbanks by W, see esp. 1776:4n. (See Moorman I, 15n.)

---

for specific conjecture concerning other visits. Various aspects of this problem are discussed in more detail below in the text and the notes.

PW (Knight, 1882–89) X, 421, quotes from a letter of Henry Inman, who painted W's portrait in 1844, to Henry Reed, 23 June 1845: "[The poet and his wife] had known each other from the early period of infancy, having gone to the same school at three years of age." The precision of Inman's statement seems to indicate that W's memory of what must have been his first experience with any sort of schooling and perhaps his first acquaintance with MH was definite; and neither plain reason nor the slight evidence available concerning W's presence in Penrith now implies that he was mistaken. It is likely that W also attended Dame Ann Birkett's school during the long visits of 1775–76 and winter 1776–77, and at least some of the time between that winter and his entering Hawkshead School in May 1779 (see 1774:2; 1775:2; 1776:3; 1776:4). Probably MH attended with W most or all of these times.

W's remarks on *LY* 328 cannot be said definitely to refer to Ann Birkett and her school as *Mem* I, 33, implies (also *Sara Coleridge and Henry Reed*, ed. L. N. Broughton, Ithaca, 1937, 100); but see esp. Moorman I, 15.

3. [c the year beginning 1774 Apr 7]

[W age four. The first clearly recollected childhood experiences described in W's poetry perhaps belong to this year.

Perhaps during this year W first worries over the problem of divine permission of evil. (See *Letters and Journals of Caroline Fox*, ed. H. N. Pym, London, 1882, I, 305.)][3]

4. June 9

Christopher Wordsworth (d. 2 Feb 1846), fourth son of JW Sr. and AW, born at Cockermouth at 8:30 PM. (W Family Bibles in the possession of Mrs. Dickson and DCP.)

5. July 8

CW baptized at Cockermouth. (Cockermouth PR.)[4]

1775

1. [c the year beginning 1775 Apr 7]

[W age five. Some chance exists that the earliest experiences W recalled as having contributed to the growth of his poetic mind occur during the part of this year spent at Cockermouth. (See 1775:2; 1774:3.)]

2. [c May 15–1776 c Apr]

[W and other members of his family probably live with W's grandparents at Penrith. W probably attends Dame Ann Birkett's infant school (see 1773:2). W perhaps returns to Cockermouth by c Apr 1776 (see 1776:1).

[3] See *Prel* I.291–304 and *app crit*, *Prel₂* I.288–300. The *app crit* contains the lines "Beloved Derwent, fairest of all streams,/ Was it for this that I, a four years child." But it will be remembered that in the final versions of the same passage (*Prel* I.291, *Prel₂* I.288) W gives his age as five. The activities concerned (running, bathing, and the like) are quite as appropriate for "a four years child" as a "five"; but as none of the events of his early childhood mentioned in his poetry can be quite precisely dated, this period is somewhat arbitrarily suggested as the time of the first events which W could consciously later recall as having made an active contribution to the growth of his poetic mind. The Fox reference records W's 1842 statement that he had "quaked in bed" over the paradox of evil when "four years old."

[4] The W Family Bibles fail to record the date of this event.

W perhaps now learns, or by now has learned, to ride a horse. The incident of W's discovery, near Penrith Beacon, of the murderer's gibbet perhaps occurs at this time. (W refers to these events: *Prel* XI.279–316 and *app crit, Prel*₂ XII.225–61.)][1]

1776

1. [c Apr (–Oct)]

[W joins RW at Gilbanks' school. (He remains until Oct.) (See 1774:2n.) He studies Latin. (*Mem* I, 10.)]

2. [Oct]

[W and RW are withdrawn from Gilbanks' school. (See 1774:2n.)]

3. [c Nov 11–1779 c May 15]

[It is possible that W and other members of his family spend much time during this period both at Penrith, with W attending Dame Ann Birkett's school, and at Cockermouth, with W carrying on further study under Gilbanks or some other master. (*Mem* I, 17, 33; Moorman I, 15–16. See 1773:2; 1776:4.)][1]

---

[1] The *Prel* passages make clear that W was at least learning, if he had not already learned, to ride. Since this experience must have occurred while W was visiting at Penrith, and when he was still very young, the dates of greatest probability would be either now or c 11 Nov 1776–c 15 May 1777, although a yet later date remains possible. The date I have chosen is thus highly conjectural. The *app crit* shows that W altered this passage often in his different drafts of it, once (in MS D) stating that the events took place when he was six years old (that is, during the year beginning 7 Apr 1776). Neither the first known draft (in MS V) nor the 1850 version makes mention of a year. My date is based on the statement in the 1805 version, "I was then not six years old" (XI.280), plus the remark in MS V that he was in "the twilight of re-memberable life," a description which would less fit an age of six or older than it would five. Moorman I, 69, implies a date of 1775 for the incidents, and Schneider 62 also places them in W's sixth year (that is, at age five).

[1] As indicated above, there is no evidence that W attended Gilbank's school except Apr–Oct 1776 (see 1776:1). JW Sr.'s accounts contain no record of expenditure on W or RW in this period, but the boys were surely receiving schooling somewhere. Evidence already noted suggests that W may well have spent the winter of 1776–77 in Penrith, and W was definitely in Penrith shortly before his mother's death in early Mar 1778 (see *Mem* I, 9). DW never returned to her Cockermouth home (in her youth) after late 1777 or early 1778 (see 1777:1). Also to be noted is GGW's remark in his

4. [c Nov 11–1777 c May 15]

[W and other members of his family probably live with W's grandparents at Penrith. W probably attends the infant school of Dame Ann Birkett. (See 1773:2.)]

1777

1. [c or soon after Dec 25, or very early 1778]

[Possibly after celebration of Christmas with her family at Cockermouth] DW departs from her father's house for the last time during her childhood. (*EL* 516.)[1]

1778

1. [c Mar 8]

Ann Wordsworth, mother of W, dies at the Cookson house in Penrith [perhaps of pneumonia. Her illness had probably lasted two

---

[1] DW to Lady Beaumont, 7 Aug 1805. DW says that this event took place "when I was six, a few months before my mother's death." She became six on 25 Dec 1777, and her mother died c 8 Mar 1778.

Notes on the Family Accounts (DCP): "Mr. Cookson's bill as mercer presented at Whitsuntide 1779 was exceptionally heavy (£75.13.2) and we know he paid the Entrance fee at Hawkshead. It may have been included on his bill as well as the charges for Education at Penrith & outfit for Hawkshead." But W's remark that he learned more Latin in a fortnight from the usher at Hawkshead than "during two preceding years at the school of Cockermouth" (*Mem* I, 10) cannot be overlooked. It seems unlikely that Dame Ann Birkett at Penrith taught Latin (see, for example, Moorman I, 15). W could have studied Latin elsewhere at Cockermouth—perhaps under his father—before or after Gilbanks, but my guess would be that JW Sr.'s accounts fail to note further actual payments to Gilbanks or some other master for W, and that the poet was making a general summary of a period spent in (perhaps intermittent) formal study, possibly both at Cockermouth and Penrith, from 1776 until he entered Hawkshead.

JW Sr. kept both a maidservant and a nurse under hire from Whitsuntide 1777 through Martinmas 1779, fairly surely at Cockermouth; so the entire family could not have been continuously at Penrith during that time.

On residence of the children at Cockermouth from now until the death of JW Sr. (30 Dec 1783) see also 1778:4, and entries for all vacations through 1783.

and one-half months.] (JW Sr.'s Accounts, DCP; GGW, Notes on Family Accounts, DCP.) [W refers to this event esp.: *Prel* II.294–96, *Prel*$_2$ II.279–81; *Prel* V.256–60, *Prel*$_2$ V.256–60. On W's last memory of his mother see *Mem* I, 9.][1]

2. Mar 11

Ann Wordsworth is buried at Penrith. (Robertson 63.)

3. June 13 –[probably 1787 May]

DW departs from Penrith in the care of her cousins Mr. [William] and Miss [Elizabeth] Threlkeld, for Halifax, Yorkshire. [DW regularly makes her home with Miss Threlkeld at Halifax probably until May 1787.] (JW Sr.'s Accounts, DCP; GGW *Cornhill* 419–20.)[2]

4. [c Dec 25]

[All the W boys probably spend Christmas at Cockermouth with their father. (*EL* 559.)][3]

---

[1] Moorman I, 18, suggests that the fatal illness was pneumonia. It was probably caught by sleeping in a damp bed on a visit to the house of a friend in London (see *Mem* I, 8; EdS *DW* 5). Records in the family accounts of payments to the apothecary are abnormally heavy for the 2½ months ending 8 Mar. It is from this fact that the length of AW's illness is determined, and it is possibly also from this that GGW *Cornhill* reaches its determination of the exact date of AW's death, which is given by no other authority. GGW's Notes also point out that the apothecary has a different name from his predecessors in the account book, and would be a Penrith rather than a Cockermouth man.

[2] On this period see EdS *DW* 5–10. GGW remarks in his Notes on the Family Accounts (DCP) that "there is no mention of [DW's] ever leaving Yorkshire between 1778 and 1787, nor of her Father visiting her there." W recalls his sister's departure in *To a Butterfly* ("Stay near me") IF note. The note in the accounts reads "Dolly Left Penrith for Halifax in a Chaise with Mr Threlkeld and Miss Threlkeld on Saturday 13th June 1778. Mr Cookson gave Miss Threlkeld 5 gns towards her conveyance &c." (cf EdS *DW* 5 and Moorman I, 18). Miss Threlkeld was the first cousin of DW's mother. She was the daughter of William Cookson's sister Elizabeth Cookson Threlkeld (see *EL* 567). William Threlkeld was Miss Threlkeld's brother; he is mentioned by DW *EL* 12, 14.

[3] I assume now and hereafter (from DW's remark, *EL* 559, that during the time she spent at Halifax her brothers "always" kept Christmas "with rejoicing" in her "Father's house") that W and his brothers spent Christmas at Cockermouth every

1779

1. [Probably c May 15 (–1787 perhaps c June 20)]

W and RW [depart from Penrith and] enter the Hawkshead Free Grammar School. [W refers to this event: *Prel* I.307–09, *Prel*₂ I.303–06.] They lodge and board with Hugh and Ann Tyson for 5 guineas (each) per half year. [W remains a student here until perhaps c 20 June 1787.] (JW Sr.'s Accounts, DCP. See 1787:12; Appendix II,D.) The Rev. James Peake (1745?–1803), M.A. of St. John's College, Cambridge, is headmaster. (Venn; *Mem* I, 38.)[1]

2. [Probably c May 15–1787 perhaps c Oct 7]

[References in W's own writings to his years at Hawkshead which are capable of relatively specific dating are entered in the text or notes.

[1] JW Sr.'s note: "Richard and Wm (Sons) went to Hawkeshead School at Whits 1779. N.B. Mr Cookson pd the ffee to the Master &c on Entrance." The strong implication that the boys were accompanied to school by Mr. Cookson suggests a departure from Penrith. GGW *Cornhill* 415 states that the entrance at Whitsuntide means "after the summer holidays"—impossible even if the religious feast were the intended referent; but, as indicated 1773:2n, JW Sr.'s use of the phrase "Whitsuntide" throughout his accounts leaves no doubt that he employed it to refer to the Scottish term day of 15 May.

PREL 516 points out that in the following autumn W had seen ten summers, even though *Prel* I.310–11 states that he had not seen nine and the V text (PREL 161 *app crit*) that he had not seen eight. *EL* 269 (W to Miss Taylor, 9 Apr 1801) remarks that he entered Hawkshead before he was nine. The phrasing of *Prel*₂ I.306–07, "Ere I had told Ten birth-days," is accurate.

year from 1778 through 1783. How much more time during the year the boys could have spent there is quite uncertain. See 1776:3; 1776:4. It is possible, of course, that the amount of time spent in Cockermouth during the long Penrith visit was quite small. JW and CW, however, attended Gilbanks' school at Cockermouth in 1781; they must have been living with their father at that time. W's statement in *V of E* 435, that his heart "lost a home" when his father died, while metaphoric, perhaps carries some suggestion of dependence on a physical home. In the absence of evidence to the contrary, the chance of short visits by W to Cockermouth at times other than Christmas, at least during vacations, during the period between the deaths of his mother and father can not be excluded. See also the discussions of the several Hawkshead vacations below.

On this period generally see Moorman I, 22–85. References capable of only imprecise dating have seemed too numerous for inclusion in the text at this point. For these passages, many of them important, see Appendix II.]

3. [Possibly c May 15–c May 29]

[During his first two weeks or so at Hawkshead] W advances rapidly in Latin under the instruction of Joseph Shaw (1756?–1825), usher at Hawkshead School. (*Mem* I, 10; Venn.)[2]

4. [Perhaps during early weeks after c May 15 (ff)]

[W establishes a fishing companionship with Tom Park, saddler, with whom he does his first Hawkshead fishing, and Mr. John Harrison, the village schoolmaster. (Later W fishes further afield, including the Brathay, with Park and his father George.) (TWT *W's Hawkshead* I, 8; TWT *Hawkshead Church* 47. See *The River Duddon* IF note; 1782:8.)]

5. [June 18, 19]

At twilight [18 June] W discovers the clothes of a drowned man beside Esthwaite Lake. Next day he watches searchers find the body. (TWT *W's Hawkshead* I, 3–4.) [W refers to these events: *Prel* V.450–81, *Prel*₂ V.426–59. See also *PB* 576–80.][3]

---

[2] W possibly did not proceed to his studies of Latin quite immediately; nor need he have been aiming at strict chronological accuracy when he said that he learned more Latin in two weeks from Shaw than during two preceding years at Cockermouth. This date is offered, therefore, only as a rather arbitrary conjecture for the time of an event that W remembered gratefully the rest of his life. Shaw left for Stafford Grammar School in 1780 (Venn).

[3] TWT confirms that the lake was Esthwaite (as does Moorman I, 9–10), gives the date of the drowning, and identifies the victim as James Jackson, schoolmaster at Sawrey. If W were correct in saying that these events occurred within a week of his arrival (*Prel* V.450–54, *Prel*₂ V.426–30), he would have come to Hawkshead after Whitsuntide. But there is little likelihood that he did come so late (see 1779:1), and the word "week" probably simply expresses the fact that the time between his arrival and this memorable occasion was very brief.

6. [Perhaps c June 20–perhaps c Aug 4]

[W and RW probably return home with their father for summer vacation perhaps c 20 June. They possibly divide their vacation between Cockermouth and Penrith. (They return to Hawkshead perhaps c 4 Aug.) (GGW *Cornhill* 416; TWT *W's Hawkshead* I, 5.)][4]

7. [Perhaps c Aug 4]

[W and RW probably return to Hawkshead from Cockermouth or Penrith. (See 1779:6n.)]

8. [Probably c Dec 11–probably c 1780 Jan 10, perhaps Jan 20]

[W and RW return to Cockermouth or Penrith for Christmas vacation. They possibly divide their vacation between Cockermouth

---

[4] GGW *Cornhill* 416 states—probably upon the evidence of the family accounts— that holidays at Hawkshead normally began "about June 20 and December 20," and that the boys returned to Hawkshead "about August 4 and January 20." He also suggests (on the basis of the family accounts for 1784 and 1791) that an Easter holiday was an annual event. I assume generally that the boys' departure from Hawkshead for vacations and their return afterwards coincide with the time of discharge of bills there by JW Sr. or, later, the administrators of his estate—whenever such payments occur close to the dates cited by GGW. Such discharge of bills cannot, of course, be taken as certain proof that the boys left school, but I have supposed whenever there is no evidence to the contrary that the boys did spend their vacations in Penrith or Cockermouth. I have also assumed that they left Hawkshead every Christmas vacation. When a relevant entry appears in the family accounts for only one or the other of the dates of the vacation and no other evidence applies, I use the days which GGW gives (as above) for the date not indicated by the accounts. When no relevant information whatever appears in the accounts, the dates are offered conjecturally only; in these circumstances the likelihood would be greater than otherwise that the boys did not go home at all.

No direct evidence bears on the present presumed departure. TWT *W's Hawkshead* states, however (it is not clear upon what evidence), that JW Sr. came to see the Hawkshead attorney John Gibson on business about the end of school this year, and indicates that the boys left with him. If the boys departed now, their destination was probably Cockermouth, but it is normally impossible during the time of JW Sr.'s life to be sure either of the boys' destination when leaving school or their point of departure when returning (exceptions are duly cited). All that looks clear is that Christmas day was spent by the boys at Cockermouth during their father's lifetime. (DW's statement, *EL* 559, that between the deaths of their parents the boys "always" spent Christmas in "rejoicing" in their father's house points more to Christmas day than the full vacation. See 1778:4.)

and Penrith. (They return to Hawkshead probably c 10 Jan, perhaps 20 Jan, 1780.) (JW Sr.'s Accounts, DCP; *EL* 559. See 1779:6n.)][5]

9. [c Dec 25]

[The W boys probably spend Christmas with their father in Cockermouth. (*EL* 559. See 1779:6n.)]

1780

1. [Probably c Jan 10–perhaps c Jan 20]

[Probably departing from Cockermouth on or about 10 Jan, and possibly spending a few days in Penrith (up to perhaps c 20 Jan) on the way, W and RW return to Hawkshead. (JW Sr.'s Accounts, DCP. See 1779:6n.)][1]

2. [c Mar 26]

[(Easter.) W and RW possibly receive a short vacation. (See 1779:6n; 1784:6.)]

3. [Possibly during the year beginning 1780 Apr 7 (or possibly during that beginning 1783 Apr 7)]

W age ten. [Possibly during this year (or possibly when age thirteen)] W becomes conscious of "loving words in tuneful order" for their own sakes. [W refers to this event: *Prel*₂ V.552–83; *Prel* V.575–607. See 1783:3.][2]

---

[5] Among discharges of Hawkshead bills noted for 11 Dec 1779 by JW Sr. is one of £10/10/– for "Hugh Tyson for half a Year's Board from Entry." This and the other bills are discharged on the same day. The accounts note a bill from "Mr Crackenthorp" on JW Sr. (£1/13/8) under 25 Dec, a fact which perhaps points to the boys' having been taken first to Penrith and then having been sent or fetched to Cockermouth about Christmas day, with the bill conveyed at the same time.

[1] JW Sr. notes payment of the bill of 25 Dec (see 1779:8n) on 10 Jan 1780 by sending the money "per Boys." This date would mark the termination of the month evidently usually given for Christmas holidays at Hawkshead School (if the vacation began c 11 Dec 1779 as assumed above). The boys might have gone to Penrith only to meet a relative and thence to proceed to school at once; they might have stayed at Penrith a few days and returned to school nearer 20 Jan (see 1779:6n); or they might have proceeded directly to Hawkshead from Cockermouth.

[2] W states in *Prel* V.575–81 that he might have seen thirteen years when this event took place. In both *Prel* and *Prel*₂ he qualifies his estimate of his age by a subjunctive—

4. [Probably c June 13 (–perhaps Aug 4)]

[W and RW probably return to Cockermouth or Penrith for summer vacation. (They return to Hawkshead perhaps 4 Aug.) (JW Sr.'s Accounts, DCP. See 1779:6n.)]³

5. [Perhaps c Aug 4]

[W and RW probably return to Hawkshead from Cockermouth or Penrith. (See 1779:6n.)]

6. [Probably Oct]

JW and CW enter the Rev. Mr. Gilbank's school at Cockermouth. (JW Sr.'s Accounts, DCP.)⁴

³ Bills of £11/8/6 and £5/6/10 from Hugh Tyson and "Mr Crackanthorp" were discharged by JW Sr. on 13 June.

⁴ The following entries in JW Sr.'s accounts refer to the attendance of JW and CW at Gilbanks' school:

		John and Christopher—my Sons	
1781	Mar 5°	For their Entrance	0/10/0
		Two Quarters	1/ 4/0
	12° Decr	Three Quarters	1/16/
		5° Mar 1781 pd revd Mr Gilbanks	1/14/0
		12° Decr pd Mr. Gilbanks to this time	1/12/0

(The second payment to Mr Gilbanks apparently leaves a balance of £–/4/– owing Gilbanks.) On the attendance of W and RW at this school see 1774:2.

---

he "might" have seen so many years—and adds "or less." A final determination would depend to a great extent on a full understanding of the sense that W means to apply to such words as "conscious" and "love" here and of how closely he means to link the readings in the poets mentioned in subsequent lines with the flowering of his own "fancy" and his first consciousness of his creative powers, an event which can be dated very roughly in W's thirteenth year (see 1783:8). W clearly means to say, however, that the event was not casual, but connected closely with a growing intellectual, critical, and poetic faculty. I use the date simply as a suggestion for a year before which the experience described probably did not occur. It would hardly, also, have occurred after the commencement of his own creative efforts. (See also Appendix III.)

It seems quite possible that most of the reading described in the passage took place after the arrival of William Taylor as headmaster in 1781 or 1782 (see Moorman I, 50–51). On the first poem from which W later remembered receiving pleasure (probably one of two poems on spring by Lucy Aikin) see *Mem* II, 304 (*Mem, R,* II, 306) and Moorman I, 54.

7. [Perhaps c Dec 20 (–probably 1781 c Jan 17)]

[W and RW return to Cockermouth or Penrith for Christmas vacation. (They return to Hawkshead probably c 17 Jan 1781.) (*EL* 559. See 1779:6n.)]

8. [Between perhaps c Dec 20 and 1781 probably c Jan 17]

[During Christmas holidays.] The Rev. James Peake resigns headmastership of Hawkshead School. He is succeeded by the Rev. Edward Christian. (TWT, information to Mrs. J. P. Hogan; tablet at Hawkshead School. See *Mem* I, 38.)[5]

9. [c Dec 25]

[The W boys probably spend Christmas with their father in Cockermouth. (*EL* 559. See 1779:6n.)]

1781

1. [During this year (–1786 June 12)]

The Rev. William Taylor ([1754]–1786), M. A., fellow of Emmanuel College, Cambridge, becomes headmaster of Hawkshead School. (He retains this post until his death, 12 June 1786.) (*Mem* I, 38; Venn; tablet at Hawkshead School. See A. Craig Gibson, "The Lakelands of Lancashire. No. I—Hawkshead Town, Church and School," *Transactions of the Historic Society of Lancashire and Cheshire* N.S. V, 1865, 139–60.)

[Taylor contributes to the character of "Matthew." See esp. *Matthew* and IF note; *Address to the Scholars of the Village School of*——; *The Two April Mornings; The Fountain;* two elegies on Matthew,

---

[5] I am indebted to the late Mrs. Hogan for knowledge of this exact date. Christian (baptized 3 Mar 1758–1823) was an elder brother of Fletcher Christian of the *Bounty*. He had distinguished himself as a Cambridge undergraduate and was later a fellow of St. John's College, Cambridge, and advocate for the W family in their suit against Lord Lowther. (Venn; Moorman I, 90 and *passim*.) Moorman I, 90n, expresses doubt that Christian was resident at Hawkshead School.

PW IV, 452–55. On Taylor see also *Prel* X.490–515, *Prel*₂ X.531–52. See also esp. Moorman I, 49–50; Schneider 76–79.][1]

2. [Perhaps c Jan 15–c July 15]

[DW perhaps attends school in Hipperholme, near Halifax, during this half year. (JW Sr.'s Accounts, DCP.)][2]

3. [Probably c Jan 17]

[W and RW probably return to Hawkshead from Cockermouth or Penrith. (JW Sr.'s Accounts, DCP. See 1779:6n.)][3]

4. [c Apr 15]

[(Easter.) W and RW possibly receive a short vacation. (See 1779:6n; 1784:6.)]

5. [Summer]

[W and RW probably spend all summer at Hawkshead. RW is ill during this time. (JW Sr.'s Accounts, DCP.)][4]

---

[1] *Mem* I, 38, gives a date of 1782 for this event. A tablet on display at the school (and described more extensively by Gibson) presents a list of Hawkshead headmasters, with the dates of their assumption of duties. It is probably the best authority currently available for such information. It indicates that Edward Christian was headmaster only in 1781, and that Taylor succeeded him during that same year.

Taylor's tombstone at Cartmel Priory states that he died at the age of "32 Years 2 Months and 13 Days."

[2] JW Sr.'s accounts note payment of £6 for DW for "Half a Year's Board at Hipperholme," with the comment that this charge was included in "G. Simpson's Bill of Schoolmaster's Bills" which was sent JW Sr. 16 July 1781. Reference is made also to DW's board at Halifax from 15 July 1781 "to the time Dolly goes to Hipperholme." It thus seems possible that DW spent more time at Hipperholme, or intended to, than the half-year cited, but evidence is insufficient for more detailed conjecture.

[3] JW Sr. records: "1781 Janry 17° paid Hugh Tyson in full 11/13/7."

[4] See also GGW *Cornhill* 417. JW Sr. sent payment to Hawkshead for bills through Whitsuntide by Mr. Cookson's servant on 1 July. The boys probably did not leave before this payment was made, and other entries offer strong indication that

6. [Perhaps c Dec 20 (—probably 1782 c Jan 24)]

[W and RW probably return to Cockermouth for Christmas vacation. (They return to Hawkshead probably c 24 Jan 1782.) (*EL* 559. See 1779:6n.)]

7. [c Dec 25]

[The W boys probably spend Christmas with their father in Cockermouth. (*EL* 559. See 1779:6n.)][5]

1782

1. [Perhaps during this year or 1783 (ff)]

[Hugh and Ann Tyson move from Hawkshead to the nearby hamlet of Colthouse, their last residence. (TWT in the Program of the Wordsworth Centenary celebration at Hawkshead, 1950.)][1]

---

[5] JW Sr.'s Accounts record the purchase of four volumes of *Gil Blas* ($\pounds$-/8/-) under 27 Dec.

[1] In William Bennett's MS record of "An Evening with Wordsworth," DCP (the evening was 11 Nov 1846), note is made of W's having remarked in a discussion of his Hawkshead years that "during a great part" of the time "he lodged at Colthouse." See also Moorman I, 84–85; PREL 532.

---

the boys did not leave between 1 July and Sept either; the sums must refer to bills accumulated after the earlier date:

1781	Gave Mr Tyson for Additional Trouble		
	and Attendce upon Richard	1/1/0	
	Gave Subscription to Books	/10/0	1/11/0
	Also ffee to Dr Atkinson for Journey to		
	attend Richard		1/11/6
	Septr 1781 pd at Hawkshead-as on		
	the ot Side		1/11/0
	At same time pd Mr Crackanthorp		
	what he pd ye Dr		1/11/6

I assume that if RW stayed the summer, and was ill, W would have remained also.

2. [During this year]

[A remote chance may exist that W visits Dovedale.][2]

3. [Probably c Jan 24]

[W and RW probably return to Hawkshead from Cockermouth or Penrith. They are accompanied by JW, who, having been withdrawn from Gilbanks' school, enters Hawkshead School. (JW Sr.'s Accounts, DCP. See 1779:6n; 1782:6.)][3]

4. [c Mar 31]

[(Easter.) W, RW, JW possibly receive a short vacation. (See 1779:6n; 1784:6.)]

5. [Possibly late spring]

[W and some friends, including his schoolmate John Benson, go on a birds'-nesting expedition for ravens' eggs on the Yew Dale Crags, during which Benson becomes crag-fast. A rescue is effected by Frank and Jonathan Castlehow. (TWT *W's Hawkshead* I, 15–16; TWT *Hawkshead Church* 43.)][4]

6. [Probably c June 16 (—perhaps c Aug 4)]

[W, RW, JW probably return to Cockermouth or Penrith for summer vacation. (They return to Hawkshead perhaps c 4 Aug.) (JW Sr.'s Accounts, DCP. See 1779:6n.)][5]

[2] The fragment *Cambridge to Hawkshead*, quoted Moorman I, 105, and in part Schneider 112, is probably to be dated 8 June 1788 (see 1788:17); it contains a description of part of a Dovedale scene as it was "about six years ago." It seems likely, however, in absence of any other evidence of such a trip, that W was drawing on the information of a guidebook or other report rather than on personal observation.

[3] JW Sr. records payment of £15/4/1 to Hugh Tyson and others under 24 Jan.

[4] See also Schneider 266. TWT gives this specific date, but not his evidence for it. His information came from the granddaughter of another member of this expedition, Fletcher Raincock. The group was led by Tom Usher (a Hawkshead waller) and Will Tyson; other Hawkshead boys along were Edward Birkett and Raincock's brother William. On the Castlehows see also 1784:10.

[5] JW Sr.'s Accounts record the discharge of bills from Hugh Tyson (£24/10/5) "for the 3 Boys . . . to Whits" on 16 June. This entry plus the fact that CW did not

7. [Perhaps c Aug 4]

[W, RW, JW probably return to Hawkshead from Cockermouth or Penrith. (See 1779:6n.)]

8. [Possibly summer]

[W and an older man go fishing on the Duddon in the rain, and W has to be carried back. (See *The River Duddon* IF note; TWT *W's Hawkshead*, I, 17–18; 1779:4.)][6]

9. [Perhaps c Dec 20 (—probably 1783 c Jan 14)]

[W, RW, JW return to Cockermouth or Penrith for Christmas vacation. (They return to Hawkshead probably c 14 Jan 1783.) (*EL* 559. See 1779:6n.)]

10. [c Dec 25]

[The W boys probably spend Christmas with their father in Cockermouth. (*EL* 559. See 1779:6n.)]

1783

1. [Perhaps during this year]

[This is perhaps the year during which Hugh and Ann Tyson move from Hawkshead to Colthouse. (See 1782:1.)]

2. [Probably c Jan 14]

[W, RW, JW probably return to Hawkshead from Cockermouth or Penrith. (JW Sr.'s Accounts, DCP. See 1779:6n.)][1]

---

[6] TWT dates the incident this summer. The basis for the date is not made clear, but W's companion is stated to be John Martin, 40, of Out Gate, a weaver.

[1] JW Sr.'s accounts read: "1783 Jan: 14 pd Tyson per rect 25/8/11½."

---

enter Hawkshead till 1785 (and thus could not have been the third boy) make it plain that JW entered Hawkshead after Christmas. JW was at Gilbanks' school until Dec 1781 (see 1780:6n). For a possible summer event see 1782:2.

3. [Possibly during the year beginning 1783 Apr 7]

W age thirteen. [Possibly during this year] W first becomes conscious of "loving words in tuneful order." [W refers to this event: *Prel* V.575–607. See 1780:3.]

4. [c Apr 20]

[(Easter.) W, RW, JW possibly receive a short vacation. (See 1779:6n; 1784:6.)]

5. [Perhaps c June 20 (—perhaps c Aug 4)]

[W, RW, JW probably return to Cockermouth or Penrith for summer vacation. (They return to Hawkshead perhaps c 4 Aug.) (See 1779:6n.)]

6. [Perhaps c Aug 4]

[W, RW, JW probably return to Hawkshead from Cockermouth or Penrith. (See 1779:6n.)]

7. [Perhaps shortly after c Aug 4]

[Some chance possibly exists that W writes his first verses shortly after his return to school. (See 1784:13; Appendix III.)]

8. [Possibly late summer and thereabouts]

[Possibly in his "fourteenth summer" W, becoming aware of "that dim similitude which links our mortal feelings with external forms," experiences while on a picnic on Coniston Water the thoughts and wishes recorded in PREL 582–83 (MS V), *Prel*$_2$ VIII.458–75 and *app crit* (PREL 298); *Extract from the Conclusion of a Poem, Composed in Anticipation of Leaving School;* also (the first poetic record of the event), *V of E* 498–513.

Possibly about this time occurs in W the first flowering of the operation of "fancy." (W refers to this event: *Prel* VIII.511–623, *Prel*$_2$ VIII.365–450.)][2]

---

[2] As only one MS (*Prel* MS V) contains a reference to W's age at the time of the incident on Coniston Water, this date is hardly certain. But other dates attaching

9. [Perhaps c Dec 19]

W goes out into the fields in stormy weather and watches from a crag for the horses which are to carry him, RW, and JW home. [W refers to this event: *Prel* XI.345–64, *Prel*₂ XII.287–305; *V of E* 418–25.][3]

10. [Perhaps c Dec 20 (—probably 1784 Jan 19)]

[W, RW, JW probably return to Cockermouth for Christmas vacation. (They return to Hawkshead probably c 19 Jan 1784.) (*EL* 559. See 1779:6n.) They find their father ill, apparently from having spent a shelterless winter night lost during his return from conducting two inquests in the Seigniory of Millom (but see 1783:11n). (GGW, Notes on Family Accounts, DCP; HCR *Diary* II, 27. See Moorman I, 68; 1774:1.)][4]

11. Dec 30

John Wordsworth Sr. dies at Cockermouth about 12:30 [PM?] (W Family Bible, DCP; Robertson 98.) His estate totals nearly £10,500.

[3] W states (*Prel* XI.345–46, *Prel*₂ XII.287–88) that this event occurred the day before the beginning of the holidays. On the situation of the crag see PREL 615. (W was uncertain in later years about the number of horses coming—*Prel* XI.349 and *app crit*, *Prel*₂ XII.291—probably there were two plus the groom's. See PREL 615; Moorman I, 68n.) Although *V of E* 418–27 seems to imply that W already knew of his father's death now (see Moorman I, 68n), the lines particularly suggesting this impossibility— "Long, long, upon yon naked rock/ Alone, I bore the bitter shock" (422–23)— probably, although colored by later experience, refer mainly to the "shock" of "the wind and sleety rain/ And all the business of the elements." And his eyes were most likely "swimming" (424) as a result of the weather, "trite reflections of morality," and "anxiety of hope."

[4] Supplementary evidence that the boys traveled directly to Cockermouth is found in *Prel* XI.365–66, *Prel*₂ XII.306–07, where W states that his father died "ere [he] had been ten days/ A dweller in [his] Father's House" (see 1783:11).

with more or less probability to the growth of W's poetic powers and practice (see esp. 1780:3; Appendix III) tend in some degree to confirm it. If W did not leave Hawkshead during this summer, the event need not, of course, have been "late," but there is no reason to suppose that the boys did not spend some time at Cockermouth or Penrith or both.

W states (*Prel*₂ VIII.451–58) that the "season" of the incident was that in which the "slender cords" of fancy were being woven. I cite this time for such weaving in default of better evidence. An attempt at great precision in the matter would be foolish.

(GGW, Notes on Family Accounts, DCP.) RW of Whitehaven and CCC hereafter take responsibility for the children. (*Mem* I, 44; GGW, Notes on Family Accounts, DCP; Moorman I, 71.) [W refers to this event: *Prel* II.294–96, *Prel*₂ II.279–81; *Prel* XI.364–89, *Prel*₂ XI.305–35; also *V of E* 424–37.]⁵

1784

1. Jan 2

John Wordsworth Sr. is buried at Cockermouth. (Cockermouth PR.) W, RW, JW attend the funeral. [W refers to this event: *Prel* XI.367–68, *Prel*₂ XI.308–09. See also *MY* I, 165.]¹

2. [Probably c Jan 3–probably c Jan 19]

[The W boys probably finish their vacation at Penrith. (Administrators' Accounts, CRH. See 1784:3.]

3. [Probably c Jan 19]

[W, RW, JW probably return to Hawkshead from Penrith. (Administrators' Accounts, CRH. See 1779:6n.)]²

⁵ EdS omits two lines interpolated by W into MS A of *V of E* (see *PW* I, 368) that help to clarify his reaction to the death of his father, particularly his ambiguous remark "I mourn because I mourned no more" (*V of E* 433): "For ah the storm was soon at rest/ Soon broke the Sun upon my breast" (435/436). The Cockermouth PR gives the cause of JW Sr.'s death as "dropsy"; his recent exposure (see 1783:10) may have served simply to accelerate the decline of an already weak constitution.

An itemization in round figures of JW Sr.'s estate is made by GGW: Cash £225, sale of effects (mostly 5, 6, 7, and 8 May 1784; see 1784:7) £328; miscellaneous debts £2400; Cookson debts (left unsettled and no interest paid—GGW) £782; capital value of Sockbridge property £1375; ditto Cockermouth property £400; ditto Ravenglass property £350; Lowther debts £4625. Total £10,485. See also Moorman I, 71.

W includes a brief sketch of his financial history between this point and 1805 in a letter to Sir George Beaumont of 20 Feb 1805; see *EL* 450–51.

¹ *Prel*₂ XI.308–09 implies that all of W's brothers were at the funeral, as do MSS D and E (see *app crit*). But *MY* I, 165, shows that CW was in Penrith. DW was, of course, in Yorkshire (see EdS's note, *MY* I, 165). Moorman I, 68, gives 5 Jan as the date of the burial.

² Payment of various sums including "Hugh Tyson's Bill" (£22/7/4) and £1/6/6 to "the three boys" is recorded under 19 Jan 1784.

4. Feb 28 (ff)

Hugh Tyson dies at Colthouse. (Moorman I, 84.) (The W boys continue to reside at his house, future payments being made by the administrators to Ann Tyson.)(Administrators' Accounts, CRH.)

5. [Possibly during the year beginning 1784 Apr 7 (more probably during that beginning 1785 Apr 7)]

W age fourteen. [Possibly during this year (more probably during that beginning 7 Apr 1785)] W reaches a determination to supply the defects in natural imagery in previous poets. (See *EW* IF note; Appendix III; 1785:3.)

6. [Perhaps c Apr 11–c Apr 21]

[(Easter, 11 Apr.) W, RW, JW probably spend a short Easter vacation at Penrith. (Administrators' Accounts, CRH; GGW *Cornhill* 416.)][3]

7. [May 5, 6, 7, 8]

[A sale of personal effects, esp. furniture, of JW Sr. takes place at Cockermouth. £260 is realized. Various other effects of JW Sr. have been sold before this time. (GGW, Notes on Family Accounts, DCP. See 1783:11.)][4]

---

[3] The date of the beginning of this presumed vacation is of course quite uncertain, and based only on the actual date of Easter this year. The assumption of the vacation itself is based on CCC's accounts as administrator, which contain the following entries:

| [Apr] 21st | Paid the boys | 12/6 |
| | Boys going to Hawkshead | 7/6 |

Another entry under 13 May, for payment of £-/5/- to John Bell for horsehire to Hawkshead, is less clear in its significance, but possibly refers to delayed payment of charges arising from the boys' return on 21 Apr.

[4] The administrator's accounts of RW of Whitehaven show an entry dated 9 May recording expenditure of 19/6 on chaisehire to and from Cockermouth for his wife's and his attendance at "the sale for the benefit of the children." GGW notes the sale previous to this time of such items as JW Sr.'s watch and rings, a silver coffee pot, and port and Madeira amounting to some five and a half cases. The key to JW Sr.'s house was delivered to Lord Lonsdale's agent, Satterthwaite, on 24 May (GGW,

8. May 24

Sir James Lowther is created Baron Lowther, of Lowther (Westmorland), Baron of the Barony of Kendal (Westmorland), Baron of the Barony of Burgh (Cumberland), Viscount of Lonsdale (Westmorland and County Palatine of Lancaster), Viscount of Lowther (Westmorland), and Earl of Lonsdale (Westmorland and County Palatine of Lancaster). (*The Complete Peerage*, ed. H. A. Doubleday and Lord Howard de Walden, London, 1932, VIII, 134.)[5]

9. [Perhaps c June 21, and 1784 summer]

[W, RW, JW possibly return to Penrith, perhaps c 21 June. It is likely, however, that much of, or the entire, summer vacation is passed by some of the boys at Hawkshead. (Administrators' Accounts, CRH. See 1779:6n.)][6]

---

[5] The editors point out that these titles were Lowther's harvest from having given the younger Pitt his first seat in Parliament (as Member for Appleby, 1781–84).

[6] CCC's accounts record payment of numerous items relating to the boys' expenses, including £26/8/9 to "Mrs Tyson" and horsehire from Hawkshead (£-/5/-) on 21 June. But a large sum (£22/1/5) is again paid Ann Tyson in an entry apparently for Sept (and another in Jan 1785), suggesting that the boys may have spent much time at Hawkshead in the summer.

The family accounts tend to confirm the accuracy of the remark of GGW *Cornhill* 416 that after the death of JW Sr. it was ordinarily the practice of the boys to spend their summers at Penrith and their Christmas holidays at Whitehaven—or, he might have added, at Branthwaite (see Moorman I, 71). (RW of Branthwaite makes an entry in his accounts, apparently under the date of 31 July 1790, for £8/12/-, for, among other things, "Carrying Richd, Wm, John and Christr from Branthwaite to Hawkshead School at Sevl dift times.") I have made it my regular assumption that whoever entered expenses on the beginning or end of a vacation was the relative whose guest W was going to be, or had just been. Where no such evidence applies, I follow the suggestions of the authorities just noted. W probably moved between one relative's home and another's during vacations, but the accounts offer only one detailed indication of such a move, a mere ten-mile trip from Branthwaite to Whitehaven (see 1786:17).

Notes on Family Accounts, DCP). (On Satterthwaite see esp. *EL* 516. The same reference, incidentally, indicates that W spent some brief time with Satterthwaite's son [James], probably before 1800, but I have been unable to specify the occasion. The younger Satterthwaite was a friend of CW's.)

10. [Early Sept]

[An arrest of members of the Castlehow family is attempted at Hawkshead. Some chance possibly exists that W composed verses on this event. (TWT *W's Hawkshead* II, 6–8. See 1784:11–14.)][7]

11. [c Sept 20]

[W is almost certainly in Keswick. (GGW, transcriptions from administrators' accounts, DCP.)][8]

12. [Possibly between c Sept 20 and Sept 30]

[W, RW?, JW? return to Hawkshead from Penrith or elsewhere. (See 1784:11; 1784:9.)]

13. [Probably after Sept 20, perhaps early Oct]

W composes his first verses. [They are assigned by William Taylor, and are on the subject of The Summer Vacation. (See Appendix III; 1784:10–12; 1784:16.)]

14. [Possibly autumn, or an indeterminate time after]

[W possibly composes verses on the attempted arrest of the Castlehows at Hawkshead. (See Appendix III; 1784:10.)]

---

[7] On the Castlehows see also 1782:5. The breeches of one of the Castlehows fell down as he attempted to flee, and Ruth Castlehow helped her brother Jonathan escape by dressing like him and diverting the ensuing chase to herself. The acting churchwarden and writing master at Hawkshead, Joseph Varty, was among the forces of the law deluded on this occasion, and W is said to have composed verses on the event which irritated Varty. TWT does not give the basis for his dating, nor for the belief that W was its laureate. W seems to have been absent from Hawkshead later in Sept, but his presence there earlier in the month is not impossible (see 1784:9).

[8] The accounts of RW of Branthwaite contain an entry for £–/–/8 under 20 Sept 1784 for payment of postage of a letter "from Master William Wordsworth at Keswick for some books etc." This seems fairly clear evidence of W's whereabouts around this time—unless, as is unlikely, "Keswick" was a slip. Concerning W's (and perhaps other of the boys') return to school CCC's accounts record entries of £–/7/4 and £–/6/8 under Sept, without specific dates. See 1784:9. I have arrived at no adequate explanation for W's presence in Keswick around the 20th.

15. [Perhaps c Dec 20 (–perhaps c 1785 Jan 20)]

[W, RW, JW probably travel to Whitehaven or Branthwaite for Christmas vacation. (They return to Hawkshead perhaps c 20 Jan 1785.) (See 1779:6n; 1784:9n.)]

16. [Between perhaps c Dec 20 and 1785 perhaps c Jan 20]

[Perhaps during this Christmas vacation W attends a dance at Egremont (six miles from Whitehaven) and afterwards composes what he later remembered as his first "voluntary" verse. These lines probably had as their subject The Return to School and were perhaps entitled *The Pleasure of Change.* (See Appendix III; 1779:6n; 1784:13.)]

1785

1. [Perhaps c Jan 20]

[W, RW, JW probably return to Hawkshead from Whitehaven or Branthwaite. (See 1779:6n; 1784:9n.)][1]

2. [c Mar 27]

[(Easter.) W, RW, JW possibly receive a short vacation. (See 1779:6n; 1784:6.)]

3. [Perhaps during the year beginning 1785 Apr 7]

W age fifteen. [Perhaps during this year] W reaches a determination to supply the defects in natural imagery in previous poets. (See *EW* IF note; Appendix III; 1784:5.)

4. [Shortly before June, and probably June]

Hawkshead School celebrates its bicentenary, [probably in June]. In response to an assignment by William Taylor, W [in June or shortly before] composes for the occasion his first surviving poem, *Lines*

---

[1] CCC's accounts (CRH) record payments to "Mrs Tyson" (£27/7/11½) and other expenses of the boys only under the general date of Jan.

Written as a School Exercise at Hawkshead. (See Appendix III; Moorman I, 56; TWT *W's Hawkshead* II, 9; *Mem* I, 10–13.)[2]

5. [Perhaps c June 20 (–perhaps c Aug 4)]

[W, RW, JW probably return to Penrith for summer vacation. (They return to Hawkshead perhaps c 4 Aug.) (See 1779:6n; 1784:9n.)]

6. [Perhaps c Aug 4]

[W, RW, JW probably return to Hawkshead from Penrith. They are probably accompanied by CW, who enters Hawkshead School. (See 1779:6n; 1784:9n; Administrators' Accounts, CRH.)][3]

7. [Perhaps c Aug 4–probably c Dec 19]

[W, RW, JW, CW probably live together with Ann Tyson. (GGW *Cornhill* 418.) During this period the boys receive instruction in dancing. (Administrators' Accounts, CRH; 1785:6; 1785:8.)][4]

---

[2] The letters Patent founding the school are dated " 10th of April, 27 Eliz" [1585] (H. S. Cowper, *Hawkshead*, London, 1899, 463). W says (*Mem* I, 10) that the lines were written for "the completion of the second centenary from the foundation of the school in 1585." The true "completion" of the school's second hundred years would thus have occurred in 1786; but it is natural to suppose that the celebration took place in the spring of 1785, and at the close of the second year. Moorman I, 56, assumes that the event took place in 1785 "when [W] was fifteen" (that is, after 7 Apr), and TWT *W's Hawkshead* II, 9 (possibly drawing on additional evidence), places it this June. The ending of the title of the poem as given *Mem* I, 10n, "anno aetatis 14," is based on a phrase in the title of a copy of the poem (almost certainly the source of the *Mem* text) made about 1830 by DW in a family commonplace book: "Copy of a poem written by William Wordsworth as a School exercise. He was then fourteen years old." A comment added to a very early MS (of unknown autograph) in DCP is: "Composed at the age of 14, as declared by his sister Miss Wordsworth and confirmed by Mrs. Wordsworth. Rydal Mount, 30th October, 1850. [signed] Edward Quillinan." It is likely, however, that if the celebration took place at the end of the school year, most of the poem was composed near this time—after W's fifteenth birthday. A date of 1784 is out of the question.

[3] An expenditure of £1/11/6 for "Entrance Money for Christopher" is noted in CCC's accounts under the date of 10 Dec, but it can be assumed that CW entered at the regular beginning of the term. The next entry shows that he took dancing lessons with his brothers during the autumn.

[4] Hawkshead bills paid at the end of Christmas vacation 1785–1786 are not itemized, so that one cannot be certain that the Tyson bill included all four boys; but there

8. [Probably c Dec 19 (–1786 probably between c Jan 11 and c Jan 14)]

[W, RW, JW, CW probably travel to Whitehaven for Christmas vacation. RW withdraws from the school. (The other brothers return to Hawkshead probably between c 11 and 14 Jan 1786.) (Administrators' Accounts, CRH; GGW *Cornhill* 415–16. See 1786:4; 1784:9n.)][5]

1786

1. [During this year]

[On writings of W possibly of this year see below and GCL 6–13. W perhaps during this year composes:
The Death of a Starling
Lesbia
Beauty and Moonlight, an Ode, Fragment
(See GCL 10.)
W perhaps engages in some composition on *V of E* during this year, but see GCL 13n.]

2. [Probably between c Jan 11 and Jan 14]

[W, JW, CW probably return to Hawkshead from Whitehaven. (Administrators' Accounts, CRH.)][1]

3. Jan 26

RW of Whitehaven records the purchase of "two books" for W under this date. (Administrators' Accounts, CRH.)

---

[5] The accounts of RW of Whitehaven record payment to John Buckham "for Chaise Driver, &c [from] Hawkshead" (£2/18/8) under 19 Dec.

[1] RW of Whitehaven records payment of a total of £1/13/6 cash to his nephews W, JW, and CW under 11 Jan 1786 and "Bills at Hawkshead and Chaisehire" (£36/-/-) under 14 Jan 1786.

---

could not be much doubt that GGW is right. The dancing lessons are indicated by CCC's accounts, which read:

Decr 10	Paid Mr Mingay, Dancing master for teaching Richard William John and Christopher to dance	5/4/–

4. [Probably c Feb 18 (–1789 c Jan)]

[RW is articled to his cousin RW of Branthwaite. (He resides at Branthwaite free of charge until c Jan 1789.) (Administrators' Accounts, CRH; GGW, Notes on Family Accounts, DCP; *EY* 24n.)][2]

5. Mar 13

CCC records the purchase of a Hedrick's Lexicon for W under this date. (Administrators' Accounts, CRH.)

6. [c Apr 7 (c this time generally)]

[(W's "seventeenth year was come.") W refers to the character of his mind about this time: *Prel* II.395–434, *Prel*$_2$ II.376–418.]

7. [c Apr 16]

[(Easter.) W, JW, CW perhaps receive a short vacation. (See 1779:6n; 1784:6.)][3]

8. [Between c June 5 and June 12]

[Within about a week of his death, William Taylor calls the upper boys at Hawkshead into his chamber and takes leave of them. (W refers to this event: *Prel* X.501–07, *Prel*$_2$ X.537–44; *Address to the Scholars of the Village School of* —— 5–11. See also *Mem* I, 38.)][4]

---

[2] Moorman I, 76, states that RW, having left school in 1785, "went immediately to London to become a solicitor." TWT *W's Hawkshead* II, 12, and Shaver *RES* also seem to suscribe to this view. But the accounts of RW of Branthwaite contain the record of an administrators' note of 18 Feb 1786 for £121 for "Clerks Fee with their nephew Richard." CCC wrote to RW at Branthwaite in June 1786 (CRH), and correspondence of autumn 1789 concerns fees to be paid for RW to Messrs Parkin and Lambert between Jan and early Mar 1789 (see 1789:3). *EY* 24n indicates that RW departed from Cumberland for London on 20 Jan 1789.

[3] RW of Whitehaven notes paying £-/10/6 to "my nephew William" under 1 May (Administrators' Accounts, CRH); the significance of the entry is not clear.

[4] *Prel*$_2$ X.537–44 does not date the incident so closely as does *Prel*. *Address to the Scholars of the Village School of* —— implies that W kissed Taylor's cheek before he died and (what seems more doubtful) raised his hand after his death. Both versions of

9. June 12

The Rev. William Taylor dies, age thirty-two. (Gravestone, Cartmel Priory.) [W refers to this event *Prel* X.494. See PREL 600–01; *Prel* references cited 1786:8.]

10. [Probably c June 15]

The Rev. William Taylor is buried in the churchyard of Cartmel Priory. (See *Prel* X.490–500, *Prel*₂ X.531–36; 1786:9.)

11. [Probably c June 24 (-perhaps c Aug 4)]

[W, JW, CW probably return to Penrith for summer vacation. (They return to Hawkshead perhaps c 4 Aug.) (Administrators' Accounts, CRH.)][5]

12. [Aug] (–1828 Dec)

The Rev. Thomas Bowman (baptized 2 Apr 1761–Dec 1828), Fellow of Trinity College, Cambridge, and assistant to William Taylor from 1785, becomes headmaster of Hawkshead School. (He retains this post until his death.) (TWT *Hawkshead Church* 33; Venn; *The Registers of the Parish of Askham*, comp. M. E. Noble, London, 1904, 164.)[6]

13. [Perhaps c Aug 4]

W, JW, CW probably return to Hawkshead from Penrith. (See 1779:6n; 1784:9n.)]

[5] CCC records payment to Ann Tyson of £32/19/7 under 26 June for "the Hawkshead bills paid at midsummer 1786." Midsummer quarter day was 24 June. Ann Tyson's account book contains a bill for W and JW for letters, cakes, and the like dated "June 19 Day 1786" (Moorman *Transactions* 155); it was presumably prepared in anticipation of the boys' departure.

[6] TWT further reports that Bowman taught W for two years (1785–87), and that his son Thomas used to say he believed that his father aided W more by lending him books than by his instruction, although W "did well enough under him" in both Classics and Mathematics.

Prel agree that Taylor said to W, "My head will soon lie low." Moorman I, 58, notes the appearance of a quite similar phrase in *A Ballad* (*PW* I, 265–67) 42. PREL 600–01 gives an imprecise but essentially accurate quotation of Taylor's epitaph, with its excerpt from Gray's *Elegy*.

14. [Shortly before Aug 7; Aug 7]

[Probably on or shortly before 7 Aug,] W composes *Anacreon*. He dates a fair copy of the poem at Hawkshead on 7 Aug. (MS, DCP.)[7]

15. Aug 8

CCC records the purchase of a copy of Demosthenes for W. (Administrators' Accounts, CRH.)[8]

16. [Aug 30]

RW of Branthwaite and RW deliver personally at Lowther Hall the claim of JW Sr.'s administrators on behalf of the estate of JW Sr. on Lord Lonsdale:

Balance of General Cash Account	£1192	14	9¾
Law Charges	£3432	8	10
	£4625	3	7¾

[This claim had taken two and one-half years to complete. (Letter of RW to John Richardson, 26 June 1802, DCP; CRH; GGW, Notes on Lonsdale Suit, DCP.)]

17. [Probably c Dec 19–probably c Jan 15]

[W, JW, CW probably travel to Branthwaite for Christmas vacation. They possibly divide their vacation between Branthwaite

---

[7] The text of *PW* is taken from a fair copy on two loose quarto sheets dated, as on *PW* I, 262, "Hawkshead, August 7th, 1786"—not, as EdS seems to imply, from the version (also—originally—a fair copy) in Nb Verse 4. The latter is only a fragment; all but the concluding lines (from "The Cot, the scene of Peace and Love") were written on leaves that have been torn from the book. This version differs from the printed one (and the other copy) only in such matters as capitalization, and the fact that both MS copies are so similar probably indicates that they date from the same general time. The Verse 4 copy, however, has lost its fairness through various additions and corrections; and these drafts as well as drafts on a later page in the Nb suggest that W worked on the poem after 7 Aug. But no fair copy survives incorporating any of this new material. This date may thus be taken as representing the time by which the poem as now known was completed.

[8] Possibly W purchased the book before his departure from Penrith and CCC entered the amount only now.

and Whitehaven. They return to Hawkshead probably c 15 Jan 1787. (Administrators' Accounts, CRH. See 1779:6n; 1784:9n.)][9]

1787

1. [During this year]

[On writings of W possibly of this year see below and GCL 2, 6–10, 12–21.

W perhaps during this year writes:

On the Death of an Unfortunate Lady (unpublished)

A Winter's Evening—Fragment of an Ode to Winter (unpublished)

Prose fragment concerning dreamlike shapes seen by W while lying in bed (unpublished; cf PREL 533.)

W perhaps engages in some composition on *V* cf *E* in the very early part of the year; but see GCL 13n.]

2. [Probably early this year, certainly before c Mar]

W composes *Sonnet, on Seeing Miss Helen Maria Williams Weep at a Tale of Distress.* (See 1787:7.)

3. [Probably c Jan 15]

[W, JW, CW probably return to Hawkshead from Whitehaven. Administrators' Accounts, CRH. See 1786:17.)][1]

4. [Shortly before Mar 2; Mar 2]

[Probably on or shortly before 2 Mar] W composes *Sonnet Written by Mr. —— Immediately after the Death of His Wife.* He dates a fair copy of the poem on 2 Mar. (MS, DCP.)[2]

---

[9] An entry of £1/16/–, dated 19 Dec, appears in the accounts of RW of Branthwaite for "Chaise hire for the Boys from Hawkshead and Exps." Since end of holiday bills are paid by RW of Whitehaven (see 1787:3), it seems not unlikely that the boys were with their uncle RW before the end of vacation.

[1] The accounts of RW of Whitehaven record payment of £35/1/– to W for discharge of Hawkshead bills and chaisehire and expenses to Hawkshead under 15 Jan 1787.

[2] The poem appears in MS (DCP) on a loose quarto sheet like those containing *Anacreon*, the fragments *On the Death of an Unfortunate Lady* and *A Winter's Evening—*

5. [Probably spring–summer, and on into early 1788]

[Probably in spring and summer] W composes the bulk of *The Vale of Esthwaite*. (See GCL 13n.) [Some composition probably extends into early 1788. The first version of the lines now known as *Extract from the Conclusion of a Poem, Composed in Anticipation of Leaving School* is probably composed at this time as part of *V of E*. (See GCL 13.)]

6. [Shortly before Mar 23, 24; Mar 23, 24]

[Probably on or shortly before 23, 24 Mar] W composes *A Ballad*. He dates a fair copy of the poem on 23, 24 Mar. (MS, DCP.)[3]

[3] *A Ballad* (on which see also Appendix II, C5) is fairly copied on seven pages toward the end of DC MS Verse 4. The leaves on which the poem appears have been torn out and replaced. A loose quarto sheet also contains another fair copy of the last three stanzas of the poem (it is clearly the last page of a full fair copy), which contain no differences of chronological significance from the Nb version. To the loose copy W appends the dates March 23 & 24, 1787. W seems to have meant that he composed the poem on the days mentioned. One may at least assume that he composed it either then or shortly before.

Fragment of an Ode to Winter (on the last two poems see GCL 14), and the dated stanzas from *A Ballad* (see 1787:6). A close comparison of this poem with the *Sonnet, on Seeing Miss Helen Maria Williams Weep at a Tale of Distress* suggests that the two poems must date from roughly the same time and would assure W's authorship of the sonnet on Miss Williams did not better information exist. Both poems, for example, use dashes for caesuras in markedly similar places: one in the first line, after a brief sentence; one after six syllables in the third line; and one after four syllables in a later line. Both show extreme fondness for the locution formed by an abstract (or nearly abstract) noun in the possessive, followed by an adjective, followed by a noun (like "Despair's dark midnight"). The themes, images, even vocabulary and rhymes of the sestets of both are quite similar and in some points identical. It seems reasonable to conjecture that both sonnets were composed in early 1787.

In the IF note to *Miscellaneous Sonnets* W states that the only sonnet he composed before 1801 was "an irregular one at school." W surely remembered the sonnet on Helen Maria Williams in 1846 (see 1787:7n), but that poem deviates from the regular Shakespearean pattern only in having three hexameter lines. The *Sonnet Written by Mr. —* is definitely irregular, and possibly was what he had in mind as he dictated the IF note, although no sure conclusion is possible.

7. [Probably c Apr 1]

W's first published poem, *Sonnet, on Seeing Miss Helen Maria Williams Weep at a Tale of Distress* appears in *The European Magazine* for Mar 1787 over the name "Axiologus."[4]

8. [c Apr 8]

[(Easter.) W, JW, CW possibly receive a short vacation. (See 1779:6n; 1784:6.)]

9. [Probably May]

DW returns from Halifax to the Cooksons' at Penrith. (*EL* 12. See 1778:3.)[5]

[4] Contemporary newspapers indicate that many London monthlies appeared on or about the first day of the month following that for which the issue was dated. Where an advertisement for a given issue of a magazine has not been discovered—as here and frequently below—the date of publication is surmised in accordance with this fact.

The difficulties which scholars have long experienced concerning the attribution of this poem to W could have been avoided if the quotation—imperfect as it is—by Knight (*PW*, Knight, 1882–89, IV, 22) of a virtual acknowledgement by W of his authorship of the poem had not been lost sight of after being last mentioned, apparently, in *PW* (Dowden) V, 176. EdS includes the sonnet in *PW* (I, 269), but gives no reason for doing so; he may or may not have known of W's comment. W's note, pointed out to me by Miss Landon, is in a copy of *EW* (DCP) presented by the poet to his son William 16 Mar 1846; it reads in part: "Previous to the appearance of these two Attempts [*EW* and *DS*] I had not published anything, except a sonnet printed in the European Magazine June or July 1786 when I was a School-Boy. The Sonnet was signe[d] Axiologus." Both Miss Landon and I have failed to find any poem in *The European Magazine* of about June or July 1786 that fits this description. W must have been thinking of the sonnet on Miss Williams.

Fink 4n remarks that these verses "appeared in the *European Magazine* for February 1787, not in the March issue as is often stated." The copies belonging to the Cambridge University Library and BM, however, show that W's poem appears in a section of the March issue misheaded "For February, 1787./ POETRY." Pagination, signatures of the gatherings, the relationship of the contents of this gathering to those of the following—and the fact that the date "For March, 1787" appears as a running head within (fourth leaf recto) the gathering containing W's poem—put the matter beyond doubt.

[5] *EL* 12 is probably the source of EdS's remark on the subject, EdS *DW* 10. On *EL* 12 DW states (probably on 1787 Dec 14; see 1787:31) that it has been seven months since she and her Halifax friend Jane Pollard parted.

10. [May 1]

The administrators of the estate of JW Sr. determine to bring action against Lord Lonsdale for the sum owed by him to the estate. (GGW, Notes on Lonsdale Suit, DCP. See 1786:16.)

11. [Perhaps before c June 20]

[On leaving school] W, John Millar [Miller], R. H. Greenwood, and T. H. Gawthrop present Hoole's translation of Tasso's *Gerusalemme Liberata* and Gillies' *History of Greece* to the school library. (See A. E[arle], "The Library at Hawkshead Grammar School, and the School-days of Wordsworth," *The Eagle*, XVIII, 1894, 386.)[6]

12. [Perhaps c June 20]

Summer vacation begins at Hawkshead School (See 1779:6n; 1787:13.)

13. [Perhaps c June 27 (–Aug 5)]

CCC having willfully delayed for a week sending horses to Hawks-head for the boys, W hires a horse and rides to Penrith to investigate. CCC then sends for JW and CW. [They return to Hawkshead 5 Aug.] (*EL* 3; 1779:6n; 1787:17.)

14. [Perhaps c June 27–Oct 20–23; 1788 summer; 1789 summer]

[W refers to his reunion with his sister and his activities, during these periods, with DW and MH (not with DW in 1789), esp. their visits to Brougham Castle and the Beacon: *Prel* VI.208–45, *Prel*$_2$ VI.190–236; PREL 551–52; *Prel* XI.316–26, *Prel*$_2$ XI.261–69.][7]

---

[6] The spelling "Millar" is that inscribed in the books themselves. Millar is described as being of "Presal" (Preesall, Lancs), and is probably identical with the John Miller "of Lancs" who matriculated at Jesus College, Cambridge, Michaelmas 1787 (Venn).

[7] *Prel* VI.214–18, *Prel*$_2$ VI.199–203 would actually refer to June–July 1787 rather than July–August 1787 as suggested PREL 551; but PREL 551–52 is undoubtedly correct in suggesting that W must have been thinking of summer 1787 when speaking of his reunion with his sister "after separation desolate." The same source is equally correct in suggesting that the passages cited describing W's activities with MH and DW combine events of 1787, 1788, and 1789, if such qualifications are noted as: (a) DW was not in Penrith summer 1789 (see 1788:28) nor, perhaps, was MH (*EY* 31n); (b) Margaret Hutchinson was perhaps among those wandering with W (see Margoliouth 52–53); and (c) it is doubtful that W did any wandering in or near Penrith in 1789 (see all entries referring to W's summer vacation 1789, esp. 1789:7n). *EL* 526 perhaps refers to these periods.

15. July 5

W is admitted as a sizar at St. John's College, Cambridge, tutor Edward Frewen. (Venn; Scott *Admissions* IV, 56, 571.)

16. [Probably July 22]

DW writes to Jane Pollard [from Penrith]: DW's description of her brothers. The humiliating life and unhappiness of the W children at the Cooksons'. Discussion of Lonsdale debt and the children's financial prospects. Suggestions that W is subject to chronic poor health. (*EL* 1–5.)[8]

[8] EdS dates the letter "[summer—1787]" (*EL* I). It is written on a Sunday, and W, JW, and CW have been at home at least four days: DW writes of JW's having helped her on the previous Wednesday. W had perhaps arrived c 27 June (see 1787:13), probably in any case in late June or very early July, with JW and CW following him two days or so later. As DW says that she, W, JW, and CW have shed tears together "many a time," as she has had time to form distinct impressions of her brothers and write them down (evidently not having seen them since 1778), and as she is looking forward uneasily to her brothers' departure for Hawkshead—not likely behavior immediately after their arrival—it seems fairly certain that the letter was not written on Sunday 1 July.

DW's next surviving letter, also to JP, was begun on a "Monday" (*EL* 5), the day after the boys' departure for Hawkshead the same summer. CCC's accounts (CRH) record payment of Hawkshead bills under the date of 5 Aug, and Ann Tyson's ledger notes a loan of £-/10/0 beneath the heading "William Wordsworth account" under the same date (Moorman *Transactions* 153–54). It therefore looks clear that the Monday in question was that of 6 Aug. Likewise clear is that DW has heard from JP since last writing herself (*EL* 7); so that it seems quite impossible (evidence below will add further confirmation) that *EL* no. 1 could date from Sunday 5 Aug.

The letter begun 6 Aug contains the remark that DW thinks it better "not to have any stated time for writing" (*EL* 8), as they have lately had up till now. In *EL* no. 1, dated on a Sunday, she tells JP to "write on Sunday [that is, the following Sunday] and depend upon an answer"; she had earlier urged her (*EL* 2) to write at "the appointed time." In the letter begun 6 Aug, a Monday, she apologizes for not having written on the "appointed day"—the day before, Sunday. These remarks indicate that DW and JP had an agreement to write on set days, and that the days were alternate Sundays. DW had delayed a week beyond her fixed time before writing *EL* no. 1 (*EL* 1–2), and *EL* no. 2 appears to involve her second offense of delay (*EL* 5); her care in apologizing implies also that JP had been keeping her end of the bargain. Thus JP had probably written to DW Sunday 29 July, and DW had probably written *some* letter to JP on 22 July. If *EL* no. 1 was in fact the letter of 22 July, the date it *should* have been written (in terms of the agreement) would be 15 July. More likely than not

17. [Aug 5 (–perhaps c Oct 7)]

W accompanies JW and CW to Hawkshead from Penrith as they return to school. [He departs perhaps c 7 Oct.] (Administrators' Accounts, CRH; *EL* 5. See 1787:19.)

18. [Probably Aug 6, 7]

DW writes to Jane Pollard [from Penrith]: W's departure [for Hawkshead]; her distressing prospects for the winter; her life at Penrith. Her father's estate and the Lonsdale debt. W's plans for Cambridge and later. Her reading. (*EL* 5–8. On date see 1787:16n.)[9]

19. [Perhaps c Oct 7; perhaps c Oct 7–perhaps shortly before, fairly certainly by, Oct 23]

[Perhaps c 7 Oct W returns to Penrith from Hawkshead. He departs perhaps shortly before, fairly certainly by, c 23 Oct. (Moorman *Transactions* 154; Administrators' Accounts, CRH.)

During W's visit in Penrith DW prepares his clothes for Cambridge. W obtains Burns's *Poems*, 1786, for DW at the book club. (W has already read them. See *At the Grave of Burns*.) (*EL*, 10, 12. On dates see 1787:18; 1787:20.)][10]

20. [Perhaps shortly before, fairly certainly by, Oct 23 (–probably Oct 30)]

W sets out to Cambridge from Penrith. [He is perhaps accompanied by his uncle William Cookson,] and he is accompanied or soon joined

[9] DW's letter, begun on Monday 6 Aug, was concluded "Tuesday." EdS's date is "[Aug 5 or 6.]."

[10] W was charged for 9 weeks' board by Ann Tyson. Nine weeks from 5 Aug (see 1787:17) is 6 or 7 Oct (or even 8 Oct) depending on how the days of arrival and departure are counted. Ann Tyson's bookkeeping methods are of course not fully known; I have assumed, somewhat arbitrarily, that she counted the day of W's arrival but not the day of his trip home. This calculation would suggest a return to Penrith on 7 Oct.

such a letter would have been in reply to a letter written on 8 July. Since, as remarked above, it seems unlikely that *EL* no. 1 was written Sunday 1 July or before, and since (in view of the probable sequence of the exchange between the girls through the rest of July) there seems no reasonable way to suppose that DW wrote to JP on 8 July, Sunday 22 July is probably the best choice for a date for this letter.

by his cousin John Myers (1767–1821), who, like W, is entering St. John's College. [He arrives at Cambridge probably 30 Oct.] (Administrators' Accounts, CRH; *EL* 7, 10, 565. See 1787:23.)[11]

21. [Between perhaps shortly before, certainly by, Oct 23 and Oct 30]

W and John Myers (see 1787:20) stop three or four days in York with Mary Myers Robinson (Myers' sister and W's cousin) and her husband Capt. Hugh Robinson. (*EL* 11; *Robinson of the White House, Appleby,* 100.)[12]

During this journey to Cambridge W for the first time hears "the voice of Woman utter blasphemy" and sees woman abandoned "to open shame" and "the pride of public vice." [W refers to this event: *Prel* VII.412–28, *Prel*₂ VII.382–93.][13]

---

[11] Moorman I, 88, suggests a departure about 23 Oct. DW states (*EL* 10) that W was with her three weeks before leaving for Cambridge. W is not likely to have returned from Hawkshead much before 7 Oct; but the accounts of CCC record payment of £15/10/– in cash on 20 Oct, and CCC would hardly have given W this large amount long before the time of his departure; this fact and the length of W's journey southward (which seems to have included a three or four days' visit in York) render it likely that despite DW's comment W departed from Penrith by about the date suggested by Mrs. Moorman.

DW writes on [7 Aug] 1787 that William Cookson is to accompany W to Cambridge (*EL* 7); but this is the only basis I know for supposing that he did so. (Schneider I states, and Moorman I, 88, implies, that he did; DW's reference to the completed trip on *EL* 11 does not mention him. See also 1787:21, which does not either.)

[12] A copy of *Robinson of the White House* (anonymous, late nineteenth century) is in the DC Library. It contains (same page) two anecdotes concerning this trip which I have not seen quoted elsewhere:

"Wordsworth... went up as a Freshman with [Myers], October 1787. In passing through York they wished to find the house of Captain Robinson, who then lived in Micklegate. Wordsworth inquired his way of a man in the street, who answered 'I'll show you if you'll give me sixpence,' on which Wordsworth said to his cousin, 'Well, John, I can see that we are in Yorkshire now.' They found the house, and greeted, the one his sister, the other his first cousin. 'I hope, William, you mean to take a good degree,' said Captain Robinson. 'I will either be Senior Wrangler or nothing,' replied Wordsworth. 'And he *was* nothing—at Cambridge,' said the shrewd old lady who heard and related this [Mary Myers Robinson], and who survived her beloved cousin nearly two years."

[13] These events occurred, W says, when he had advanced southward "Two hundred miles." Moorman I, 88, suggests Stamford or Grantham as possible locations.

75

22. [Perhaps c Oct 23]

W composes a Farewell to Helvellyn (in prose), "What is it that tells my soul the sun is setting [?]" (MS, DCP. See 1787:21.)[14]

23. [Probably Oct 30–1789 c Jan, 1791 Jan 21]

[Probably arriving in Cambridge (at the Hoop Inn), on 30 Oct, W comes into residence at St. John's College, Cambridge on that day His tutor [probably until c Jan 1789] is Edward Frewen. W remains student here until 21 Jan 1791. (Scott *Admissions* IV, 56, 571. See 1792:14n; 1791:5.) [W refers to the arrival: *Prel* III.1–15, *Prel* III.1–17.][15]

24. [Probably Oct 30–1791 Jan 21]

[References in W's own writings to his years at Cambridge which are capable of relatively specific dating are entered in the text or notes On this period generally see esp. Schneider *passim* and Moorman I 86–153. Many of the references mentioned in the text or notes are said by W to apply to his first year (and probably largely do so apply), but must include feelings and experiences of his later Cambridge years as well. Other references, incapable of specific dating, include:

1. *Prel* VIII.641–77, *Prel*₂ VIII.495–529. (W an idler among academic bowers; growth of his mind at Cambridge; his attention to moral subjects.)
2. *Prel* IX.225–32, *Prel*₂ IX.222–32. (Cambridge as something of a republic.)
3. *Prel* XI.224–42, *Prel*₂ XII.174–92. (When first called from native hills, he feels, and nothing else; the same heart is with him in the Alps. Thus this description probably applies to his feelings through the entire Cambridge period.)

[14] This Farewell occupies a page in MS Verse 3 (which gave EdS MS A of *V of E*) It is a kind of Ossianic prose poem, although it may have been meant to serve as draft work for verse. Much of the passage is a plea to "the spirit of these mountains," who sits enthroned on Helvellyn, to bid the mist break from his forehead and to nod the speaker thrice "farewell." The subject suggests a time (which is not contradicted by anything else in the Nb) about that of W's departure for Cambridge.

[15] John Myers came into residence the same day (Scott *Admissions* IV, 394). Concerning Hawkshead students now at or entering Cambridge see esp. Schneider 1–3

4. *Mem* I, 13–15 (Autobiog Mem); *Mem* II, 463–64 (*Mem*, R, II, 472–73). (Failure to write verses upon the death of the master of St. John's—see 1789:4. He studies Italian under Agostino Isola; feels envy toward his fellow student in Italian, possibly William Mathews.)

5. *Monument of Mrs. Howard* IF note. (Sees Pitt often at Cambridge and in House of Commons.)

6. Worth note here also is *The Gentleman's Magazine* LXIV (1794), 252. (At Cambridge W meets a now unidentifiable future reviewer of *EW* and *DS* who hears W speak warmly of the beauties of the North.)][16]

25. [Oct 30–1788 early June]

[W's first school year at Cambridge. W appears to refer primarily or entirely to this period in the following passages. Experiences or feelings of later years may in some cases, however, play a part in his descriptions. (See also 1787:24.)

1. *Prel* III, *Prel*₂ III. Esp.:
 a. *Prel* III.16–167, *Prel*₂ III.18–169. (Early observations and impressions of Cambridge; his manner of living. He feels that he is not for that time or place. The growth of his mind there.)

[16] Schneider deals with all major aspects of W's years at Cambridge, and makes many useful suggestions about his college reading, his probable preparations for examinations, and the like. Moorman deals with all these topics somewhat more briefly. Of interest also (although the most important of its contents are noted in the more widely available sources just mentioned) is *W at Cambridge*.

On Isola see Edmund Gosse, *Gray* (London, 1889) 181; Lamb *Letters* III, 86, 123, 169; Schneider 99–103; Moorman I, 99–100; entries by George Dyer (as Lamb *Letters* III, 169) and Matilda Betham in the album of Emma Isola [Moxon], HUL. It is not known when W began his studies of Italian or how long they continued, although Schneider suggests the year 1788–89. W was reading Ariosto during the summer of 1790 (see Schneider 103, 275–76); so he had almost surely begun his study by some time in 1789. On W's Italian reading generally see Schneider 103, 275–76; Moorman I, 99–100.

The inference that the fellow student of W's toward whom W felt envy was William Mathews, his friend and correspondent over the coming decade, is made by Schneider 102–03. Mathews knew some Italian before coming to Cambridge, and this suggestion is probably the best that can be made on the basis of present evidence. (See Mrs. [Anne Jackson] Mathews, *Memoirs of Charles Mathews*, London, 1838–39, I, 35.)

b. *Prel* III.202–375, *Prel*₂ III.204–371. (Observations and impression of Cambridge. His activities; his reading; a jovial evening during which he drinks deeply in honor of Milton.)

c. *Prel* III.433–39, *Prel*₂ III.426–30. (His disappointed expectation of Cambridge.)

d. *Prel* III.506–672, *Prel*₂ III.496–635. (Observations and impression of Cambridge. The growth of his mind.)

2. *Prel* XI.224–42, *Prel*₂ XII.174–92. (The character of his mind when he is first called forth from his native hills. See 1787:24.)

3. *Yarrow Visited* IF note. (College reading.)][17]

26. [Probably late this year]

W writes first version of *Dirge, Sung by a Minstrel*. (MS, DCP.)[18]

27. [Shortly after Oct 30]

W receives two exhibitions. (*W at Cambridge* 3.)

28. Nov 6

W is admitted Foundress Scholar at St. John's College. (Scott *Admissions* IV, 571.)

29. [Probably late Nov or early Dec]

DW writes to Jane Pollard [from Penrith]: Her unhappy life in her grandparents' home. Her education under her uncle [William Cookson]. Her wish to visit various friends and relations. (*EL* 8–11.)[19]

---

[17] The jovial evening (1b) was probably spent in the rooms of his Hawkshead classmate Edward Joseph Birkett (see Prel 529). On the question of whether W actually "laughed with Chaucer" while at Cambridge see esp. Moorman I, 100–01.

[18] The work on this version of the poem, for a boy, appears in Nb Verse 4 just preceding the version for a girl, which dates from Jan 1788 and possibly shortly after (see 1788:7). While certainty in the matter is not possible, one suspects that the first version did not long precede the second.

[19] *EL* 8 gives a date of "[late autumn–1787]." Since DW has had time to hear from W since his arrival at Cambridge (*EL* 11), the letter was written at least a few days after 30 Oct. She mentions the "long silence" of which she has been guilty

30. [Dec]

[W takes college examinations.] The reports of the results place him in the first class. (*W at Cambridge* 31; Schneider 13.)

31. [Probably Dec 14–16]

DW writes to Jane Pollard [from Penrith]: Her wishes to see JP and visit Halifax. Her opinions of Burns's poems. Her social life at Penrith. Thoughts and questions about Halifax and people there. (*EL* 12–14.)[20]

---

[20] EdS dates this letter as begun "Friday Decr 17th [1787]," with the final date in the PS "Sunday night Decr 16th [? 19th]" (*EL* 12, 14; bracketed dates inserted by EdS). The year is surely 1787: In Dec of 1786 DW was in Halifax; in 1788 she was in Forncett; and it has been just seven months since DW left Halifax (*EL* 12). But 17 Dec 1787 was not a Friday; nor was 19 Dec a Sunday. DW's own concluding date, "Sunday night Decr 16th," is unexceptionable from the standpoint of agreement of date and day, and can be accepted as the date on which the letter was finished. She probably misdated the letter on Friday. (The MS, DCP, makes it plain that EdS did not misread "Decr 14th," which would have been the correct date for that Friday, as "Decr 17th.") The autograph suggests that the PS up through "Telling me" *EL* 13) was written at the same time as the body of the letter ("Friday"), and that the PS from "I thank you" to the end of the letter belongs to a different time from all that precedes it—no doubt to "Sunday night." In the second part of the PS DW says that she received JP's letter on "Thursday," but since DW indicates just before her "Friday" date that she has not heard from JP, she must again be mistaken. It would seem not likely that DW erred as she noted the day of the week she was writing on *when* she wrote; probably she was being careless on Sunday in remembering the time of arrival of JP's letter. Since DW closed the first part of her letter "Friday morn eleven oclock," she could still easily have received JP's letter on Friday.

---

before writing this letter (*EL* 11), and on probably 14 Dec (*EL* 12; see 1787:31) she fears that JP may think her "very unreasonable" for being in daily expectation of hearing from JP in response to her last, which she had been "so long in writing." As there would not have been time between early Nov (the earliest possible date for this letter) and 14 Dec for DW to have written an intermediate letter capable of being construed as coming after any appreciable silence, the present letter must be the one DW is referring to on 14 Dec. If DW regarded herself as perhaps unduly impatient for a reply to this letter on 14 Dec, she was probably hoping to receive the reply within a period of not much over two weeks from the time of her writing this (I assume that she was allowing a reasonable amount of time for the passage of the letters to and fro).

32. Dec 17

W signs the Matriculation Register of Cambridge University (Scott *Admissions* IV, 571.)[21]

33. [Between c Dec 17 and 1788 Jan]

[Some chance possibly exists that during his Christmas holidays W makes a brief visit to London, his first. (See 1788:2; 1787:32n.)]

34. [Perhaps c Dec 20]

[JW and CW probably travel to Whitehaven or Branthwaite for Christmas vacation. JW withdraws from the school. (W refers to this event in "When to the Attractions of the Busy World" 67.) (Administrators' Accounts, CRH; GGW *Cornhill* 415. See 1779:6n; 1784:9n.)]

35. [c Dec 19]

William Cookson, grandfather of W, dies suddenly at Penrith. (See 1787:36; *EL* 14.)[22]

36. Dec 22

William Cookson is buried at Penrith. (Penrith. See 1787:35.)

1788

1. [Early Jan–1792 end of Feb]

[The Earl of Lonsdale receives in early Jan a summons on "Original Bill and Summons." The summons is the latest step in the suit of the administrators of the estate of JW Sr. for Lonsdale's debt to the estate (see 1786:16). Lonsdale begins a series of delays and evasions lasting

---

[21] The dates of the Cambridge terms were as follows: Michaelmas Term, 10 Oct–16 Dec; Lent Term, 13 Jan–Friday before Palm Sunday; Easter (or May) Term, eleventh day after Easter–Friday after Commencement Day (which was usually the first Tuesday in July). A matriculation took place the day after each term. Candidates for the B.A. were required to reside for "the greater part" of any term counting toward their degree. (Adam Wall, *An Account of the Different Ceremonies Observed in the Senate House of the University of Cambridge*, Cambridge, 1798, 8, 37, 38, 41–42, 67, 76, 82.)

[22] W erred when he told RW in 1813 (*MY* 567) that their grandfather died autumn 1788.

hrough 1792 Feb. (GGW, Notes on Lonsdale Suit, DCP. See 1788:10;
1788:11.)]

2. [During this year]

[On writings of W possibly of this year see below and GCL 2, 6–8,
13, 15, 22–36.

Through much of this year W is probably engaged in translating
rom Vergil, esp. *Georgics*. Some of his translation, in heroic couplets,
probably takes place in early 1788, possibly as late as summer. Other, in
blank verse, probably took place in summer or autumn or both, with
some composition perhaps slightly later. (See GCL 23; Appendix V.)

During this year W perhaps visits London for the first time. (W
refers to this event esp.: *Prel* VII.72–74, *Prel*$_2$ VII.65–68; *Prel* VIII.689–
710, *Prel*$_2$ VIII.539–59. Also see PREL 562; 1789:14.)][1]

3. [Probably early this year and/or summer]

W writes:

Drafts of an elaborate description of a storm comparing the storm
to an eagle or condor. (See GCL 22; Appendix V.)

Drafts describing someone's madness as the "shipwreck of a soul."
See GCL 22; Appendix V.)

[1] It is impossible to date with certainty W's first visit to London. Moorman I, 124,
believes it occurred at Christmas vacation 1789–90. In the first set of passages cited
from *Prel* the 1805 version remarks that in 1791 it had been "at least two years"
since he had first beheld the "mighty city"; the 1850 version says "three years."
Although several intermediate MSS omit all reference to the span of time, the periods
mentioned are not at great variance; they seem to imply plainly that W had been in
London before Christmas 1789–90 (see 1789:14), a visit that preceded his departure
for London in late Jan or Feb 1791 by only a year. W speaks of himself consistently as
having been a "transient visitant" on his first trip. How short a stay such phrasing
implies is uncertain (he had time to "pace" London's "endless streets"), but it probably refers to a period briefer than the one he seems to have spent at Christmas
1789–90. The only other occasion before early 1791 when W can be shown fairly
certainly to have been a "transient visitant" to London is summer of 1790, about 10
July, on his way to Europe—obviously not the reference of the passages.

I incline to believe that W had visited London at least briefly by very early 1789,
perhaps in 1788. Beatty *RP* 330n suggests 1788. As good a specific guess as any is
that of Schneider 63—the end of W's summer vacation in 1788. Christmas vacation
1787–88 and 1788–89 are other possibilities.

4. [Probably early this year, perhaps by late spring]

W writes:

Orpheus and Eurydice. (See GCL 24; Appendix V.)

Short prose draft forming basis for *EW* 37–42. (See GCL 24 Appendix V.)

Fragment: Simile describing the terror of a shepherd. (See GCL 24 Appendix V.)

5. [Possibly c early this year]

W composes two prose epitaphs. [This date is extremely uncertain. (See GCL 25; Appendix VI.)

6. [Perhaps c early this year]

W writes a blank verse fragment toward a poem on Milton (*PW* V, 362). (See GCL 26.)

7. Jan [and possibly shortly after]

W writes second version of *Dirge, Sung by a Minstrel.* (MS DCP.)[2]

8. [Probably late Jan, or Feb; possibly as late as Mar]

JW sails for Barbados on his first voyage. (See *EL* 15; 1788:9n.)

9. [Probably late Jan, or Feb; perhaps Jan 27, even more likely Feb 10]

DW writes to Jane Pollard [from Penrith]: The death of her grandfather William Cookson. Her longing to visit Halifax; her loneliness for JP and Halifax friends. JW has set sail for Barbados. (*EL* 14–16.)[3]

---

[2] This version (in Nb Verse 4) is headed "Cambridge Janry 88" in an autograph obviously contemporary with what follows just below it. The draft as a whole follows directly upon the first version of the *Dirge*, continues for several pages, is not all in an identical autograph, and is much corrected; it then is followed (after four leaves torn out) by two pages of a new copy of the same poem (itself with some corrections), following which five more leaves have been torn out. Probably it is justifiable to conclude that W's work on this version was extensive, and quite likely continued beyond the month in which it began.

[3] EdS suggests a date of January 1788 for this letter. He probably bases his suggestion primarily on DW's description of the interval in the correspondence with JP (*EL* 14)

10. [Between Apr 15 and May 7]

Easter Term of Court. The Earl of Lonsdale obtains an injunction, by a bill filed in the Court of the Exchequer, to stay proceedings against him by the administrators of the estate of JW Sr. on the ground that

---

or the fact that DW seems to report her grandfather's death (which occurred c 19 Dec 1787) to JP here. One difficulty is posed by DW's remark that "John has set sail for Barbadoes." GGW interprets the family accounts (Notes on the Family Accounts, DCP) as indicating that JW did no sailing until August and September of 1788, but it seems fairly clear that this is too late. A Mr. Wood was paid by RW of Whitehaven for "schooling" for JW on 24 Feb, and was again paid on 22 Oct for "teaching John navigation"; so Wood was very likely instructing JW in nautical matters early in the year. Payment for such items as dried mutton and rum was noted on 30 Jan, for cheese and soap "for Nep: John" 24 Feb, for four sea hats for John 10 Mar, for shoes for him 9 July. A guinea cash and freight for his chest are recorded for him on 6 Aug, and among later items appears a note of payment on 4 Oct for "washing John's Sea Cloaths." (Administrators' Accounts, CRH.) It is improbable that JW sailed for Barbados in Dec 1787: He left Hawkshead only about 20 Dec 1787 and had no known experience with ocean sailing previously. The entries from the accounts just noted do not give much basis for assuming that JW had sailed by late Jan, but do indicate that he had fairly surely gone to sea by late Feb or early Mar. Probably he was in the Whitehaven area around early Aug, but had again been to sea before early Oct. Probably JW did not depart on his first extended cruise *before* late Jan.

DW's information about JW's sailing could be a bit premature, but it is clearly a long time since JP had last written DW (*EL* 14), the last known letter from JP to DW having apparently reached Dorothy 14 Dec 1787 (see 1787:31n). The girls seem to have agreed that they would write one another once a month, each writing on a Sunday two weeks after the other (*EL* 16). DW's hope that in the "next six weeks" JP would let her have "twice the number of letters" she would have if she had not been "so long unable to write" could be an indication that the interval between DW's present letter and her last was six weeks, or, as seems more likely, that JP had not written for six weeks after DW's last to her. As DW did not reply to JP's letter until two weeks after JP wrote (on the "last Sunday but one"—*EL* 16), a period of something like six weeks or two months could have passed between 14 Dec 1787 and this letter. A mid-February date for this letter would put it more surely within the period by which JW was at sea. If there had in fact been an exchange between DW's last known letter (14–16 Dec 1787) and this one (DW's remarks on the death of her grandfather do not preclude the possibility), the date of the letter under discussion would be pushed into Mar, by which time JW and his four sea hats are all the more likely to have departed; but such an exchange seems rather doubtful. I am inclined to give the letter a date of probably late Jan or Feb, perhaps 27 Jan, even more likely 10 Feb. More conclusive evidence is needed before the possibility of a later date can be dismissed altogether.

JW Sr. had agreed to do all business for £100 per annum. [No agreement of the sort, evidently, had ever existed between them.] (GGW, Notes on Lonsdale Suit, DCP; H. Black, *Black's Law Dictionary*, fourth edn, St. Paul, 1951, s.v. "Easter Term.")

11. [May–1791 early Mar]

In May the administrators of the estate of JW Sr. obtain an order *nisi* to dissolve Lonsdale's injunction [see 1788:10], but various delaying tactics by Lonsdale prevent dissolution of the injunction until early Mar 1791. (GGW, Notes on Lonsdale Suit, DCP. See 1791:8.)

12. [Early June (before June 8)]

[W takes college examinations.] The reports of the results place him in the second class. (*W at Cambridge* 31. See Schneider 16, 28, 55; 1788:13.)

13. [Early June, c June 8 and after (–probably between Oct 18 or shortly after and Nov 3)]

[W travels from Cambridge to Hawkshead via Ashbourne (Derby). (W refers to his departure from Cambridge: *Prel* III.671–72, *Prel*₂ III.634–35.) He perhaps wanders extensively in Yorkshire and Lancashire on his way. (He returns to Cambridge probably between 18 Oct or shortly after and 3 Nov.) (See entries below through 1788:18; 1788:30.)][4]

14. [Summer; 1789 summer]

[During one or both summers W wanders fairly extensively in Yorkshire and Lancashire, esp. about the Appenine between the two counties. He observes cottage life in the region of the Appenine. (W refers to these activities: *Prel* VI.208–10, *Prel*₂ VI.190–95.) (See 1788:13; *The Force of Prayer* IF note.)

Probably during one or both summers W spends some time

---

[4] W says in the *Prel* passage that he had spent eight or nine months at Cambridge. Seven months would have been a more correct figure in terms of literal chronology. See the next two entries and notes.

visiting his cousin Mary Wordsworth Smith (daughter of RW of Whitehaven) at Broughton. (See *The River Duddon* IF note and Sonnet XXI; Moorman I, 122n.)

On W's activities with DW, MH, and perhaps Margaret Hutchinson during these periods—W would have seen them after his long visit (if it was one single long visit; see 1788:18) to Hawkshead in summer 1788—see 1787:14.][5]

15. [Probably c summer and autumn, and possibly slightly later]

W develops his conception of, and engages in early work on, *EW*. (See GCL 28; Appendix V.)

He develops from blank verse into heroic couplets a passage describing a female vagrant freezing with her two children. The passage forms the basis of *EW* 257–300. (See GCL 28; Appendix V.)

He develops a description of pity, *V of E* 125–30, 138–52, into heroic couplets forming the basis of *EW* 379–88. (See GCL 28; Appendix V.)

He writes *In Part from Moschus—Lament for Bion*. (See GCL 29; Appendix V.)

---

[5] PREL 532 states that W reached Kendal by coach; Moorman I, 105–06, says that W went directly from Ashbourne (see 1788:17) to Kendal, where he spent the night, then walked across the moors to Windermere Ferry and so to Hawkshead the following day. *Prel* IV.1–15, *Prel*₂ IV.1–26, which refer to the last part of his trip, offer no justification for the assumption of a coach trip. If W walked from Kendal to Hawkshead, he did not have so much baggage as would necessarily force him to come by coach from Ashbourne. (He evidently had a horse the evening he "rode over" to Dovedale. See 1788:17; Moorman I, 105). There is perhaps evidence which I have not seen for the coach ride and for W's spending the night at Kendal; on the basis of present knowledge I leave open at least the possibility that W did not come directly to Hawkshead, but wandered about for a time in Yorkshire and Lancashire.

The exact times or extent of W's "sundry wanderings" these summers appear impossible to judge, as implied in the text and notes below. PREL 551 suggests that Bolton and Fountains Abbeys were among the "works of art" (*Prel*₂ VI.190) which W sought, but the Advertisement to *The White Doe of Rylstone* shows that W first visited Bolton and the country around it in 1807. W states in the IF note to *The River Duddon* that he "was several times resident in the house of a near relative" in Broughton "during [his] college vacation, and two or three years afterwards, before taking [his] Bachelor's degree." "Before taking" should be "after taking" (see Moorman I, 122n).

16. [Probably c summer]

W writes:

Fragment: Heroic description of a warrior moving (apparently) to battle. (See GCL 30.)

Description (blank verse) of a castle, forming the basis of *Gothic Tale* 17–23. (See GCL 30; Appendix V.)

Several fragments (blank verse) of natural description. (See GCL 30; Appendix V.)

17. [1788] June 8 [and possibly shortly after]

W arrives at Ashbourne on 8 June; rides out to see Dovedale this evening. [Probably this same evening] he writes a fragmentary journal description of Dovedale. (See Moorman I, 105; *Prel* VI.208–10, *Prel*$_2$ VI.190–95.)

[Either this evening or the following day (or shortly thereafter), W probably visits a rocky recess at Ilam where Congreve was said to have written *The Old Bachelor*. (See *At Florence* IF note.)][6]

---

[6] As Mrs. Moorman remarks, the short journal entry in DCP MS Verse 7 in which W describes these events would seem to belong, on the basis of *Prel* VI.208–10, *Prel*$_2$ VI.190–95, to the summer of 1789. Such is the assumption of Schneider 112. Mrs. Moorman and EdS, however, believe that W visited Forncett at the beginning of the long vacation 1789, and I concur in this opinion. (See PREL, EdS, 608 f, g; 1789:6. On Nb Verse 7 see also Appendix V.)

In the IF note to *At Florence* W is recorded as stating that in one of his college vacation rambles he visited "at [   ] a seat near a kind of rocky cell at the source of the river [   ], on which it was said that Congreve wrote his 'Old Bachelor.'" Of the several places which vie for the honor of having been the location of the composition of *The Old Bachelor*, the one W visited must have been that at Ilam, four miles northwest of Ashbourne. "The kind of rocky cell," on a hill beside the Manifold River, is described in detail in J. C. Hodges, "The Composition of Congreve's First Play," *PMLA* LVIII (1943), 971–76. See also R. G. Howarth, "Congreve's First Play. Addendum," *PMLA* LX (1946), 596–97. Boswell describes the same scene in *Life of Johnson* (ed. G. B. Hill and L. F. Powell, Oxford, 1934–50, III, 187). The cell is not near the source of a river, but the Manifold rises at Ilam after traveling underground for several miles. W possibly visited these sights on the evening he rode out to Dovedale from Ashbourne, but he leaves no clear evidence in the matter, and the visit perhaps took place the following day or after. Summer 1789 is not an impossible date, but clearly much less likely than the present suggestion.

18. [Probably June 10 or shortly after, and nine weeks during the summer]

[Probably on 10 June or shortly after W arrives at Hawkshead via Kendal and the Windermere Ferry. (W refers to this event: *Prel* IV.1–15, *Prel*₂ IV.1–26. See also 1788:3; 1788:17.) W spends nine weeks of his vacation at Hawkshead, with Ann Tyson at Colthouse. (Moorman *Transactions* 154.)

(W refers to the time spent this summer at Hawkshead: *Prel* IV and *Prel*₂ IV *passim*. He refers to the nature and progress of his mind at this time, including his unconscious "dedication," esp.: *Prel* IV.121–246, 268–504; *Prel*₂ IV.131–255, 276–469. See also PREL 535–37; *STCL* II, 1033. On the events and impressions following immediately upon W's arrival at Hawkshead see *Prel* IV.16–91, *Prel*₂ IV.27–100.)][7]

[7] The description of W's possible manner of travel between Ashbourne and Hawkshead shows that he could not have reached Hawkshead before 10 June.

In a bill dated 6 Jan of the following year Ann Tyson charges W for nine weeks' board. It is not quite definite that W spent all nine weeks at Hawkshead on a single visit, although that appears the most probable assumption. It seems certain that W visited Penrith and Whitehaven (see 1788:23–29) and that he came to Hawkshead from Cambridge without visiting any close relatives (see 1788:13). The unambiguous statement of *Prel*₂ that the meeting with the discharged soldier took place in the autumn, when the summer months were flown, need not conflict with the 1805 statement that the event was "ere these summer months were passed away"; in 1805 W was probably using "summer months" to mean only "summer vacation."

Entries of possible relevance in the family accounts prove puzzling. CCC makes an entry for £36/8/6 cash on W's account under 21 June; an entry for £2/2/– is made by RW of Whitehaven under 28 Aug, another for the same amount by CCC under 18 Sept. A washing bill (shared with JW) is recorded as paid by RW of Whitehaven 4 Oct, and more cash, £1/1/–, noted on W's account under 5 Oct. Then two entries are made for cash (total £7/16/9) under 18 Oct by CCC. RW of Whitehaven seems always to use "remitted" for transfer of funds to W elsewhere than Whitehaven; "cash" pretty surely implies that he gave the amounts to W personally. Thus W might well have been in Whitehaven some time about 28 Aug and 5 Oct. Whether CCC's accounts can be interpreted to imply that W was in Penrith about 21 June, 18 Sept, and 18 Oct is much less certain (his bookkeeping appears ordinarily less methodical than that of RW of Whitehaven); but that is their most apparent significance. If such was the case, W was traveling much, and the only time for an extended visit to Hawkshead would have been from after c 21 June until c 28 Aug; this period would allow a visit of nine weeks. W did not, however, travel to Penrith before coming to Hawkshead. Could he have come to Hawkshead first, gone thence to Penrith, and returned? Then have traveled from Hawkshead to Whitehaven and

19. [c June 21]

[W is perhaps in Penrith on a visit of undetermined length. (Administrators' Accounts, CRH. See 1788:18n.)]

20. [Possibly this summer (probably 1789)]

[While residing at Hawkshead,] W, after a dance, encounters a discharged soldier. [W refers to this event: *Prel* IV.369–504, *Prel*₂ IV.370–469.] (See 1789:10; PREL 536; 1788:18n; 1788:25.)

---

thence twice between Whitehaven and Penrith, with possibly an autumnal visit at Hawkshead, before leaving for Cambridge? It would be difficult to believe that the pattern of his movements was so complex. (A charge by Ann Tyson on 6 Jan 1787 for £-/1/6 for horsehire in addition to board charge probably indicates a trip to Penrith or Whitehaven; but her entry offers no suggestion of the date of the trip.)

June 21 would have been a likely time for CW to be fetched to Penrith for the summer (see 1779:6n), and CCC might have been in Hawkshead then, but CW's bills were not discharged until Aug; hence one suspects that CW spent most of his summer at Hawkshead with W. (DW's remark of Feb 1793—*EL* 83—that she and CW had been separated "nearly five years last Christmas" would tend to confirm that he did not return to Penrith this summer.) The accounts show, however, that W was definitely at Hawkshead c 16 Sept 1789. How long he was there is not indicated, but this evidence nevertheless offers the best available indication for a time when W can be supposed to have met the discharged soldier in the autumn, while at Hawkshead, on a college vacation. If the meeting with the discharged soldier is considered an event of late summer vacation 1789, but recounted in *Prel*, by accident or design of condensation, as an event of summer 1788, W's movements during the period from 18 Sept through 18 Oct are to some extent simplified. I can offer no other simplification. Probably he paid at least one visit to Penrith in the late summer, sometimes about 18 Sept or 18 Oct, and at least one to Whitehaven sometime about 28 Aug or 4 Oct (where he saw JW and shared his washing bill). And it must remain a possibility that he paid two visits to each place at the times mentioned. The length of any given visit could have varied from a day to several weeks. I incline to believe, since the accounts do indicate an autumn during which W was very likely at Hawkshead and could well have met the discharged soldier (1789), that a return to Hawkshead for a visit of two or three weeks before leaving for Cambridge, as suggested Moorman I, 114, is not the most likely conjecture that can be made for this period. It seems at least quite as probable that W departed from Penrith for Cambridge (see 1788:30).

This period is chosen somewhat arbitrarily as a referent for STC's description of W's early decision to do "one thing well" (*STCL* II, 1033), a choice that would seem linked with W's becoming a "dedicated Spirit." But an exact assignment of a time for his determination, which probably became conscious only gradually, would almost certainly reflect W's actual development falsely.

21. [Probably late summer or autumn, possibly slightly later]

W writes:
The Horse. (See GCL 31; Appendix V.)
Ode to Apollo. (See GCL 31; Appendix V.)

22. Aug 27

Christopher Crackanthorpe Cookson, uncle of W, marries Charlotte Cust in Penrith. (Penrith. See Moorman I, 75.)[8]

23. [Aug 28]

[W is perhaps in Whitehaven on a visit of undetermined length. (Administrators' Accounts, CRH. See 1788:18n.)]

24. [Sept 18]

[W is perhaps in Penrith on a visit of undetermined length. (Administrators' Accounts, CRH. See 1788:18n.)]

25. [Between mid-Sept and Oct]

[W possibly leaves Penrith after a visit of undetermined length and spends some weeks at Whitehaven; then returns for another visit to Hawkshead. The meeting with the discharged soldier possibly occurs during this visit to Hawkshead (although the event more likely occurs in 1789). (See 1788:18n; 1788:24; 1788:27; 1789:10.)]

26. [Probably late 1788 and 1789, esp. summer 1789]

W composes the bulk of *An Evening Walk.* (See GCL 28.)

27. [Oct 5]

[W is perhaps in Whitehaven on a visit of undetermined length. (Administrators' Accounts, CRH. See 1788:18n.)]

---

[8] This wedding would offer no indication that W was in Penrith now; he would not have been especially anxious to wish his uncle well (and see 1788:23). The Moorman reference describes subsequent events connected with the wedding and their effect on W (see *MY* 698 on the same subject).

28. Oct 17 [–between 1793 Aug 30 and 1794 Feb 17, perhaps c 1793 Dec or c 1794 Jan]

The Rev. William Cookson marries Dorothy Cowper at Penrith 17 Oct. DW departs with them on their wedding trip to Newcastle. [She lives with them, primarily at Forncett, near Norwich, until between 30 Aug 1793 and 17 Feb 1794, perhaps c Dec 1793 or c Jan 1794.] (Penrith; *EL* 17. See 1788:29; 1793:27.)[9]

29. [Oct 18]

[W is perhaps in Penrith on a visit of undetermined length. (Administrators' Accounts, CRH; 1788:18n.)]

30. [Probably between Oct 18 or shortly after and Nov 3]

[W travels to Cambridge (perhaps from Penrith), arriving there before 4 Nov. (See 1788:29; 1788:18n; 1788:32; *EL* 17.) (W refers to his return: *Prel* VI.1–18, *Prel₂* VI.1–19.) There is a possibility that he makes his return via London. (See 1788:2n; 1789:14.)][10]

31. [Probably between Oct 18 or shortly after and Nov 3–1789 June; 1789 mid- or late Oct–1790 June]

[(School years 1788–89, 1789–90.) W refers to these two years at Cambridge: *Prel* VI.19–207, *Prel₂* VI.20–189. (The growth of W's mind during this period, his meditations. He begins to trust with firmness

[9] For DW's opinion of Dorothy Cowper in late 1787 see *EL* 10. The statement of Prel 552 that DW departed from Penrith in Nov is incorrect.

[10] Moorman I, 118, suggests that W returned to Cambridge in late Oct. DW visited Cambridge 4 Nov (see 1788:32) and found W "very well and in excellent spirits." She had left Penrith 17 Oct for Newcastle with her uncle William Cookson and his wife, and it is not clear from DW's remarks whether it had been only since 17 Oct, or much longer, that she had not seen him. EdS *DW* 22 seems to imply that W had left for Cambridge rather more than ten days before the 17th; yet if W had been in the area, he might well have made at least some effort to attend the wedding of the uncle who had showed so much kindness to DW (see *EL* 10), and CCC's accounts record entries of cash given W totaling £7/16/9 for 18 Oct, the day after this wedding (see 1788:18n). It thus seems not unlikely, although certainly not proved, that W was in Penrith about 18 Oct, and that he left for Cambridge from here 18 Oct or after. He had, as noted, arrived in Cambridge before 4 Nov.

that he can leave behind an enduring work. His walks and readings; geometry.)][11]

32. [Nov 4]

DW, William Cookson and Mrs. Cookson, having spent a fortnight in Newcastle, visit W at Cambridge on their way to Forncett. (*EL* 17. See 1788:28. Also see *Some Letters* 54.) [They visit King's College Chapel. (See *EL* 63.)][12]

33. [Dec]

[W takes college examinations.] In the reports of the results W is unclassed, but placed among "those who did not go thro' the whole of the examination & yet had considerable merit." (*W at Cambridge* 31; Schneider 95.)

34. [Dec 7–8]

DW writes to Jane Pollard from Norwich: DW has not written to JP for half a year. The wedding of her [uncle William Cookson and Dorothy Cowper]; the fortnight spent by the three in Newcastle [see 1788:28; 1788:32]. Their visit to Cambridge [4 Nov]; their arrival at Norwich [5 Nov]; a visit to Forncett [7 Nov]. Preparations for living at Forncett; plans for Christmas; description of Norwich. (*EL* 16–20.)[13]

35. [Between Dec 8 and Dec 25]

[DW and her aunt and uncle move to Forncett. (*EL* 19–21.)]

36. Dec 28

DW writes to Jane Pollard [from Forncett]: Life at Forncett. JW has gone to Jamaica; is to go to East Indies on his return, which should be Mar or Apr. (*EL* 20–23.)

---

[11] PREL xxxiv gives the date of 1788 for the time that W began to trust in his ability to leave a great work behind, but the remarks of W himself offer no grounds for such precision. This event is simply said to fall within the period of the "two winters" which he is passing "without a separate notice." (*Prel* VI.25–26, *Prel*₂ VI.22–23.)

[12] It is clear the visit took place the day before Guy Fawkes Day.

[13] DW dates her letter "Decr 6th Sunday Eveng," but no such date occurred in 1788. No doubt she began the letter Sunday 7 Dec and wrote the PS beginning "Monday morng" on 8 Dec.

1789

1. [During this year]

[On writings of W possibly of this year see below and GCL 6–8, 15, 28–29, 31–37.

W begins the study of Italian under Agostino Isola. (See 1787:24.)

Possibly this year, if not before, W first reads Crabbe. (See *LY* 1376.)]

2. [By early 1789 (more probably during 1788)]

[W probably pays a brief visit to London. (See 1788:2.)]

3. [Probably between Jan 20 and early Mar]

RW travels to London and enters the law offices of Messrs. Parkin and Lambert in Gray's Inn. (GGW, Notes on Family Accounts, DCP; Administrators' Accounts, CRH; letter of CCC to RW, 22 Mar 1789, CRH. See 1786:4n.)

4. [Mar 14 and shortly after]

[John Chevallier, Master of St. John's College, dies 14 Mar. W refuses to join the many undergraduates who write the customary elegy on the event, and thus displeases his uncle William Cookson. (*Mem* I, 13–14; London *Times*, 19 Mar 1789; Thomas Baker, *History of the College of St. John the Evangelist*, ed. J. E. B. Mayor, Cambridge, 1869, II, 1082.)][1]

5. [June]

[W takes college examinations.] In the reports of the results W is unclassed, but placed among those who "distinguished [themselves] in the Classic." (*W at Cambridge* 31–32; Schneider 105.)

---

[1] Moorman I, 95, perhaps inadvertently dates these events 1788. *The Gentleman's Magazine* LIX (1789), 279, gives Chevallier's death a date of 7 Mar 1789, but Baker and *The Times* agree on 14 Mar. For an amusing account of Chevallier's funeral and examples of the verses which were composed on this occasion, see Henry Gunning, *Reminiscences of the University Town, and the Country of Cambridge from the Year 1789* (London, 1855) I, 184–86.

6. [Probably June, and possibly part of July (–between mid-Oct, after probably Oct 14, and early Nov)]

[Probably in June W departs from Cambridge for summer vacation. He first, possibly through part of July, visits DW and the Cooksons at Forncett. (He returns to Cambridge between mid-Oct, after probably 14 Oct, and early Nov.) (See PREL, EdS, 608 f, g; Moorman I, 105n, 120; 1789:12.) W probably refers to this visit in "Sweet Was the Walk" (see GCL 37).][2]

7. [Probably late June or July, and later summer–between mid-Oct, probably after Oct 14, and early Nov]

[W travels north from Forncett, eventually arriving at Whitehaven or Penrith, probably in late June or July. (See 1789:6.) He returns to Cambridge between mid-Oct, probably after 14 Oct, and early Nov. (See 1789:12.)

He perhaps wanders fairly extensively in Yorkshire and Lancashire, esp. about the Appenine between the counties. He possibly visits a seat near Ilam where Congreve was said to have written *The Old Bachelor* (he probably paid the visit on 8 June 1788 or shortly after). He perhaps stays some time with his cousin Mary Wordsworth Smith at Broughton. He possibly walks with MH and Margaret Hutchinson in and near Penrith. (See 1788:14; 1788:17.)

(W probably does not spend time alone with Tom Hutchinson now or any other time. See Moorman I, 1957, 121.)][3]

---

[2] EdS notes that DW remarks on 30 Apr 1790 that she has not seen W "since my aunt [DW's term for her cousin Elizabeth Threlkeld] was with us," and shows that her "aunt" probably did not come at the end of the previous long vacation (nor, as remarked Moorman I, 105n, would the distance of Forncett from the Lake District allow W to visit in the middle of vacation). His conclusion is that W and Elizabeth Threlkeld were at Forncett at the beginning of W's long vacation in 1789. Note also DW's remark on 7 Dec 1788 that a visit is expected from Miss Threlkeld "in Spring" (*EL* 18). There is no way of knowing how long W's visit lasted, but if an appreciable part of the events which possibly took place elsewhere this summer (see esp. 1789:7) did in fact take place, he must have left by some time in July.

[3] Dates can be given for very few of W's activities during this summer. The only events, in fact, that can be assigned to this summer and no other are his visit to Forncett, which probably began in June, his (conjectured) presence in Whitehaven

8. July 14

A French mob storms the Bastille. (W's immediate reactions to this event are unknown. See esp. 1791:6; 1791:31.)

9. [Shortly before Sept 16]

[W is probably in Whitehaven on a visit of undetermined length. (Administrators' Accounts, CRH. See Moorman I, 122.)][4]

10. [Perhaps shortly before, fairly certainly by, Sept 16–c possibly Oct 14]

[4] A washing bill evidently of £-/8/- recorded under 8 Nov by RW of Whitehaven possibly indicates a longer visit in Whitehaven this year than last, when the washing bill was only £-/3/-. But the evidence is not imposing.

shortly before 16 Sept; his departure for Hawkshead perhaps shortly before, fairly certainly by, 16 Sept; and his passage through Penrith on his way to Cambridge probably 14 Oct (see 1789:9–11). All that can be said about the other activities mentioned is that more of them possibly occurred now, and for longer periods, than during the previous summer, when he spent nine weeks at Hawkshead; but none need be confined to this summer exclusively. W implies (see esp. *Prel* VI.208–10, *Prel*$_2$ VI.190–95) that most took place over the two college vacations when he went North. CCC's remarks about the call which W paid in Penrith on 14 Oct do not make clear whether W visited there earlier in the vacation, and thus whether he walked with MH (and perhaps Margaret Hutchinson) in the Penrith area this summer (see *Prel* VI.208–45, *Prel*$_2$ VI.190–236); DW was, of course, at Forncett. It cannot even be regarded as certain that W passed about a month at Hawkshead, as suggested Moorman I, 122–23; all that is clear is that he was in Hawkshead c 16 Sept. W could have been visiting or rambling elsewhere through much of the period (see 1789:10). Nor can it be said that W went directly to Cambridge from Penrith after 14 Oct; he could have roamed about more before arriving at college. On W's movements during the summer see the remarks of Moorman I, 120–24.

The suggestion that W stayed for a time with Tom Hutchinson (see Moorman I, 1957, 121), seems to deserve denial in the text because of the confusing indications of the document prompting it (*LY* 1324). The MS of W's letter is lost, but in the copy quoted by EdS, a remark appears about the shock occasioned by Tom Hutchinson's recent death "to me especially who for many years before our several marriages was his sole companion—we two out of a large family left by our parents, lived together." It can be noted that MW's phrasing when referring to Tom after an accident, MW *Letters* 154–55, is quite similar to that of these remarks. W frequently dictated letters to MW, especially in his later years, and these remarks become intelligible if taken, as I take them, as a comment interjected by MW, speaking for herself, into a letter which she was copying from W's dictation.

[Perhaps shortly before, fairly certainly by, 16 Sept W travels from Whitehaven to Hawkshead. He possibly remains at Hawkshead until as late as c 14 Oct. (Administrators' Accounts, CRH. See Moorman I, 122.)

It is probably during this visit at Hawkshead that W encounters the discharged soldier. (W refers to this event: *Prel* IV.369–504, *Prel*₂ IV.370–469. See PREL 536. On date see 1788:18n.)][5]

11. [Probably Oct 14]

W calls at the house of CCC in Penrith on his way to Cambridge. [He probably stays only an hour or so.] (Letter from CCC to RW, 22 Oct 1789, CRH; Moorman I, 123.)[6]

12. [Between mid-Oct, probably after Oct 14, and early Nov]

W returns to Cambridge. The exact length of time he spent on the road is unknown. (See 1789:11; 1789:7n; 1787:32n.)

13. [Dec]

[W takes college examinations.] His name does not appear in the reports of the results. (*W at Cambridge*; Schneider 156.)

14. [Between 1789 Dec and 1790 Jan]

[W takes his Christmas vacation. He probably visits London for at least part of the vacation, and sees JW. He purchases and reads Bowles's *Fourteen Sonnets*. (Moorman I, 124–25.) This is possibly W's first visit to London; but see 1788:2.][7]

---

[5] As remarked by Moorman in the reference cited, the accounts of RW of Whitehaven record the following payments for W under 16 Sept:

By Cash remitted [to W] to Hawkshead & stamps   6/6/6
By gave servants for William   /3/ .

[6] The letter says that W called "on Friday last in his road to Cambridge." Although 21 Oct was a Friday, CCC more probably means Friday 14 Oct.

[7] Mrs. Moorman shows that a remark made by W to Samuel Rogers (*Recollections of the Table-Talk of Samuel Rogers*, ed. Rev. Alexander Dyce, London, 1856, 258n) that he had purchased Bowles's *Fourteen Sonnets* when they first appeared, while on a walk with JW in London, points plainly to Christmas vacation 1789–90. CCC's accounts note transmission to JW of "cash per brother Richard" under 18 Dec 1789. One may well suppose that both W and JW stayed with RW.

1790

1. [During this year]

[On writings of W possibly of this year see below and GCL 6–8, 28, 32–39.

W probably performs one "act" and several "opponencies" as requirements leading toward his degree. (Schneider 165. See Schneider 30–32; Christopher Wordsworth, *Scholae Academicae*, Cambridge, 1877, 32–43.)]

2. [1790] Jan 25, [26]

DW writes to Jane Pollard [from Forncett] [PS written 26 Jan]: [Her "Aunt" Elizabeth Threlkeld's] displeasure at DW's long silence [see 1789:6n]. Her contented life at Forncett. JW has probably sailed for India on the *Earl of Abergavenny* [see 1790:3]; W is at Cambridge; RW in London; CW at Hawkshead. The Lonsdale suit. DW's little school. [William] Wilberforce has been visiting them over a month. (*EL* 23–26.)

3. Jan 30 (–1791 Aug 19)

The *Earl of Abergavenny* (JW aboard) sails for India, Captain John Wordsworth (cousin of W). (It reaches moorings on return 19 Aug 1791.) (Hardy 137; *EL* 45; letter of JW to RW, 24 June 1794, DCP.)

4. Mar 7

RW records a loan to W £5/5/– under this date. (RW, accounts with W and DW, 1816, DCP.)

5. Apr 30

DW writes to Jane Pollard from Forncett: The current state of DW's little school. W's indefinite prospects for the future. Description of CW. Life at Forncett. Her reading. (*EL* 26–30.)[1]

---

[1] EdS's conjecture that DW's date of 30 Apr was a slip for 30 Mar was no doubt founded on DW's remark that W "will be twenty in April" (*EL* 28). DW was being careless, however, perhaps out of long habit of thinking just that thought: the postmark on the letter (DCP) is "MA/4/[9]o."

6. [June]

[W takes college examinations.] In the reports of the results W is unclassed but placed among those who had "considerable merit in the subjects which they undertook." (*W at Cambridge* 32; Schneider 172.)

7. [June (after college examinations)–July 10]

[W's whereabouts during this period are unknown. He very probably sees no relative. (See *EL* 36, 39.)]

8. [July 10–between Sept 29 and probably Oct 19, fairly certainly late Oct]

[On 10 July W and Robert Jones leave London and spend the night at Shooter's Hill on their way toward France and a walking trip through Europe. W has probably told no relative of his departure. They return to Cambridge between 29 Sept and probably 19 Oct, fairly certainly late Oct. (Racedown Nb—see *PW* I, 325–26; *EL* 36, 39. See 1788:2n; 1790:100n; 1790:9.)

W often refers in his writings to this walking trip and to his companion, a lifelong friend. On the trip generally see esp. Moorman I, 128–49; Schneider 173–80; C. N. Coe, "Did Wordsworth Read Coxe's 'Travels in Switzerland' before Making the Tour of 1790?" *N&Q* CXCV (1950), 144–45; Max Wildi, "Wordsworth and the Simplon Pass," *English Studies* XLI (1959), 224–32. References in W's work capable of relatively specific dating are entered in the text or notes. The most important sources of such references, and other references capable of only imprecise dating include:

A. General references.

1. *DS, passim,* and its dedication. (Many references to sights and experiences of the trip.)
2. *Prel* VI.338–705, *Prel₂* VI.322–778. (General treatment of trip.)
3. *Prel* XI.241–42, *Prel₂* XII.191–92. (The heart which he carries with him in the Alps. See *Prel* XI.224–40, *Prel₂* XII.174–90.)
4. *The Tuft of Primroses* 466–80. (Casual mention of Rhone, Loire.)
5. *EL* 30–37. (Descriptive itinerary from Chartreuse through Berne.)

6. *Mem* I, 14–15 (Autobiog Mem). (Their appearance; the first days of the tour.)

(Although many poems in *Memorials of a Tour on the Continent* refer to places visited by W and Jones, I have not cited such poems except where they have some particular relevance or reference to this tour. Ordinarily they appear to have no such reference.)

B. On Jones see esp.:

   1. *DS* (Dedication)
   2. *A Character*
   3. *A Parsonage in Oxfordshire* and IF note
   4. *To the Lady E.B. and the Honourable Miss P.* IF note
   5. *Composed near Calais, on the Road Leading to Ardres, August 7, 1802*
   6. *Pastoral Character* and note
   7. *Prel* VI.339–40 and *app crit, Prel*$_2$ VI.322–24. See also PREL 554.

C. Worth note at this point are some remarks in a letter from Jones to W of 23 Feb 1821 (DCP): "I wish particularly to know your Route and whether the things you saw in Switzerland & c in 1820 brought to your recollection some times (always could not be expected) the objects you saw with far different eyes in 1790. We were early risers in 1790 and generally walked 12 or 15 miles before breakfast and after feasting on the morning Landscape how we afterwards feasted in our Dejeune(r) of whatever the house might afford!"][2]

---

[2] Moorman I, 132, evidently errs in stating that W and Jones left London and slept at Shooter's Hill on 11 July. The Racedown Nb is known to have been used extensively at Racedown, but was possibly in use much earlier (see Appendix IV). It contains a day-by-day itinerary (from Calais) of the walking trip (copied with a few errors in *Mem* I, 56–57—reproduced from this source *PW*, Knight, 1882–89, I, 309, and *PW*, Knight, 1896, I, 332–33—and *PW* I, 325–26). As indicated in Appendix IV, the time at which this itinerary was entered is uncertain, and was surely not contemporary with the main part of the trip; but the Nb seems by far the best authority presently available for determining the route of the journey. I have made occasional alterations of the spelling of this itinerary, either to correct errors in the original or to bring the place names into conformity with general modern English usage. Where such corrections are only a matter of diacritical marks, hyphens, and the like, they are silent; otherwise they are indicated by square brackets. My authority on geographical spelling has customarily been *The Columbia Lippincott Gazetteer of the World* (New York, 1952); in cases where this has proved inadequate, my authority has been either *The Times Atlas of the World* (Boston, 1955) vol. III, or Arthur Jacot, *Dictionnaire*

9. July 11

W and Jones spend the night at Canterbury. (See 1790:8n.)

10. July 12

W and Jones spend the night at Dover. (See 1790:8n.)

11. July 13

W and Jones [cross from Dover to Calais,] spend the night at Calais. [W refers to these events: *Prel* VI.355–60, *Prel*₂ VI.342–49; *Mem* I, 14–15.] (See 1790:8n.)

12. [July 14–28]

[W refers to his journey south from Calais to Chalon-sur-Saône: *Prel* VI.360–82, *Prel*₂ VI.349–74.]

13. July 14

W and Jones spend the night at Ardres. [W refers to this occasion: *Mem* I, 15; *Composed near Calais, on the Road Leading to Ardres, August 15, 1802*, esp. 9–14.] (See 1790:8n.)

14. July 15

W and Jones spend the night at Lillers. (See 1790:8n.)

Géographique de la Suisse (Lucerne, 1957). In a few instances the name of the town given in the Nb is only a confusing approximation (resembling the name of another place) of that of the town where they must really have spent the night.

W says (*Mem* I, 14) that he and Jones each had about £20 at the outset of the trip. Moorman I, 132n, provides an accurate record of the sums recorded in the administrators' accounts as given W in 1790, with the exception of two cash sums, totaling £23/2/–, noted without more precise date by RW of Branthwaite.

The article by Coe indicates strongly that William Coxe's *Travels in Switzerland* played a large part in determining the route followed by the two travelers. W may well have known the French translation and expansion of Coxe by Ramond de Carbonnières at this time also, although Wildi implies that he did not take up this version until 1791.

15. July 16

W and Jones spend the night at Arras. [W refers to this occasion: *Prel* X.449–66, *Prel₂* X.490–510.] (See 1790:8n.)[3]

16. July 17

W and Jones spend the night at Péronne. (See 1790:8n.)

17. July 18

W and Jones spend the night at a village near [Coucy-le-Château]. (See 1790:8n.)[4]

18. July 19

W and Jones spend the night at Soissons. (See 1790:8n.)

19. July 20

W and Jones spend the night at Château-Thierry. (See 1790:8n.)

20. July 21

W and Jones spend the night at Sézanne. (See 1790:8n.)

21. July 22

W and Jones spend the night at a village near Troyes. (See 1790:8n.)

22. July 23

W and Jones spend the night at [Bar-sur-Seine]. (See 1790:8n.)[5]

23. July 24

W and Jones spend the night at Chatillon [-sur-Seine]. (See 1790:8n.)

---

[3] PREL 599 says that W and Jones "passed through" Arras on 16 July.

[4] The wording of the Racedown Nb is "Village near Coucy."

[5] The Racedown Nb gives the name of the town as "Bar-le-Duc." Since W and Jones slept near Troyes the night before, a night at Bar-le-Duc would have required a walk of some fifty miles in one day. The town where they spent the night was almost surely Bar-sur-Seine, although there is possibly some chance that it was Bar-sur-Aube.

24. July 25

W and Jones spend the night at [Saint-Seine-l'Abbaye]. (See 1790:8n.)[6]

25. July 26

W and Jones [pass through Dijon, where they visit the Hospital]. They spend the night at Nuit[s-Saint-Georges]. (See 1790:8n.)[7]

26. July 27, 28

W and Jones spend the night at Chalon[-sur-Saône]. (See 1790:8n; *Stray Pleasures* IF note; *HCR & W Circle* 343–44, 372.)[8]

27. July 29

W and Jones board a boat to float down the Saône to Lyon with a company of *fédérés* returning from Paris. They spend the night along the Saône. [W refers to this event: *Prel* VI.383–421, *Prel*₂ VI.374–414.] (See 1790:8n; *Stray Pleasures* IF note; 1790:26.)[9]

28. [July 29–Aug 1]

[W and Jones travel down the Rhone—probably some of the way below Lyon on foot—at least as far as Saint-Vallier (see entries for separate days).

[6] The Racedown Nb says simply that they passed the night in a "Town in a hole." Mrs. Moorman has kindly passed on to me the opinion of Mr. Robert Farr, former British counsul at Dijon, that Saint-Seine-l'Abbaye is the place in question; and personal observation confirms that this village (hardly a town) lies in a very narrow valley. It is almost surely where the travelers rested.

[7] Robert Jones remarks to W in a letter of 23 Feb 1821, "You may remember that Dijon is the place where you and I walked the Hospital in 1790" [*sic*]. The Hospital (now disused) is still a notable sight in Dijon. I am indebted to Mrs. Moorman, who passed on to me the remarks of Mr. Farr (see 1790:24n) on this subject. Mr. Farr's suggestion that Jones's remark is a slip for "walked to" is undoubtedly correct.

[8] The IF note to *Stray Pleasures* has often been printed as giving a date of 1799 to W's observation of the floating mills on the Saône. (The most influential example is Grosart III, 33–34.) But EdS's reading, 1790, from the MS copy of the notes, DCP (*PW* II, 494), is undoubtedly correct.

[9] The river on which they floated here was not the Rhone, despite the statement of *Prel* VI.386, *Prel*₂ VI.378.

On the journey down the Saône and Rhone see PREL 556 (quotation of prose passage describing a river, from *Prel* MS B, quite possibly referring to this trip.)][10]

29. July 30

W and Jones [possibly disembark (see 1790:28) and] spend the night at Lyo[n]. (See 1790:8n.)

30. July 31

W and Jones spend the night at Condrieu. (See 1790:8n.)

31. Aug 1

W and Jones [evidently proceed at least as far south as Saint-Vallier, where W probably begins a letter to DW, but turn northeast and] spend the night at [Moras]. (*EL* 30. See 1790:8n; 1790:28n.)

32. Aug 2

W and Jones spend the night at Voreppe. (See 1790:8n.)

[10] W implies in the IF note to *Stray Pleasures* that his boat journey terminated in Lyon. Although he and Jones proceeded southward along the Rhone from that point, the distances which they traveled 31 July and 1 Aug suggest that they may have walked at least part of the time on those days. Saint-Vallier, the most southern point of the Rhone which they are known to have reached, is some twelve miles southeast of Moras, where they evidently spent the night after Condrieu. Whether their having proceeded so far south was the result of accident or design is unknown; but they apparently determined at some point to proceed to the Grande Chartreuse north of the Plateau of Chamberin, rather than via the Val d'Isère, to the south. They later crossed into the Val d'Isère, probably on the day when they reached Voreppe.

If W floated some of the way along the river south of Lyon, esp. on the second day, it might offer some explanation of the difference between the two days which *Prel* says it took them to reach the Convent of the Grande Chartreuse after leaving the *fédérés* with whom they traveled on their boat (*Prel* VI.421–24, *Prel*₂ VI.414–19) and the five days which did elapse between Lyon and the Convent. The journey from the river itself to within a few miles of the Grande Chartreuse (Voreppe) was accomplished in two days. I am unable to confirm by any primary sources the suggestion of Harper (R) 63–64 that W sailed with the *fédérés* from Lyon to Saint-Vallier; but such a hypothesis is attractive, and no primary source refutes it. W and Jones could possibly have traveled at least the better part of four days on one or more boats.

33. Aug 3

W and Jones spend the night at a village near Chartreuse. (See 1790:8n.)

34. Aug 4, 5

W and Jones spend the night at the Monastery of the Grande Chartreuse. (See 1790:8n; 1790:28n; *Prel* VI.422–23, *Prel*₂ VI.417–18.) W probably finishes a letter to DW from here. (*EL* 30.)
[W refers to the Chartreuse and Monastery:
DS 53–79 (Chartreuse, Vallombre)
Prel VI.422–23 and *app crit* (PREL 198–202), *Prel*₂ VI.420–88
The Tuft of Primroses 509–27 (see also PREL 556–57.)][11]

35. [Aug 6–17]

[On the trip from the Chartreuse through the Simplon Pass see *EL* 31–32.]

36. Aug 6

W and Jones [leave the Grande Chartreuse], spend the night at Aix[-les-Bains]. (See 1790:8n.)

37. Aug 7

W and Jones spend the night in a town in [Haute-]Savo[ie]. (See 1790:8n.)[12]

[11] As remarked by Moorman I, 137, W and Jones could not have met soldiers at the Chartreuse who were there either to expel the inmates or on any sort of domiciliary visit, despite references to the riotous soldiers in both *DS* and *Prel*. Possibly W saw some soldiers who were in the neighborhood for other than official reasons and later attached such significance to them. W and Jones were fairly certainly among the last visitors which the Monastery received (see Moorman I, 135–36). On this visit see also *HCR & W Circle* 121.

[12] The present Haute-Savoie would contain the "town in Savoy" (Racedown Nb) where the travelers slept.

38. Aug 8

W and Jones spend the night in a French town on Lake Geneva. (See 1790:8n.)

39. [Aug 8–30]

[W makes general mention of the lakes of Geneva and Zurich, Lake Como, Lago Maggiore, and the Simplon Pass in *Written in the Strangers' Book at "The Station," opposite Bowness (PW* IV, 387–88).][13]

40. Aug 9

W and Jones spend the night in Lausanne. (See 1790:8n.)

41. Aug 10

W and Jones spend the night in Villeneuve. (See 1790:8n.)

42. Aug 11

W and Jones spend the night in [Saint-Maurice]. (See 1790:8n.)

43. Aug 12, 13

[On 12 Aug, in their walk from Saint-Maurice toward Chamonix, W and Jones see the green valley which W describes in *Prel* VI.446–52, *Prel*$_2$ VI.517–23, probably also (his first poetic treatment of the scene) in *Septimi Gades* 13–18. The valley is the Valley of the Trient. (See 1790:8n; *DWJ* II, 280–81, 294.) It is at least possible that they spend the night of 12 Aug in this valley.

Probably on 12 Aug they see Mont Blanc for the first time. (W refers to this event: *Prel* VI.452–56, *Prel*$_2$ VI.523–28.) Probably on the same day, as they come past the Col de Balme, they meet the Alpine boy whom W mentions in *DS* 440–41. (See *DWJ* II, 282.) Probably on the same day they have their first sight of the Vale of Chamonix. (W refers to this event: *Prel* VI.456–68, *Prel*$_2$ VI.528–40. He refers to the Vale of Chamonix in *DS* 680–712.)

---

[13] The experiences W describes here are probably much more for the sake of quick rhymes than for transmission of autobiographical data to posterity, and have not been separately listed.

They probably reach Chamonix and spend the night there on 12 Aug. On 12 and/or 13 Aug they visit, perhaps dine, or even stay at the Union Inn at Chamonix (see *DWJ* II, 284). They spend the night of 13 Aug in Chamonix. (See 1790:8n.)][14]

44. Aug 14

W and Jones spend the night in [Martigny-Ville]. (See 1790:8n.)[15]

45. Aug 15

W and Jones spend the night in a village [east of] Sion. (See 1790:8n.)

46. Aug 16

W and Jones spend the night in Brig. (See 1790:8n.)

[14] Evidence on their resting place 12 Aug is confusing. The Racedown Nb says they slept at Chamo[nix] 12 and 13 Aug, and there is almost never reason to suppose that this record is incorrect. *Septimi Gades* 13–18 pretty clearly refers to the Valley of the Trient, which "seeks" the "Rhone" below; and W says he "sheltered his pilgrim head" here. But Martigny, where they slept 14 Aug, is close by this valley, through some of which at least they would have passed that day, and *Septimi Gades* could refer to that night. DS 680–712 describes the Vale of Chamonix by sunset, a sight which they might have seen as they approached Chamonix 12 Aug, or as easily on 13 Aug. Both versions of *Prel* agree that they saw Mont Blanc on the same day as their first sight of their pastoral valley, but the 1805 version indicates that they were reconciled to realities after their sight of Mont Blanc by the "wondrous Vale of Chamouny" on "the following morn," while the 1850 version indicates that they first saw Mont Blanc and the Vale at much the same time. They must have seen the Vale if they came even within five or six miles of Chamonix on this day, and I suspect that the best conjecture would be that they did in fact reach Chamonix 12 Aug and see its Vale some time before, perhaps by sunset. A sight of the Vale on one of the two following mornings (perhaps as they retraced their steps toward Martigny), could perhaps have been so impressive as to be distinguished in W's mind for some time from earlier sights of it.

[15] The Racedown Nb gives only a German spelling for Martigny, "Murtinach" (which should be "Martinach"). It is possible that Martigny-Bourg, two miles from Martigny-Ville, was where they spent the night, but more likely the Nb refers to the larger and better-known Martigny-Ville.

47. Aug 17

[W and Jones join a band of muleteers on their way up the Simplon Pass. They eat lunch probably at the old Stockalber Spittal, are parted from the muleteers, lose their way, and eventually discover that they have crossed the Alps. They descend through the Ravine of Gondo and spend the night (during which W does not sleep) at the Spittal of Gondo. (W refers to these events: *Prel* VI.488–580 and *app crit, Prel*₂ VI.557–648.) (See 1790:8n; *DWJ* II, 258–60; Max Wildi, "Wordsworth and the Simplon Pass," *English Studies* XLI, 1959, 224–32; also Moorman I, 138–42.)][16]

48. [Aug 17–18]

[W refers to the river Toce, which he and Jones follow during these days, in *DS* 178–83.]

49. [Aug 18–20]

[W refers to his early impressions of Italy, esp. as far as Lake Como: *Prel* VI.581–616, *Prel*₂ VI.649–87; *DS* 717; *EL* 32.]

50. Aug 18

W and Jones spend the night at M[e]rgozz[o]. (See 1790:8n.)

51. Aug 19

W and Jones walk along Lago Maggiore [to which W refers in *Dion* 1–2 *app crit*] probably passing through Locarno [to which W refers in *DS* 176–77]. They spend the night in a village beyond Lago Maggiore. (See 1790:8n.)

52. Aug 20

W and Jones [pass by the Lake of Lugano (to which W refers in *DS* 718)] and spend the night in a village on [Lake] Como. (See 1790:8n.)

[16] The Racedown Nb says this night was spent at the "Spital." (The only example in *OED* of the word "spital" in English is taken from *G &S*.) On the spital, and for a detailed reconstruction of the day's events, see Wildi. *DWJ* states that the travelers were kept from sleep (see *Prel* references) by reasons other than simply the noise of the torrent. One shares Mrs. Moorman's and Wildi's curiosity as to why thirty years later W refused to enter the building where he had spent the night (see *DWJ* II, 259).

53. [Aug 20–22]

[W refers to scenes and possible events at Lake Como: *DS* 215–42; *Prel* VI.617–57, *Prel*₂ VI.688–726 (see below). See also *EL* 32–33, 36; *DWJ* I, 101.

W and Jones take a path on the western side of the lake from "the foot of the water to its head" (*DS* 90n).]

54. Aug 21

[W and Jones probably first go to sleep in Gravedona. They are deceived by the church clock, leave Gravedona, and spend most of the night in or near a village beyond Gravedona. (W refers to these events: *Prel* VI.621–57, *Prel*₂ VI.691–726; *DS* 215–37.) (See 1790:8n.)][17]

55. Aug 22

[Probably on this day] W and Jones are parted by a storm and spend much or all the night wandering in the forests between Gravedona and Chiavenna. [Part of W's wanderings are on the path on the west side of Lake Como.] W finally reaches Samol[a]co; Jones finally reaches Chiavenna. (See 1790:54n; 1790:8n; *DWJ* II, 219–20, 243–45.)

[17] The description in *Prel* of the events of the night is so distinct that I am inclined to accept its statement that they "left" Gravedona as a result of their deception by the clock and spent the larger part of the night beyond the town. The statement of the Racedown Nb that they slept in a "village beyond Gravedona" may be reconciled with *Prel* in the manner suggested in the text. But it is at least possible that they began their night in the "village," and that W's memory was not precise. The statement of *Prel* is that they sat up on their "second night" in sight of Como. W's memory appears sound in this case. It would not have been the third night, when the Racedown Nb confirms that they spent the night apart; nor is there any intelligible reason why W should have remembered the night as distinguished from the first if it were not other than the first.

DWJ records that W saw the moon hanging over "Mount Colico" [Monte Legnone] the night he wandered alone, and that he walked down to the shore, "then most dismal" from the storm. This source also comments that the incident of the separation is recorded in [*Prel*]; as remarked Moorman I, 144n, however, it is not. Possibly this sight of the moon was fused in his mind with the moon as they saw it on the night of 22 Aug. *DS* 215–42 clearly draws on the experiences of 22 Aug; the moon, similar to that in the description of *Prel* ("waning" and "red," with the water "slinking"), hangs above a hill.

56. Aug 23

W and Jones sleep at So[az]za. (See 1790:8n.)

57. [Aug 24–30]

[On the trip from Soazza to Lake of Zurich see *EL* 33. The travelers follow Valle Mesolcina to its head; pass the Adula Gruppe to Hinterrhein (and Splügen—see 1790:58); follow Rhine through the Grisons to Reichenau; turn up other branch of Rhine and follow it to Tschamut. Thence they proceed north at the Urserental and follow the Reuss to Altdorf; thence along the Lake to Lucerne, thence to Zurich. (See 1790:58–65; *DWJ* II, 198; *HCR & W Circle* 637.)]

58. Aug 24

W and Jones spend the night at Spl[ügen]. [W refers to the "infant Rhine" in the chasms of Via Mala in *DS* 184–91; on this passage see also Appendix V.] (See 1790:8n.)

59. Aug 25

W and Jones spend the night at Fl[i]ms. (See 1790:8n.)

60. Aug 26

W and Jones spend the night at Di[s]entis. [W refers to the Urserental in *DS* 243–44.] (See 1790:8n.)

61. [Aug 26–27]

[W refers to the Reuss, Valley of Schöllenen, and Urserental in *DS* 243–82. See also *DWJ* II, 188–89 (W and Jones descend through Valley of Schöllenen; the Reuss rages).]

62. [Aug 28–29]

[W refers to the Lake of Uri and the Lake of Lucerne, of which Uri forms a part in *DS* 283–366.]

63. Aug 28

W and Jones spend the night at Flüelen. (See 1790:8n.)

64. Aug 29

W and Jones spend the night at Lucerne. (See 1790:8n.)

65. Aug 30

W and Jones probably pass through Zurich. They spend the night in a village on the Lake of Zurich. (See 1790:8n; *EL* 33.)[18]

66. [Aug 31–Sept 14]

[On the trip from the Lake of Zurich to Lauterbrunnen see *EL* 33–35. They travel along the Lake of Zurich to Richterswil; visit Einsiedeln; proceed to Glarus; visit the Valley of Glarus; proceed to Lake of Constance via Lake of Wallenstadt and Canton of Appenzell. Thence they travel along the Rhine to the Falls of the Rhine; follow the Rhine down c eight leagues from Schaffhausen; cross it and proceed via Baden to Lucerne; thence to Grindelwald (and Lauterbrunnen). (See 1790:67–83.)]

67. Aug 31

W and Jones spend the night at Einsied[eln]. [W refers to Einsiedeln in *DS* 654–79.] (See 1790:8n.)

68. Sept 1, 2

W and Jones spend the night at Glarus. On 2 Sept they spend the day visiting the Valley of Glarus. (See 1790:8n; *EL* 33.)

[18] W's phrasing on *EL* 33 is: "To Lucerne, and thence to Zurich. From Zurich, along the banks of the lake, we continued our route." W may be using the name Zurich as synonymous with the lake, but the phrasing indicates that he had in fact passed through Zurich itself before proceeding southeast along the lake. To have walked from Lucerne to Zurich and thence along the lake would probably have meant a walk of well over thirty miles, and W and Jones seldom came close to the "thirteen leagues" (counting a league as three miles—see *EL* 38) that W mentions to DW as having traversed "several times" (*EL* 36). But 30 Aug was perhaps a day when they did approach that figure.

69. Sept 3

W and Jones spend the night at a village [beyond Walle(n)stadt]. (See 1790:8n.)[19]

70. Sept 4

W and Jones spend the night in a village on the road to Appenzell. (See 1790:8n.)

71. Sept 5

W and Jones spend the night in Appenzell. (See 1790:8n.)

72. Sept 6 (–Sept 16)

W and Jones spend the night at Ke[ss]will, on the Lake of Constance. W here begins a letter to DW [probably his second of the trip]. (He is to finish it 16 Sept at Bern.): Their expenses to this point have amounted to not more than £12. Description of his itinerary from the Grande Chartreuse; observations on the places visited and their inhabitants. His departure from England without informing any relative of his plans. Their appearance. His hopes of having a two or three weeks' visit with DW before returning to Cambridge. (*EL* 30–37.)

73. Sept 7

W and Jones spend the night along the Rhine. (See 1790:8n; 1790:74.)

74. Sept 8

[Probably on this day (if not, 7 Sept)] W and Jones visit the Falls of the Rhine at Schaffhausen. They spend the night along the Rhine. (See 1790:8n; *EL* 33.)[20]

75. Sept 9

W and Jones spend the night on the road to Lucern[e]. (See 1790:8n.)

[19] The phrasing of the MS is "beyond the lake of Wallesstadt." The lake referred to is no doubt Wallen.

[20] Unless W and Jones traveled an unusually long distance on 7 Sept, their visit to the falls would have occurred on 8 Sept.

76. Sept 10

W and Jones spend the night in Lucern[e]. (See 1790:8n.)

77. [Sept 11, 12]

[Sachseln, along the Aare, Unterwalden. W refers to this area: *DS* 414–41, 492–509, and IF note. (The Aare. The secluded scenes of Unterwalden. The valley filled with mist based on scenery of the region of which major features are Lungern and Sarnen—on which see also *DWJ* II, 135–41.)][21]

78. Sept 11

W and Jones spend the night in Sa[chseln]. (See 1790:8n.)

79. Sept 12

[On this day] W and Jones are treated rudely by officials stationed at the border of the cantons of Bern and Unterwalden to collect tolls. They spend the night in a village on the Aare. (See 1790:8n; *DWJ* II, 134.)[22]

80. Sept 13

W and Jones spend the night in Grindelwa[l]d. (See 1790:8n.)

81. Sept 14

W works on his letter to DW (see 1790:72). W and Jones have difficulty [this day] recrossing a stream [after viewing] a waterfall in

[21] W says the passage begins "in solemn shapes," but this phrase appears only toward the end of a description of a valley in which mist plays only a minor part (*DS* 263–82). The really notable mist-filled valley of *DS* appears lines 492–509 (496 begins "A solemn sea!"; the scene as a whole contributes heavily to W's description of his climbing of Mount Snowdon in *Prel*). Probably it is to this passage that W refers. On *DS* 440–41 see also 1790:43.

[22] The rudeness of the officials, *DWJ* notes, was "owing to the jealousies and disorders of the French Revolution."

the Valley of Lauterbrunnen. They spend the night at Lauterbrunnen. (*EL* 34; MS Verse 4, DCP. See 1790:8n.)[23]

82. Sept 15

W and Jones spend the night [c nine miles] from Bern. (See 1790:8n.)[24]

83. Sept 16

[W and Jones pass through Bern.] At Bern W concludes his letter to DW begun Sept 6. They spend the night at Av[e]nches. (See 1790:8n.)[25]

84. [Sept 17–18]

[W refers to the marsh at Anet (Ins) and the Lake of Neuchatel in *DS* 715–16.]

85. Sept 17

W and Jones spend the night in a village in the [Val de Travers]. (See 1790:8n.)[26]

[23] The prose fragment in Verse 4 which describes their danger in recrossing the stream (see Moorman I, 146) locates the incident in "the heart" of the valley, and remarks also that on returning down the valley, they discovered a torrent of water rolling over the spot, beneath a bridge, where they had eaten lunch two hours earlier. *DS* 211–14 may owe something to the second incident. Both occasions illustrate the rapid changes which the melting snows can cause in streams of this region. W and Jones could not have been in the Valley of Lauterbrunnen two hours after lunch the following day, when they slept "three leagues" from Bern; so these events must belong to 14 Sept.

[24] The phrasing of the Racedown Nb is "3 leagues" from Bern. DW understood W's "league" as meaning three miles (*EL* 36, 38), and I am assuming that she and W had a common definition of the term. The entry for 20 Sept is based upon a similar calculation from "4 leagues" from Basel; that for 22 Sept on "6 leagues" from Strasbourg; that for 27 Sept on "2 leagues" from Coblenz; and that for 29 Sept on "3 leagues" from Aix-la-Chapelle.

[25] EdS's suggestion of Av[r]anches (for the Nb's "Avanches") would have W walking several hundred miles this day. Avenches is eighteen miles southwest of Bern.

[26] A map or gazetteer indicates the only possible reading for the name of the valley, which is not easy to make out in the MS.

86. Sept 18

W and Jones spend the night in a village in the [Val Saint-]Imier. (See 1790:8n.)

87. Sept 19

W and Jones spend the night in a village beyond Pierre Pertui[s]. (See 1790:8n.)

88. Sept 20

W and Jones spend the night in a village [c twelve miles] from Basel. (See 1790:8n; 1790:82n.)

89. [Sept 21 or 22]

W and Jones buy a boat in Basel. (*Mem* I, 57n; 1790:90; 1790:91.)

90. Sept 21

W and Jones spend the night in Basel. (See 1790:8n.)

91. Sept 22 (–Sept 28)

W and Jones embark in a boat purchased in Basel for a trip down the Rhine to Cologne. (The trip ends 28 Sept.) They spend the night in a town [c eighteen miles] from Strasbourg. (See 1790:8n; 1790: 82n.)

[W refers to this trip: *Author's Voyage down the Rhine* (published 1822 in *Memorials of a Tour on the Continent, 1820*, but subsequently omitted; later adapted for *Ecclesiastical Sonnets* III.xii). See also *DWJ* II, 57.]

92. Sept 23

W and Jones spend the night [along the Rhine, probably at Speyer]. (See 1790:8n.)[27]

[27] EdS and the Racedown Nb use the French spelling "Spires." *Author's Voyage down the Rhine* and *Ecclesiastical Sonnets* III.xii mention the sight of "spires" along the river, but there can be little question in this case as to W's resting place.

93. Sept 24

W and Jones spend the night in a village on the Rhine. (See 1790:8n.)

94. [Sept 25]

[Where W and Jones spent this night is not known. (See 1790:8n.)][28]

95. Sept 26

W and Jones spend the night at [Mainz]. (See 1790:8n.)

96. Sept 27

W and Jones spend the night in a village on the Rhine [c six miles] from Coblenz. (See 1790:8n; 1790:82n.)

97. [Sept 28 or 29]

W and Jones sell the boat they purchased in Basel. (*Mem* I, 57n. See Moorman I, 147.)

98. Sept 28

W and Jones spend the night in Cologne. (See 1790:8n.)

99. Sept 29

W and Jones spend the night in a village [c nine miles] from Aix-la-Chapelle. (See 1790:8n; 1790:82n.)

100. [Between Sept 29 and probably Oct 19, fairly certainly by late Oct]

[W and Jones return to England, perhaps via Calais, probably by 19 Oct. They fairly certainly arrive at Cambridge by late Oct. Nothing more, aside from their meeting with Belgian troops on their way to the Channel (W refers to this event: *Prel* VI.689–92, *Prel*₂ VI.762–65), is known of their movements during this period. (Administrators'

---

[28] The Racedown Nb has a blank at this point.

Accounts, CRH; *Mem* I, 57n. See *EL* 37; Schneider 180; 1787:32n; 1790:99.)][29]

101. [1790] Oct 6

DW writes to Jane Pollard from Forncett: Her "Aunt" Threlkeld's approaching marriage to William Rawson. W's European walking tour described, with extensive quotation from W's letter of 6–16 Sept (W is not yet returned). News and queries about relations and

[29] On 14 Sept they had planned to travel from Cologne to Ostend and there take the packet to Margate (*EL* 34). L. A. Willoughby ("Wordsworth and Germany," *German Studies Presented to H. G. Fielder*, Oxford, 1938, 348) agrees that this was their route. They reached Cologne as planned, but *Mem* I, 57n, says they crossed from Calais. The source of the statement of *Mem* may or may not be W himself; the route must remain in doubt, although *Mem* can perhaps be given greater credence than W's statement of his plans on 14 Sept. If the travelers walked from Aix-la-Chapelle to Calais, the journey would probably have taken not less than ten days (see Harper I, 92), and if to Ostend possibly a day or two less. On 14 Sept W had hoped to be in England "by the 10th of October." Moorman I, 149, suggests that they did cross from Calais at or about that time and proceed directly to Cambridge. DW's not having heard of W's return by 6 Oct (*EL* 38) is not necessarily proof that he was not back. RW of Whitehaven, however, records remission of £30 to W under 19 Oct (Administrators' Accounts, CRH); W had fairly certainly reached the shores of England by then.

Concerning W's return to Cambridge itself, PREL 562 suggests that he reached there only in early Nov, and Schneider 180 says (on the basis of *EL* 37) they arrived at the "last possible moment," 10 Nov. One obvious aspect of the matter is that a projected visit to Forncett after his return (*EL* 37) did not take place (see *DWJ* II, 86; also Moorman I, 149). Another is that W spent "six weeks" (or thereabouts) at Forncett at Christmas vacation (*EL* 46); this fact implies that W left Cambridge in early Dec, for he had to be back by mid-Jan for Senate House examinations. In order to have left c early Dec and still have resided at Cambridge during the greater part of Michaelmas Term (as he was required to do if the term was to count toward his degree—see 1787:32n) he would have had to be in Cambridge by late Oct.

Among the drafts of the accounts between RW and W and DW in 1816 appears this item, charged to W:

> 1790 Nov 6   To cash paid Messrs Wilkinson & Crosthwaite
>   on account of their bill for wine   5/5/–.

The entry, crossed off the draft, does not appear in the final accounts; that it adds much to evidence already cited about the date of W's return is doubtful, but it perhaps offers some indication of one of W's early concerns upon arrival.

friends, at Halifax and elsewhere. Life at Forncett, DW's little school. (*EL* 37–43.)

102. [Probably early Dec–1791 mid-Jan]

W pays a visit [of six weeks or thereabouts] at Forncett. He and DW walk much in the garden there. (*EL* 46. See also *EL* 92–93; *DWJ* II, 86.) [W probably refers to this visit in "Sweet Was the Walk." (See GCL 37.)]

1 7 9 1

1. [After 1790, but esp. probably between 1795 Nov 20 and 1797 c Mar–June 4–7]

W shakes off domination of "lesser faculties"; stands a creative soul. [W refers to this event: *Prel* XI.243–57, *Prel*₂ XII.193–207. (See 1795:50.)]

2. [During this year]

[On writings of W possibly of this year see below and GCL 6–8, 28, 32–40. By some time during this year W has perhaps composed something corresponding to *The Female Vagrant*. None of this work, if written down, has survived in a form earlier than as incorporated in *SP*. (See Appendix XII.)]

3. [c Jan 10–16]

[W perhaps spends the week before his Senate House examinations largely employed in reading *Clarissa Harlowe*. (*Mem* I, 48.)]

4. [Jan 17–21]

[W takes Senate House examinations 17 Jan.] He qualifies for his B.A. degree; is classed among *hoi polloi*. (Christopher Wordsworth, *Scholae Academicae*, Cambridge, 1877, 44–45; Schneider 189, 283; information based on MS Grace Book Λ at the office of the Registry, Cambridge. See 1791:5.)[1]

[1] The Senate House examinations always began at eight on the morning of the Monday after Epiphany se'nnight; admission to the B.A. took place the following Friday.

5. Jan 21

W admitted to B.A. degree at Cambridge University. (Scott *Admissions* IV, 571. See 1791:4; Moorman I, 153.)

6. [Perhaps late Jan, certainly after Jan 17–probably late May ff]

[Perhaps in late Jan, certainly after 17 Jan, W travels to London from Cambridge. (W refers to his departure from Cambridge: *Prel* VII.57–62, *Prel₂* VII.52–57.) He departs from London probably late May. (See *EL* 48; 1791:10. On this visit generally see Moorman I, 153–60.)

In London: W lives alone (see *Prel* VII.75–76; Moorman I, 153). He sees his "Aunt" Rawson before 23 May (*EL* 43, 45).

A. References in W's writing to this visit include the following. Many of the experiences here recorded possibly draw on other, esp. longer, visits as well.

1. *Prel* VII.63–411, 435–740 and *app crit*; *Prel₂* VII.58–381, 400–771. (His life in London; sights and impressions; growth of his mind at this time.)
2. *Prel* VIII.62–81, *Prel₂* VIII.70–75. (Feels power of nature in the city.)
3. *Prel* VIII.678–859, *Prel₂* VIII.530–675. (London and its significance to his growing mind.)
4. *Prel* VIII.860–70, *Prel₂* VIII.676–86. (W's fellow beings still less to him than Nature.)
5. *Prel* IX.18–30, *Prel₂* IX.23–33. (His life in London.)
6. *Monument of Mrs Howard* IF note. (Hears Pitt at Commons. See 1787:24.)
7. *EL* 48, 56. (His life in London.)

B. References probably including this visit and other, esp. later, visits:

1. *Excursion passim* and IF note (esp. *PW* V, 374–75). In frequent residences in London in early Revolutionary period W finds many contributions to character of the Solitary, esp. in Joseph Fawcett.
2. (Through 1797 visit) *TA* 25–57 ("But oft, in lonely rooms ... How often has my spirit turned to thee." Cf W's phrasing *EL* 48.)][2]

---

[2] On W and Fawcett in London during this period generally see esp. M. Ray Adams, "Joseph Fawcett and Wordsworth's Solitary," *PMLA* XLVIII (1933), 508–28. On Fawcett see *DNB*.

7. Jan 28

RW of Whitehaven records remission of £60 to W under this date. (Administrators' Accounts, CRH. See Moorman I, 154n.)

8. Feb 28; [early Mar]

The Earl of Lonsdale's injunction (see 1788:10) is ordered dissolved unless the plaintiff pays £4000 into court in a week. [Lonsdale evidently fails to comply with this order, and the injunction is dissolved.] (GGW, Notes on Lonsdale Suit, DCP.)

9. May 19

RW of Whitehaven records remission of £20 to W under this date. (Administrators' Accounts, CRH. See Moorman I, 154n.)

10. [Probably late May, perhaps by May 23–probably early Sept, by Sept 14]

[Probably in late May, perhaps by 23 May, W travels to Wales, where he stays for nearly four months, visiting at Plas-yn-Llan, Llangynhafal, with Robert Jones and three of his sisters, and walking with Jones. He departs probably early Sept, by 14 Sept. (*EL* 45–48. See esp. *EL* 51; Lloyd 338; entries below through 1791:19; 1793:21. On W's later references to this trip see Appendix VII; 1791:13.)][3]

11. [1791] May 23

DW writes to Jane Pollard from Forncett: Her long delay in writing. Her hopes to visit Halifax in two or three years. W in Wales; JW expected on the *Abergavenny* in about a month. The hopeful appearance of the Lonsdale suit. W's visit to Forncett last winter. Life at Forncett. Inquiries about mutual acquaintances. (*EL* 43–47.)

[3] DW writes JP on 23 May that W is "now in Wales" (*EL* 45), but there is nothing in her remarks about him to indicate that she has heard from him since his arrival there. Her assumption could be based on recent information from W about his immediate plans, rather than on present certainty. W's remarks on 17 June that he left London "about three weeks" ago would be very loose indeed if he had in fact reached Plas-yn-Llan by 23 May.

12. [1791] June 17

W writes to William Mathews from Plas-yn-Llan: W departed from London about three weeks ago after a visit of four months. His life in London. Inquiries about Mathews and Terrot. His visit in Wales; an intended walking tour through northern Wales with Jones. (*EL* 47–50. See Lloyd 338.)

13. [Probably between June 17 and Aug 3]

W and Jones make a walking tour of northern Wales. (See 1791:12; 1791:15.)

[Much of the itinerary of the travelers remains in doubt. It is probable that they visit Cader Idris, Menai, the Conway, the Dee, and make their ascent of Snowdon. They probably visit the Aberystwyth–Devil's Bridge area; they possibly also visit Thomas Pennant and Thomas Thomas of Pennant Melangell. At the home of Thomas, W is threatened with a carving knife by a Welsh priest. For more detailed discussion and references see Appendix VII. The following references in W's writings definitely or probably allude to places visited now: *DS*, Dedication. (Names a number of places visited. See Appendix VII.) *Excursion* VII.1–30. (W hears the singing of an "accomplished Master."

The passage implies that W visited Penmaenmawr, as well as Cader Idris and Snowdon.)

Prel XIII.1–84, *Prel*₂ XIV.1–86. (The climbing of Snowdon.)]

14. [1791] June 26

DW writes to Jane Pollard from Forncett: Hears often from W; his enjoyment of his visit in Wales; W and his intellectual character described; W reads Italian, Spanish, French, Greek, Latin, English. The Lonsdale suit. Life at Forncett. DW's financial prospects. (*EL* 50–54.)

15. [1791] Aug 3

W writes to William Mathews from Plas-yn-Llan: Attempts to raise Mathews' low spirits. Has visited "the greater part of North Wales." Knows almost nothing of modern literature except three volumes of *Tristram Shandy* and a little of the *Spectator*. Did little [reading and, presumably, writing] in [London] and has done none since coming to Wales. His interest in modern Italian literature. His good spirits. Their friends Terrot and [R. H.] Greenwood. (*EL* 54–56.)[4]

16. Aug 18 (and 1792 autumn)

CW is admitted as pensioner to Trinity College, Cambridge, 18 Aug. [He comes into residence autumn 1792.] (Venn; *Trinity College Admissions*, ed. W. W. Rouse Ball and J. A. Venn, London, 1913–16.)

17. Aug 19

The *Earl of Abergavenny* (JW aboard) reaches moorings in England. (It had sailed 30 Jan 1790.) (Hardy 137; *EL* 45.)

18. [Perhaps late Aug (ff)]

A verdict is given in the Lonsdale suit in favor of the administrators of the estate of JW Sr. The matter is referred to an arbitrator, probably for settlement of the amount to be paid by Lonsdale. But the arbitration is delayed and not concluded (see 1792:4). (GGW, Notes on Lonsdale Suit, DCP. See *EL* 52–63; Moorman I, 167–69.)

19. [Probably early Sept, by Sept 14]

W, having received an offer from his cousin John Robinson of a curacy in Harwich, departs from Wales and travels to London in order to inform Robinson that he is not of age for Anglican orders. (*EL* 56–57.)[5]

[4] EdS dates this letter 13 Aug as a result of a mistake by Knight (*Letters of the Wordsworth Family*, London, 1907, I, 30). The MS (BM) shows that the date is 3 Aug. Knight dates the letter correctly in a brief reference to it *PW* (Knight, 1882–89) IX, 59.

[5] The offer no doubt arrived shortly before W's departure, but the date of the departure is unknown. Jones left [Plas-yn-Llan] when W did, and was at Chester "some time" before returning home on 21 Sept. (*EL* 56–57.) It would be safe to suggest that Jones was absent at least a week. I do not know the basis of the statement of T. H. Bowen (*English* VIII, 1950, 18) that W left Jones in the third week in Sept.

20. [Probably between early Sept and Sept 27 (–probably mid- or late Oct, esp. c Oct 23)]

W [sees John Robinson] and proceeds from London to Cambridge. [He remains at Cambridge until probably mid- or late Oct, esp. c 23 Oct.] (*EL* 57. See 1791:19; 1791:21; 1791:24.)[6]

21. [1791] Sept 29

W writes to William Mathews from Cambridge: His travel from Wales to Cambridge via London. Efforts to cheer and advise Mathews. His intention is to stay in Cambridge "till the University fills." (*EL* 56–57.)[7]

22. Oct 9

DW writes to Jane Pollard from Forncett: The Lonsdale suit. JW has arrived [see 1791:17]; CW has entered at Trinity [see 1791:16], should be at Cambridge within a year; W at Cambridge. Wilberforce is visiting at Forncett. W is to study Oriental languages. (*EL* 59–60. See *EL* 61.)[8]

23. Oct 16

Samuel Taylor Coleridge comes into residence at Jesus College, Cambridge. (Hanson 29.)

[6] W probably saw Robinson at his home, Wike House, Syon Hill, Isleworth, Middlesex. (See *DNB*; Moorman I, 158; G. J. Aungier, *The History and Antiquities of Syon Monastery; The Parish of Isleworth; and The Chapelry of Hounslow*, London, 1840, 212.) W had plainly gone on to Cambridge before the arrival of the letter from Mathews which had been forwarded from Wales by Jones on or after the 21st (see *EL* 56–57; 1791:19); the letter had to be forwarded a second time, from London, before reaching him on the morning of 29 Sept. The probable date of the second forwarding was the 28th; W had no doubt left London before then. No record of W's visit to Cambridge has been discovered.

[7] EdS dates this letter 23 Sept as a result of a mistake by Knight—*PW* (1882–89) IX, 60, and *Letters of the Wordsworth Family* (London, 1907) I, 33. The MS (BM) shows that the date is 29 Sept.

[8] Wilberforce visited the Cooksons 7–10 Oct (R. A. and Samuel Wilberforce, *The Life of William Wilberforce*, London, 1838, I, 315).

24. [Probably mid- or late Oct, esp. c Oct 23 (–probably Nov 22)]

[W travels to London from Cambridge. (He remains in London until probably 22 Nov.) (*EL* 59–60. See 1791:20; 1791:25.)][9]

25. [Nov 6 or 7]

W, RW meet in London. W states his determination to travel to France immediately and pass the time there previous to his taking orders. Asks RW to request £40 from RW of Whitehaven for him, which will maintain him until following summer. (Letter of RW to RW of Whitehaven, 7 Nov 1791, DCP.)[10]

26. Nov 10

RW of Whitehaven records remission of £40 to W under this date. (Administrators' Accounts, CRH.)[11]

27. [Probably Nov 22 –Nov 26]

[Probably on 22 Nov] W travels to Brighton from London on his way to France, which he reaches 27 Nov. (He remains there until 26 Nov.) (*EL* 60, 66.) [W refers to this trip from England to France: *Prel* IX.31–39, *Prel*$_2$ IX.34–41.][12]

[9] W's statement on 29 Sept that he meant to stay "until the University fills," is not unambiguous, but would normally indicate an intended departure about mid- or late Oct (see 1787:32n). On the length of W's visit in London see entries below through 1791:27. JRM astutely suggests that W's comment in his 23 Nov letter to Mathews, that he has daily expected to have the course of his winter activities "determined" for "this month past," indicates the length of the period he has just spent in London.

[10] RW, who had been away (apparently in the North), arrived back in London the night of 6 Nov, and found W there. It is not clear whether he saw W the night of the 6th or on the 7th.

[11] W thus went to France twice as "rich in monies" as Moorman I, 175, states; the remittance is recorded Moorman I, 154n.

[12] As pointed out by JRM, W writes to Mathews from Brighton on 23 Nov (Wednesday), and on 19 Dec W says that he was delayed there from "Tuesday till Saturday Evening." It can be concluded that W arrived Tuesday 22 Nov (probably making the trip down by coach). W also remarks (*EL* 66) that he arrived in Orléans "just a fortnight" after leaving London; one suspects that W is thinking of a fortnight

28. [1791] Nov 23

W writes to William Mathews from Brighton: W on his way to Orléans for the winter. Plans and worries about his future; intentions of studying Oriental languages in preparation for taking orders upon his return. (*EL* 60–62.)

29. [Probably between Nov 23 and Nov 26]

While waiting for a ship from Brighton to France, W calls on Miss Charlotte Smith, who gives him letters of introduction for France, including one for Helen Maria Williams in Orléans (see 1791:36) and "Letters for Paris." [He perhaps reads and possibly copies poems of Miss Smith's in MS (esp. nos. 49 and 51 of *Elegaic Sonnets*, 1792).] (*EL* 66; Mr. Bishop C. Hunt.)[13]

30. [Probably Nov 26]

[On the evening of this day W departs from Brighton to cross the Channel to Dieppe. (*EL* 66. See 1791:27n.)]

---

[13] As JRM remarks, if W had called on Miss Smith before writing Mathews on the 23rd, he would probably have mentioned the fact to his friend. The addressees of the letters for Paris are unknown. One good guess would be Brissot (see 1791:34). JRM suggests another possibility, W's later friends John Frederick Pinney and his brother Azariah; yet another might be "Walking" Stewart (see 1791:34). Mr. Hunt's unpublished Oxford thesis, "Wordsworth's Marginalia in Dove Cottage, to 1805: A Study of His Relationship to Charlotte Smith, Milton, and Certain Poets in Anderson's Anthology," points out that copies by W of the two sonnets noted, which he wrote into his copy of the 1789 edition of Miss Smith's *Elegaic Sonnets* (DCP), appear to represent states of the poem intermediate between earlier published versions in *Celestina*, 1791, and the texts as they appeared in the edition of the *Sonnets* of 1792. W was perhaps copying the poems from memory, and to some degree mingling recollections of earlier and later versions, or else saw intermediate versions of the poems in MS at Miss Smith's; he could possibly have made some sort of copies of the poems there.

---

based on corresponding weekdays. He arrived in Orléans Tuesday 6 Dec. EdS's statement (*EL* 66) that W was in Brighton from Tuesday 6 Dec must be a careless slip. The statement of the 1805 *Prel* that W had been in London a year is, of course, far from accurate chronologically.

31. [Nov 27–1792 perhaps Nov or early Dec, fairly certainly by Dec 22 (ff)]

[On the morning of 27 Nov W arrives in Dieppe. He travels to Rouen, arriving there the same night. He departs from France finally perhaps Nov or early Dec 1792, fairly certainly returning to England by 22 Dec 1792. (See 1792:37; 1792:39.)

On W's visit to France generally see esp. Moorman I, 171–210; *Mem* I, 70–77. References in W's writings to this visit, or to the visit and an indefinite period following, not capable of precise dating, include:
1. *Prel* IX.217–66, *Prel*₂ IX.215–62. (Early events of Revolution as part of Nature's course.)
2. *Prel* X.658–757, *Prel*₂ XI.74–172. (Probably from this visit until a time by late 1795. W, in a pleasant exercise of hope and joy, philosophizes on the management of nations.)
3. *Prel* IX.555–934, *Prel*₂ IX.553–85, *Vaudracour and Julia*. (Probably 1792. W hears at least the basic elements of the story of Vaudracour and Julia in France. On W's source see PREL 591; Shaver *RES*; C. L. Shaver, *TLS* 21 Feb 1958, 101; F. M. Todd, *Politics and the Poet* (London, 1958) 221–25; Beatty *RP* 214–16. On W and the poem generally see esp. *Vaudracour and Julia* IF note; Shaver *RES*; 1791:36.)
4. *Excursion*, esp. II.164–303 and *app crit* (*PW* V, 48). (Probably from now until late 1795. The Solitary's early enthusiasm for the Revolution and the course of his mind in regard to it, including his later disillusionment, may be taken as partly based on W's own attitudes.)
5. *The Emigrant Mother* and IF note. (W sees French fugitives "during the time of the French Revolution.")
6. Worth note also is *Mem* II, 491 (*Mem*, R, II, 501–02). (W knows ecclesiastics in France; thinks highly of them as a class. Religion in town and country.)]

32. [1791–92 winter]
[It is probably during this period that Nature becomes subordinate to man in W's affections, as described in *Prel* VIII.482–85, *Prel*₂ VIII. 347–51. (See also PREL 580; 1791:36.)][14]

[14] All dating of points in W's psychological growth in the present study is, of course, undertaken simply as clarification of W's own descriptions of what he re-

33. [Probably Nov 28, 29]

W remains in Rouen [waiting for the Paris "diligence"]. (*EL* 66. See 1791:27n.)

34. [Probably Nov 30–Dec 5; 1792 probably Oct 29–perhaps late Nov or early Dec, fairly certainly by Dec 22]

[On 30 Nov W travels from Rouen to Paris, arriving at night. He departs probably 5 Dec. (W refers to this visit: *Prel* IX.40–79, *Prel*$_2$ IX.42–80.)

During this period he visits the National Assembly, introduced by a member (Brissot?); he probably visits the Jacobin Club. He changes £20 for 643 livres. (*EL* 66, 68; *Mem* I, 73. See 1791:27n.)

James Watt, Jr., is possibly an associate of W's at this time. (J. P. Muirhead, *Blackwood's Magazine* 221, June 1927, 205–06; Muirhead, *The Life of James Watt*, London, 1859, 479–80); but the chance of such an acquaintance is extremely remote. Probably both now and in the following autumn (see 1792:31) W forms many acquaintances among the Girondins. He is perhaps at both times acquainted with

---

membered, or thought he did, and does not deal with problems of the "real" accuracy of these descriptions. It is probably much more nearly correct to say with PREL 580 that nature became subordinated to man in W's affections when he had passed "two-and-twenty summers" (*Prel*$_2$ VIII.349), rather than when he had passed "three-and-twenty" (*Prel* VIII.483). (This new state of W's feelings must be distinguished from the state described *Prel* VIII.624–40, *Prel*$_2$ VIII.476–94, when, even before W's arrival at Cambridge, man had become to him the crown "of all visible natures"—that is, the crown of all the visible objects which his primary love, Nature, presented to his sight—see *Prel* VIII.860–70, *Prel*$_2$ VIII.676–86.) The poet's phrasing in *TA* 75–85 raises a possible problem: Here W plainly says that nature was "all in all" to him during the summer of 1793 (see Appendix VII), a statement in apparent agreement with the earlier *Prel* reading cited, and indicates that any deep concern with humanity resulted from recognitions of a later date. The development of W's affections could not have been other than gradual, but the *Prel* description of his feelings while in France leaves no doubt that an essential change, more than the formation of a "bond unknown," must have occurred during this visit abroad, probably before, during, and after his twenty-third summer. His new attitude toward man need not have precluded a later period of compulsive seeking of strong excitements, and escape from the oppressions of various problems, by means of external nature. See Moorman I, 232–33; 1793:17.

"Walking" Stewart and is struck by his eloquence. (*Mem* I, 74; Moorman I, 172, 205–07; *Collected Writings of Thomas De Quincey*, ed. David Masson, London, 1896–97, III, 96, 106.)]15

15 W possibly had a letter of introduction to Brissot from Charlotte Smith. While W later denied having lived "in the same house" with Brissot (BM MSS Add 41,325) upon his return to Paris next year, he never denied having had contacts with this revolutionary, who had many close English associations. (See 1791:29n; Moorman I, 172, 202n.) JRM suggests that W visited the Jacobin Club on Friday, 2 Dec (see F. A. Aulard, *La Société des Jacobins*, Paris, 1889–97, III, 268–71). He could have attended Friday or Sunday, but the Friday meeting was livelier, and *Mem* I, 73, offers at least a little indication that W attended a lively meeting. JRM mentions the possibility of a meeting with John Frederick and Azariah Pinney at this time.

Alger's evidence for identifying as James Watt, Jr., the anonymous English Constitutional Whig who inspired a fervid ceremony at the Jacobin Club on [6 and] 18 Dec is "a letter from the London Constitutional Society thanking the Jacobins for their reception of Cooper and Watt" (p. 45n). The letter is quoted by Aulard (III, 621–23), and has no bearing on events before Mar–Apr 1792. A letter from Watt and Thomas Cooper of 6 Mar 1792, just following their arrival in France, to Thomas Walker of the Manchester Constitutional Society requesting to be made delegates to the Jacobin Club and other patriotic societies ("We look upon it that this will be an extremely good introduction") suggests that Watt had no entrée to the Jacobins— an impossible case had he evoked the impassioned ceremonies of the previous Dec (see *The Original*, ed. Blanchard Jerrold, London, 1874, I, 82–83; Aulard III, 272–75, 290). Watt's whereabouts between 4 Nov 1791 and Feb 1792 are, however, not known (see *Memoirs of the Manchester Literary and Philosophical Society*, third series, IX, 1883, 173; Eric Robinson, "An English Jacobin: James Watt, Junior, 1769–1848," *Cambridge Historical Journal* XI, 1953–55, 349–55), and W is recorded by Muirhead (*Life of Watt*, 480) as having said that he found Watt in Paris "before him." Eric Robinson has kindly passed on information concerning Watt's movements in late 1792: Watt departed Paris, apparently for the last time, for Nantes 7 Oct 1792; Nantes for Bordeaux 20 Oct; Bordeaux for Marseilles 28 Oct; Marseilles for Leghorn 18 Nov (Nb of Watt's traveling expenses, found by Mr. Robinson at Birmingham Reference Library). Watt's father writes on 8 Jan 1793 of having heard from him from Leghorn "last week" (MS, Birmingham Reference Library), and Watt wrote to his father from Naples 15 Jan (BM Add MS 38, 650, fol. 88). W hence could hardly have met Watt in Paris in late 1792, although Watt could conceivably have traveled to Nantes via Orléans, W's residence. Watt is unlikely to have returned to Paris in late 1793 because of his uneasy political position there (Muirhead, 479–80; personal communication from Mr. Robinson; see 1793:26n), although I have not traced his movements between 6 Sept 1793, when he noted by endorsement receipt of a letter from his father in Genoa, and 5 Nov, when he received letters in Frankfurt (MSS, Birmingham Reference Library). Evidence seems to weigh against any meeting of W and Watt in Paris, but a faint chance may remain of a 1791 or 1793 encounter. W possibly

35. [Probably Dec 5]

W departs from Paris for Orléans. (*EL* 66. See 1791:27n.)

36. [Probably Dec 6 and shortly after–probably shortly before 1792 Oct 29]

Probably on 6 Dec W arrives in Orléans. On this day or shortly after he takes lodgings with M. Gellet-Duvivier. He departs from Orléans finally probably shortly before 29 Oct 1792. (*EL* 66. See 1791:27n; 1792:31; Moorman I, 175.)

W refers to the period of his residence in Orléans and Blois generally: *Prel* IX.80–125, *Prel*₂ IX.81–124 (W becomes a patriot, gives heart to people—see 1791:31); *DS* 740–73 (the Loire region, esp. the Loiret; refers esp. to 1792 Oct). See also *DS* 760n (visits La Source); *The Tuft of Primroses* 466.

Also on 6 Dec or shortly after W finds that Helen Maria Williams, to whom he has a letter of introduction from Charlotte Smith, and whom he expected to find in Orléans, has departed. (*EL* 66–67.)

Perhaps on 6 Dec or shortly after W becomes acquainted with the (André-Augustin) Dufours, and, through them, with Paul Vallon and his sister Marie-Anne (Annette) Vallon. (*AV* 8–11, 110–11; Moorman I, 178. See *AV* and *WFD passim.*) W frequently passes evenings at the Dufours' hereafter (*EL* 67). (*Prel* IX.555–934, *Prel*₂ IX.553–85, and *Vaudracour and Julia* probably draw heavily on experiences and emotions arising from W's relationship with Annette Vallon.)][16]

[16] On the reason for W's choice of Orléans for his destination see Moorman I, 174–75. In *Prel* W fuses the activities of his visits to Blois and Orléans into an apparent single visit. H. M. Williams had left Orléans for Paris just before W's arrival. (JRM, drawing on evidence of H. M. Williams, *Letters from France*, Boston, 1792, 49; see 1791:29.)

The assumption that the Dufour household was where W often spent his evenings is based on the known later close relationship between the Vallons, the Dufours, and W (see esp. *WFD* 28–29). JRM, building on *AV* 11–12, suggests that Paul and Annette, the latter visiting from Blois, were lodging at the Dufours', where Annette very likely gave birth to her child in 1792 (see *WFD*). Moorman I, 178, states the basis for the conclusion that W met Annette in Orléans: There is no other conceivable reason why W should have left Orléans as soon as he did (see 1792:2) for Blois (cf W's comments *EL* 67).

---

spoke loosely to Muirhead of contemporary reports of Watt, or Muirhead may have recorded W's remarks incorrectly.

37. [Probably between Dec 6 and 1792 perhaps late Nov or early Dec; esp. after mid-May 1792]

W composes the bulk of *Descriptive Sketches*. [No passages are known definitely to date before 1792 mid-May.] (*DS* IF note; W, MS note in presentation copy of *EW*, 16 Mar 1846, DCP. See 1792:10; 1792:27; 1792:28; Appendix V.)[17]

38. [1791] Dec 7

DW writes to Jane Pollard from Forncett: Life at Forncett; the girls' health; King's College Chapel. The Lonsdale suit under arbitration by Mr. Burrow; her hopes for a speedy conclusion to the affair. DW's grandmother's generosity; her plans to present the W children £100 apiece [see 1792:5]. Summary of financial condition and prospects of the W children: The four younger children hope for £1000 apiece eventually. JW's plan to sail on *Thetis* in the spring. W's visit to Orléans to learn French in order to be a companion to a young gentleman; he will study oriental languages in England, if he settles here on his return. The Cookson children. (*EL* 62–65.)

39. [Dec 18 ff]

W calls on Mr. Foxlow, an Englishman who owns a cotton factory in Orléans, [on 18 Dec. The Foxlows probably later introduce him to the "best society" of Orléans.] (*EL* 67; Moorman I, 174. See 1792:2.)

40. Dec 19

W writes to RW from Orléans: His trip to Orléans from England. His call on Charlotte Smith [at Brighton]. Living arrangements in Orléans. The recent departure of Helen Maria Williams; Foxlow [see

[17] W's MS note of 1846 was kindly brought to my attention by Miss Landon. The IF note says that "much the greatest part" of the poem was composed on the banks of the Loire during 1791, 1792. In view of the time of W's arrival in France little could have been done in 1791. Moorman I, 196, dates the writing of DS summer and early autumn 1792. Parts, of course, could have been written before W's trip to France (any time after the 1790 walking trip), or any time up the date of the poem's publication (28 Jan 1793); these parts, however, if they exist, must be few. Virtually no MS work on the poem survives; the additions and corrections in the Huntington Library copy of *DS* appear, on stylistic grounds, to date not long after the publication of the poem (see esp. *PW* I, 42–81 *app crit*; *PW* I, 324–25; Appendix IV).

1791:39]. Has passed several evenings [at the Dufours' (see 1791:36)].
The anti-Revolutionary attitudes of the wealthy here. Expects to enjoy
Orléans. (*EL* 66–68.)

41. [Probably c late Dec–1792 Apr 30, early May]

JW arrives at Forncett for a visit of four months [probably c late
Dec. He departs 1792 Apr 30.] RW visits Forncett, [probably c 17
Mar]; gives DW a gown, later [by early May] a hat. (*EL* 68–72;
EY 71n.)

1792

1. [During this year]

[On writings of W possibly of this year see below and GCL 7,
32–35, 38–41.]

2. [Probably between Jan and mid-Apr, possibly by Feb 3–Sept or
Oct]

[Probably between Jan and mid-Apr, possibly by 3 Feb, W departs
from Orléans, takes up residence in Blois. He departs possibly between
3 and 6 Sept, perhaps later Sept or Oct 1793. (See 1791:36; 1792:3;
1792:11; 1792:22; 1792:25; *EL* 74; *Mem* I, 74; Moorman I, 178–79.)

(W perhaps refers esp. to his society at Blois: *Prel* IX.113–23, *Prel*₂
IX.113–22—JRM.) W becomes acquainted with Michel Beaupuy. W
refers to his activities and talks with Beaupuy, and the importance of
their association esp.: *Prel* IX.126–554, *Prel*₂ IX.125–552. Events of this
period probably contribute to *Prel* IX.555–934, *Prel*₂ IX.553–85;
Vaudracour and Julia. See also PREL 588–89.][1]

---

[1] W's remark to Mathews on 19 May that he had received his letter as he was
preparing to leave Orléans, and that since his arrival at Blois "day after day and week
after week" have "stolen insensibly" over his head, suggests that he has been at Blois
at least a month. PREL 585 assumes that this comment points to a time not later than
Mar. On Beaupuy see esp. George Bussière and Emile Legouis, *Le Général Michel
Beaupuy* (Paris, 1891).
JRM suggests that Orléans is where W "loitered" for "a short time," and Blois
the "noisier world" into which he withdrew, and where he met officers (*Prel* IX.113–
23; *Prel*₂ IX.113–22). Although W implies that his change of "world" was social,

3. Feb 3

On 3 Feb two Englishmen are granted permission to attend the meetings of the "Friends of the Constitution" at Blois. [W is possibly one of the Englishmen. He has thus possibly by this time traveled from Orléans to reside in Blois.] (Harper I, 155; *EL* 74. See 1792:2; Moorman I, 193.)[2]

4. [End of Feb (ff)]

[Lord Lonsdale alleges the cause of the Wordsworth suit to be abated by the coming of age of one of the W children. (The matter of the suit evidently rests at this point indefinitely.) (GGW, Notes on Lonsdale Suit, DCP. See 1791:18.)]

5. [Probably before Apr 26]

DW's grandmother makes her a present of £100. (*EL* 64; letter of CCC to RW, 30 Apr 1793, CRH. See 1793:10.)

6. [Apr 30]

JW departs from Forncett after a visit of four months to travel to Cumberland [via London]. (*EL* 68, 69, 72. See 1791:41.)

7. May

RW records under this general date a credit of £68 to W and DW as their share of a sum of £136 received from [their Uncle] Cookson

---

[2] Moorman doubts that W was one of the Englishmen; her reason, that this would be "an early date" for W to be in Blois, seems, however, not especially strong. JRM believes that W was in fact one of the two, and suggests that Edmund Dayrell, who bought an estate near Blois in Feb 1792 (see Alger 237), was the other. Harper I, 168, notes that an officer with a name like Beaupuis or Beaupuy gave an address to this club on 22 and 29 Jan; W possibly met Beaupuy here.

and came about "gradually," a geographical move could have been a major force in bringing about a change of his associates. The same authority also infers that the royalist gambling society (see *Prel* IX.115) belonged to Orléans, and that W might have attended the Royal Academy of Sciences at that city (JRM draws on Anatole Bailly, *Les Archives de l'Académie d'Orléans*, Orléans, 1872).

on account of an intended present from [their Aunt] Cookson. (RW, accounts with W and DW, 1816, DCP. See *EL* 63–64; 1792:8.)[3]

8. [Probably between May 1 and May 8]

DW writes to RW [from Forncett]: Thanks RW for a present of a beaver hat. The £100 gift [from her grandmother (see 1792:5)]. Has not heard from W since [30 Apr]. (*EL* 68. See *EL* 72; 1792:7. On date see 1792:9.)

9. May 8

DW writes to Jane Pollard [from Forncett]: Inquiries about Halifax acquaintances; her dimming prospects of visiting Halifax. She expects to visit London as the Cooksons travel to Windsor for three months; expects to see RW, perhaps W, in London. JW has spent four months at Forncett; departed [30 Apr] for Cumberland; will sail to America or West Indies from Whitehaven. RW another visitor at Forncett; he brought her a gown; sent a hat. Transcription of W's "Sweet Was the Walk." (*EL* 70–74.)[4]

[3] The accounts indicate that this present had nothing to do with the £100 which DW's grandmother gave her. The £100 remained with CCC for at least a year.

[4] EdS quotes the date of letter no. 23 as "Tuesday May 6th, 1792," but the figure 6 has been corrected, probably by DW, to an 8. The correct date for that Tuesday would be 8 May. The date of JW's departure, 30 Apr, is set by DW's remark that he left "last Monday."

The dates of EdS's letters nos. 21 and 22 can probably be set more precisely than his "[spring–1792]." Number 21 was written after the departure of JW, and the day after receipt of the hat from RW; reference to the hat in no. 23 strongly implies that no. 23 was written after no. 21; despite DW's phrasing in no. 21, "if John is still in London," she must have been fairly sure he was, since the note was enclosed in a parcel of silk being sent to JW (*EL* 68). DW had had no reason to suppose he had left London by 8 May (*EL* 72). Number 21 can thus be dated between 1 May (the day after JW left; she could hardly refer to him as she did on the very day of his departure) and 8 May. She says she has not heard from W since JW's departure, a remark more appropriate a few days after JW's departure than immediately after.

DW assumed on 8 May (letter no. 23) that JW had not left London, but in letter no. 22 she notes that she has just (the same day) received a letter from JW from Penrith (*EL* 69): He had traveled there via London and Newcastle, where he stopped three or four days, and wrote to DW the day after his arrival in Penrith. Number 22 was finished "Monday evening." Which Monday is not certain, but a good guess is

10. May 10–Oct

Four hundred soldiers are now quartered at the Grande Chartreuse. [W appears to imply—*DS* 53–79, PREL 198–202 *app crit*, *Prel*₂ VI.418–78—that this occupation took place in 1790.] (See 1790:34n; Moorman I, 136–37, 196.) [*DS* 53–79 is probably composed at or after this time (see 1790:34n).]

11. May 19

W writes to William Mathews from Blois: W's delay in writing Mathews. Suggests that Mathews explore possibilities of literary work in London. Intention of taking orders this winter or next spring; his uncle will give him a title [see 1792:12]. Mutual friends—Jones, Terrot. Mathews' low spirits. Events of, comments on, the French Revolution. Expectation of returning to England in autumn or early winter. (*EL* 74–77.)[5]

12. [Possibly May 21; probably May 28]

DW writes to RW [from Forncett]: Thanks RW for the hat [see 1792:8]. JW has arrived in Penrith. Uncle Cookson has offered W a

---

[5] As first pointed out to me by Professor Shaver the MS of this letter (BM) shows that its date is 19 May. EdS dates it 17 May as the result of an error by Knight, *PW* (1882–89) IX, 64, and *Letters of the Wordsworth Family* (London, 1907) I, 42.

---

possible. At the time of no. 21, DW had not heard from W since JW's departure from Forncett; now it has been "about a week" since both she and her uncle received letters from W. JW probably left London shortly after DW's letter of 8 May (*EL* 68, 69, 72), but distances and coach speeds (a mail coach averaged about seven miles per hour—see Paterson; Joyce 290, 399–400), plus his visit in Newcastle, show that well over a week must have passed before DW could have received JW's letter. JW reached Penrith by 22 May ("John, your Brother, paid me a Visit yesterday": letter of Rev. Thomas Myers to RW, 23 May, CRH). RW of Whitehaven notes a charge of 7/6 for carriage of JW's sea chest from Newcastle under 23 May (Administrators' Accounts, CRH). The charge was most likely recorded about the time of the arrival of the sea chest; the chest would have taken a few days at most to come, and probably was not dispatched long—if at all—after JW left Newcastle. JW thus probably traveled to Penrith shortly before, certainly by, 22 May. Unless DW was mistaken concerning JW's whereabouts at the time of her letter of 8 May, Monday 14 May is an impossible date for this letter. May 21 or 28 thus become the likely dates, with (in view of the sea chest) the 28th the more probable.

title for orders; W intends to accept it; related problems [see 1791:25]. The children at Forncett have recovered from [inoculation for small-pox]. Her present from her aunt [see 1792:7]. CW looks forward to Cambridge. (*EL* 68–70. On date see 1792:9n.)

13. June 11, 14 and shortly after

Dorothy Crackanthorpe Cookson, grandmother of W, dies at Penrith 11 June. She is buried 14 June. (Penrith; CRH *Transactions* 148.) [JW] is [still] at Penrith 14 June; CW is expected the beginning of next week [c 19 June]. CCC inherits Newbiggin Hall. (Letter of CCC to RW, 14 June 1793, CRH *Transactions* 148; Moorman I, 5. On the W children's inheritance see esp. 1794:3.)

14. June 23

RW of Whitehaven records payment of £30 to the Rev. James Wood, W's tutor at Cambridge, on W's account under this date. (Administrators' Accounts, CRH. See *EL* 353–54.)[6]

15. [Probably between late July and 1793 Apr 26]

[JW probably sails to the West Indies or America. If so, he returns by 26 Apr 1793. (See 1793:9n; *EL* 72; Administrators' Accounts, CRH.][7]

---

[6] W's tutor at entrance was Edward Frewen, but Frewen was instituted rector of the united college living of Thorrington cum Frating, Essex, on 14 Feb 1788. His fellowship at St. John's was filled in Mar 1789, and he was married in June 1789. Wood was probably W's tutor from Jan 1789. (*W at Cambridge* 2–9; Venn; Scott *Admissions* III, 717, and IV, 56.) *EL* shows that W's debt to Wood was not paid in full before Dec 1803.

[7] JW's earlier plan to sail on the *Thetis* in spring 1792 (*EL* 64) was not followed; the *Thetis* returned from that voyage 19 June 1793 (Hardy). The later plan for a voyage to the West Indies or America more likely was followed, although no evidence indicates the exact time of his sailing or return. CCC, however, wrote RW on 31 July (CRH) that [JW] had left him "last week" and "gone to Whitehaven." RW of Whitehaven records payment of bills, probably of recent date, for JW in late Feb and early Mar 1793 (Administrators' Accounts, CRH).

16. July 17

Christopher Crackanthorpe Cookson takes new legal surname Crackanthorpe, his name now becoming Christopher Crackanthorpe Crackanthorpe. (W. P. W. Phillimore and E. A. Fry, *An Index to Changes of Name*, London, 1905. See CRH *Transactions* 148.)

17. July 27

Beaupuy's regiment (the thirty-second) leaves Blois for active service on the Rhine frontier. (George Bussière and Emile Legouis, *Le Général Michel Beaupuy*, Paris, 1891, 43.)

18. July 31

DW and the Cooksons leave Forncett on their way to Windsor. (*EL* 78.)

19. Probably Aug 1–8, 9, or 10

[Probably on 1 Aug] DW arrives in London. [She departs probably 8, 9, or 10 Aug.] She sees RW; makes purchases. (*EL* 78–79; RW, accounts with W and DW, 1816, DCP.)[8]

20. Aug 10

Louis XVI dethroned. W is still in Blois. (*Mem* I, 15.)

21. Aug 27

RW records receipt of £20 from RW of Whitehaven, [remitted c 21 Aug,] to forward to W, under this date. [RW probably writes to W at once on this subject.] (RW, draft account with W and DW, DCP; letter of RW to RW of Whitehaven, 27 Aug 1792, DCP; Administrators' Accounts, CRH. See Moorman I, 200; *EL* 77; 1791:25; 1791:26; 1792:24.)

---

[8] DW says that she quit London for Windsor "exactly a week" after arriving there but also that she traveled to Windsor on 9 or 10 Aug (the trip must have been accomplished within a single day). She made purchases totaling £7/15/5 from Mr. Birtwhistle; RW records payment of the bill under 6 Aug 1792.

22. [Perhaps c Sept ff]

[Annette Vallon returns to Orléans perhaps c Sept; she probably stays at the Dufours'. (See 1792:25.)]

23. [Sept 2–6]

[The September massacres take place in Paris. (W possibly travels to Orléans before the end of this period.) (See 1792:25.)]

24. Sept 3

W writes to RW from Blois: Arrangements to receive his £20 [see 1792:21]. Expects to return to London in Oct and stay with RW and J. L. Wilkinson [on whom see esp. Shaver *RES*] while he arranges publication [of *EW* and *DS*]. (*EL* 77.)[9]

25. [Possibly between Sept 3 and Sept 6, perhaps later Sept or Oct]

[W returns to Orléans from Blois. (*Mem* I, 15; *Mem* II, 491, *Mem*, R, II, 501—W in conversation with Ellis Yarnall 18 Aug 1849. See Moorman I, 200–01; 1791:36, 1792:22; 1792:23.)][10]

---

[9] The postmark "Sept 10.92" quoted by EdS and mentioned Moorman I, 200n, is, as Professor Shaver first informed me, that of the General Post Office in London, and would signify the date of the arrival of the letter there.

[10] W twice stated in his late years that he was in Orléans at the time of the September massacres; these took place 2–6 Sept. His statement could be true only if he had set off almost at once after writing his letter to RW from Blois on 3 Sept. W's memory may have erred on this point; or it is perhaps possible that he was considering the violent events that took place in Orléans in mid-Sept (described by JRM and Moorman I, 201, esp. from material in the Public Records Office, London) as some sort of offshoot of the events in Paris and entitled to the same name. Yarnall's report, however, has W remarking (ironically, it appears) to his wife, after mentioning his presence in Orléans now, "I wonder how I came to stay there so long, and at a period so exciting"—as if the excitement were in Paris. W was expecting to receive money from RW at Blois (*EL* 77); on the other hand, he was pretty certainly in Orléans by sometime in Oct (*DS* 760–773). As Moorman I, 200, notes, W was planning to stay in Blois when he wrote on 3 Sept, and if he left for Orléans shortly after writing RW, the move must have been sudden and unexpected. W's remarks probably offer better evidence for the return to Orléans at this time than any conjecture about the remarks' doubtfulness offers against it. Nor is evidence available to show whether he may have returned to Blois later in the month, or whether he made arrangements to receive his money in Orléans. Anyhow, the time of W's return to Orléans must have been roughly that of Annette's return thither.

26. Sept 21

[W perhaps attends the celebration in honor of the Republic at Orléans on this day. (JRM; *AV* 24; E. Bimbinet, *Histoire de la Ville d'Orléans*, Orléans, 1884–88, V, 1225. See 1792:27.)]

27. Sept 22; [between Sept 22 and early Jan]

On 22 Sept the French Republic is proclaimed. [The foundation of the Republic is the probable subject of *DS* 774–809. These lines were thus probably composed between 22 Sept and early Jan.] (See 1791:37; 1791:27; 1793:3; Moorman I, 201.)

28. [Probably Oct; probably between Oct and early Jan]

[W refers to sights and walks in the region of the Loire and Loiret, including visit(s?) to La Source, apparently esp. in Oct, in *DS* 740–73. These lines were thus probably composed between Oct time and early Jan. (See 1791:36; Moorman I, 201.)][11]

29. [1792] Oct 16

DW writes to Jane Pollard from Windsor: Her and the Cooksons' trip to Windsor via London. Windsor; the royal family and their manner of life. DW's activities at Windsor; her "entrée" at an Egham Race Ball. They are to leave Windsor in three weeks. (*EL* 78–82.)

30. [Perhaps late Oct]

[Before leaving Orléans, W authorizes André-Augustin Dufour to represent him at the baptism of Annette Vallon's child. (*WFD* 28–29; *AV* 25; Moorman I, 201–02. On Dufour see 1791:36.)]

31. [Probably shortly before Oct 29]

[W departs from Orléans, possibly on foot; travels to Paris. (W refers to this event: *Prel* X.1–39, esp. 1–8, *Prel₂* X.1–47, esp. 1–11.) (See 1792:32.)]

---

[11] Mrs. Moorman's suggestion that W finished his work on *DS* before his departure for Paris and England (shortly before 29 Oct) is entirely possible but cannot be confirmed.

32. [Probably Oct 29 (–probably between Oct 29 and Dec 22)]

[Probably on 29 Oct W arrives in Paris. (He departs perhaps Nov or early Dec, certainly by 22 Dec.) (*Prel* X.83–125, *Prel₂* X.94–145. See PREL 595; 1792:37.) (W refers to his return to Paris and his first night there: *Prel* X.38–82 and *app crit*, *Prel₂* X.48–93.)]

33. [Probably Oct 29–perhaps late Nov or early Dec, fairly certainly by Dec 22]

[W in Paris. (See 1792:32; 1792:37.) (W refers to the time of this visit: *Prel* X.100–189 and *app crit*, *Prel₂* X.113–221—his intense reactions to Revolutionary events.)

James Losh and Felix Vaughan are perhaps also in Paris, and W possibly knows them here. (See Schneider 202; P. A. Brown, *The French Revolution in English History*, London, 1923, 91; Richard Welford, *Men of Mark 'Twixt Tyne and Tweed*, London, 1895, III, 83–84; Alger 47–48; H. Lonsdale, *The Worthies of Cumberland*, London, 1873, 186–87; Moorman I, 205–07.) W probably has many acquaintances among the Girondins, including Brissot, at this time. (W probably refers to these contacts: *Prel* X.195–96, *Prel₂* X.229–30.) (See 1791:34; 1793:26; *Mem* I, 76–77.)][12]

34. Nov 3

RW admitted to Staple Inn. (E. Williams, *Staple Inn*, London, 1906, 178.)

---

[12] As noted by JRM, the statement that W stayed in the same house with Brissot in Paris appears to have been made first by the anonymous author of the biographical memoir prefacing the 1828 Galignani edition of W's poems. W possessed a copy of this edition (see *LY* 336; W Soc *Transactions* VI, 257—sale catalogue), and is not known to have commented on this statement, but Mrs. Moorman (I, 202) has observed that he denied the suggestion in a note written in Barron Field's MS Memoirs of Wordsworth (BM Add MS 41, 325). One wonders whether Field took his information from the Galignani edition (his phrasing is, "He is said . . . to have lived") or had it some other way. On the possibility of W's knowing James Watt, Jr., in Paris at this time see 1791:34n. Margoliouth's suggestion (Margoliouth 11) that *Prel* X.180–89 (*Prel₂* X.211–21), which speaks of the potential power of "the virtue of one paramount mind," may refer to a search by W for journalistic work in Paris seems forced (see esp. PREL 595–96).

35. Nov 18

A great banquet of English Radicals takes place at White's Hotel, Paris; [W possibly attends]. (JRM; J. G. Alger, *Paris, 1789–94*, London, 1902, 325–29. See 1792:37.)[13]

36. [Perhaps late Nov or early Dec, certainly by Dec 22–1795 Sept 26]

[W refers to this period: *Prel* XIII.334–67, *Prel*$_2$ XIV.349–69. (London chiefly his home; his undomestic Wanderer's life; Raisley Calvert.) (See 1795:34.)]

37. [Perhaps late Nov or early Dec, fairly certainly by Dec 22–1793 perhaps late June, probably early July]

[W returns to London from Paris perhaps in late Nov or early Dec, fairly surely by Dec 22. (See 1792:39; *AV* 25–26; Moorman I, 208–09.) (W refers to his return: *Prel* X.190–92, *Prel*$_2$ X.222–25.) He departs perhaps late June, probably early July 1793. (See 1793:18.) (W refers to events and his feelings around the time of his return and during his London visit: *Prel* X.189–227, *Prel*$_2$ X.221–262.) (See also 1791:6; 1791:31; Moorman I, 211–30.)

In London W probably lives with RW and J. L. Wilkinson. While living with them W tells Wilkinson the story of *Vaudracour and Julia* and speaks of his plan to turn it into a novel. (Shaver *RES*; *EL* 77; Moorman I, 211.) He makes final preparations for publication of *DS* by late Jan (see 1793:3; Shaver *RES*).

W's specific activities during this visit are largely unknown. He eats supper a number of times with Samuel Nicholson of Cateaton St. and goes to hear Joseph Fawcett preach (*Excursion* IF note; JRM). He sees his cousins Mr. and Mrs. Rawson; they invite him to visit them (at Halifax) (*EL* 94). He perhaps meets James Gray and James Perry of *The Morning Chronicle* (see *EL* 130; Moorman I, 298).][14]

[13] No list of the guests has survived.

[14] Lack of funds to remain abroad longer, as stated by W, was the probable reason for his return to England. DW's phrasing on 22 Dec, that W was in London and writes her "regularly," appears to mean that he has been writing her regularly *from* London; and there would hardly be any basis for speaking of "regular" letters unless

38. Dec 15

Anne-Caroline Wordsworth (d. 8 July 1862), only child of William Wordsworth and Marie-Anne Vallon, born and baptized in Orléans. (*WFD* 28–29; *AV* 113.)[15]

39. Dec 22

DW writes [to an unknown correspondent from Forncett]: W is in London; writes to DW regularly. (*EL* 82.)[16]

1793

1. [During this year]

[On writings of W possibly of this year see below and GCL 7, 32–34, 38, 39, 41–45.]

---

[15] The birth almost surely took place at the home of the Dufours (see 1791:36; 1792:30; Moorman I, 178–87). Anne-Caroline's tombstone records her birth as on 6 Dec (*AV* 113), but her certificate of baptism (see *WFD* 28–29) must be correct. Her marriage certificate indicates that she customarily used the name Wordsworth (*WFD* 33–36).

[16] *Mem* I, 77, is the only source for this brief passage from an otherwise unknown letter.

---

he had been writing for some two weeks at least. W's manner of speaking of his return visit to Paris implies that he must have remained in that city for a period of not less than about a fortnight, although there is no basis for certainty on the point. There seems little reason, however, to conclude with EdS *DW* 35 that W was still in Paris on 15 Dec, when his child was born, and none at all with Harper (*WFD* 27) and PREL 585 that he perhaps returned as late as Jan 1793 (PREL 596 gives the date as Dec 1792). Some of W's own remarks about the length of his visit in France are plainly inaccurate. Autobiog Mem (*Mem* I, 15) says "fifteen or sixteen months"; *Prel*₂ X.236–37 says the leaves fell, and winter came on, twice while he was there. But his earliest remarks on the subject seem more definitely in accord with the known facts: *Prel* X.203 says he was abroad "a whole year," and in a letter to John Scott (*MY* 668) he gives the length of his visit as "upwards of twelve months." In deference to these comments, I have conjectured that his return occurred not before late Nov.

JRM astutely suggests that a comment of W's to Losh (*EL* 190) that he has not forgotten Losh's "apprehensions from sea-sickness" possibly points to W's and Losh's having returned together. JRM appears to be the first to have identified W's friend Nicholson as Samuel Nicholson, haberdasher.

2. [Probably early this year (by July 10)]

[W's break with his Uncle Cookson probably becomes definite at this time. (Joseph Farington, *The Farington Diary*, London, 1922–28, II, 230; Moorman I, 212–13; *EL* 97–98, 107–08.)]¹

3. [Probably late Jan or early Feb]

W sends copies of *EW*, *DS* to Forncett. DW, CW [who is at Forncett on vacation] analyze the poems in detail, prepare a criticism. [CW evidently carries the MS to Cambridge for the comments of friends there.] (*EL* 85–86. See 1793:4.)²

4. Jan 29

An Evening Walk, Descriptive Sketches are published in London. (*MC*. See Shaver *RES* 57n.)

5. Feb 1

France declares war on England. (See 1793:7.)

6. Feb 2

RW credits to W and DW under this date the receipt from CCC of two fifths of one third of a £500 legacy from Richard Crackan-thorpe (great-grandfather of W; buried 14 Apr 1752) to the children of his daughter Dorothy Crackanthorpe Cookson. This share amounts to £66/13/4. (RW, draft account with W and DW, 1816, DCP; *Parish Registers of Newbiggin, Westmorland*, comp. J. F. Haswell, CWAA Soc, 1928; *EL* 567.)³

7. [Feb 11–between 1795 Nov 20 and late 1796]

[On 11 Feb 1793 England declares war on France. (See 1793:5.) W writes of his feelings concerning this event: *Prel* X.228–90, *Prel₂*

---

¹ Dr. Cookson said in 1804 that the coolness had been caused by W's espousal of "French principles." Cookson's phrase is ambiguous, but in any case, as Mrs. Moorman suggests, Annette must have played a significant part in the matter.

² CW apparently took a long vacation, although W was perhaps able to send his poems to Forncett shortly before they were published.

³ On Richard Crackanthorpe's will and later family arrangements in connection with it see CRH *Transactions*.

X.263–314; *Prel* X.758–74, *Prel*₂ XI.173–88. (On *Prel* X.259–64, *Prel*₂
X.283–88, see 1793:29.)

W refers to the period following this event: *Prel* X.774–91, *Prel*₂
XI.188–205 (wild theories are afloat). See *Excursion*, esp. the character
of the Solitary, and IF note (W sees the Solitary's state of mind exhibited
often with England's rupture with France 1793); aspects of the character
of W's own mind now and in the years immediately succeeding are
undoubtedly depicted in the Solitary. (See 1791:6; 1791:31; 1794:26;
1795:9.)

The moral crisis precipitated in part by this event reaches its climax
between 20 Nov 1795 and late 1796. (See 1795:49.)]

8. Feb 16

William Godwin's *An Inquiry Concerning Political Justice* is published.
London Chronicle. See 1795:9 and other references cited there.)

DW writes to Jane Pollard from Forncett: CW's recent visit to
Forncett; description of CW and W; her affection for her brothers.
EW and *DS*]; DW's comments on them; her and CW's "bulky
criticism" of the poems [see 1793:3]. Mutual acquaintances. (*EL* 82–87.)

9. [Probably c Apr 1]

A review of *EW*, *DS* appears in *The Analytical Review* (XV, Mar
1793). (See 1787:7n.)

10. [Perhaps Apr, fairly certainly before c Apr 26]

DW writes to RW [from Forncett]: Encourages RW to talk
seriously [with Uncle Cookson] about settling their affairs with CCC,
and about the division of her grandmother's estate [see 1794:3]. DW's
£100 [see 1792:5]; she has received a year's interest from CCC. (*EL*
108; 1793:11n.)[4]

---

[4] On CCC's financial arrangements with the children see esp. 1783:11; 1793:6; *EL*
117–19. EdS's date is "[Forncett, 1793]." The letter was most likely written before
any arrangements to transfer DW's £100 to JW had begun (see 1793:11n); and she
speaks as if she expected to receive future interest on the sum from CCC. In view of
the interest she has already received, it is probably at least a year since the present
from her grandmother. The present was still news between 1 and 8 May 1792 (see
1792:8). No record of a £100 present to W survives (cf 1791:38).

11. May 22 (–1794 Sept 20)

The *Earl of Abergavenny*, JW fifth mate, sails for China, Captain John Wordsworth (cousin of W). (It reaches moorings on return 20 Sept 1794.) (Hardy; Shaver *Transactions* 223–24. See *EL* 118.)[5]

12. [Probably June or shortly after]

W writes *A Letter to the Bishop of Llandaff*. (C. W. Roberts, "The Influence of Godwin on Wordsworth's Letter to the Bishop of Llandaff," *Stud Phil* XXIX, 1932, 588–602.)[6]

13. [Probably 1793 June 5]

DW writes to Jane Pollard [from Forncett]: DW has obtained her uncle's consent to visit Halifax; hopes to arrive before winter, and stay not less than six months. (*EL* 87–88.)[7]

---

[5] This sailing, under the captaincy of JW's cousin, was undoubtedly that referred to by DW in her letter of 30 Aug 1793, although Hardy records the destination of the voyage as China instead of, as DW had supposed, the East Indies. JW wrote CCC from Gravesend 26 Apr asking for the £100 of DW's in the Carlisle Bank (MS letter, DCP; see 1792:5), and another letter (also DCP) shows that a draft for £100 was made out by Thomas James of Penrith on behalf of CCC on 16 May. This draft was no doubt forwarded at once to RW, but probably did not reach JW before he sailed: DW is still speaking of the propriety of JW's taking out "her £100" in early 1795 (*EL* 132), and she did not receive another such sum, from any source, between now and then. RW's accounts with JW, DCP, record a credit of £100 to JW from a loan from DW for "May" 1793; and the same accounts record a payment of £100 into the hands of JW's bankers under 13 July 1795.

[6] A note by Miss Darbishire with the MS (DCP) shows both that the MS is largely in an unknown autograph, and that corrections and passages in W's hand prove close and immediate cooperation with his copyist; the copyist was not simply reproducing another MS. The tone of W's references to the death of Louis XVI (which occurred on 21 Jan) indicates that that event must have taken place not long before he wrote. W probably wrote his pamphlet in June or, at the latest, shortly after.

[7] The date of this letter is determined from that of her next (Sunday 16 June) and the day of the week on which this one was written, Wednesday. In the letter of 16 June DW says she had hoped JP would reply to the earlier by return mail; she had been looking for the reply as early as 12 June, the Wednesday previous to 16 June. Thus DW's former letter must date from Wednesday 5 June.

14. [1793 probably soon after June 5]

W writes to DW [from London; only a fragment of his letter survives]: W's pleasure in DW's pleasure in the prospect of visiting Halifax; his determination to see her as soon as he has found an engagement. (*EL* 98–99.)[8]

15. [1793] June 16

DW writes to Jane Pollard from Forncett: Vain hope for a letter from JP; DW's projected visit to Halifax; Aunt Cookson's new baby [George]. W's activities and prospects; his 1790 visit to Forncett [see 1790:102]. DW's recent study of French. (*EL* 88–93.)[9]

16. [Probably mid- or late June or early July, certainly before July 12]

W writes to DW [from London; only a fragment of his letter survives]: W's and DW's plan to meet not to be affected by his trip with Calvert; a meeting will perhaps be possible at Halifax. (*EL* 99. See 1793:18, 1793:19.)

17. [c 1793 summer–between 1795 Nov 20 and 1797 probably c Mar]

[W refers to his attitude toward nature during this period: *TA*, esp. 66–85 (his love of sitting in judgment on nature; nature has no interest unborrowed from the eye); *Prel* XI.138–99, *Prel*₂ XII.93–151 (his eye is the master of his heart). (See PREL 611—cf *EL* 128.) Possibly W has some sight of "a new world" c summer 1793 (*Prel* XII.354–79, *Prel*₂ XIII.350–78). (See esp. 1797: 2.)][10]

---

[8] W, like JP, was one of the first to hear about the trip to Halifax; DW apparently wrote him a special letter on the subject (*EL* 98). His reply probably was not long delayed.

[9] On George Cookson see Venn.

[10] W's compulsive seeking of external nature and domination of it by his "eye" is to be distinguished from his earlier, more innocent and uncritical "enthusiasm for nature in all her various forms" when to leave behind the "most sublime and beautiful" areas of the Alps was like "quitting a beloved friend" (see *EL* 34; Appendices I, II; 1787:24, 3; 1790:8, A3; *Prel* XI.224–57, *Prel*₂ XII.174–207).

18. [Perhaps late June, probably early July–late July or early Aug]

[Perhaps late June, probably early July, W and William Calvert travel from London to Isle of Wight, where they spend c a month in view of the English fleet, which is preparing for war with France. (*EL* 94–95; *G&S* Advertisement; RW, accounts with W and DW, 1816, DCP.)

Probably at the Isle of Wight W writes "How Sweet to Walk along the Woody Steep" (*PW* I, 307–08) (Racedown Nb. See Appendix IV).

("How Sweet" refers to this visit. W refers to it also: *Prel* X.291–307, *Prel*₂ X.315–30; *G&S* Advertisement.)][11]

19. July 10–12

DW writes to Jane Pollard [from Forncett]: DW's projected visit to Halifax; W will perhaps join them there. W's tour with Calvert which will last until Oct; W described; his possible visit to Halifax; his search for employment; his lack of favor with his near relations except JW, CW—the cause being his natural disposition; W compared to Edwin in Beattie's *The Minstrel*; his trip to Halifax to be regarded as a secret; fragmentary quotations from two of W's letters [see 1793:14; 1793:16]. Life at Forncett; DW's Uncle and Aunt Cookson; a present

[11] The exact location of their residence during their visit on the Isle of Wight is unknown, but see Moorman I, 230. The chronology of W's movements during early and mid-summer is generally difficult to determine. One cannot be certain that W and Calvert drove directly to the Isle of Wight, and DW's *EL* phrasing does not clearly indicate that they had left London by 10 July. An advance of 5 guineas to W by RW upon his departure "with Mr Wm Calvert" is recorded in RW's accounts without specific date. It can be assumed that W spent something like a month on the Isle of Wight, that he wandered two or three days on or near Salisbury Plain, and that the rest of his travels—from London to Salisbury Plain by "whiskey" and thence to North Wales on foot—took some twelve days or more. DW had heard from W from North Wales by 30 Aug; he would thus have written her by 27 Aug (Paterson Joyce 290, 399–400). Calculated on such a basis, W's departure from London would have been by c 10–12 July.

As remarked in Appendix IV, evidence other than this fragment exists to indicate that the Racedown Nb, in which "How Sweet to Walk" appears, was in use before Racedown. It is most reasonable to suppose that "How Sweet," in couplets like those of *DS*, dates from, or near, the time of his visit to the Isle of Wight.

of 5 guineas from her Aunt. Failure of a plan for W to teach Lord Bellmore's son. (*EL* 93–101.)

20. [Probably late July]

STC learns of W's reputation, [the result of *EW* or *DS* or both,] in a literary society at Exeter. (Christopher Wordsworth, *Social Life at the English Universities*, Cambridge, England, 1874, 589; *STCL* I, 57–61, 57n.) [It is probably at this time that STC becomes acquainted with *DS* (see *BL* iv).]

21. [Probably late July or early Aug–between late Aug, perhaps after c Sept 15, and early Oct]

[In late July or early Aug W, William Calvert depart from Isle of Wight. Somewhere near Salisbury their "whiskey" is broken by the horse, and Calvert rides off. W wanders about (probably between Salisbury and Bath) two or three days, probably at least two days mainly on Salisbury Plain. He naps in Stonehenge c noon of one day. During his wandering here he has the visionary or near visionary experiences recorded *Prel* XII.312–53, *Prel*$_2$ XIII.312–49, and forming the basis of *PW* I, 100, 104 *app crit*. (W refers to Salisbury Plain: *G&S*; *PW* I, 94–127, 330–41 *passim* and *app crit*. He refers to Stonehenge also in *Excursion* III.143–48.) (See 1793:18; *G&S* Advertisement; *Mem* I, 81–82; *Prel* XII.337–38, *Prel*$_2$ XIII.336–37; *MLR* LIII, 1958, 546–47; Moorman I, 231–36.)

From Salisbury Plain W travels, mostly on foot, to North Wales, to the home of Robert Jones, Plas-yn-Llan, Llangynhafal. He proceeds via Bath to Bristol and thence (having crossed the Severn by water) up the Wye. He passes Tintern Abbey. (He refers to his journey in *TA*, esp. 66–85. See *G&S* IF note; *The Tuft of Primroses* 466–80.) At Goodrich Castle he meets the little girl described in *We Are Seven* (*We Are Seven* and IF note). Near Builth he meets a tinker who later contributes to his conception of Peter Bell; walks down to near Hay with him *PB* IF note; *PW* II, 530). He proceeds northward (from near Hay) to Jones's house (see Appendix VII), which he probably reaches by 27 Aug. (See 1793:18n.) He departs probably between late Aug, perhaps after c 15 Sept, and early Oct. (See 1793:26.)

Probably during this trip and possibly shortly after (but probably in any case by some time in Sept) W composes:

At least the bulk of *SP* in form of MS 1. (*Prel* XII.357–59; *Prel$_2$* XIII.352–54; Appendix XII. See GCL 45; 1793:26.)

"In Vain Did Time and Nature Toil To Throw" (unpublished sonnet). (Miss Landon. See GCL 44.)

"The Western Clouds a Deepening Gloom Display" (unpublished elegaic quatrains). (Miss Landon. See GCL 44.)][12]

22. [Probably c Aug 1]

A review of *EW* appears in *The Critical Review* (VIII, July 1793). (See Peek 8n; 1787:7n.)

23. [Aug 9]

DW writes to RW from Forncett: She has lost her purse containing 6 guineas [see 1793:19]. Asks advice and, if possible, aid. (*EL* 102–03.)[13]

---

[12] Concerning the setting of *SP* and *G&S*, JRM notes (from *The Gentleman's Magazine* LXIII, 1793, 856–57) that a violent storm swept southern England 7 Aug 1793. Miss Landon has pointed out to me a number of reasons for supposing that the castles referred to in the unpublished poems are Welsh (the longer poem, for example, appears to deal with Chepstow, which W would have passed near the mouth of the Wye). The sonnet follows the Isle of Wight fragment ("How Sweet to Walk") in the Racedown Nb (see Appendix IV; 1793:18n); and both are in a Bowlesean mood of melancholy meditation. I am in agreement with Miss Landon that castles which W must have seen during this walk offer the best guess for the sources of W's inspiration. The poems describe landscapes as if they were before the speaker's eyes; it is likely that W composed his poems some time fairly soon after being present at the scenes. On the meeting with the little girl of *We Are Seven* see also *Recollections of the Table Talk of Samuel Rogers* (London, 1856), 175n.

[13] The "Friday afternoon" of the PS indicates the day of the PS itself; and the urgent nature of the letter indicates that the rest must date from Friday also. An endorsement, probably by RW, noting "ten pounds" for "6th June 1793," apparently has no relevance to the problem of the date, as no parallel entry appears on later accounts of RW with DW; but an entry in a draft account of 1816 reads: "1793 Aug 11 to Cash sent Miss DW per post 10/-/–." DW thanks RW for this sum (she thought it was a present) on "Monday August 12th"; it had been sent "by the very next post" (*EL* 107). The earlier letter thus almost certainly dates from Friday 9 Aug.

24. [1793] Aug 12

DW writes to RW from Forncett: Thanks RW for a £10 note. *EL* 103. See 1793:23.)

25. [By Aug 27]

W writes to DW from Plas-yn-Llan (letter not surviving except for a few words quoted by DW): The abrupt conclusion of his tour with Calvert. Jones's house. (See *EL* 105; 1793:21n.)

26. [Late Aug–probably mid-Oct; esp. between perhaps c Sept 15 and probably c mid-Oct]

[W spends part of this period in Wales with Jones; he is perhaps still there as late as c 15 Sept. (See 1793:29.)

During this period (certainly by early Oct) W probably returns to France. He witnesses the execution of Gorsas in Paris on 7 Oct, and returns to England by about mid-Oct. W's flight from Paris is possibly hastened by the advice of Thomas Bailie. (Thomas Carlyle, *Reminiscences*, ed. C. E. Norton, London, 1887, 303; Alger 145; Alaric A. Watts, *Alaric Watts*, London, 1884, II, 286–87; H. W. Piper, *The Active Universe*, London, 1962, 66–67. See 1791:34n.)][14]

[14] It has often been observed that Carlyle's report of W's statement that he had witnessed the execution of Gorsas, which took place 7 Oct 1793, is the only evidence pointing to a visit by W to Paris in 1793. Nothing vaguely resembling the events of which W spoke to Carlyle happened in 1792, however, and Carlyle's memory seems altogether clear. There seems little chance that W was not in Paris at the time of the death of Gorsas. (James Muirhead's records of W's remarks—noted Moorman I, 205–06—are not consistent: In *Blackwood's Magazine* 221, June 1927, 733, W is quoted as having said that he went to Paris in "1792 and 1793"; in *James Watt*, London, 1859, 480, that he went in "1792 or 1793." But neither reading adds much weight to any side of the balance.) On the possibility of W's having known James Watt, Jr., in Paris at this time see 1791:34n. The only other relevant information is Alaric Watts's story that an "old republican" named "Bailey"—probably Thomas Bailie (see the Piper reference)—had warned W in Paris that his life was in danger because of his connection with the Mountain, whereupon W had "decamped with great precipitation." W's attachment was actually with the Girondins, of course, rivals of the Mountain, but a slip could have occurred at some point in the course of the transmission of the story. Such advice to W, it is to be noted, would have been not especially likely in late 1792 but extremely appropriate around early Oct 1793; that month saw the trial and execution not simply of Gorsas, but of the larger part of the Girondins. A general arrest of Englishmen took place 14–15 Oct (see Alger).

27. [1793] Aug 30; [between Aug 30 and 1794 Feb 17, perhaps c 1793 Dec or c 1794 Jan (–early Apr)]

DW writes to Jane Pollard from Forncett on 30 Aug: Impatient to visit Halifax; hopes to arrive by Christmas. The sudden end of W's and Calvert's trip together at Salisbury [see 1793:18] where W has walked to Jones's house in North Wales. Her impatience to see W. Her health; the loss of her 6 guineas; RW's present of £10 [see 1793:23; 1793:24]. RW, CW in North; JW at sea [see 1793:11]. Injunctions for secrecy concerning W's possible visit to Halifax [see 1793:19]. (*EL* 104–08.)

[Between 30 Aug and 17 Feb 1794, perhaps c Dec 1793 or c Jan 1794, DW travels from Forncett to Halifax, where she stays with her cousin Elizabeth T. Rawson and her husband William. She departs probably early Apr. (*EL* 104–08, 110–13. See 1794:2; 1794:6.)][15]

28. [Probably c Sept 2]

A review of *DS* appears in *The Critical Review* (VIII, Aug 1793). (See Peek 8n; 1787:7n.)

29. Sept 8–[c Sept 15]

On 8 Sept the English are defeated in the battle of Hondeschoote. [W writes of his feelings upon hearing of this event: *Prel* X.259–64, *Prel*₂ X.283–88. W is possibly still in Wales c 15 Sept after the first news of the event probably arrives. (Moorman I, 224. See *Prel* X.259–75, *Prel*₂ X.283–99.)][16]

---

[15] The time of DW's removal to Halifax is uncertain (cf EdS *DW* 48). She had hoped to travel there by Christmas (*EL* 104–05), and W is unclear on 17 Feb 1794 as to how long he has been visiting her at Halifax (*EL* 108–09). He would probably have made an effort to reach her there soon after her arrival.

[16] Mrs. Moorman interprets the lines from *Prel*, which refer to Hondeschoote and W's inabilities to offer prayers or praises "in the Congregation" for his country's victories, to mean that W was still in Wales (the only place W was likely to attend a church where such prayers were offered) at about the time of this battle. W's ambiguous phrasing makes it unclear, however, that there was a direct connection between W's political feelings while he sat in church and this particular battle; no certainty is possible. News concerning the battle itself would not have reached Plas-yn-Llan before 14 Sept; the first general report in England was in a *London Gazette Extraordinary* of 12 Sept. The report was reprinted in the *Times* on 13 Sept. The first Sunday after 14 Sept was 15 Sept.

30. [Probably c Oct 1]

A review of *EW* appears in *The European Magazine* (XXIV, Sept 1793). (See Cornell opp. p. 161; 1787:7n.)

31. Oct 7

Gorsas is executed in Paris. [W witnesses this event.] (See 1793:26.)

32. [Probably c mid-Oct–1794 Feb 17, early Apr]

[Probably c mid-Oct W returns from France. He travels about in—so far as is known—northwest England. (See *EL* 108; 1793:26.) His exact movements are unclear. He probably visits Whitehaven c Christmas (see 1793:35). He visits Keswick (probably Windy Brow) (*EL* 108; see Moorman I, 243). He also stays for a time with Mrs. John Spedding at Armathwaite Hall, probably just before traveling to Halifax (*EL* 112). By 17 Feb 1794 W travels to Halifax, where he stays with DW at the home of Elizabeth Threlkeld Rawson and her husband (William). He departs probably early Apr. (*EL* 108–09. See 1794:6.)

(W refers to Windy Brow in *Kendal and Windermere Railway*, Grosart II, 327: A "shrewd and sensible" woman under whose roof W lives "for some time in the Vale of Keswick" comments on the spread of the curious habit that folk have nowadays of talking about "prospects." DW describes this family, evidently tenants at Windy Brow, *EL* 111–12.)][17]

33. [Probably c Nov 1]

A review of *EW* and *DS* [by Thomas Holcroft] appears in *The Monthly Review* (XII, Oct 1793). (See Peek 8n; 1787:7n; H. W. Garrod, *Wordsworth: Lectures and Essays*, Oxford, 1927, 39n.)

---

[17] Either now or in a later visit to Windy Brow W has with him, and leaves there, among other books, a *Guide du voyageur en Suisse*, R. Crackanthorpe's *Treatise of the Fifth General Council Held at Constantinople*, 533, and two volumes of RW's four-volume set of Blackstone (letter of RW to W, 15 May 1799, DCP; see *LY* 1342). A letter from Mrs. Mary Stanger, daughter of William Calvert, to Professor Knight (DCP) reports: "Whilst a Bachelor Wm Wordsworth paid [Calvert] one or more visits his means were restricted & so *was his wardrobe*! I have heard my father say." *PW* (Knight, 1882–89) IX, 88, states that while at Halifax W gave Mr. Rawson's nephew lessons in French.

34. Nov 4

CW, STC, and others discuss the review noted 1793:32, also W'
poems themselves, in Cambridge on 4 Nov. STC speaks of W'
reputation among a literary society at Exeter (see 1793:20). [Dewhurst
Bilsborrow speaks of his reputation among Erasmus Darwin, Miss
Seward, and others at Derby. (Christopher Wordsworth, *Social Life a*
the English Universities, Cambridge, Eng., 1874, 589.)

35. [c Christmas]

[W probably visits Whitehaven. The length of his visit is unknown
Moorman I, 242–43; 1793:36. On W's movements generally both
now, before, and after see 1793:32.)]

36. Dec. 26

RW of Whitehaven records an advance of £20 cash to W under
this date. (Administrators' Accounts, CRH. See Moorman I, 239n.)[18]

1794

1. [During this year]

[On writings of W possibly of this year see below and GCL 28,
32–34, 38, 41, 45–46.]
RW records under this general date a £10 cash advance to W
from Joseph Lough of Penrith. [The advance is perhaps made at the end
of the year, when W is in Penrith, but certainty is impossible.] (RW,
accounts with W and DW, 1816, DCP.)

2. [1794] Feb 17

W writes to William Mathews from Halifax: His recent wanderings [see 1793:31]. He is now at [the Rawsons']. Approval of Mathews'

[18] RW of Whitehaven also charges payment of a bill of £1/11/– to W's account
under 11 Jan 1794, further proof of a visit to Whitehaven about this time, although
RW's notation need not, of course, imply that W was still in Whitehaven 11 Jan.

abandonment of [plans to study for priesthood]; the priesthood attended by more inconveniences than any other profession. W does nothing; cannot determine self to be a priest, is uninterested in law. His intention of resuming study of Italian immediately, and of instructing DW in it. Terrot, Myers. Inquiries about the Portuguese nation. (*EL* 108–10.)

3. Mar 1

RW credits to W and DW under this date a two fifths part of one third of the personal estate of their grandmother Dorothy [Crackan-thorpe] Cookson. This share amounts to £57/9/14. (RW, accounts with W and DW, 1816, DCP.)[1]

4. Mar 10

RW of Whitehaven records remission of 5 guineas to DW at Halifax under this date. (Administrators' Accounts, CRH.)

5. [Probably c Apr 1]

A review of *EW* and *DS* appears in *The Gentleman's Magazine* (LXIV, Mar 1794). (See Peek 8n; 1787:7n.)

6. [Probably early Apr (–mid-May, almost certainly by May 23)]

[W, DW probably travel to Kendal from Halifax by coach in early Apr. From Kendal they walk to Grasmere, where they spend a night, and whence DW writes to her "Aunt" Rawson; that day they stop at Staveley, drink a basin of milk, and DW puts on silk stockings after washing her feet in a brook; later during this day they stop to eat beside a rill entering Windermere near Low Wood. (W refers to this meal in "There is a Little Unpretending Rill," and *app crit*. See *PW* III, 4–5 and IF note.) They reach Grasmere at sunset. (*EL* 110–11, 113–14; *DWJ* I, 104, 182. See Moorman I, 243–44.) The following day

---

[1] The sum is noted in a draft of the accounts as entered on 1 Mar 1793, but the record of the final accounts, as described in the text, is correct: RW had learned of the amount of the Wordsworth share of Dorothy Cookson's estate (£143/13/4) only on 23 Feb 1794 (CRH *Transactions* 149).

they walk from Grasmere to Windy Brow, Keswick. (They depart probably c mid-May, by 23 May.) (*EL* 111. See 1794:13.)]²

7. [Probably between early Apr and late in the year]

[Probably at Windy Brow, and possibly later in the year] W composes corrections and additions for *EW*. He enters various corrections and additions on the large margins of DC MS Verse 10 (a copy of *EW* made up by pasting pages of the published poem on larger sheets). (Windy Brow Nb and MS Verse 10, DCP. See *PW* I, 4–38, 319–20; *EL* 116; 1794:6.)³

8. [Probably between early Apr and mid-May, almost certainly by May 23]

[At Windy Brow:] W composes *Inscription for a Seat by the Pathway Side Ascending to Windy Brow*. (Windy Brow Nb, DCP [and title of poem]; 1794:6; 1794:7.)

MS 1 of *SP* is written. (See GCL 45; Appendix XII; 1794:6; 1794:7; 1794:16.)

---

² DW's phrasing concerning their departure from Halifax, that they "set forward by coach towards Whitehaven, and thence to Kendal" is ambiguous; at least a remote possibility may exist that they went to Whitehaven first. But since Whitehaven is well the other side of Kendal from Halifax, and a visit there first would imply a most curious itinerary, it seems by far the best guess that their journey was as described above (see Moorman I, 243). The "unpretending rill" is identified more exactly *PW* III, 419. The rest at Staveley must have taken place now rather than 1799; they almost surely went through Staveley in a post chaise in 1799. Whether William Calvert passed any time at Windy Brow during W's and DW's visit is uncertain; cf *EL* 112 and *STCL* II, 670.

³ EdS's "1794" variants are mostly taken from Verse 10 (cf *PW* I, 320), though a few in fact come (not so specified) from the Windy Brow Nb. Common readings indicate that the work of Verse 10 is later than that of the Windy Brow Nb. Probably much of the new work of Verse 10 can be regarded as Windy Brow composition; but W's remarks of 23 May indicate that he was not then done with *EW* altogether. His attendance on Raisley Calvert put an end to significant composition from late 1794 (see *EL* 128), and I doubt that he resumed work on the poem once he had reached London in early 1795. The earlier date may be regarded as the time by which W concluded work on *EW*. The *EW* "Corrections and additions" (so titled) face the MS of *SP* in the Windy Brow Nb; they are followed by *Septimi Gades*, *From the French*, and *From the Greek* (see Appendix IV); the last is immediately followed by *Inscription for a Seat*.

9. [Probably mid- or late Apr]

DW writes [to an unknown correspondent from Windy Brow, Keswick]: W's and her trip from Halifax to Windy Brow; she intends to stay a few weeks longer. (*EL* 110.)⁴

10. [Mid-Apr, probably between Apr 15 and Apr 19]

W and DW visit Mrs. [John] Spedding and her two daughters at Armathwaite for three nights. (*EL* 112, 113.)⁵

11. [1794 c Apr 21]

DW writes to Jane Pollard from Windy Brow: Their trip from Grasmere to Windy Brow. She has been here over a fortnight; intends staying a few weeks longer. Windy Brow described. W intends to lodge there until he finds employment. She and W have been visiting the Speddings at Armathwaite [see 1794:10]. Relatives and mutual acquaintances. (*EL* 110–13.)⁶

12. [1794] Apr 21

DW writes to Mrs. CCC from Windy Brow: She has been spending three days at Armathwaite with the Speddings; she replies to Mrs. CCC's censures of her conduct, which she supposes to refer to expenses and her personal protection: Her expenses low (their diet described) and her protection excellent. Defense of her extensive walking. Intention of staying at Windy Brow a few weeks longer. She has advanced splendidly in French; has begun study of Italian.

⁴ The phrasing of this fragment has many similarities to that of the letter to JP of c 21 Apr, but no indication exists whether DW has or has not been at Windy Brow "above a fortnight" when she wrote it, or whether plans for a visit of "a few weeks" more there implies a longer or shorter period than that of the possible "three or four weeks'" further stay she mentions to JP. Probably by early May DW's plans about her departure, even as expressed to the unsympathetic Mrs. CCC, would not have been so vague.

⁵ DW's phrasing on 21 Apr, that they "have been staying" there three nights (or three days) does not make it quite certain that they have just returned, but the chances are that they returned not much more than a day or so before.

⁶ W, DW have just been at the Speddings', and the letter is thus of about the same time as DW's letter to Mrs. CCC of 21 Apr (see 1794:12).

The Speddings. (*EL* 113–14.) [Mrs. CCC's censures probably contribute to, but do not offer the primary occasion for, *To a Young Lady Who Had Been Reproached*. (Miss Landon. Cf *DWJ* I, 100–01, 103, 108.)]

13. [Probably c mid-May, by May 23–between June 18 and Aug 21]

[Probably c mid-May, by 23 May, Raisley Calvert offers W a share of his income. (*EL* 123; Moorman I, 251. See the rest of this entry.)

Probably c mid-May, by 23 May, W, DW travel to Whitehaven where they remain until sometime between 18 June and probably c but by 21 Aug. (*EL* 114. See 1794:22.) Their route almost certainly takes them through Cockermouth, where they see their father's house. DW refers to the visit *EL* 516. It is possible that W refers to this visit in two fragments: "Derwent Again I Hear Thy Evening Call" (unpublished) and the lines quoted as *PW* V, 340, *I*. (Miss Landon. See Moorman I, 248; GCL 8a, 54.) They probably also travel via Branthwaite, where they see their uncle RW of Whitehaven, who is quite ill. (See *EL* 117; Eds *DW* 54.)

DW stays with Mrs. John W (wife of Captain W) for at least part of her visit at Whitehaven. (*EL* 118–19.) W stays at the home of RW of Whitehaven for at least part of his visit. (*EL* 114, 117. See Moorman I, 249.)

W probably does not have the dream of the Bedouin (described *Prel* V.49–165; *Prel*$_2$ V.50–165) now or any other time. (See Moorman I, 250; PREL 539; J. W. Smyser, "Wordsworth's Dream of Poetry and Science: *The Prelude*, V," *PMLA* LXXI, 1956, 269–75.)][7]

[7] The date of their journey to Whitehaven is not perfectly clear: W wrote to Mathews from Whitehaven on 23 May having received a letter dated 11 May from Mathews only the day before. Mathews' letter was probably addressed to Halifax (whence W wrote his latest surviving letter to Mathews on 17 Feb) or to Keswick (see *EL* 114, 117); W would have received it either at Keswick or Whitehaven (hardly Branthwaite) on 22 May. Depending on the route of the letter and the number of times it was forwarded, W could have left Windy Brow by 13 May, the earliest possible date for the arrival of the letter there (Paterson, Joyce 290, 399–400). DW's comments on 21 Apr (*EL* 114) and to JP about that time (*EL* 111), that they mean to stay in Keswick "a few" or "perhaps three or four" weeks longer do not appear to indicate that they planned to leave much before 13 May.

Since W wrote to RW by 21 May describing his uncle's bad health, it is probable

14. [Probably mid-May, by May 20, certainly by May 21]

[W writes to RW (letter not surviving): Asks for money for DW (probably £10). Describes the bad health of RW of Whitehaven. (*EL* 117; RW, accounts with W and DW, 1816, DCP. See 1794:15.)][8]

15. May 23

RW records remission of £10 note to DW under this date. (RW, accounts with W and DW, 1816, DCP.) RW writes to W from Staple Inn: Encloses £10 note; has forwarded W's Italian Grammar, Tasso, Ariosto to him at Keswick. (DCP; this letter is described *EL* 117n.)

16. [1794] May 23

W writes to William Mathews from Whitehaven: His living in London now financially out of the question. Possible establishment of a monthly miscellany. W declares his political sentiments: he is a democrat now and always will be. Details, questions concerning the miscellany. Is correcting, adding to *EW, DS*; the circumstances of these poems' publication; asks Mathews to call at the publishers and inquire about their sale. [*SP*], written last summer, is ready for the press. (*EL* 114–17. See 1794:13n.)

17. [1794] May 28

DW writes to RW [from Whitehaven]: The £10 note has arrived. Uncle RW improved, but will never enjoy good health. W intends to stay at Keswick until he finds employment. After three more weeks at Whitehaven DW will travel to Rampside for a fortnight, after which she means to travel to Armathwaite to visit Mrs. Spedding; thence to Newbiggin; thence to Halifax. Her anxiety to have their

---

[8] Distances and coach speeds (Paterson; Joyce 290, 399–400) and usual times for transit of letters between this area and London indicate that if RW responded on 23 May, W's letter could not have been dispatched later than 21 May, and was very likely sent a day earlier than that.

---

that he had been in Branthwaite by that date; if not, it is almost certain that he had checked personally with his Whitehaven relatives on the subject—and hence had left Keswick—by then.

affairs settled; the Lonsdale suit; CCC's delay in reaching a settlement. Uncle RW's health. (*EL* 117–19.)[9]

18. [Probably 1794 June 15 or 22]

W writes to William Mathews from Whitehaven: His political opinions—disapproval of monarchy and aristocracy, of the British Constitution; he recoils from sudden change and revolution. The enlightened friend of mankind will explain the general principles of political justice. W an enemy of violence; wants absolute freedom of investigation; rejects inflammatory addresses. The miscellany [see 1794:16]—title, contents, kinds of essays. Their probable supporters and readers. [Raisley Calvert] has offered W a share of his income. W will not come to town soon. He has written little prose. First steps in starting the magazine; news from the Continent is desirable for it. (*EL* 119–25.)[10]

19. June 16

RW of Whitehaven dies, aged 51. (*Miscellania Genealogica et Heraldica* N.S. IV, 1884, 42.)[11]

20. [Probably June 15 or 22–probably early Dec]

[DW's movements during this period are known only roughly. She perhaps visits her cousins the Barkers for a fortnight at Rampside, spends some time with the Speddings at Armathwaite, and visits CCC

[9] Despite the implication of *EL* 117, both the writer's address and the year are taken from postmarks.

[10] The faint postmark of this letter, which was begun on a "Sunday," appears to read JU/19 or JU/29; so that the letter—partly in the hand of DW—probably dates from Sunday 15 June or 22 June. W had had time to become apprehensive about a long silence by Mathews, whose last letter W had probably received 22 May and replied to on 23 May (*EL* 114).

[11] Moorman I, 124, states that RW of Whitehaven's widow claimed £400 from W after her husband's death; elsewhere (I, 249) the same work indicates that the claim was £460, and first put forward 1797. The first such claim that I can find evidence for is Robinson W's, for £250, in early May 1797 (see *LY* 1337–38; Moorman I, 338). The amount finally paid, however, came to £412 (*MY* 698), which probably included interest.

at Newbiggin. (See 1794:18; 1794:21; 1794:22; 1794:32; *EL* 114, 118, 134–35.)][12]

21. [Probably between June 15 or 22 and c but by Aug 21]

[DW travels to Rampside from Whitehaven to visit her cousin Elizabeth W Barker (daughter of RW of Whitehaven) and her husband Francis. W probably accompanies her as far as Broughton (see below). (*EL* 118, 565. See 1794:18n.) From that point W perhaps returns to Whitehaven or travels to Keswick (or travels on to Rampside for a visit of unknown length).

W probably in any case returns to Keswick for at least one visit of undetermined duration (*EL* 125), and possibly spends some time with his cousin Mary W Smith (daughter of RW of Whitehaven) and her husband John in Broughton. (*River Duddon* xxi; *River Duddon* IF note; Moorman I, 122n; *EL* 565. See 1794:22.)][13]

22. [Probably c but by Aug 21–probably Sept 21 or 28; c Aug 20 or 21]

[Probably c but by 21 Aug, and after a visit to Keswick, W travels to Rampside to visit his cousins the Barkers (see 1794:21). He returns to Keswick (Windy Brow) probably 21 or 28 Sept. (W refers to the visit in

---

[12] DW's statement of her plans on 28 May is the only basis for guesses about her travels during this period. Real proof is lacking either for a visit to Rampside or to Armathwaite; on the other hand, no evidence exists that she was not at Rampside during part or all W's visit there weeks later. Her comments in Apr 1795 (*EL* 134–35) seem small grounds for supposing that she spent "some months" at Newbiggin (cf EdS *DW* 54–55); they do not constitute definite indication that she was there at all (although alternative interpretations of her remarks might admittedly seem far-fetched). The only certain facts are that DW saw CCC between mid-June 1794 and the time of her letter of Apr 1795. She refers twice to her "meeting" with her uncle, and in no way indicates that she spent any extended time with him, even though she was prompted to see him as a result of complimentary remarks which he had made to the Misses Griffith (in Newcastle). The meeting or visit appears to have taken place before DW returned to Newcastle in Dec.

[13] The phrasing of *EL* 125 implies a familiarity with the progress of Raisley Calvert's illness that would be unlikely for W to have assumed had he not seen Calvert since late May. As W was most probably at Rampside for an extended visit just before returning to Keswick 21 or 28 Sept, it is reasonable to suppose that W visited Windy Brow during the early summer.

Elegaic Stanzas 1–32.) On a day during this visit, probably c 20 or 21 Aug, W visits grave of William Taylor at Cartmel Priory, hears of death of Robespierre. (W refers to this day: *Prel* X.467–567, *Prel*₂ X.511–603. See PREL 600; 1794:23.) Probably while at Rampside W sees the family of Dr. Roger Baldwin at Aldingham, including Cecilia Baldwin and her brother John, a college acquaintance of W's. (*EL* 125–26, 190; *STCL* I, 433; Venn. See Moorman I, 257.)][14]

23. July 28 ff

Robespierre is executed 28 July. [W refers to this event and its consequences: *Prel* X.530–657, *Prel*₂ X.568–603, XI.1–73. (Authority puts on a milder face in France. W's reaction to subsequent events of the Revolution. His revulsion at events in Britain.) (On W's earliest news of the death of Robespierre see 1794:22.)]

24. Sept 20

The *Earl of Abergavenny* (JW fifth mate) reaches moorings in England. (It had sailed 22 May 1793.) (Hardy; Shaver *Transactions* 223–24. See *EL* 132, 118; 1793:11.)

25. [Probably Sept 21 or 28]

W travels to Keswick (Windy Brow) [probably from Rampside]. (*EL* 125–26. See 1794:22.)

[14] W wrote William Calvert on Wednesday 1 Oct that he had returned to Keswick "last Sunday" after having been detained "in Lancashire." *Elegaic Stanzas* refers to a four weeks' visit in the neighborhood of Piel Castle, and there is no evidence extant pointing to any other period during which W remained so long continuously in that part of Lancashire. Rampside is the one place W is likely to have visited for any length of time which is in sight of Piel Castle. "Last Sunday" could refer either to 21 or 28 Sept. PREL 600 points out that the first mention of the fall of Robespierre appeared in *The Times* on 16 Aug, and more accurate reports on 18 and 19 Aug; any of these reports would have reached the North about two days later. Thus, since W heard of the fall of Robespierre on Leven Sands, close to Rampside (see Moorman I, 257–60), he was doubtless visiting in that area by 21 Aug. W's phrasing on 1 Oct implies that if he stopped in Whitehaven or elsewhere on his return to Windy Brow, it could not have been for long; but no sure conclusion can be reached about which Sunday he returned to Windy Brow. "Four weeks," in *Elegaic Stanzas*, would have so much greater imaginative accuracy than "five weeks" that it is doubtful that W would have used the latter figure even if it were better chronology.

26. [Oct ff]

[Pichegru embarks on a conquest of the Low Countries in Oct. This campaign is the most spectacular of early campaigns of conquest by revolutionary France; its date may stand as a probable date after which W's disillusionment with France begins. (See 1798:7.) For the present W sticks more firmly to old tenets. (W refers to this time: *Prel* X.792–805, *Prel*₂ XI.206–22.) (See 1795:9; PREL 603–06. See also T. C. Grattan, *Beaten Paths*, London, 1865, II, 120—about this time W knows French well; later wishes to forget it in his "abhorrence of Revolutionary excesses.")]

27. [1794] Oct 1

W writes to William Calvert from Keswick: Returned to Keswick last Sunday [see 1794:22]. Raisley Calvert's health and determination to travel to Lisbon; W offers to accompany him there, if assisted financially. Raisley's will: All real and personal property to be left to William Calvert, with a £600 legacy to W [depending on the legal aspect of W's affairs (see 1794:28)]. (*EL* 125–26. See Moorman I, 251–53; 1794:30.)

28. Oct 9

W and Raisley Calvert set off from Keswick for Lisbon (see 1794:26); reach Penrith [and probably spend the night there]. (See 1794:29.)

29. [1794] Oct 10

W and Raisley Calvert return to Keswick from Penrith, Calvert having found himself too ill to undertake the proposed trip to Lisbon.

W writes to RW from Keswick: The abortive trip. Calvert's will: Calvert means to leave him £600, but hesitates because of the W debt to their Aunt Wordsworth [widow of RW of Whitehaven] and the heirs of RW of Whitehaven. Asks RW to bond himself to pay any debt to their aunt, if such payment becomes necessary, rather than let W's legacy be seized. Calvert will not leave him the legacy if there is any prospect of its seizure by others. (*LY* 1329–31.)

30. [1794 probably Oct 17]

W writes to RW [from Keswick]: Thanks RW for having undertaken the bond [requested in W's letter of 10 Oct]; Raisley wishes the bond made with a penalty of £400 to secure any legacy to W from claims of heirs of RW of Whitehaven. He has determined to leave W £900. Problems in drawing up the will. (*LY* 1331–32.)[15]

31. Nov 7

W writes to William Mathews from Keswick: Concurs with Mathews [in Mathews' decision to give up plans for a magazine (see 1794:16, 1794:18). Calvert's] present health and the impossibility of W's leaving him; W's determination to come to London when possible; inquiries about chances of work on an opposition newspaper. He does not reprobate those who, unlike him, believe in the necessity of the present war. [Mathews' friend] Burleigh. W has used Jones ill. [John] Myers. CW's success at the university. His desire to be in London; tiresomeness of Lake scenery; lack of time for anything except attendance on Calvert. Title of *SP*. (*EL* 126–28.)

32. [Probably early Dec–probably late Mar or Apr]

[Probably in early Dec DW travels to Newcastle (it is not clear from where—see 1794:20). She stays with the Griffiths (*EL* 131–32). She departs probably late Mar or Apr 1795. (*EL* 132n. See 1795:13.)][16]

33. [Probably between shortly before Dec 25 and Jan 7]

[Shortly before 25 Dec] W writes the first part of a letter to William Mathews [possibly from Penrith, whence he has perhaps moved by this

---

[15] This letter is written in reply to one to W from RW dated 13 Oct (DCP) which was in turn written in reply to W's letter of 10 Oct. W states also that a day has elapsed between his receipt of RW's letter and his writing of this one. The postmark indicates that W's letter reached London on the 20th (DCP). If the mail took about its usual time in transit, W probably wrote on the 17th.

[16] There is no proof that DW spent all this time in Newcastle, but she was probably the chief reason for W's visit there in Jan 1795; and there is no evidence of her having departed between then and 11 Mar (*EL* 132n)—unless the perplexing question of when, where, and how long she saw CCC bears on the case (see *EL* 134–35; 1795:13).

time; otherwise, from Keswick]: Calvert worsens daily. The acquittal of Tooke. W's determination to come to London [after Calvert's death]. Possible types of periodical writing which he might do—translation from French and Italian gazettes, some political comment. Nervous headaches disqualify him for parliamentary reporting. (*EL* 128–30.)

[If W and Calvert have not already moved from Keswick to Penrith, they do so at this time, but probably some days before 7 Jan. (*EL* 131.)]

On 7 Jan W finishes his letter to Mathews: W is now, and has been for some time, in Penrith at the Robin H[ood] Inn. (*EL* 130–31.)[17]

1795

1. [During this year]

[On writings of W possibly of this year see below and GCL 6, 8, 32–35, 45, 47.]

2. [c Jan 9]

Raisley Calvert dies [at Penrith]. (See 1794:33; 1795:4; Harper I, 249n; Moorman I, 253.)

[On Calvert's legacy see esp. 1794:30; 1795:3; *EL* 450.

(W refers to Calvert: *To the Memory of Raisley Calvert* and IF note; *Prel* XIII.349–67, *Prel₂* XIV.354–69.)]

3. [Probably between c Jan 9 and c early Apr]

W receives £5 from Calvert's estate. (See *LY* 1338–39; 1795:2; 1795:26. Cf Moorman I, 273.)

4. [Jan 12]

Raisley Calvert is buried at Greystoke, Cumberland. (Moorman I, 253; PREL 511.) [W probably attends the funeral. (*EL* 131.)]

---

[17] W states on 7 Jan that he has neglected his letter "upwards of a fortnight"; 25 Dec would have begun a fourteen-day fortnight. On W in Penrith see also 1794:1. Horne Tooke was acquitted on 22 Nov 1794.

5. [Probably between Jan 12 and Jan 31–perhaps Feb, certainly by late Feb]

[Probably between 12 and 31 Jan] W travels to Newcastle. He departs perhaps Feb, certainly by late Feb. (*EL* 131–32. See 1795:4; 1795:8; 1795:9.) Some chance possibly exists that during this visit W hears the story forming the basis of *PB's* description of Peter Bell's wives (see *PB* IF note).][1]

6. Jan 16

RW records remission of £5 to DW at Newcastle under this date. (RW, accounts with W and DW, 1816, DCP. See 1795:7.)[2]

7. [1795] Jan 16

DW writes to RW from Newcastle: Raisley Calvert's death; his will. Thanks RW for £5. She expects W to be in London in a fortnight or three weeks. RW should consult with JW on the propriety of JW's taking her £100 [on his voyage (see 1793:10n; 1795:19)]. Rogerson, a young Newcastle man lately moved to London. (*EL* 131–32. See 1795:6.)

8. Jan 31

RW records remission of a bill, value £10, to W at Newcastle under this date. (RW, accounts with W and DW, 1816, DCP.)

9. [Perhaps Feb, certainly by late Feb–probably between Aug 15 and Aug 21]

[Perhaps in Feb, certainly by late Feb, W travels to London from Newcastle. (See *EL* 127–28, 132.) He departs probably between 15 and 18 Aug. (See 1795:25.) (W refers to this period: *Prel* X.792–901. *Prel*₂

---

[1] Since W says only that the "lawless creature" with many wives lived in County Durham, and was the subject of comment there, he could easily have heard about him elsewhere, perhaps in Cumberland or Westmorland. This is, however, W's only definitely known visit to this area before writing *Peter Bell*.

[2] RW probably failed to record this sum on the day it was sent; it is possible, however, that DW misdated the letter described in the next entry.

XI.206–305. On this visit see esp. Schneider 222–29; Moorman I, 260–70; *EL* 129–31; EdS *DW* 58.)

This period may be counted that of W's firmest adherence to the doctrines of William Godwin. (See entries below through 1795:25.) It is probably during this visit that W, if he ever does so at all, tells a young student at the Temple to "throw away his books of chemistry and read Godwin on necessity." (*The Spirit of the Age*; see *The Complete Works of William Hazlitt*, ed. P. P. Howe, London, 1930–34, XI, 17.)

W probably lives for a time, esp. c Mar–Apr, at 15 Chalton Street, Sommers Town. (*STCL* I, 154; Woof.)

W meets Basil Montagu; notes the danger, esp. to Montagu's child, Basil, of certain of his wild habits, and helps Montagu eradicate them. W probably lives with Montagu for a time at Lincoln's Inn; both perhaps making some use of the chambers of JFP Jr. as well. (Unpublished MS Autobiography of Basil Montagu, DCP; *EL* 155–56; *LY* 1335; PP.) Before W departs from London, he agrees with Montagu to take little Basil to live with him and DW (*EL* 137–42; see below in this entry).

W's friends here probably include William Mathews (see *EL passim*), Francis Wrangham (see esp. *EL* 143, 145), JFP Jr., Aza P (see below in this entry), W's cousin John Myers (*LY* 1335), James Losh, John Tweddell (see 1795:10; *EL* 190), George Dyer, and perhaps the general literary circle of John Tobin, of Lincoln's Inn, including James Tobin, his brother. (JRM, noting esp. Miss Benger's *Memoir of John Tobin*, London, 1820; Woof. See also Moorman I, 267.) W, CW probably meet in London (*EL* 139).

W or Wrangham or both probably compose an imitation of Juvenal VIII.1–86 (not surviving, unless *Juvenal* 163–73 represents a revision of present work on 85–86). (See Appendix XIV.) W reads Wrangham *SP* (probably in form of MS 1). (See Appendix XII; *EL* 145.)

Probably by shortly before 24 July W meets Aza P. (See 1795:21; 1795:25; also 1791:34n.) By 27 July JFP Jr. offers W the use of Racedown, a family house in Dorset, rent-free, and W accepts the offer. (Evans and Pinney 9n; *EL* 137–42; PP.)][3]

[3] W was probably in Newcastle at the end of Jan and/or early Feb (see 1795:8), and there is very little direct evidence about any aspect of his London residence, or

10. Feb 27

W drinks tea at [William] Frend's, with William Godwin, [Thomas] H[olcrof]t, [James] Losh, [John] Tweddell, Jona[tha]n Raine, [Thomas] Edwards, [Godfrey] Higgins, [William] French, and [George] Dyer. This is W's first known meeting with Godwin. (Godwin Diary. See Schneider 222; Moorman I, 263–64.) [If this occasion marks the commencement of the W–Godwin acquaintance, it is most likely this evening that Godwin later remembered as the one in which he converted W "from the doctrine of self-love to that of benevolence." (See Schneider 222–23.)]

11. Feb 28

W calls on Godwin, [probably in the morning]. (Godwin Diary. See Schneider 224; Moorman I, 264.)

12. Mar 10

W breakfasts with Godwin. (Godwin Diary. See Schneider 224; Moorman I, 264.)

13. [Probably late Mar or Apr and more than 3 weeks following]

[Probably in late Mar or early Apr] DW travels to Sockburn-on-Tees, near Northallerton, from Newcastle, to visit the Hutchinsons.

---

even when it began. On 16 Jan DW had said that she expected W to be in London "in a fortnight or three weeks at furthest." He was not there so soon, but his frequently expressed desire to be in London justifies a conjecture that he was on his way there before February was far advanced.

Montagu's phrasing in his autobiography does not make it certain that W shared his lodgings, but the references in *EL* and *LY* are strongly suggestive, when taken together with Montagu's remarks, of his having done so. The amount cut away from Montagu's MS is only four fifths of a page (cf Moorman I, 261n); some canceled words appear at the top of the next page: "habits in which he found me." The rest of the passage is quoted *EL* 138n, except that "childbed, two years later I settled in Lincoln's Inn Chambers." should read "childbed. After an interval of two years I, by the assistance of Mr Lane, settled in Lincoln's Inn." Woof points out that the frequency of visits between W and Godwin around Mar–Apr are suggestive of W's residing in Sommers Town, the home of Godwin, at that time. JFP Jr. had entered Lincoln's Inn 27 July 1793 (*The Records of the Honorable Society of Lincoln's Inn. Admissions*, Lincoln's Inn, 1896). On 27 July 1795 JFP Sr. wrote that his son had let Racedown to a friend of his (PP).

[After spending probably more than three weeks there,] she returns to Halifax. [Probably shortly after her arrival, but in Apr,] she writes to Jane Pollard from Sockburn: It will be three weeks before she arrives at Halifax. The H's and their farm; her decision to stay longer there than originally planned; her activities there. A surprisingly friendly visit with CCC [see 1794:20]. Pitt's powder tax. (*EL* 132–36. See 1795:16.)[4]

14. Mar 25

W calls on Godwin, [probably in the morning]. (Godwin Diary. See Schneider 224; Moorman I, 264.)

15. Mar 31

W calls on Godwin. (Godwin Diary. See Moorman I, 264.)[5]

16. [Apr or May, certainly by late May]

DW returns to Halifax from Sockburn-on-Tees. (See 1795:13.)

17. Apr 9

W breakfasts with Godwin. (Godwin Diary. See Moorman I, 264; 1795:15n.)

18. Apr 22

W calls on Godwin. (Godwin Diary. See Moorman I, 264.)

[4] DW was still in Newcastle 11 Mar, and had not, evidently, by that time informed her "Aunt" Rawson of her exact plans about returning to Halifax (*EL* 132n). As her original plans appear to have been for a relatively short visit to Sockburn (*EL* 133), her "aunt" would probably have known by now if DW had been planning on immediate departure from Newcastle; so the earliest really likely time for the departure is probably late Mar. It is unknown, however, how long DW had been with the Hutchinsons when she wrote JP that she planned to stay three weeks longer (*EL* 132–33); the only clue—her statement in her "April" letter that "when I came I had no intention of staying longer than till yesterday"—implies that she had only been there a few days; hence she probably came not earlier than late Mar. If she carried out her plan of staying three weeks at Sockburn, she would have been in Halifax by late May at latest. On the problem of when DW saw CCC see 1794:20.

[5] An oversight must lie behind the statement of Schneider 224 that there were no visits by W or Godwin to each other between 25 Mar and 14 July. I find no record of a visit, however, on 28 Mar (cf Moorman I, 264).

19. May 24 (–1797 Feb 13)

The *Osterly*, JW fourth mate, sails for China. (It reaches moorings on return 13 Feb 1797.) (Hardy.)

20. July 14

Godwin calls on W, [probably in the morning]. (Godwin Diary. See Schneider 224; Moorman I, 264.)

21. [Perhaps shortly before July 24]

W, Montagu, Wrangham are all in London, but leave for a visit to Cobham. [W probably returns by 29 July. They probably all see Aza P briefly on the day of their departure.] (Letter of Aza P to JFP Sr., 31 July 1795, PP.)[6]

22. July 29

[Godwin calls on W. (Godwin Diary. Cf Schneider 224.)][7]

23. Aug 15

W and Ma[t]hews call on Godwin, probably in the late afternoon or evening; Godwin is not at home. (Godwin Diary. See Moorman I, 264. Cf Schneider 224.)

24. Aug 18

Godwin calls on W; W is not at home. [W has probably left London for Bristol by this time.] (Godwin Diary. See Schneider 224; 1795:25.)

---

[6] A typed copy of the letter from Aza P to his father, among the PP, is endorsed "July 31st 1795," and the letter is dated "Lincoln's Inn Friday Morn." The best guess seems to be that Aza P wrote on the Friday previous to 31 July, that is, 24 July. A passage reads: "I have taken possession of my Brothers Apartments by Mr. Montagu's desire, and am consequently at no expense for lodgings. When I arrived Mr Montagu, Wrangham and Mr Wordsworth were all in Town, but intended leaving it the same Eveg for Cobham, which they performed and left me the sole management of his Chambers and Servants."

[7] Godwin's phrasing is "Call on Wordsworth & Foulkes, nah." Godwin was usually meticulous about placing "nah" (not at home) after the name of each person to whom it applied, and it is probable that he did find W at home.

25. [Probably between Aug 15 and Aug 18–probably Aug 21, probably Sept 26]

[Probably between 15 and 18 Aug W departs for Bristol, arriving there probably by 21 Aug. He had been with Mathews the night before his departure from London. He remains in Bristol until 26 Sept, visiting at the home of J. F. Pinney Sr., 7 Great George Street. (*LY* 1333–34; Stanley Hutton, *Bristol and Its Famous Associations*, Bristol, 1907, 113n; 1795:24; 1795:34.) W leaves several books at Montagu's in London. (*LY* 1334–35; *EL* 155.)

(W's departure from London is probably at least a partial referent of *Prel* I.1–54, *Prel*₂ I.1–45, also *Prel* VII.1–9, *Prel*₂ VII.1–8—see esp. 1795:34.)

During this visit in Bristol W meets Robert Southey, who contributes three lines to *Juvenal*. (*EL* 144–45; *LY* 1333–34.) He probably meets Joseph Cottle at this time. (See Moorman I, 271; *EL* 149n.) Probably either by 1 Sept or toward the end of the visit he meets Samuel Taylor Coleridge. His introductions to STC and Southey possibly take place at the same time; if so, the meeting more likely takes place in late Aug than toward the end of W's visit. STC perhaps hears W read *SP*. (*EL* 144, 149; *LY* 1263; *The Farington Diary*, London, 1928, VI, 36; Moorman I, 270–71. On the *SP* reading see 1796:48; *BL* I, 58; *STCNB* 6n.)

Probably at Bristol W composes an imitation of Juvenal VIII. 87–124; also composes *Juvenal* 1–28. (*EL* 143–45. See Appendix XIV.)

It is not probable that W visits Racedown during this period. (See 1795:37; Moorman I, 276–78.) W perhaps makes some sort of contact at this time with William Rawson, husband of Elizabeth Threlkeld (*EL* 142).][8]

[8] PREL 605 states that W traveled to Bristol early in Sept. As pointed out Moorman I, 270, W arrived at Racedown 26 Sept, and he later wrote Mathews that he was in Bristol "at least five weeks." If he left Bristol on 26 Sept, as seems likely, he would probably have arrived there on or before 21 Aug. He was still in London on 15 Aug (see 1795:23) and with Mathews at least part of the day. He indicates elsewhere (*LY* 1334–35) that he was with Mathews "the evening before he left town." Possibly the evening mentioned was that of the 15th. JFP Sr. wrote to JFP Jr. on 15 Aug from Bristol that Aza P, who had returned from London the previous Thursday, had told

26. Aug 20

RW [possibly belatedly] records receipt of £5 of the Calvert legacy on W's account under this date. (RW, correspondence with William Calvert, DCP. See 1795:3.)

27. Aug 21

The Birth of Love is published in *The Morning Chronicle* [sent in, with introductory note, by Francis Wrangham]. (See GCL 41.)

---

him that W was to arrive "tomorrow or next day." (He also had been told that DW would arrive "a day or two after," and that the W's, with little Basil, would set off for Racedown "about Wednesday.") (PP.)

W perhaps met Southey before 1 Sept, when Southey changed his residence from Bristol to Bath (Jack Simmonds, *Southey*, London, 1945, 55; EKC 44). He did not, in any event, get to know Southey well at this time (*LY* 1333–34; *EL* 155; *STCL* I, 336; Southey, *Works*, Boston, 1854, IV, 5–6). The problem of when precisely W met STC cannot be solved on the basis of present evidence: Mrs. Moorman notes that their acquaintance may have begun "in a lodgings," or at a political society meeting (see *LY* 1263; *Farington Diary* VI, 36). It is possible but not likely that the political society met in someone's lodgings; it is more possible that W heard and saw STC at a meeting without actually making his acquaintance there. W's late, uncertain memory was that he "saw" STC, Southey, and Edith [Fricker] (soon to be Mrs. Southey) for the first time all together at the lodgings just mentioned. While the length of STC's absence from Bristol in early Sept is not clear beyond the facts that he was probably at Stowey 12 Sept and certainly on 19 Sept, Mrs. Moorman's conclusion, that the meeting took place close to the time of W's departure for Racedown, seems as good as any yet advanced. Its main advantage is that it avoids the necessity of having to suppose incorrect STC's statement that he wrote *Lines . . . at Shurton Bars* before he knew W. Southey could have come over from Bath to Bristol for a visit, and have been present for a meeting, at almost any time. STC may nevertheless have erred about the *Lines . . . at Shurton Bars*; the two poets could have met, in the presence of Southey, in late Aug or early Sept. (The comment of Sara Coleridge *fille* that the meeting was in a house of Pinney's while STC was on an excursion—see *BL* (1847) II, 345–46—must inaccurately look forward to Racedown.)

Cottle's remark (*Reminiscences* 174) that a visit to STC at Stowey had been "the means" of his own introduction to W is an obvious absurdity. A line has been drawn through Barron Field's repetition of this statement in his Memoirs of W, BM Add MS 41, 325, and it appears that W was the drawer of the line.

"Her Eyes Are Wild" IF note records that W heard of the Mad Mother from "a lady of Bristol." The incident cannot be dated exactly, but probably occurred between this time and c 16 May 1798 (see GCL 67).

28. Aug 25

Two bills toward payment to W of the Calvert legacy are dated on this day. One, for £250, falls due one month hence; the second, for £50, falls due two months hence. (*LY* 1338.)

29. [1795] Sept 2, [3]

DW writes to Jane Pollard Marshall from Halifax: JPM's recent marriage. Life at Halifax. A recent visit there by CW. The plan for residing in Dorset (a secret); they are to take care of little Basil Montagu and a "natural daughter" of their cousin Tom Myers. Their expected income £170–180 per annum. The arrangement with the Pinneys about Racedown. Montagu and little Basil. W's finances; he has recently been offered 10 guineas for a work that did not take much time [perhaps *SP*]. DW regrets leaving Halifax. Mr. Rawson is to see W at Bristol. Plans for travel to Racedown. Life at Halifax. (*EL* 136–42.)[9]

30. Sept 14

RW records remission of £5 to DW under this date. (RW, accounts with W and DW, 1816, DCP.)

31. [Sept 14]

W writes to RW [in Penrith] from Bristol: Galway, a friend of Montagu's, has offered a rent charge to W for £500 by 10 Oct. W can procure £300 from Calvert [see 1795:28]; probably RW will have to borrow £200. Asks RW's assistance and advice. Expects arrival of DW at Bristol within a week. (*LY* 1332–33.)[10]

32. [Sept 22]

DW arrives at Bristol from Forncett. [Little Basil is perhaps with her.] (Letter of Eliza Pinney to JFP Sr., 23 Sept 1795, PP; *EL* 142; 1795:31; 1795:34.)[11]

[9] While the first paragraph was no doubt begun the day the letter is dated, the second paragraph commences "I was interrupted yesterday in writing."

[10] The postmark of 16 Sept and W's "Monday afternoon" establish the date of the letter.

[11] Eliza Pinney remarks of DW who, she says, arrived "last night": "I like her manner and appearance extremely, she is very animated, and unaffected."

33. Sept 25

A bill for £250 of the Calvert legacy comes due. RW records receipt of the sum under this date. (*LY* 1338–39; RW, correspondence with William Calvert, DCP. See 1795:28.)

34. [Probably Sept 26–1797 probably July 2]

[Probably on 26 Sept] W, DW, [and probably little Basil Montagu] travel to Racedown from Bristol. They arrive c midnight 26 Sept. (Gill Diary; Evans and Pinney 15; *EL* 142; Paterson; Joyce 290, 399–400.) [(This trip to Racedown and their residence there probably contribute to the content of *Prel* I.1–271, *Prel*₂ I.1–269; see also *Prel* VII.1–9, *Prel*₂ VII.1–8.) They reside at Racedown until probably 2 July, possibly 1 or 3 July 1797. (See 1797:33.)

During their residence here DW writes to an unknown correspondent from Racedown. Possibly only a fragment survives of one letter, in which the pleasant situation of their home is described. In the same letter or another she refers to W's dexterity with a spade. In the same letter or another she speaks of the local scenery. (*Mem* I, 94.)

On W's residence at Racedown generally see Moorman I, 279–320; Evans and Pinney. References in W's writings to this period incapable of specific dating include:

OMT and IF note. (A meeting with an old man. See *OMT*; Appendix XV.)

The *Glow-worm* and n. (The incident described takes place at Racedown.)

Worth note here is *The Life and Correspondence of the Late Robert Southey*, ed. C. C. Southey (London, 1849) I, 63. (W smells a patch of stock; it is like "a vision of Paradise.")][12]

---

[12] According to Cary's *Roads* (1798), the distance from Bristol to Blackdown totaled about 52½ miles; Racedown lay a mile from Blackdown. The Wordsworths' mode and speed of transportation is unknown, but in view of their late time of arrival, it seems probable that they had left Bristol the same day. Their original plan, anyhow, had been to come down by chaise (*EL* 142). The Gill Diary makes no mention of little Basil, but he probably came now or shortly after (see *EL* 142). The opening lines of *Prel* appear the only basis for the supposition that the journey was made on foot.

Prel I.1–115, *Prel*₂ I.1–107, so far as can now be determined, do not describe any

35. Sept 26–1798 [June 25]

[W refers to the period of his residence at Racedown and Alfoxden: *Excursion* III.659–705. (The Solitary's self-evaluation probably draws heavily on this period.) *Excursion* IF note (concerning *Excursion* I, *RC*). (Several passages describing Margaret in her affliction are taken from observations in Dorset, Somerset.)]

36. [Between Sept 26 and Nov 20]

W makes extensive revisions on [the MS 1 version of *SP*, adding much or all of the character and story of the sailor]. (*EL* 145. See Appendix XII; 1795:34.)

37. Sept 29

W, DW go to Harlescombe (a nearby farm of the Pinneys') and settle how they are to get butter, eggs, and the like. W certifies an

---

single journey made by W. The poet's emotions upon traveling to Racedown, leaving London and Bristol behind, are bound to have contributed. Chances are much against a solitary walking trip to Racedown before DW's arrival (see 1795:25), and there is little cause to suppose that W and DW walked down. Nor was Racedown in a "known" vale insofar as personal experience was concerned, nor did W make a "choice" of this destination at any time very near his actual departure for it (see 1795:9). Grasmere, in 1799, was certainly a chosen vale to which he perhaps set out with cheer on parting with STC in late Nov, and again, even more elatedly and with high purpose (although he was not alone and did not loiter) in Dec: one of these occasions possibly provided the impetus for the composition of the passage as it now stands. He apparently made a "choice" of a visit to Jones at the "known" Vale of Clyde in the summer of 1793; and his departure from London to visit Jones in the same vale in 1791 (and possibly—if not likely—a "choice" of a visit to the "known" Vale of Keswick in autumn 1793) could also be among occasions contributing. In terms of the application of the lines to a departure from a "City," the best conjecture of the chronological referent for the lines—if such a conjecture must be made— appears the traditional one of his trip to Racedown (even if by coach) and his residence there, commencing in "autumn." (See PREL 512; Moorman I, 276–77.)

Aza P's remark concerning "poor Rosinate" (see Moorman I, 320) probably does not, as I was first informed by Miss Landon, refer to a tradition that W rode a horse to Lyme, forgot it, and walked back. The Gill Diary shows that a horse died at Racedown on 11 Mar, shortly before Aza P's remark. The tradition does not seem well enough substantiated for inclusion in the text.

It appears that the last quotation from a lost letter by DW on *Mem* I, 94, is to be dated in the Racedown period rather than 1799, the date of the preceding quotation.

inventory of the furnishings of Racedown House. (Gill Diary; Inventory, in possession of Mrs. Marsden-Smedley; Evans and Pinney 9–11.)[13]

38. Oct–1796 Oct 1

W lends Basil Montagu £300 in Oct for "a sort of irregularly secured annuity" on which [Montagu proposes to pay] W 10 percent up to 1 Oct 1796. (*LY* 1336. See 1796:59.)[14]

39. Oct 4

S. T. Coleridge marries Sara Fricker at Bristol. (EKC 47; Stanley Hutton, *Bristol and Its Famous Associations*, Bristol, 1907, 106.)[15]

40. [Perhaps Oct 19 or 20]

W walks to Lyme, attempts to see Leader, [a friend of Mathews',] but fails. He returns to Racedown for dinner. (*LY* 1334.)

41. Oct 20

J. Gill calls on Mrs. Pinney of Blackdown, partly at the desire of DW, who has not yet called on her. (Gill Diary.)

42. [1795 perhaps Oct 20 or 21]–Oct 24

On [perhaps 20 or 21 Oct] W begins a letter to William Mathews from Racedown: His Bristol visit. Mathews' friends the Clones.

[13] I am grateful to Mrs. Basil Marsden-Smedley for the valuable opportunity of examining the Racedown inventory. The inventory itself is twice dated 7 Sept by Gill, but the date plainly has no connection with any activities of W in early Sept.

[14] By late Oct W had received £305 of the Calvert legacy (see 1795:43). When this agreement with Montagu was formalized or what its terms were cannot be told; W had received dated bills covering £300 on 25 Aug; he tells RW simply that the interest from Montagu was to have come due "more than a month" after 17 Aug 1796. On Montagu's financial dealings with W generally see Moorman I, 269–70, 296–97.

[15] Their first child, David Hartley, was born 19 Sept 1796 (see *Memoir and Letters of Sara Coleridge*, 1873, 2). Births of their other children, which took place after the commencement of close acquaintance with the W's, are noted in the text.

W saw STC in Bristol, but only a little [see 1795:25]. Met Southey also; his good opinion of Southey. Racedown; local poverty. His walk to Lyme and vain attempt to see Leader [see 1795:40]. W wishes to trade Mathews his copy of [Trenchard and Gordon, *Letters of Cato*, London, 1755] for Bell's [*Fugitive Poetry*, vol. X (*Poems in the Stanza of Spenser*)], which contains *The Minstrel* and [Mickle's] *Sir Martyn*. (*EY* 153–54; Moorman I, 1965, 287.) [The letter is concluded 24 Oct. (See 1795:44.)]

43. [Probably Oct 23]

Leader (see 1795:40) rides over from Lyme to Racedown, where he dines, and then returns to Lyme. (*EY* 154; Gill Diary.)[16]

44. Oct 24

W finishes his letter to Mathews from Racedown (see 1795:42): Leader has come to dine with him [see 1795:43]. Asks Mathews to send him a copy of the catalogue that he had asked Mathews to make of the books W left at Montagu's. The library at Racedown. [John] Myers. Asks Mathews to order six pairs of shoes for him from W's shoemaker at Lincoln's Inn. (*EY* 153–56.)[17]

45. Oct 25

A bill for £50 of the Calvert legacy comes due. RW records receipt of the sum under this date. (*LY* 1338–39; RW, correspondence with William Calvert, DCP. See 1795:28.)

46. Nov 13

Mr. and Mrs. Pinney [of Blackdown] pay a visit to W and DW. (Gill Diary; Cary's *Roads*, 1799. See Evans and Pinney 11.)[18]

[16] Gill's Diary records a visit from Leader 26 Oct, but Gill dates were frequently inaccurate, and this is probably the visit to which he refers.

[17] The shoemaker was probably R. Hilton, whom RW paid, on W's behalf, 3 guineas on 2 July 1796 and £3 on 18 Apr 1799 (when he also paid £2 for DW).

[18] It seems certain that the visit which Gill records by "Mr & Mrs Py" on this date was paid by the Blackdown Pinneys, on whom Gill had called at DW's request 20 Oct, and not by JFP Sr. and his wife (see Evans and Pinney 11, 15–16). The elder Pinneys could hardly have come from Bristol for a call, and the Gill Diary offers no indication that a visit longer than a call was paid.

47. Nov 15

A parcel arrives from Bristol for W. Gill asks W [not for the first time] to compare his own signed inventory of the Racedown furnishings with Gill's and sign the latter, at [JFP Sr.'s] request. W says he will do so soon. (Gill Diary.)[19]

48. [1795] Nov 20

W writes to Francis Wrangham from Racedown: Discussion of *Juvenal* [see Appendix XIV]; some verses for *Juvenal*, of which Southey supplied a couplet; other matters concerning the poem. W wants to receive the *Morning Chronicle*. Invites Wrangham to Racedown. W wishes to sell [*SP*], which he has altered extensively since reading it to Wrangham [see Appendix XII]. (*EL* 143–45.)

49. [Probably between 1795 Nov 20 and late 1796; esp. early 1796]

[Whatever approximation W makes of "yielding up moral questions in despair" and turning toward mathematics for secure mental activity and support—his soul's "last and lowest ebb"—probably occurs at this time, esp. in early 1796. DW, nature, and STC aid in his emergence from this crisis with greater strength and knowledge. W writes of this time: *Prel* X.900–30, *Prel*₂ XI.304–56.

Spring of 1796 is probably the spring which W sees return when he is "dead to deeper hope," as described in *Prel* XI.24–120, *Prel*₂ XII.33–93. (See PREL 610; 1795:50; 1796:58.)][20]

---

[19] W's inventory was evidently the one he had signed 29 Sept.

[20] The progress of a recovery from emotional and philosophical depression can hardly be minutely chronologized, but it seems fair to suppose that this was the period of the "crisis" of W's "strong disease." STC was "about this time" first known to W, and W was passing his days in DW's sight; so the poet is surely referring to the Racedown period. W was still much, and positively, concerned with moral questions soon after his arrival in Dorset, in view of the nature and extent of his alterations to *SP*. He was positively—if not cheerfully—engaged on such topics again in his composition of *The Borderers* by late 1796, after which time such considerations in one way or another underlie virtually all his work. His poetic output in early 1796 was small: He composed a little of *Juvenal* c Mar–Apr, but while these lines are in a sense "moral"

50. [Probably between 1795 Nov 20 and 1797 probably c Mar–June 4–7]

[At this time, as he later recalls, W shakes off the habit of letting his "eye dominate his heart" (see 1793:17) and again stands in the presence of nature "a sensitive and creative soul," as described in *Prel* XI.243–57, *Prel*₂ XII.193–207. (See 1795:49; 1796:58; 1797:2.)][21]

51. [1795] Nov 30

DW writes to Jane Marshall from Racedown: A recent fire from which JPM escaped. Life at Racedown: little Basil; servants; routine; scenery; the house; neighbors. An expected but unmaterialized visit from Montagu. W has received a letter [from Annette] since arrival at Racedown—one of a half-dozen she has written but which have not arrived. Aunt Cookson's new child [Anne]. Postal, other difficulties at Racedown; the countryside; local poverty. Mutual acquaintances. (*EL* 146–48, 567.)

---

[21] W's full emergence from his earlier habit, while prepared for more or less unconsciously over many years, must have been closely related to emergence from the depressions and uncertainties described in the preceding entry, although W of course says that he still "gloried" in nature through that period (*Prel* XI.20–41, *Prel*₂ XII.29–43). I have taken W's early work on the *RC* as the clearest indication about this time of an attitude toward nature distinctly different from that described in *Prel* XI.138–99, *Prel*₂ XII.93–151.

---

he did not consider them "writing" (see *EL* 154–56); and *The Convict*, *Fragment of a Gothic Tale*, and *XVI* (probably between late Mar and Oct), if also "moral," show few signs of philosophical vigor; even less do *Address to the Ocean* and "The Hour Bell Sounds." In *The Borderers*, however, he has not only set aside a number of his earlier basically Godwinian moral assumptions, but is once again engaged in really extensive composition—on

> Those mysteries of passion which have made,
> And shall continue evermore to make . . .
> One brotherhood of all the human race.

W and STC probably began direct correspondence between 6 Mar and 13 May 1796 (see 1796:19), a fact which would contribute to W's recollection that it was now that STC lent him help in regulating his soul (although "living help" must mainly look forward to Alfoxden, when W was no longer in a state of serious depression). In any event, mention of STC's part in W's recovery is removed in *Prel*₂.

52. Dec 9

A bill for £220 toward payment to W of the Calvert legacy is dated on this day. It falls due in one month. (*LY* 1338.)

53. Dec 17

The gardener comes to grind the apples for cider. Gill tells W to inform the gardener of several jobs he wants done. (Gill Diary.)

54. [Probably Dec 23]

W, DW, Gill dine at the home of the Pinneys of Blackdown. (Gill Diary.)[22]

1796

1. [During this year]

[On writings of W possibly of this year see below and GCL 6, 8, 32–35, 47–56.]

RW records under this general date an advance of 6 guineas to W, for, and to be repaid by, Basil Montagu. [The sum is apparently never repaid.] RW also records under the same date payment of several tailor's bills for W [amounts unknown, but see 1796:30]. (RW, accounts with W and DW, 1816, DCP.)

2. [Perhaps early 1796, more probably between Mar 21 and early Oct]

W writes:

Drafts edited by EdS as *XVI a, b* (*PW* I, 292–95) [perhaps as part of an effort to recast independently the story of the Female Vagrant]. (See Appendices XII, XVI.)

The Convict. (See Appendix XVI.)

Drafts edited by EdS as *Fragment of a Gothic Tale.* [Some chance possibly exists that the poem was written between late May and early Oct. (See Appendix XVI.)]

---

[22] Gill's record of this event appears to be part of his 25 Dec entry, but "1796" is written beside the line in question; so absolute certainty is not possible.

3. [Jan (by Jan 20)]

W lends £200 to Charles Douglas. (*LY* 1336. See esp. 1796:10.)

4. [Probably Jan 2]–Jan 7, 10

[Probably on 2 Jan JFP Jr. and Aza P] arrive at Racedown for a visit [as paying guests]. JFP departs 7 Jan, Aza P 10 Jan. One of the brothers brings W a copy of Southey's *Joan of Arc*, a gift from Cottle. Other books are perhaps brought, including Madame Roland's *Memoirs* and H. M. Williams' *Letters*, 1795. (*EL* 140, 149–50; Gill Diary; Landon *BNYPL*.) [On the activities of the household during the visit see *EL* 150–51; Evans and Pinney 12–13.][1]

5. [After Jan 2, probably early in the year]

W composes "The Hour Bell Sounds." (Landon *BNYPL*; Appendix XVI.)

6. Jan 7

JFP Jr. departs from Racedown for Bristol. (Gill Diary.)

7. [Probably Jan 7 or later Jan]

W writes to Joseph Cottle from Racedown: Thanks Cottle for the gift of Southey's *Joan of Arc* [see 1796:4] W had hoped to send the MS of *SP* with his note, but unforeseen engagements have prevented him. Is now at leisure, expects to send the MS in a few days. Compliments to STC. (*EL* 149; Cornell 2298; P. M. Zall, "Old Knight Revisited," *PMLA* LXXI, 1956, 1177. See 1798:18.)[2]

---

[1] Blurring—apparently deliberate—in Gill's Diary prevents certainty concerning the date of the arrival, but Gill seems to have recorded in an entry for 3 Jan that the Pinneys arrived "[yes]terday." A record of extra household furnishings taken from the storeroom is almost certainly entered under 3 Jan. DW's remark on 7 Mar that the Pinneys visited "one week at Christmas" was probably not meant to be especially exact.

[2] W states that he has been delayed in transmitting *SP* to Cottle by "unforseen engagements," but that he is "now at leisure." One suspects that the "unforseen engagements" were connected with the visits of JFP Jr. and Aza P in early Jan. "Mr. Pinney's" arrival preceded the letter, inasmuch as part of W's reason for writing

8. [Jan 9]

[A bill for £220 of the Calvert legacy come due to W. (*LY* 1338–39. See 1795:52; 1796:9.)]

9. Jan 10

RW records receipt of £220 of the Calvert legacy on W's account under this date. (RW, correspondence with William Calvert, DCP. See 1796:8.)

Aza P departs from Racedown for Crewkerne and London. (Gill Diary.)

10. Jan 20

Basil Montagu signs a bond for the payment of the £200 loaned Douglas (see 1796:3) and interest on demand. (*LY* 1336–37. See esp. 1796:47; 1796:74.)

11. [Feb 1]

[W inquires about having the tenants fetch coal. (Gill Diary.)]

12. Feb 10 [–Mar 6]

JFP Jr. (and his man Rawlins) arrive at Racedown. [They depart 6 Mar.] (Gill Diary; *EL* 150, 153.)

13. Feb 11

DW takes the sugar jar from Gill's Room. (Gill Diary.)

14. Feb 12

JFP Jr. takes a great part of Gill's newspapers to pack up "his picture of Leda naked" for Bristol, and also takes Gill's *Town and Country* magazines for the amusement of W [and the others]. (Gill Diary.)

---

was to thank Cottle for Southey's *Joan of Arc*, which Pinney had brought. The MS at Cornell exhibits no definite sign of having passed through the mails; so the letter may have been carried by one of the Pinneys. Probably W's leisure presupposes the departure of at least one of the brothers, neither of whom appears to have visited Racedown later in the month.

15. Feb 17

[On this day the Pinneys of Blackdown probably come to dine. (Gill Diary; *EL* 152.)][3]

16. Feb 24 [–Mar 6]

Aza P arrives at Racedown from London. [He departs 6 Mar.] (Gill Diary; *EL* 150, 153.)

17. Mar 1

W, JFP Jr., Aza P go to Crewkerne to dine. W finds a letter for DW from JPM there. They assist at a fire and arrive back between 12 and 1 AM. (Gill Diary; *EL* 150.)

18. [Mar 6 ff, esp. by Mar 25]

JFP Jr., [presumably his man Rawlins,] and Aza P depart from Racedown [6 Mar] (they had arrived 10, 24 Feb respectively). Aza P takes with him the MS of *SP*, which he delivers to Cottle at Bristol; Cottle gives it to STC, who, probably by 25 Mar, interleaves it with white paper for comments and works out a plan for its publication (500 copies) and the sale of copies to the readers of *The Watchman*. (*EL* 150, 153; Gill Diary; Evans and Pinney 12–13; EKC 75; *STCL* I, 216n. See 1796:29.)

19. [Probably between Mar 6 and May 13 and thereabouts]

[The earliest direct correspondence between W and STC takes place. Probably about this time STC encourages W to publish *SP*. (See 1796:18; 1796:27 and references there cited; *G&S* IF note; 1795:49—on STC's help in "regulating W's soul.")][4]

---

[3] Gill notes that many table implements were loaned to W at this time; he records that everything "except knives & forks" were returned by some time on the 18th. The very large number of items involved (for example, "2 doz Plates") indicates that it was at this time that W's had the "grand rout," and not at the "Christmas" [early Jan] visit of the Bristol Pinneys, as suggested Evans and Pinney 15–16.

[4] Aza P must have remembered imprecisely when he said he had spent three weeks on his visit to Racedown (see 1796:18). STC apparently did not have W's address until after 6 Mar (Aza P to W: "I gave him [STC] your address"); it is hard to

20. Mar 7

W hews wood and roots up hedges for an hour and a half in the morning. [Later] he writes to Francis Wrangham from Racedown: Wrangham's induction [to rectory of Hunmanby, Yorkshire]; Wrangham's projected volume of poems. W's determination to bring [*Juvenal*] to a speedy conclusion. The Pinneys' visit. His desire for a [London] newspaper. Invites Wrangham to Racedown. Intends to publish [at least *SP* (see 1796:18)]; can Wrangham obtain him some purchasers? Little Basil. (*EL* 152–53.)

21. [1796 Mar 7]

DW writes to Jane Marshall [from Racedown]: The fire at Mr. Marshall's mill. A fire at Crewkerne, attended by W [1 Mar]. Mutual acquaintances; Montagu; the Pinneys' visit; the Pinneys described; their activities during the visit. Weather; coal at Racedown; little Basil; Margaret Hutchinson [see 1796:25]; a dinner at Racedown attended by the Blackdown Pinneys [see 1796:15]. W to publish a poem [see 1796:20]; DW studying Italian; her reading. (*EL* 149–52.)

22. [Probably between Mar 7 and Apr]

W composes imitation of Juvenal VIII.163–230, 254–75 (*Juvenal* 29–162), only surviving version of VIII.85–86 (*Juvenal* 163–73). (See Appendix XIV.)

23. Mar 9

DW returns items borrowed from storeroom to Gill. (Gill Diary.)

24. [1796] Mar 21

W writes to William Mathews from Racedown: Inquires about Mathews; Southey is a coxcomb [cf 1795:42]. Life at Racedown. W

---

imagine STC's referring to W on 13 May as a "very dear friend" had he not heard from W at least once, and STC had probably written W first (see Evans and Pinney 12–13). *Letters, Conversations, and Recollections of S. T. Coleridge* (London, 1836) I, 205, possibly refers to an incident of W's and STC's early correspondence: STC writes to inquire if W is a Christian; W replies that "when [he is] a good man, *then* [he is] a Christian."

has been reading industriously; writing is out of the question, but he attempts satires. The catalogue of W's books at Montagu's [see 1795:45]; asks Mathews to have the books nailed up in a box, including four volumes of Gilpin [see esp. Appendix XVI]. Compliments to [John] Myers. Invitation to Racedown. DW's and his Italian reading. The second edition of *Political Justice*, which Montagu has sent him; its writing criticized. Holcroft's *Man of Ten Thousand* ("such stuff"). (*EL* 154–56.)[5]

25. [c Mar 29], Apr 1

Margaret Hutchinson dies [c 29 Mar]. She is buried at Sockburn on 1 Apr. (Sockburn PR, Mr. W. Tynemouth. See Margoliouth 52–56; Moorman I, 424–25; *EL* 152.)

26. [Probably between mid-Apr and mid-Nov, certainly by Nov 21]

W composes *Address to the Ocean*. [Some chance may exist that the composition took place before mid-Apr.] (See Appendix XVI.)

27. May 13

STC refers to W as a "very dear friend," and in his opinion "the best poet of the age." W has read STC's *Religious Musings*. (*STCL* I, 215–16. See 1796:19; Moorman I, 283–94.)

28. [May 15]

J. Hitchcock, farmer at Racedown, goes to Lyme for coal for W. (Gill Diary. See Evans and Pinney 16.)

29. [Perhaps late May]

STC sends [his MS of *SP* (see 1796:18)] to Charles Lamb in London, who [reads it] "not without delight." (Lamb *Letters* I, 8, 9. See 1796:32.)

---

[5] RW enters payment for porterage and for booking a box for [W] to Racedown (£-/-/8) under 28 May (RW, accounts with W and DW, 1816, DCP). The box possibly contained W's books; but see Appendix XVI.

30. May 23

RW records repayment to Birtwhistle what he has paid "Thos Stubbs, Taylor," on W's account (£7/2/6) and payment of Birtwhistle's own bill on W for goods (£1/8/6) under this date. (RW, accounts with W and DW, 1816, DCP.)

31. May 26

RW records remission of a bill, value £5, to W at Racedown under this date. (RW, accounts with DW and W, 1816, DCP.)

32. [June 1–probably July 9]

[On 1 June W departs for London. (Gill Diary. See Moorman I, 292.) He arrives back at Racedown probably 9 July. (See 1796:48; 1796:49.)

In London: W perhaps meets Charles Lamb. Lamb possibly returns to W the MS of *SP* sent him by STC. (See Lamb *Letters* I, 8, 9; 1796:29; 1796:48; *LY* 442.)][6]

33. [June 5]

DW and Gill walk to Crewkerne, where they find a letter from W. (Gill Diary.)[7]

34. June 7

W and JFP Jr. or Aza P call on Godwin after dinner. [W] and Godwin eat supper at Montagu's. (Godwin Diary. See Moorman I, 297.)[8]

35. June 10

DW, Gill walk to Crewkerne. (Gill Diary.)

---

[6] The Gill Diary gives "June 2nd Wednesday" for W's departure, but the correct date for the first Wednesday of June is 1 June. (Cf Moorman I, 292.)

[7] Gill says "Sunday" the 6th, but 6 June was a Monday (see 1796:32n).

[8] Godwin's entry: "Wodsworth [*sic*] & Pinney call: sup, w. W., at Montagu's." Godwin normally uses the initial "W" to refer to Mary Wollstonecraft, but the context here leaves little doubt that he is speaking of the poet.

36. June 12

DW, Gill walk to Crewkerne. (Gill Diary.)

37. [Probably June 16–probably June 18]

JFP Sr. and Jr. arrive at Racedown. [They depart probably 18 June.] (Gill Diary.)[9]

38. [Probably June 18]

JFP Sr. and Jr. depart from Racedown [this morning]. (Gill Diary. See 1796:37.)

39. June 18

W, Godwin, [John] Stoddart, [James or John] Tobin meet at Montagu's. (Godwin Diary. See Moorman I, 297.)

On this day W's name is taken off the St. John's College Boards. (Scott *Admissions* IV, 56.)

40. June 19

W, [John] Stoddart, Godwin eat supper at Montagu's. (Godwin Diary. See Moorman I, 297.)

41. June 20, [24]

A letter from Mr. Pinney of Sherborne arrives at Racedown concerning the sending of the perambulator. DW wishes the perambulator kept till she can measure the distance to Crewkerne, [but it is evidently sent away on Friday 24 June]. (Gill Diary. Concerning this occasion, and the perambulator, see Moorman I, 298n; Evans and Pinney 17.)

42. June 25

W, Godwin, [Robert?] Allen, [James or John] Tobin meet at [John] Stoddart's. (Godwin Diary. See Moorman I, 297.)

[9] Gill's diary is confusing: An entry dated 16 June (a Thursday) states that [JFP Sr. and Jr.] "came to RaceDown & remained untill Saturday Morning," when they left for Sherborne and Bristol. It would appear somewhat more likely for Gill to write the entry in late, but under the date of the arrival, than for him to wait from the Saturday of their departure (following an unknown time of arrival) until the next Thursday before making any note at all of the visit. (See Moorman I, 298n.)

43. [Probably between the latter half of 1796 and early 1797, possibly as late as 1797 summer]

W writes *Argument for Suicide*. (See Appendix XVII; GCL 51.)

44. [Probably between the latter half, probably late, 1796 and 1797 late Feb; possibly as late as 1797 summer]

W composes the bulk of the first version of *The Borderers* MS 1 (including MS A). [Some composition possibly extends into summer 1797. Probably also at this time] W composes his Prefatory Essay for *The Borderers*. (See Appendix X; GCL 52; *PW* I, 342–43, 345–49.)

45. [Probably between the latter half of 1796 and 1797 early June]

W composes:
Description of a Beggar (the core of *OCB*). (See Appendix XV; GCL 53.)
Old Man Travelling. Animal Tranquillity and Decay. (See Appendix XV; GCL 53.) Fragment: "Yet Once Again." (See Appendix XVII; GCL 54.)

46. [Probably between the latter half, even more probably late, 1796 and 1797 c Mar]

W writes the Baker's Cart fragment (*PW* I, 315–16). (See Appendices XIII, XVII; GCL 55.)

47. July 2

In London: Basil Montagu and Charles Douglas sign a promissory note to W for £220, due 1 Jan 1797, in return for a loan from W of £200. [See 1796:3; 1796:10.] [W is thus probably still in London.]

RW records receipt of £30 of the Calvert legacy on W's account under this date. (RW, correspondence with William Calvert, DCP; *LY* 1339.)

RW records payment of a bill of Mr. Hilton [shoemaker] on W for 3 guineas, and a loan to W of 2 guineas cash under this date. (RW, accounts with W and DW, 1816, DCP.)[10]

[10] Hilton's bill perhaps concerned W's order of shoes made through Mathews 24 Oct 1795.

48. [Probably between July 2 and July 9]

W returns to Racedown from London, arriving 9 July. [A chance possibly exists that his return is via Bristol, and that he sees STC there and recites *SP* to him; but more likely W returns more directly.] (See Moorman I, 292–93; Gill Diary; 1795:25.)[11]

49. [Probably July 9]

W arrives at Racedown from London. (Gill Diary.)[12]

50. July 14

Gill gives W a tumbler from his lock-up room. (Gill Diary.)

51. [July] 23

Gill lends W four sheets of gilt-edged paper and the [*Weekly*] *Entertainers* from his newspapers. (Gill Diary. See Moorman I, 298–99.)

---

[11] The possibility of a visit to Bristol depends on the likelihood of W's having made his "recitation" of a poem, apparently *SP*, to STC at this time (see *BL* I, 58). It is remotely possible that STC failed to read the poem before sending it to Lamb, although Aza P's comments of 25 Mar (Evans and Pinney 12–13) make such a supposition most doubtful. Mrs. Moorman's suggestion is that W's powers were given a "new revelation" to STC upon a recitation now of the poem which STC had in fact read earlier (I, 293). But STC had already come to regard W as the "best poet of his age" by 13 May (*STCL* I, 215–16); it is hard to believe that the "sudden effect" had occurred after STC arrived at that opinion, and equally hard to imagine what other work (it would not have been *EW* and *DS*—see *BL* iv) could have brought him to this high estimate. One guess might be that STC had heard W recite the poem in Bristol in Sept 1795 and that he was confirmed in a first high estimate of W's powers by later comments of mutual friends in Bristol and his reading of the revised *SP* this spring— circumstances of this kind could have tended to lead STC in later years to remember the earlier recitation as a rather more remarkable occasion than it had actually seemed at the time. The 1805 *Prel* speaks of STC's response as one that occurred after "perusing" the verse. The poets would indeed have been very nearly "strangers" in both late 1795 and early 1796 before they opened their correspondence, probably between 6 Mar and 13 May. STC would probably have done his perusing by early in the period of their first correspondence.

[12] The relevant Gill Diary entry is boxed in between the entries evidently for 4 July and "Friday" 10 July, and states that W arrived "Saturday even." The Friday in question was no doubt Friday 8 July, and as W was most likely still in London on 2 July, the Saturday of W's arrival was probably that of 9 July (cf Moorman I, 292).

52. Aug 17

Montagu signs a new annuity bond to W on the £300 which he had received from W Oct 1795. RW pays for a stamp, enrollment, and a certificate. (*LY* 1336; RW, accounts with W and DW, 1816, DCP.)

53. [Probably Aug 23]

W picks the first French beans from the garden. (Gill Diary.)[13]

54. Sept 1

[W takes out an insurance policy on the life of Basil Montagu.] RW records payment of costs of entering the policy at the Equitable Insurance Office, Blackfriars Bridge, and one year's premium (£7/10/6) totaling £8/14/– under this date. Montagu is to repay the annual premium to RW.

Also under this date RW records payment of a draft of W's on him plus other unspecified items to W's charge totaling £3/13/3. (RW, accounts with W and DW, 1816, DCP; *LY* 1337.)

55. Sept 7

Gill goes to Crewkerne. Writes a memo [to remember] "Mr. W's Letters." (Gill Diary.)

56. [Sept 20–Sept 25 or Oct 1 and thereabouts]

[On 20 Sept] JFP [Jr.] and a Mr. Moncrief arrive at Racedown. [They depart 25 Sept or 1 Oct. Possibly Aza P pays a visit about this time also.] (Gill Diary.)[14]

[13] Gill's entry begins 22 Aug and contains a notation of W's picking the beans on "Tuesday." The best guess appears to be that the Tuesday in question was 23 Aug.

[14] The Gill Diary notes the arrival as being "19 Tuesday." The Tuesday in question was the 20th. Aza P wrote Mr. Berington, Cheltenham, on 16 Sept that he was "about to set out for Dorsetshire" for a shooting party (PP). Although the Gill Diary makes no mention of his presence at Racedown about this time, the fact is by no means assurance that he did not come.

57. [Sept 25 or Oct 1]

JFP [Jr.] and Moncrief depart from Racedown. (Gill Diary.)[15]

58. [Probably c late this year–1797 c Mar]

[W probably refers to this period: *Prel* XII.20–219, *Prel*₂ XIII. 16–220. (Moderated and composed, W finds man again an object of his love. He attempts to find what is of real worth in ordinary laborers; turns to lonely roads, wanders about; finds love and noble emotions in humble people.) (See PREL 615–16. On date see 1795:50; 1797:2.)]

59. [Perhaps by c Oct 1]

W receives [£30?] representing income from a 10 percent annuity from £300 of W's which Montagu has held since Oct 1795. (*LY* 1336–37. See 1796:52.)[16]

60. [Probably Oct 4 (–perhaps Oct 6)]

JFP [Jr.] and Moncrief return to Racedown. [They depart perhaps 6 Oct.] (Gill Diary.)[17]

61. [Perhaps Oct 6]

JFP [Jr.] and Moncrief depart from Racedown. (Gill Diary. See 1796:60n.)

[15] An entry in the Gill Diary belonging to sometime between 20 Sept and 3 Oct (but which there seems no way to date more exactly) notes that the visitors left on "Sunday"; the Sunday could have been either of the two between these dates, as cited.

[16] W says on 9 May 1797 (*LY* 1336) that he has received the interest "up to the 1st of October last"; the time of its receipt is not known. His remarks make it clear that £13 of the total interest due him from Montagu and Douglas by 1 Jan had not yet been paid by 9 May. What is not certain is whether the missing £13 was owed from interest on the Montagu annuity or on the Montagu-Douglas note (see *LY* 1336) or both. W's phrasing seems to me more suggestive of its having been owed on the note.

[17] Gill records their arrival on "Octr 3d Tuesday," and appears to note their departure on "Tuesday Octr 5th." I have assumed that Gill meant an arrival on Tuesday 4 Oct and a departure on Thursday the 6th, but the matter is far from certain.

62. Oct 19

Michel Beaupuy dies at the Battle of the Elz. (Emile Legouis and Georges Bussière, *Le Général Michel Beaupuy*, Paris, 1891, 168–170.)

63. [Probably Oct 22]

A person from Lyme comes to see W. (Gill Diary.)[18]

64. Oct 23 (and Nov 7)

On 23 Oct W writes to the editor of *The Weekly Entertainer* from Racedown: An extract was recently published in the *Entertainer* from a work purporting to be by Fletcher Christian. The work is spurious. (W's letter is published 7 Nov.) (JRM *RES*. See Moorman I, 299–300.)

65. Oct 24

DW writes [to an unknown correspondent from Racedown]: W is "ardent in the composition of a tragedy." (*Mem* I, 96. See Appendix X.)

66. Oct 31

J. Gill carries some coal to Mr. Pinney of Blackdown which W had borrowed. (Gill Diary.)

67. Nov 7

W's letter of 23 Oct (see 1796:64) to the editor of *The Weekly Entertainer* is published in that magazine. (JRM *RES*. See Moorman I, 299–300.)

68. Nov 8 [–probably Nov 11]

JFP [Jr. ?] arrives at Racedown in the evening. [He departs probably 11 Nov.] (Gill Diary.)

69. [Probably Nov 11]

JFP [Jr. ?] departs from Racedown for Bristol. (Gill Diary.)[19]

---

[18] Gill notes on Monday 24 Oct that the visitor came "Saturday."

[19] Gill notes that JFP departed for Bristol Friday 12 [Nov]; the Friday in question would have been 11 Nov.

70. Nov 21

W borrows a guinea from Gill. (See Evans and Pinney 17.)

Address to the Ocean, signed "W.W." [and by W] appears in *The Weekly Entertainer*. (See JRM *RES*.)

71. [Probably c Nov 28–1797 June 4]

[Mary Hutchinson and her brother Henry arrive at Racedown c 28 Nov. Henry departs the following morning. MH departs 4 June 1797. (Landon *BNYPL*. See 1797:25; *HCR & W Circle* 444; EdS *DW* 73n; Henry Hutchinson, *Retrospect of a Retired Mariner*, Stockton, Eng., 1836, iv.) (W appears to refer to MH at the time of this visit: *Prel* XI.199–223, *Prel*₂ XII.151–73.)]

72. [Probably between c Nov 28 and 1797 June 4]

W composes:

Inscription for a Seat by a Road Side, Half Way up a Steep Hill Facing the South (*PW* I, 301–02), a revision of *Inscription for a Seat by the Pathway Side Ascending to Windy Brow* (*PW* I, 300). (Racedown Nb, DCP. See 1794:8.)[20]

Stanzas (incomplete, not published), probably toward the poem which eventually developed into *The Three Graves*, about "Mary," "Edward," and a sexton. The stanza is that of *The Three Graves* as published *PW* I, 308–12, *STCPW* I, 269–84. (Racedown Nb, DCP.)[21]

The Three Graves, Part II. (Racedown Nb, DCP.)

---

[20] This poem was published in the *MP* of 21 Oct 1800 (see Woof *SB* 178–80), doubtless sent in by STC (see esp. *PW* I, 372). EdS points out that part of the MS is in the hand of MH. Most or all the work probably dates from the time of her visit (see 1796:71). Its position in the Nb suggests that the work dates after the entry of *Septimius and Acme*, and probably after *Lesbia*, and before the work on *The Three Graves* (including the unpublished work described below).

[21] The unpublished verses seem to relate that Mary is walking in the churchyard with Edward's greyhound. The greyhound races away to the woods. Mary, self-deluded, joyfully supposes that the dog has discovered its master, whom she has thought dead. A large part or all the story appears to be told by the sexton. The MS is evidently partly in the hand of MH; the time of her visit is a reasonable guess for

73. [Probably c Nov 29]

Henry Hutchinson departs from Racedown early in the morning. (Landon *BNYPL*. See Henry Hutchinson, *Retrospect of a Retired Mariner*, Stockton, Eng., 1836, iv; 1796:71.)

74. [Probably c Dec]

Charles Douglas pays Montagu £100 of the £200 which W had loaned Douglas Jan 1796, for which Montagu had signed a bond 20 Jan, and for which both had signed a promissory note 2 July. (*LY* 1336–37.)

75. Dec

RW records the purchase of 100 yards of Irish Linen and 3 yards of cambric under this date. He shares the price equally with W, W's half being £9/1/10. (RW, accounts with W and DW, 1816, DCP.)[22]

76. Dec 24

Gill notes expenditure of 10d for DW's "Diary." (See Evans and Pinney 17.)

---

[22] DW made RW shirts from this material. Whether she put it to other uses is unknown.

---

the date. STC's description of *The Three Graves*, and some of his own work on it, show that it is supposed to be "narrated by an old Sexton." This story does not appear to belong to any part of *The Three Graves* presently surviving in verse or STC's prose description, but the characters and narrator seem the same (and a phrase in this MS, "barren wife," is used twice by STC—lines 22, 200). Very likely this was work done before the plan of *The Three Graves* had reached its final form. STC would probably not have known about the poem before 4 June 1797; W probably handed over this work, and *The Three Graves* generally, to STC between 4 June and sometime in July 1797 (see *PW* I, 374). STC said in *The Friend* of 21 Sept 1809 that his verses for *The Three Graves* were composed "somewhat more than twelve years ago," which would point to summer of 1797 (some work was perhaps later—see 1798:99). *The Three Graves*, Part II also appears to be partly in the hand of MH, and probably belongs to the same general date as the unpublished stanzas.

77. Dec 26

Snow is very deep at Racedown. Gill consults with W. (Gill Diary.)

1797

1. [During this year]

[On writings of W possibly of this year see below and GCL 6, 8, 20, 32–35, 51–60.]

2. [Probably c early 1797, esp. c Mar–early 1798, esp. Mar–May]

[This period is probably the primary referent of *Prel* XII.220–379, *Prel₂* XIII.221–378. (W determines to write about the nobility of the common man, and about the human heart; forms the hope of producing a work of "a power like one of Nature's"; has sight of a "new world … fit to be transmitted.")][1]

---

[1] The complexity of W's synthesis in *Prel* XI–XIII (*Prel₂* XII–XIV) of experiences preceding his post-Godwinian "ebb" and experiences connected with his recovery, heightened especially by the various uses made throughout these books of phrases like "then," "at that time," "now," "that very day," "about this time," "once more," "about this period" (see esp. XI. 111, 200, 230, 234, 235, 293; XII.21, 69, 168, 220, 278, 313, 360, 370), skillfully dissolves clear temporal boundaries between earlier attitudes or events seen in retrospect as contributive to the recovery and attitudes and events of the period of the recovery itself. In regard to XII.354–79 (*Prel₂* XIII.350–78), it is possible that W began to think of "transmitting" some sort of "new world" about the time of *SP* MS 1—or the 1794 additions to *EW*; parts even of *DS* would support similar speculation. In *Prel* XII, however, the journey across Salisbury Plain (312–53) is described as having taken place "at" the time (313) when W was coming to comprehend the prophetic power of the Poet, which is in turn described as being "about" the time (278) of his determination to write inspiring and "oracular" verse on the subject of the "heart of man." The "about this period" preceding W's statement that he seemed to have sight of a new world may hence refer to the "period" of the visit to Salisbury Plain and the verses which the visit inspired or to the period that is the basic subject of XII as a whole, that of W's emotional and intellectual recovery; the elaboration of chronological ambiguities through the preceding books prevents clear distinction. While *SP* assumes a nobility in the common man, and *The Borderers* the importance of common emotions, no major work of W's until *RC* makes an unremitting effort to subsume both these

191

3. [Probably early 1797, perhaps after Feb 8, and by July]

W composes *Lines Left upon a Seat in a Yew-tree*. (Racedown Nb. See GCL 20.)[2]

4. [Probably early 1797, certainly by Mar 29]

W composes *Written on the Thames near Richmond* (as Cornell opp. p. 400), from materials perhaps dating back to between 1789 and 1791. (Cornell, opp. p. 400. See Appendix IV.)[3]

---

[2] Drafts for lines 33–46, 50–55, 60–61, and 63–64 of this poem, plus other lines not used in the final version, appear in the Racedown Nb. A fair copy of lines 1–13 in the hand of MH (see *PW* I, 92, *app crit*) also appears, followed by stubs of four leaves which could well have contained more of the work. It seems probable that the poem was well conceived, and in something approaching final form, before the end of MH's visit to Racedown, probably c 28 Nov 1796–4 June 1797. The version of the poem which STC evidently knew c 17 July 1797 (see *STCL* I, 334), and no doubt Lamb also from his visit of probably c 7–14 July 1797 (Lamb *Letters* I, 112), certainly contained some version of lines 48 ff (on the subject of contempt). Jonathan Wordsworth's forthcoming study of *RC* notes a probable debt of *LLSYT* to Southey's *Inscription for a Cavern*, published in Southey's *Poems* 8 Feb (London; see *The Times*). W might have known Southey's verses earlier, or may not have received the *Poems* until after c 25 Feb (see *EL* 162). Evidence is inconclusive, but chances favor a date after 8 Feb. The poem in any case may be said to date probably from early 1797, fairly certainly by July. Something resembling a few lines may come from as early as mid-1787 (see GCL 20). A copy of lines 36–64 appears on a loose sheet in the HUL with the added note "The Female Vagrant to follow": this copy was possibly part of the preparation for production of *LB* in 1798. In the complicated construction of that volume either *Lewti* or *The Nightingale* (or both) finally were placed between *LLSYT* and *FV*.

[3] The poem was copied into Cottle's MS Book 29 Mar 1797. W would probably have thought, on such an occasion, of copying out a recent poem.

---

subjects within a context consciously handled to express "The excellence, pure spirit and best power/ Both of the object seen, and eye that sees" in regard to theme, character, and (STC's remarks notwithstanding) image. Any "clear sight" (*Prel₂* XIII.369) of W's "new world" can probably be assigned to this general period. (See also esp. R. D. Havens, *The Mind of a Poet*, Baltimore, 1941, 602–03.)

Many of the poems of *LB*, esp. of Mar–May 1798, are devoted to related subjects, and confirm his intense interest in the goals described in *Prel*. Although his conception of a great philosophical poem possibly was worked out before early 1798, it is not until that time that he was engaged in work (*The Recluse*) in deliberate pursuance of that aim. (See entries covering early 1798.)

5. [By c Jan 1?]

[W receives possibly as little as £7 or as much as £20 interest from Basil Montagu and Charles Douglas. (See *LY* 1336–37; 1796:59n.)]

6. Jan 5

RW records payment for Miss Threlkeld of £1/19/4½ for DW under this date. (RW, accounts with W and DW, 1816, DCP.)

7. Feb 13

The *Osterly* (JW fourth mate) reaches moorings in England. (It had sailed 24 May 1795.) (Hardy.)

8. [Probably c but by Feb 25]

W writes to Francis Wrangham [from Racedown]: Adaptation of lines from Juvenal VIII [see Appendix XIV]. W gives up all thought of taking pupils. W has nearly finished a first draft of [*The Borderers* (see Appendix X)]. Inquiry about Wrangham's [*Poems*]. Plain living at Racedown. (*EL* 156–62; *LY* 1388.)

9. [Probably c Mar–Apr]

W composes the conclusion of *The Ruined Cottage*, later used as *Excursion* I.871–916. (See Appendix XIII.)

10. [Probably between c Mar and June 4–7; possibly between June 4–7 and July 7–14, and later in the year (–early 1798)]

[Probably between c Mar and 4–7 June] W composes the fragments of *RC* in the Racedown Nb, *RC* MS A, and probably an early version of *RC*. [Other *RC* work, including the passages in the Christabel Nb, is possibly also composed now or between 4–7 June and 7–14 July or even later in the year. (The Christabel passages are almost certainly in existence by, but more probably composed in, early 1798.)] (See Appendices IX, XIII.)

[Probably between c Mar and 4–7 June] W writes *Incipient Madness*. (See Appendix XIII.)

11. [Mar 15 (–Mar 19)]

Basil Montagu arrives at Racedown [from London] while W and DW are still in bed. (He departs 19 Mar.) (*EL* 163, 165. See 1797:12.)[4]

12. Mar 19 –[shortly after Mar 30]

W, Basil Montagu depart for Bristol. (See 1797:13; 1797:11.) [W returns to Racedown shortly after 30 Mar. He perhaps sees STC in Bristol.] (See entries below through 1797:18, esp. 1797:17.)[5]

13. [1797] Mar 19

DW writes to RW [from Racedown]: Comments, questions about shirts DW is making for RW. W, Montagu departed for Bristol this morning. MH still at Racedown. (*EL* 162–63.)

DW writes to Jane Marshall from Racedown this evening: W's and DW's system of raising little Basil Montagu. W, Montagu (Sr.) gone to Bristol. MH at Racedown. W is "the life of the whole house." (*EL* 163–66.)

14. Mar 20

James Losh forwards a large packet of books, pamphlets, and magazines to W. (Losh Diary.)[6]

[4] DW wrote on Sunday 19 Mar that Montagu had arrived the preceding Wednesday.

An amusing entry appears in a Nb of Tom Wedgwood's (Wedgwood Museum, Barlaston); it cannot be dated, but its place in the Nb is generally suggestive of 1797 or 1798: "basil Montagu thinking he saw a cow in his bed room—his eyes open—Wordsworth expostulating with him on the unreasonableness of the idea. At last *b* says. It is gone—how coud it go, the door being shut?"

[5] This visit to Bristol appears to be the only remotely possible referent of an alleged quotation from a letter from W to Mathews in James Gillman's *Life of Samuel Taylor Coleridge* (London, 1834), 74–75: "To-morrow I am going to Bristol to see those two extraordinary young men, Southey and Coleridge." Gillman's statement that the letter was written from Alfoxden is clearly impossible, and Southey is not likely to have been in Bristol now (see 1797:17n). The quotation does not seem to justify an entry in the text.

[6] For contents see Moorman I, 309–10.

15. Mar 27

W drinks tea at Mrs. Spedding's [in Bristol] with Losh, also Mr., Mrs., two Misses Hanson; eats supper with Mr. and Mrs. [John] Wedgwood, the Misses Wedgwood, Montagu, and Losh [probably at the Wedgwoods' residence, Cote House, Bristol]. (Losh Diary. See Moorman I, 310.)[7]

16. Mar 28

W walks and pays calls with Montagu and Losh, [possibly having earlier breakfasted with them and Thomas Ward]. (Losh Diary.)[8]

17. Mar 29; [probably Mar 29 or 30, and shortly after ff]

[W visits Joseph Cottle in Bristol] 29 Mar. He enters *Written on the Thames near Richmond* in Cottle's MS book. (Cornell, opp. p. 400. See GCL 33.)

[Having parted from Montagu, who returns to London, W returns to Racedown, setting out probably 29 or 30 Mar and arriving shortly after. He visits, probably briefly, with STC at Nether Stowey on his way. A chance possibly exists that Southey is also present. STC possibly accompanies W to Stowey from Bristol. W, STC discuss Southey's poems. W meets Thomas Poole. Poole, in the course of a walk, tells W and STC some parts of the story of John Walford. The poets request Poole to draw up the story in writing. (*STCL* I, 319, 320, 325; Poole *B and B*; Moorman I, 310.)][9]

[7] Moorman I (as cited) indicates that W moved to Bath after a week in Bristol. Evidence for this possibility seems only slight. W was surely in Bristol on the 27th and on the 29th. In any event, the proximity of Bath and Bristol would have allowed W to travel back and forth quickly.

[8] Losh's Diary reads: "Breakfast with Ward calls walks & c with Montagu and Wordsworth."

[9] The suggestion that W perhaps saw STC in Bristol is based on the fact of STC's having been in Bristol 23 Mar (see *STCL* I, 321). STC's return to Nether Stowey perhaps took place about the same time as W's trip there, if STC's reference to his feeling of depression on "the Saturday, the Sunday" after his arrival and to W's conversations, evidently of that time, as "rousing him somewhat" is taken together with (a) W's plan on 19 Mar to remain away from Racedown "a week or ten days" or "about a fortnight" (*EL* 163, 165) and (b) the fact that 30 Mar was a Friday (and

18. [Probably between Mar 29 or 30 and 1798 c May 16, 1798 July 2]

[Probably between 29 or 30 Mar and 2 July 1798 W hears from Poole the story of *The Farmer of Tilsbury Vale*. (See *Farmer* IF note; 1797:17; 1798:153.)

Probably between 29 or 30 Mar and c 16 May 1798 W hears from Poole at least the closing words of the story of *The Idiot Boy*. (See *The Idiot Boy* IF note; 1798:131; 1798:135.)]

19. [Perhaps c Apr–May, fairly certainly between Mar 29 and autumn]

W composes *A Somersetshire Tragedy*, [based on information from Thomas Poole]. (See 1797:17; Poole *B and B*; Bateson 130–32.)

20. [Apr 14; c Apr 14]

[On 14 Apr James Losh writes to W, and about that time sends him another large parcel of pamphlets (see 1797:14), contents unknown. (Losh Diary.)]

21. [1797] May 9 [and shortly after]

W writes to RW from Racedown on 9 May: DW ill upwards of a fortnight; little Basil has been very ill; W has a cold. Account of

---

31 Mar a Saturday)—although as STC's depression apparently lasted about a fortnight after his return, the younger poet could have gone home about a week before W came to visit him there.

A note with Poole's narrative of "John Walford" states that the friends at whose request the narrative was written were "Messrs. Southey and Wordsworth." Whether the note, dated 27 Feb 1833, is Poole's is not clear, and it seems unlikely that Southey was present (see C. Southey, *The Life and Correspondence of Robert Southey*, London, 1850, I, 305–11, and above, 1797:12n; cf Sandford II, 237). Poole himself, however, finishes the text of his article with the remark that "This narrative was drawn up in March 1797." As the narrative is fairly lengthy, it was probably not concluded in the month of Mar; but W would probably not have waited much longer than a month or so to write his poem about Walford. It seems moderately safe to assume that W would not have paid prolonged attention to the unrelievedly depressing materials of *A Somersetshire Tragedy* after he had worked extensively on *RC* or come to some understanding of the significance of *RC* for him—certainly not after late 1797, at which time he was in any case mainly concerned with readying *The Borderers* for the stage.

W's loans, totaling £500 [from Calvert legacy] to Montagu and Douglas; past financial arrangements with Montagu. W seeks advice concerning Robinson W's recent application to him for £250 of the sum advanced by the W's of Whitehaven to the W children. (*LY* 1335–38.)[10]

[Perhaps shortly after W receives £13 interest from Montagu. (See *LY* 1336; 1796:59.)]

22. May 16

The end of the Venetian Republic is proclaimed. W later writes of this event in *On the Extinction of the Venetian Republic.*

23. May 23

RW records receipt of £10 of the Calvert legacy on W's account under this date. (RW, correspondence with William Calvert, 1798, DCP; *LY* 1339.)

24. [1797] May 28

DW writes to RW [from Racedown]: Repeats W's request for advice about claims of Robinson W [see 1797:21]. Six shirts ready for RW. [*The Borderers*] nearly finished; their hopes of Sheridan's seeing it [see Appendix X]. (*EL* 166–67.)

25. [Probably June 4]

MH departs from Racedown, taking four shirts to RW in London. (She had arrived c 28 Nov 1796.)

Before MH's departure, W and DW write to RW: Renewed requests for advice about claims of Robinson W [see 1797:21; 1797:24]. MH carries the letter to RW. (*EL* 167–68; MS, DCP.)[11]

---

[10] On DW's illness see *EL* 254. EdS gives the date of the letter as "7th May," but the figure in the date on the MS looks like a 9.

[11] The letter is dated "Sunday morning June 5th." The Sunday referred to must be that of 4 June.

26. [Probably between June 4 and June 7 (–June 28)]

STC arrives at Racedown at teatime or before on a day [probably between 4 and 7 June. (He probably remains until 28 June.)] At his arrival he cuts off an angle in the road by leaping over a gate and bounding across a field. W's *RC* is read first; after tea STC repeats two and a half acts of his *Osorio*.

The next morning W reads *The Borderers*. (*EL* 168–69; *LY* 1263; *STCL* I, 325. See Appendices X, XIII; 1797:31.)[12]

27. [Probably between June 4 and sometime in July]

[W hands over *The Three Graves* to STC. (See 1796:72.)]

28. [Probably 1797 between June 6 and July 2]

DW writes [to MH] from Racedown: Description of STC. His visit to Racedown [see 1797:26]. Readings of *RC*, two and a half acts of *Osorio*, *The Borderers*. (*EL* 168–69. See 1797:33.)[13]

29. [1797 June 10]

STC writes to J. P. Estlin [from Racedown]: DW transcribes in this letter lines from *RC* corresponding to *Excursion* I.880–916. (*STCL* I, 327–28. See Appendix XIII.)

[12] Present evidence permits no certainty about the date of STC's arrival. The two facts available seem to be (a) that he arrived after MH's departure, which took place 4 June, and (b) that he arrived before Thursday 8 June (*STCL* I, 325). The *STCL* reference makes extensive mention of *The Borderers*; such references must have been inspired by the reading of the play mentioned *EL* 169, and this reading took place the morning after STC's arrival. So STC probably arrived at least a day before writing his letter of 8 June.

[13] The only certainties in dating this fragment are: (a) It was written on or after the "next morning" following STC's arrival (see 1797:26)—and probably after, or "this morning" would have been the phrase used to describe the time of the reading of *The Borderers*. (b) It was written before W and DW departed for Stowey. With regard to (a), it would be unusual to refer to "next morning" in describing the morning of a preceding day; "yesterday morning" would seem a rather more likely expression. I should conclude that, as 7 June was the first day, by any calculation, on which STC could be said to have arrived three days before, the letter was written not before 6 June. Moorman I, 317, and I agree with *EL* 167, 168, that the letter was written to MH.

30. [1797] June 12

W writes to RW from Racedown: Renewed requests for advice about claims of Robinson W [see 1797:21; 1797:24; 1797:25]. (*EL* 168.)[14]

31. [June 28]

STC returns to Nether Stowey from Racedown. (*STCL* I, 329.)[15]

32. [Between June 29 and probably July 2, possibly July 1 or 3]

[STC returns to Racedown from Nether Stowey. (See 1797:31; 1797:33.)]

33. [Probably July 2, possibly July 1 or 3–probably July 16, probably 1798 July 2]

STC, [having returned to Racedown,] brings W and DW back to Nether Stowey [probably 2 July, possibly 1 or 3 July. W, DW depart from Nether Stowey probably 16 July. They depart from the neighborhood finally probably 2 July 1798.] (*STCL* I, 334, 336; *EL* 170–71. See 1797:40; 1798:152.)

[On this period generally see esp. Moorman I, 321–400. W refers to the Alfoxden–Nether Stowey area: *Prel* XIII.386–410, *Prel*₂ XIV.388–414. (Walks with STC on the Quantock Hills; plans for *LB*. The passage refers esp. to spring 1798.)][16]

---

[14] These claims were not settled until Dec 1812 (see *MY* 698).

[15] STC wrote to Cottle 29 June that he had "returned from Wordsworth's last night." It is probable that he had not returned before this date, although such a trip is suggested by Campbell and others—for example, EdS *DW* 74—evidently on the basis of STC's remark of 8 June (*STCL* I, 325) that he meant to be at Stowey by the next Friday (which would have been 16 June). Margoliouth 4 thinks it most likely, as do I, that STC stayed on till the end of the month. Chronological conclusions based on STC's statements of his plans are based on shaky evidence.

[16] STC says that he brought DW back (*STCL* I, 336) and, elsewhere in the same letter, that he brought W and DW back (*STCL* I, 334). The conveyance, incidentally, was probably Poole's one-horse chaise (see *STCL* I, 329, 336; Moorman I, 321; Margoliouth 4). Could W have walked much of the distance? There seems no basis for supposing in any event that W and DW did not come at the same time.

The exact date of the W's arrival at Stowey is not altogether certain. *STCL* I, 330 (following EKC 77), gives it definitely as 2 July, and Margoliouth 4, 20, shares this judgment. I would agree with Mrs. Moorman (I, 321n) that it was "probably" on 2

34. [July 4]

In a ramble W and DW see Alfoxden for the first time. (*EL* 170–71.)[17]

35. July 4

DW writes [to MH from Nether Stowey]: The Stowey area described. (*EL* 170, 167n. See *Mem* I, 102.)

36. [Probably between July 4 and July 7]

W and DW discover that Alfoxden is to be let. (*EL* 170. See 1797:38.)

---

[17] The letter which *Mem* quotes as belonging to 4 July (see 1797:35) surely refers to the waterfall at Alfoxden (see Moorman I, 325); DW's letter of 14 Aug indicates that they had discovered Alfoxden on the day of the earlier letter.

July. DW later said in a letter dated 14 Aug (a Monday) that she and W stayed "a fortnight" at STC's cottage before moving to Alfoxden, and that their removal to the larger house took place "a month yesterday" (*EL* 170–71). But the date of that move is likewise uncertain. EdS *DW* 77, *EL* 170n, and *STCL* I, 332, all indicate belief that the W's moved on 14 July; Margoliouth 16 suggests "probably Sunday 16 July," a conclusion with which Moorman I, 321, agrees, and which appears to me correct: DW's 14 Aug date cannot be relied upon (W's dating of his letter of "Friday, August 16"—*EL* 171–72—is badly off; see 1797:55). But in her "month yesterday" she is probably remembering either an exact date (13 July), or a day of the week. On the latter basis, if her 14 Aug date (a Monday) is correct, a "month yesterday" would be Sunday 16 July. Charles Lamb pretty surely left Nether Stowey 14 July (see 1797:39), and later in the month asked STC (Lamb *Letters* I, 112) whether W and DW had "left yet," a question inappropriate had the W's left within hours of his own departure. Additional evidence appears in the report of Thomas Jones of Alfoxden to the spy Walsh that he had waited on table at the large dinner at W's "the Sunday after Wordsworth came" (Eagleston 83). If Jones is accurate—he was no intellectual giant, but he lived right at Alfoxden House—W could not have moved before Sunday 16 July: the great dinner included Thelwall, who had not arrived by the 16th (see 1797:44). On the other hand, the move had been made by the 17th, for STC spent the night at Alfoxden that night (Sandford I, 232–33). The most probable date for the move, then, seems 16 July, although the 15th or 17th is not an impossible alternative.

To return, finally, to the question of the date of the W's arrival at STC's, the fortnight's visit there which DW mentions would have begun, if the move to Alfoxden was made 16 July, on 2 July. One cannot be sure, of course, that DW means to indicate precisely fourteen days by her phrasing, but the assumption seems justified that the arrival was not before 1 July or after 3 July.

37. [Probably c July 7–probably July 14]

[Probably c 7 July Charles Lamb arrives at Nether Stowey for a visit. He departs probably 14 July. This is Lamb's first meeting with DW; he had perhaps met W in summer 1796 (see 1796:32). During this visit he probably hears or reads *LLSYT* and some version of *RC*. (*STCL* I, 334; Lamb *Letters* I, 112, and II, 126–27. See Appendix XIII.)][18]

38. July 7

W and John Bartholomew, lessor of Alfoxden House, sign an agreement leasing the house to W for one year "from Midsummer last" for £23. Thomas Poole is witness. (MS copy of lease, BM. Cf Sandford I, 225–26.)[19]

39. [Probably July 14]

Charles Lamb departs from Nether Stowey. [He had arrived probably c 7 July.] (See 1797:37n.)

40. [Probably July 16–1798 probably June 25]

[Probably on 16 July W and DW move into Alfoxden House. They reside there until probably 25 June 1798. (See 1797:33; 1798:152.) STC and Sara C perhaps come with them. Sara returns to Stowey probably on 17 July; STC probably visits for several days. (See 1797:41.)

---

[18] STC remarks that Lamb arrived at Stowey shortly after the W's, stayed for "a week," and left on a Friday morning (*STCL* I, 334). EKG 78 is surely correct in assuming that Lamb's departure was Friday 14 July; whether his arrival was Friday 7 July, as suggested by Chambers, depends on what STC meant by "a week." The 7th seems the best guess.

The "inscription" to which Lamb refers might be *Inscription for a Seat by a Road Side* (*PW* I, 301–02), but Lamb's phrasing is more suggestive of *LLSYT* (both poems were work done during MH's winter-spring visit); STC makes an indirect but almost certain reference to *LLSYT* in the letter of his cited above.

[19] *STCL* I, 332, gives 14 July for the signing, as do Moorman I, 325, Harper (R) 239–40, and Margoliouth 16n. JRM reads the badly written date on this lease as 7 July, as do I ("This 7th day of July 1797").

(This residence at Alfoxden probably contributes to *Prel* I.116–271, *Prel*₂ I.108–269—see 1795:34.)

W here observes his primary model for Simon Lee, Christopher Tricky, who lives near the entrance to Alfoxden Park. (*Simon Lee* IF note; W. H. P. Greswell, *The Land of Quantock*, Taunton, 1903, 285–86.) By c 16 May 1798 the incident occurs, near Holford, on which *The Last of the Flock* is based. (*The Last of the Flock* IF note.)][20]

41. [July 17 and very shortly after]

[STC spends the night of 17 July at Alfoxden, probably as part of a visit of several days. STC spends much time at Alfoxden in the immediate future. (Sandford I, 232–33; *STCL* I, 336. See 1797:40; Moorman I, 326–27.)]

42. July 18–[probably c, certainly by, July 27]

John Thelwall, who had arrived at Stowey 17 July, and Sara C arrive at Alfoxden before breakfast. W, DW, STC, Sara C, and Thelwall make "a most philosophical party." During this day W, STC, and Thelwall ramble near the house, discussing literature and politics. (Sandford I, 232–33.) [This ramble is probably the occasion of an incident recorded in different versions in *Anecdote for Fathers* IF note, STC *Table Talk* (ed. T. Ashe, London, 1884), 103, and Mrs. Andrew Crosse, *Red-letter Days of My Life* (London, 1892), 102: Thelwall perhaps remarks that a lovely scene here makes a man forget the jarring and conflicts of the world—or the necessity of treason. See also *STCL* I, 337: This ramble perhaps hurts STC's scalded foot.

Thelwall departs from the neighborhood probably c, certainly by, 27 July (see 1797:47). (On W and Thelwall see also Sandford I, 235; *PW* V, 471. For a comment on W and DW at this time see Thelwall, *Lines Written at Bridgewater*, quoted *STCL* I, 339.)]

[20] The conjecture of Moorman I, 326, that STC went over to Alfoxden when the W's moved there is reasonable. On a possible visit of James Losh to Alfoxden see *LY* 56n; what evidence EdS is drawing on in his record of this visit is unclear. W states that *Ruth* was suggested by an "account I had of a wanderer in Somersetshire" (IF note). W's ambiguous phrasing may indicate that he heard the account in Somersetshire; if so, the Alfoxden residence is the most likely occasion, but certainty is impossible.

43. [Probably July 21]

W, DW, STC, Sara C, Thelwall all walk back to Stowey. The discussion primarily concerns politics. (James Dykes Campbell, *Samuel Taylor Coleridge*, London, 1894, 73. See Moorman I, 327.)

44. [Probably July 23]

[*The Borderers* is perhaps read "under the trees" at Alfoxden. Later the W's entertain fourteen people for dinner, including the Coleridges, Poole, Thelwall, Willmott (lessor of Woodlands), perhaps also Thomas Ward, Mr. and Mrs. Cruikshank, and (though not very likely) Basil Montagu. (*STCL* I, 332; Eagleston 83; Sandford I, 235–36; G. W. Meyer, "Wordsworth and the Spy Hunt," *American Scholar* XX, Winter, 1950–51, 52.)][21]

45. [Probably between July 23 and Aug 18]

[W returns to Racedown for Peggy (their servant) and little Basil. Finds £22 there for him. (*EL* 171. See 1797:54.)][22]

46. July 25

RW records receipt of £20 of the Calvert legacy on W's account under this date. (RW, correspondence with William Calvert, 1798, DCP; *LY* 1339.)[23]

---

[21] Meyer's date must be based on Thomas Jones's report to the spy that he waited on the dinner "the Sunday after Wordsworth came" to Alfoxden. Thelwall had not arrived Sunday, 16 July, and he was gone well before 30 July. (Eagleston, Sandford, *STCL* as cited; see 1797:47). STC's note to Poole (*STCL* I, 332) must refer to meat for the dinner (Moorman I, 331–32), and thus must have been written 22 July. The Cruikshanks were to be lessors of Alfoxden after the W's (see *EL* 188); they are mentioned often in *STCL*.

[22] The £22 was probably mostly if not all from the Calvert legacy. Whether the date of 25 July W later gave the receipt of £20 from Calvert's estate represents merely the date of the remittance itself or the date he received it is unclear, but RW's accounts record the sum under the same date (see 1797:46). As W states that the £22 had been waiting for him "some time" when he found it, and as he could not have gone to Racedown until after 23 July, the date was probably that of the remittance. This suggestion would point toward W's having made his trip rather after 25 July, probably sometime in Aug. But there is no real evidence on which to establish W's whereabouts between 23 July and 16 Aug.

[23] Moorman I, 269, indicates that £775 had been paid by the end of 1796; W's figures, however, imply that the sum had even now reached only £585 (see also 1798:167).

47. [Probably c, certainly by, July 27]

Thelwall departs from Alfoxden and Stowey. (See Thelwall, *Lines Written at Bridgewater . . . on the 27th of July, 1797; STCL* I, 338–39.)

48. Aug 8, 11

On 8 Aug Dr. Lysons, of Bath, writes the Duke of Portland, Home Secretary, about the suspicious behavior of the Wordsworths. On 11 Aug he writes again from Bath on the same subject. (Eagleston 79–80.)

49. Aug 11

G. Walsh, government spy, writes the permanent undersecretary of state about frequent visitors at Alfoxden, and about late rambles and inquiries concerning local topography by the inhabitants of Alfoxden, as reported to him by C. Mogg, of the Farm House, Alfoxden. (Eagleston 80–81.)[24]

50. [Perhaps c Aug 14, certainly shortly before Aug 19]

[STC pays a brief visit to Bristol, esp. to see Mrs. Barbauld. (*Illustrated London News*, 22 Apr 1893, 500; *STCL* I, 340–44. See 1797:56.)]

51. [Aug 14 ff]

[Basil Montagu and probably JFP Jr. or Aza P arrive at Alfoxden. The time of their departure is uncertain; the visit probably lasts only a few days. (Eagleston 83. See Moorman I, 332.)]

52. Aug 14

DW writes [to MH] from Alfoxden: Their visit with STC in early July. Description of Alfoxden. (*EL* 170–71, 167–68.)

53. Aug 15

G. Walsh, the spy, arrives at Stowey; he writes to the Home Office that Alfoxden appears to him the nest of a gang of disaffected Englishmen. (Eagleston 82.)

---

[24] On the spy generally see also *BL* x; Sandford I, 235–43; G. W. Meyer, "Wordsworth and the Spy Hunt," *American Scholar* XX (Winter, 1950–51), 50–56.

54. Aug 16

G. Walsh writes to the Home Office: Reports on Poole and others. Has learned from Thomas Jones of Alfoxden about the great dinner [23 July] and how W has lately been [to Racedown] and brought back [Peggy and little Basil (see 1797:45)]. The arrival of [Basil Montagu and one of the Pinneys (see 1797:51)]. (Eagleston 82–83.)[25]

55. [Aug 18]

W writes to Joseph Cottle from Alfoxden: Thanks Cottle for 2 guineas and proffered financial assistance; will not need the assistance now (Poole has let him have £25, and he found £22 at Racedown). They are now settled at Alfoxden. (*EL* 171–72.)[26]

56. [Probably c and certainly by Aug 19]

Richard Reynell arrives for a visit at Nether Stowey. [George] Burnett is visiting STC. Reynell sees W twice during his visit, [at least once by 19 Aug]. (*Illustrated London News*, 22 Apr 1893, 500; *STCL* I, 340–41.)[27]

57. Aug 23

RW records payment of £5 loaned W by John Myers under this date. (RW, accounts with W and DW, 1816, DCP.)[28]

58. Aug 31

RW pays, for W, £7/10/6, [premium on £300 policy on Basil Montagu's life,] on this date. (RW, accounts with W and DW, 1816, DCP; receipt, DCP. See esp. 1796:54.)

59. [Probably between c Sept and Nov 12, and between Nov 20 and Dec 8]

W revises *The Borderers* for the stage at the suggestion of [Thomas] Knight. (See Appendix X.)

[25] Nothing further is known of the present activities of the spy.
[26] W's date, "Friday, August 16," did not occur this year. If he wrote on a Friday, as is probable, it must have been the 18th.
[27] STC was away when Reynell arrived; he returned 19 Aug. Reynell visited Alfoxden the day of his arrival.
[28] There is no record of when Myers made the loan to W; probably it was during W's last or next-to-last London visit.

60. [Probably early Sept]

[W advances] £-/5/- for Mary W. Godwin through [Francis Tweddell], who draws on RW. (RW, accounts with W and DW, 1816, DCP.)[29]

61. [Probably c Sept 6 (–probably mid-Sept, by Sept 15)]

STC sets off from Nether Stowey to visit W. L. Bowles at Shaftsbury, [taking *Osorio* with him. (The length of his absence is unknown, but he returns probably c mid-Sept, by 15 Sept.)] (*STCL* I, 344–46; *EL* 172.)

62. [1797] Sept 13

W writes to Joseph Cottle [from Alfoxden]: Thanks Cottle for proffered financial assistance. Proposes to be in Bristol within three weeks. STC set off a week ago with [*Osorio*] to see Bowles. (*EL* 172.)

63. [Probably mid-Sept, by Sept 15]

STC returns to Nether Stowey from a visit to W. L. Bowles. (See 1797:61.)

64. [Probably Sept 14–perhaps Sept 18 ff]

[Probably on 14 Sept Charles Lloyd arrives at Alfoxden hoping to hear the latter part of *The Borderers*. W is ill. The Wedgwoods are expected perhaps 16 Sept. Lloyd intends to stay until Monday 18 Sept. (*STCL* I, 345–46.)

This visit or the visit of the Wordsworths to London later this year is possibly the occasion of Lloyd's telling DW that STC is a villain; later (perhaps next Mar) he writes her on this subject. (EKC *RES*; EKC 95; Moorman I, 395. See 1797:81.)]

65. [Perhaps Sept 16 (–perhaps Sept 21)]

[Perhaps on 16 Sept] Tom Wedgwood and probably John Wedgwood (if not the latter, then James Tobin) arrive at Alfoxden for a visit

---

[29] Mary Godwin died on 10 Sept. RW's phrasing runs "advanced Mr Tweddall for Mrs Godwin," and the date is given as "Septr."

of five days. [They depart perhaps 21 Sept.] (*STCL* I, 345–46; Litchfield 51.)[30]

66. [Sept 17]

[Probably this evening Tom Wedgwood and others, probably including W, visit Nether Stowey. They call on Poole, but find him not at home. (Letter of Wedgwood to Poole, 18 Sept 1797, BM Add MS 35, 345, fol. 83.)]

67. [Perhaps Sept 18]

Charles Lloyd departs from Alfoxden. [He had arrived probably 14 Sept.] (*STCL* I, 345–46.)

68. [Perhaps Sept 21]

Tom [and John] Wedgwood depart from Alfoxden after a visit of five days. (See 1797:65.)

69. [Between Sept 21 and Oct 9]

[Some chance perhaps exists that W visits Bristol at this time. (See *EL* 172; 1797:64; 1797:65; 1797:68; 1797:71.)]

70. Sept 22 (–1799 Aug 1)

The *Duke of Montrose*, JW second mate, sails for "Coast and Bay." (It reaches moorings on return 1 Aug 1799.) (Hardy.)

[30] Litchfield quotes a passage from Tom's Nb which begins "Time, entering the garden at Langford, Sept 15," and appears to imply plainly that Tom and his companion returned *from* their trip to Alfoxden on 15 Sept, but the date of Tom's letter from Alfoxden, 18 Sept, also seems quite certain. I have been unable to locate the Nb quoted by Litchfield (I examined similar ones at the Wedgwood Museum, Barlaston) in order to check the passage in question. On the basis of present evidence, one appears to have no choice but to admit that Tom must be somehow referring to his departure for, rather than return from, Alfoxden.

David Erdman (*BNYPL* LX, 1956, 433n) and Litchfield 52n express a belief that Tom's companion was Tobin, but Lloyd's remark (*STCL* I, 346) that "the Wedgwoods are coming" seems to me the most convincing evidence on the subject.

71. Oct 9

W visits Thomas Poole. Charlotte Poole and STC are present. (Sandford I, 244.)[31]

72. [Probably between c Oct 11 and Oct 13]

STC is absent a day or two from Nether Stowey; his whereabouts are unknown. [He probably returns 13 Oct.] (*STCL* I, 349.)[32]

73. [Perhaps c Nov]

W receives [£40?] from Montagu, payment for one year, one month, on his annuity of £300, and for the insurance policy on his life. (See *LY* 1336, 1339; 1796:54.)

74. [Early Nov]

W, DW, STC make a short walking tour to Lynton, via the coast. [They possibly sleep a night at Porlock.] They sleep a night at Lynton. They visit the Valley of Stones. (*EL* 174. See 1797:79n.)

[This expedition gives rise to a plan to make the Valley of Stones the scene for a prose tale by W and STC in the manner of Gessner's *Death of Abel* (see *First Acquaintance* 120; Moorman I, 346–47); and probably within a few days *The Wanderings of Cain* is begun, but the plan for cooperative effort on it fails. (See STC's preface to *The Wanderings of Cain; We Are Seven* IF note; 1797:79n.)

This expedition is probably the occasion on which STC retires, perhaps to Ash Farm near Porlock, possibly as a result of an attack of dysentery, and writes *Kubla Khan*.][33]

---

[31] Sandford notes also that Penelope Poole once refused, at a similar gathering at Poole's home, to sing "Come, ever smiling Liberty" to Poole's friends because "she knew what they meant with their liberty!"

[32] On the question of whether *Kubla Khan* was composed during this absence see 1797:74n.

[33] *STCL* I, 348–49, concludes that *Kubla Khan* was composed a few days before 14 Oct, and EKC 100–03 seems to reach the same conclusion. Moorman I, 346, states

75. [Perhaps early Nov]

DW writes [to MH? from Alfoxden]: Their tour of early Nov [see 1797:74]. (*EL* 174.)[34]

76. [Early Nov, probably by Nov 4]

DW writes to RW from Alfoxden: Requests RW to pay premium on insurance on Montagu's life when due [see 1797:58]; Montagu will be in London in a week or two, or in Jan. Renewed requests for advice on Robinson W's claims [see 1797:21; 1797:24; 1797:25; 1797:30]. Difficulties in making RW's shirts. Thanks RW for £5. (*EL* 173.)[35]

---

[34] The sole basis for suggesting the addressee of this letter and the letters of 20 Nov and 21 Dec is that the only letters to an unidentified recipient dating earlier in the year fairly certainly went to MH (see *EL* 167–68n).

[35] This letter (DCP) seems definitely dated "November 11" by DW; but it is postmarked 6 Nov. The error in dating is serious even by Dorothean standards, but it looks more probable that she was wrong than that the post office was. Distances and coach speeds (Paterson; Joyce 290, 399–400), as well as the relation of the dates of other letters of this period and their postmarks, indicate that the letter was almost certainly dispatched by 4 Nov. It is possible that DW's "11" represents the two vertical lines of a "4," but other samples of her 4's usually have a firm crossmark (for a later example see Cornell opp. p. 256).

"late September or October 1797." See also Wylie Sypher, "Coleridge's Somerset: a Byway to Xanadu," *Philological Quarterly* XVIII (1939), 353–66; Alice Snyder, *TLS*, 2 Aug 1934, 541. In his letter of probably 14 Oct 1797 (*STCL* I, 349–52) STC does say he has been absent "a day or two," and some of his phrasing is suggestive of *Kubla Khan* and vaguely descriptive of scenes like those near Porlock (see *STCL* I, 349; Sypher). I agree, however, with the opinion of Margoliouth 18 that this early Nov walking trip was the occasion of the poem's composition. Margoliouth does not explain the basis of his conjecture, but it makes sense to suppose that STC should have retired to a farm "between Porlock and Linton" on this trip, for he was certainly (which cannot be said of the early Oct date) in that neighborhood. If his illness involved dysentery from the onset (see *STCL* I, 349), an immediate retirement would have been necessary. Nothing whatever is known of STC's movements during his absence of "a day or two" in early Oct, and it is hard to perceive why he would have traveled so far—well over twenty miles—merely to sequestrate himself for such a brief time if sickness was the cause of his leaving Stowey—least of all if his sickness was actually dysentery.

77. [Probably by Nov 6 (–1798 probably Jan 4 or 5)]

Probably by 6 Nov Basil Montagu is in the Alfoxden–Nether Stowey neighborhood, perhaps at Alfoxden. (He departs probably 4 or 5 Jan 1798.) (*EL* 173. See 1797:76; 1798:4.)][36]

78. [Probably c Nov 10–Nov 11]

W reads in Shelvocke. (*We Are Seven* IF note; 1797:79. See also *AM* n in *The Poems of Coleridge*, ed. Derwent and Sara Coleridge, London, 1852.)

79. [Probably between Nov 12 and Nov 20]

[Probably on 12 Nov W, DW, and STC depart on a walking tour at c 4:30 PM. They return probably by 20 Nov. (*EL* 174.) On 12 Nov W and STC lay plans for a poem which became *The Ancient Mariner* to contribute to the expenses of the tour; that evening or possibly a day later they abandon their attempt to do the poem conjointly. The plan of a volume which eventually ended as *Lyrical Ballads* is probably evolved also on 12 Nov, or certainly in the course of the tour. Their route perhaps takes them through Watchet (they possibly spend the night there), and it perhaps leads also through Dulverton. (*EL* 174; *We Are Seven* IF note; *AM* n in *Sybilline Leaves*, 1817; *AM* n in *The Poems of Coleridge*, ed. Derwent and Sara Coleridge, London, 1852; *Mem* II, 444, *Mem*, R, II, 454; *BL* xiv; Moorman I, 346–49; *HCR Diary* III, 86.)][37]

---

[36] Miss Margaret Crum, in her unpublished doctoral dissertation on the "Literary Friendships of Basil Montagu," expresses a belief that an anecdote about W told by B. W. Proctor (*Autobiographical Fragment*, Boston, 1877, 141) came to him from his son-in-law Montagu; if so, the event is likely to have occurred during this autumn and winter visit: "A most reliable friend" informed Proctor that during a visit to W in "the period of his poverty" he met the poet coming out of a wood with a "vast quantity" of nuts in "a bag or apron before him." The nuts were "for the purpose of helping out the scanty meal to which the family had to sit down on that day."

[37] DW writes on 20 Nov, a Tuesday, that they "set out last Monday." *EL* 174 makes it probable there were two tours about this time. The simplest and most convincing way to reconcile the partly conflicting evidence concerning the travelers' routes and the events of their trip seems to me that of Mrs. Moorman (with whom I disagree only on the date of *Kubla Khan*). On W's contributions to *AM* see the references cited.

80. Nov 20

DW writes [to MH? from Alfoxden]: The second recent tour [see 1797:79]. *The Borderers* has been sent to the managers of the Covent Garden Theatre. (*EL* 174–75, 167–68n. See *STCL* I, 358; 1797:75n.)

81. [Probably between Nov 20 and Dec 1–possibly Dec 15]

[Probably between 20 Nov and 1 Dec, W, DW travel to London in hope of revising *The Borderers* to suit it for the London stage. They stay at Samuel Nicholson's, 15 Cateaton St. (*EL* 174–75; Moorman I, 350–51; *TLS* LVIII, 1959, 341.) Basil Montagu probably takes care of little Basil in their absence (see *EL* 173, 175). They remain in London until possibly 15 Dec (see *EL* 174–75). W alters *The Borderers* at least somewhat by 8 Dec (see 1797:82).

During their visit DW and probably W dine at Southey's three times and call there once or twice. Possibly Charles Lloyd tells DW here that STC is a villain (later, perhaps next Mar, Lloyd writes her on the same subject; but see 1797:64). (*EL* 196; EKC *RES* 78–80; EKC 95; Moorman I, 395.)][38]

82. Dec 8

DW writes to CW from Samuel Nicholson's, London: W has altered *The Borderers* here at the suggestion of a principal actor at Covent Garden [probably Thomas Knight]. They are still awaiting word on the fate of the play. (*TLS* LVIII, 1959, 341; *The Borderers* IF note. See 1797:83.)

83. Dec 13

W and [James or John] Tobin call on Godwin. (Godwin Diary; See Moorman I, 351.)

W writes to Joseph Cottle from London: Thanks Cottle for the volumes of Amos Cottle's [translation of *Edda Saemundar Hinns Frøda*],

[38] Southey had almost certainly seen W and DW in London by 3 Dec (BM Add MS 30, 927). In the letter of DW's published in *TLS*, DW says they have been in town over a week. This visit was possibly the occasion of DW's first meeting with Southey; on her reaction see *EL* 481.

passed on to him sometime since by STC. He and DW plan to leave London Friday and travel to Bristol, arriving there Friday night. [Thomas] Harris, [manager of Covent Garden,] has rejected his play. (*EL* 174–75.)

84. Dec 14

The Convict appears in *MP* over the signature "Mortimer." [The poem was almost certainly sent in by STC under his contract with Daniel Stuart of the *MP*.] (See Woof *SB* 160–64; Moorman I, 351–52; R. A. Potts in *The Athenaeum*, 13 Aug 1904.)

85. [Possibly Dec 15–1798 probably Jan 3]

[Possibly on 15 Dec] W and DW depart from London for Bristol. [They perhaps arrive in Bristol sometime the following day. (*EL* 175; Paterson; Joyce 290, 399–400. See 1797:83.) They remain in Bristol until probably 3 Jan, perhaps spending some time under the roof of Cottle's father and mother.] (*EL* 175; *LY* 349. See 1798:3.)[39]

86. Dec 21

DW writes [to MH? probably from Bristol]: She, W have been in London on account of the play. Both W's and STC's plays have been rejected. (*EL* 175. See 1797:85; 1797:75n.)[40]

1798

1. [During this year]

[On writings of W possibly of this year see below and GCL 32, 33, 53, 57, 60–84.]

---

[39] W writes on Wednesday 13 Dec that they are to depart "Friday"; whether they did so is uncertain. The distance from London to Bristol was some 114 or 120 miles, depending on the route; even a mail coach needed over fifteen hours.

[40] Probably there is as good reason to suppose that this letter is to MH as there was to suppose that DW's letters of perhaps early Nov and 20 Nov were.

2. [Perhaps by c Jan 1]

W receives [£20?], representing 10 percent interest on the sum of £200 loaned by W to Charles Douglas in Jan 1796 (see 1796:3; 1796:47; 1796:74). The principal of the sum is not repaid as planned on 1 Jan. (*LY* 1336–37. See 1796:59; Moorman I, 296–97.)

3. [Probably Jan 3]

W and DW travel to Alfoxden. [from Bristol] (*EL* 175.)[1]

4. [Probably Jan 4 or 5]

Basil Montagu departs from Alfoxden or its neighborhood carrying five shirts for RW in London. (*EL* 175.)[2]

5. [1798] Jan 6

DW writes to RW from Alfoxden: Their arrival at Alfoxden from London, via Bristol. Montagu carrying five shirts for RW. Matters concerning clothes purchased in London, and a parcel "entrusted to Mr Knight." A message from [William Cookson] about newspapers. (*EL* 175.)

6. [Probably Jan 11 (–Feb 9)]

STC departs from Stowey for Shrewsbury and a short visit to Bristol. [He returns 9 Feb.] (*STCL* I, 369–70. See 1798:32.)

7. [Late Jan ff]

[Ménard enters Switzerland in late Jan with 15,000 troops and marches to Lausanne. This is the first military step in the French occupation of Switzerland. W later remembered that from the time of French violation of Swiss independence his heart turned against

[1] DW writes on 6 Jan, a Saturday, that they arrived from Bristol "Wednesday night." Presumably they left Bristol the same day.

[2] He probably would not have left with RW's shirts before the Wordsworths' return. He was supposed to be in Bristol the 6th, when DW wrote; so he probably departed before the 6th. He left the shirts at Nether Stowey (see Moorman I, 352); they did not get sent on till probably 24 Apr (*EL* 191).

Bonaparte and France and that he parted in feeling from the Whigs. See *Thought of a Briton on the Subjugation of Switzerland; The Convention of Cintra* (esp. Grosart I, 39). (See also *LY* 57; PREL 603–06; 1794:25.)]

8. Jan 20

DW [perhaps begins] her Alfoxden Journal. She makes a fragmentary entry [probably on this day] in the Alfoxden Nb, but does not continue her journal there. (Alfoxden Nb; *DWJ* I, 3.)[3]

9. Jan 21

[W,] DW walk on the hilltops and sit under the firs in the park. (*DWJ* I, 3. See 1798:8n.)

10. Jan 22

[W,] DW walk through the wood to Holford. (*DWJ* I, 3. See 1798:8n.)

11. Jan 23

[W,] DW go out walking at 3 PM; return after sundown. (*DWJ* I, 3–4. See 1798:8n.)

12. Jan 24

[W,] DW walk between [c 3:30] and [c 5:30] PM. (*DWJ* I, 4. See 1798:8n.)

13. Jan 25 [–before late Oct 1800]

[W,] DW walk to Poole's after tea. [On the road, going or coming, they see the scene recorded in *A Night-Piece.*] (*DWJ* I, 4. See 1798:8n.)

[3] On the probability of DW's having kept a journal earlier at Alfoxden or Racedown see 1796:76; Moorman I, 354. Knight, the last editor to see the MS of the Journal, knew of no earlier work of this kind (*Journals of Dorothy Wordsworth*, ed. William Knight, London, 1919, I, viii). It appears reasonable to assume, esp. from DW's frequent use of "we," that, unless the contrary is indicated by DW herself, W accompanied her on the walks she records. Little Basil was surely along often too, but I have not tried to guess when, and have mentioned him only when DW does. The village in which STC lived is described as "Nether Stowey" in entries based on *DWJ*, although DW regularly drops the "Nether."

[W probably composes *A Night-Piece* extempore, at least in substantial part. Composition of the poem in EdS's "MS" form probably takes place this day or shortly after, and the poem is certainly completed by late Oct 1800. (*A Night-Piece* and IF note. See *PW* II, 503; Appendix IX.)][4]

14. [Probably between Jan 25 and Mar 5 (–1800 late Oct)]

[W forms his conception of *The Recluse*. (*EL* 188, 190; *STCL* I, 391. See *PW* V, 363–64.) W engages in composition on *RC, OCB*, the Discharged Soldier (*Prel* IV.363–504, *Prel*₂ IV.370–469). He expands the significance and use of the character of the Pedlar in *RC* and designs use of *RC* in *The Recluse*. He probably composes *RC* materials in the Christabel Nb, the Alfoxden Nb, and in *RC* MS B, and mainly in that order, including materials contributive to *Prel* II.416–34, *Prel* III.124–67. (Some composition in MS B, esp. of concluding passages, probably takes place shortly after 5 Mar, esp. 6 Mar–c 10 Mar—see esp. 1798:16.) (See GCL 57; Appendices IX, XIII.)

W conceives *OCB* in its final form, and composes a version of the poem. (The poem is completed by 10 Oct 1800. See Appendix XV.) (The Discharged Soldier is completed in the form of *Prel*—18A variants —by late Oct 1800. See Appendix IX.)]

15. [Probably between Jan 25 and Mar 19]

W writes:

Fragments quoted *PW* V, 340–41, *II, i, ii, iii, iv.* (See Appendix IX.)

Lines on the Pedlar from which quotations appear on *PW* V, 413, and which include materials that contribute to *Prel* II.321–41, *Prel*₂ II.302–22. (See Appendix IX.)

16. [Perhaps between Jan 25 and Mar 5, more probably shortly after, esp. between Mar 6 and c Mar 10]

W composes conclusions to *RC* MS B, including "Addendum," corresponding to *Excursion* IV.958–68, 1207–75. [Part of this composition fairly certainly takes place between 6 Mar and c 10 Mar.] (See *PW* V, 369; Appendix XIII.)

---

[4] Although the word "compose," with W, does not necessarily mean "write," there is little cause to doubt that the poem was written down this evening or shortly after.

17. Jan 26

[W,] DW go out to walk before 2 PM. They follow the sheep tracks till they overlook the larger combe; return through the wood shortly after 4. (*DWJ* I, 4; 1798:8n.)

18. Jan 27

[W,] DW walk from 7 till [c 8:30] PM. Hear the manufacturer's dog howl at the murmur of the village stream [this experience contributes to unpublished variants for *Prel* IV.c 450–53 in the Alfoxden Nb]. (*DWJ* I, 4–5. See 1798:8n.)

19. Jan 28

[W,] DW walk "only to the mill." (*DWJ* I, 5. See 1798:8n.)

20. Jan 29

W walks to the top of the hill to see the sea. (*DWJ* I, 5. See 1798:8n.)

21. Jan 30

W calls DW into the garden to observe a singular appearance about the moon: a perfect rainbow, within the bow one star. The bow becomes a circle, then fades. They walk to the blacksmith's and baker's. (*DWJ* I, 5. See 1798:8n.)

22. Jan 31

[W,] DW start for Nether Stowey at [c 5:30] PM. They are overtaken by a storm and shelter under the hollies; leave the woods when all is clear. On their return they meet a storm of rain and hail at the Castle of Comfort. (*DWJ* I, 5. See 1798:8n.)[5]

23. Feb 1

[W,] DW set out some two hours before dinner to call on John Barthol[o]mew (see 1797:38). They shelter from the wind in a wood,

[5] The Castle of Comfort was a public house in the parish of Dodington (Poole *B* and *B*).

gather a burden of rotten boughs; sit with the window open an hour in the moonlight on their return. (*DWJ* I, 6. See 1798:8n.)[6]

24. Feb 2

[W,] DW walk through the wood and on the downs before dinner. (*DWJ* I, 6. See 1798:8n.)

25. Feb 3

[W,] DW, [and perhaps someone else] walk over the hills. [W and DW, or all three] return to dinner at 5. (*DWJ* I, 6. See 1798:8n; 1798:26; 1798:27.)[7]

---

[6] It is not clear whether they completed their call.

[7] The entries of the Alfoxden Journal for this and the following two days all mention walking with STC. But STC had been away since mid-Jan, and *STCL* I, 383–85, makes it quite plain that he did not return until 9 Feb. EKC 90, Moorman I, 353n, and Margoliouth 19, which report STC back by 2 or 3 Feb, did not have STC's previously unpublished letter (see the *STCL* reference) of 9 Feb to work with. On the other hand, no serious doubt can be cast on DW's datings at this time: her dates jibe with days of the week, even with indications of matters like the phases of the moon (she speaks of the half-moon on 25 Jan; the moon was then at its first quarter). The fact that our only knowledge of the journal is through Knight's transcription proves unfortunate here.

The suggestion of EKC 101, accepted by Margoliouth 30n, that the entry of 9 May, "wrote to Coleridge," was a mistaken reading for "wrote to Cottle" (Cot read by Knight as Col) is surely right; but conjecture as to whether another such mistake occurred here is impossible. There exists not the slightest evidence of an early Feb visit by Cottle (see esp. 1798:70). Visits and walks such as DW describes on the three successive days in question would have been most uncharacteristic for Sara C (whom DW would probably have called Mrs. Coleridge anyhow—see EKC 101; *DWJ* I, 12). They did not normally see quite so much of Poole, and DW would not so carefully have noted that W was her companion on two of the three days in walks simply to, or nearly to, Nether Stowey. "Poole" or "Tom Poole" or "William" would seem to bear little possible resemblance to "Coleridge."

The fact is that DW's phrasing is just the sort that she used in speaking of STC when he is known to have been in the neighborhood. DW at times wrote up her journal late (see, for example, *DWJ* I, 12); perhaps she mistook notes of her own, or her memory played her false, although three successive days seems too long a series of mistakes. The error is probably Knight's, but the correct reading remains in doubt.

26. Feb 4

[W,] DW walk a great part of the way to Nether Stowey [perhaps with someone] in the morning. (*DWJ* I, 7. See 1798:8n; 1798:25n.)

27. Feb 5

[Someone perhaps calls. W,] DW walk [with him] to Nether Stowey, returning by Woodlands. (*DWJ* I, 7. See 1798:8n; 1798:25n.)

28. Feb 6

[W,] DW walk to Nether Stowey over the hills, returning to tea. (*DWJ* I, 7. See 1798:8n.)

29. Feb 7

[W,] DW walk out to see cottage gardens; they go up the smaller combe to Woodlands, to the blacksmith's, the baker's, and through Holford. (*DWJ* I, 7. See 1798:8n.)

30. Feb 8

[W,] DW go up the park, over the hills, and, via a new pathway, to the combe. Sit on the heath. (*DWJ* I, 7–8. See 1798:8n.)

31. Feb 9

W gathers sticks. (*DWJ* I, 8.)

32. [Feb 9]

STC returns to Nether Stowey [having been absent since probably 11 Jan]. (*STCL* I, 383. See 1798:6.)

33. Feb 10

[W,] DW walk to Woodlands, and to the waterfall. (*DWJ* I, 8. See 1798:8n.)

34. Feb 11

[W,] DW, STC [who has probably called] walk to near Nether Stowey. (*DWJ* I, 8. See 1798:8n.)

35. Feb 12

DW walks alone to Nether Stowey. She and STC return in the evening. [STC perhaps spends the night.] (*DWJ* I, 8.)

36. Feb 13

[W,] DW, STC walk through the wood. (*DWJ* I, 8.)

"If Grief Dismiss Me Not to Them That Rest" is published in *MP* over the initials W.W. [The poem was probably sent in by STC.] (See Moorman I, 352; Landon *RES* 393; Woof *SB* 166–67. On the date of composition see GCL 36.)

Translation of a Celebrated Greek Song (*From the Greek*) also published in *MP* over the signature "Publicosa." [It was probably revised and sent in by STC.] (Landon *RES* 393; Woof *SB* 164–66. On the date of composition see GCL 7.)

37. Feb 14

W, DW gather sticks and sit in the woods. W unwell. (*DWJ* I, 8.)

38. Feb 15

W, DW, little Basil gather sticks in the further wood. DW "crosses the water with letters." (*DWJ* I, 8.)

39. Feb 16

[W,] DW go for eggs into the combe, and to the baker's; bring home a burden of sticks. It snows before they go to bed. (*DWJ* I, 8. See 1798:8n.)

40. Feb 17

A deep snow on the ground. W, STC [who has apparently called,] walk to Barthol[o]mew's and thence to Nether Stowey. W returns; he and DW walk through the woods into the combe to fetch eggs. (*DWJ* I, 8–9.)

41. Feb 18

[W,] DW walk beyond Woodlands after dinner. (*DWJ* I, 9. See 1798:8n.)

42. Feb 19

DW walks to Nether Stowey before dinner; W [apparently starts with her but is unwell and] not able to go all the way. She returns alone. (*DWJ* I, 9.)

43. Feb 20

[W,] DW walk after dinner toward Woodlands. (*DWJ* I, 9. See 1798:8n.)

44. Feb 21

STC calls in the morning. W walks through the wood with him toward Nether Stowey. (*DWJ* I, 9.)

45. Feb 22

STC calls in the morning; stays to dinner. W, DW walk after dinner to Woodlands. They meet a razor-grinder wearing a soldier's jacket and knapsack, with a boy to drag his wheel. (*DWJ* I, 9.)

46. Feb 23

W, STC, [who has evidently called,] walk in the morning. DW stays in. (*DWJ* I, 9.)

47. Feb 24

[W,] DW walk to the hilltop to look at the sea, return through the woods. (*DWJ* I, 9–10. See 1798:8n.)

48. Feb 25

[W,] DW do not walk. (*DWJ* I, 10.)

49. Feb 26

STC calls in the morning, also Mr. and Mrs. Cruikshank (see *DWJ* I, 10n). [W,] DW walk nearly to Nether Stowey with STC after dinner. Poole calls while they are absent. (*DWJ* I, 10. See 1798:8n.)

50. Feb 27

W, little Basil escort DW through the wood in the evening. She continues alone to Nether Stowey. STC returns with DW as far as the wood. (*DWJ* I, 10–11.)

51. [Probably between early Mar and c May 16]

W composes:
Goody Blake and Harry Gill. [Probably composed after 6 Mar. See 1798:62.]
The Complaint of a Forsaken Indian Woman
"Her Eyes Are Wild"
The Idiot Boy
The Last of the Flock
We Are Seven
Simon Lee
(See Reed *UTQ* 245.)

52. [Between possibly early Mar, probably early Apr, and c May 16]

[W composes *Lines Written in Early Spring*, "while sitting by the brook running down from the Comb." (*Lines Written in Early Spring* and IF note; *DWJ* I, 14–15. For other references to the same scene see 1797:42; *EL* 170.)

The incident with little Basil occurs on which *Anecdote for Fathers* is based, in front of Alfoxden House. The poem is probably written shortly after (and before c 16 May). (*Anecdote for Fathers* and IF note; *DWJ* I, 14–15. See 1798:131.)][8]

53. [Probably between Mar 1 and Mar 9, esp. Mar 6, 8, or 9]

W composes *To My Sister*. [Probably the composition took place on 6, 8, or 9 Mar.] (*To My Sister*; *DWJ* I, 11–12.)[9]

---

[8] There were some warm days in early Mar, but *DWJ* makes plain that springtime scenes of the sort described in the two poems did not occur until early Apr. Beatty's suggestion (Beatty *RP* 179), that "Kilve," in *Anecdote*, refers to Racedown and "Liswyn farm" to Alfoxden, is surely correct.

[9] There seems little reason to share the doubt of Margoliouth 23 that the poem was composed, as it itself states, on the "first mild day of March." Most early Mar days

54. Mar 1

W, DW arise early. (*DWJ* I, 11.)

55. Mar 2

[W,] DW walk with STC, [who has probably called,] part way to [Nether Stowey] in the morning; gather fir-apples afterwards. (*DWJ* I, 11.)

56. Mar 3

DW goes to the shoemaker's. W lies under the trees till her return. They then go to the secluded farmhouse in search of eggs, and return over the hill. (*DWJ* I, 11.)

57. Mar 4

W, DW walk after dinner to Woodlands. (*DWJ* I, 11.)

58. Mar 5

[W,] DW gather fir-apples, walk to the baker's and shoemaker's and through the fields toward Woodlands. They find Poole in the parlor on their return; he takes tea. (*DWJ* I, 11.)[10]

59. [1798] Mar 5, [6]

DW writes to MH from Alfoxden: *RC* has grown to 900 lines; the Pedlar's character now makes the most considerable part of the poem; DW is to copy the part concerning the cottage. They are to leave Alfoxden, which has been let. Vague future plans. W was unwell last week; is better now; his faculties seem to expand every day; he

---

[10] G. W. Meyer (*American Scholar* XX, Winter, 1950–51, 55) says that it was on the 5th that the W's were informed that Alfoxden had been rented to others. No source is given, but a conjecture that Poole came over for that purpose is justifiable.

---

were more or less agreeable, but the 6th is the first about which anything is noted like "a pleasant morning" and a "mild, pleasant afternoon." The 8th was clear and sunny after a foggy morning (but the poem refers to a pleasant morning), and the 9th had a "clear sunny morning" and was very warm. The 9th is surely the latest possible choice (see also Moorman I, 378).

composes with much increased facility; his ideas flow faster than they can be expressed.

Brief synopses and extensive quotation of *RC*, totaling 381 lines; mention of the existence of 200 lines descriptive of Pedlar, about 20 lines descriptive of the poet's feelings; [implication of the existence of other lines that (a) introduce the poem (the poet approaches a group of trees on a common at noon) and (b) describe how a fever seizes Margaret's husband]. Mention also of the part of *RC* which MH "has," and implication of the existence of "much more about the Pedlar" than is detailed above. [This MS constitutes *RC* MS B$_2$.]

A visit from Poole [5 Mar]. Thanks for a ham from Jack Hutchinson; request for a Sockburn cheese. (*EL* 176–87.)[11]

60. Mar 6

DW walks to see STC in the evening. W accompanies her as far as the wood. STC very ill from a bad tooth. [Probably DW returns to Alfoxden.] (*DWJ* I, 11; *STCL* I, 390. On this date see also 1798:53.)

61. [1798] Mar 6

W writes to James Tobin from Alfoxden: Thanks Tobin for a letter and *Gustavus Vasa*. Lewis's *The Castle Spectre*; W "easy" about [*The Borderers*]. The Wedgwoods' annuity to STC. Alfoxden let to Cr[ui]kshank; their own plans, which are not formulated. He has written 1300 lines of a poem conveying most of his knowledge, on man, nature, and society; everything comes within the scope of his plan. Needs travel books. Has not seen [Godwin's *Memoirs of the Author of A Vindication of the Rights of Woman*]; asks Tobin to pay his bill for newspapers. (*EL* 187–89.)[12]

---

[11] Although DW's letter is dated only 5 Mar, it states that Poole drank tea with them "yesterday." *DWJ* would surely have noted visits by Poole two days in a row had he paid them (nor would Knight have omitted this information in his transcription), and a visit is recorded only on the 5th. DW's letter is very long; she probably began it on the 5th, but did not finish until the 6th. Her mention of Poole comes at the end of the letter.

[12] The date of 6 May given this letter Moorman I, 609n must be a careless error. On *Gustavus Vasa* see Moorman I, 391. STC writes on 7 Mar that W has done 1200 lines of a great poem (*STCL* I, 391). What the lines—whether 1200 or W's total of

62. [Probably Mar 7 (fairly certainly between early Mar and Apr 20)]

W writes to Joseph Cottle [from Alfoxden]: Thanks Cottle for £10. Asks him to obtain Darwin's *Zoönomia* immediately, from John Wedgwood if necessary, and forward it to him by the first carrier. (*EL* 169.)[13]

63. Mar 7

W, DW drink tea at STC's. DW sees a dancing leaf [her description of which probably formed the basis of *Christabel* I, 49–52]. (*DWJ* I, 11–12.)

64. Mar 8

[W,] DW walk in the park in the morning. DW sits under the fir trees. STC comes after dinner; they do not walk again. (*DWJ* I, 12. See 1798:8n; 1798:53.)

STC's *The Old Man of the Alps* appears in *MP* over the signature

---

[13] As the letter (Victoria and Albert Museum) has a Bridgewater postmark, it dates from the Alfoxden period; a "1797" pencil endorsement does not look contemporary. A reasonable conjecture would seem to be that W wanted the *Zoönomia* in connection with work on his *Lyrical Ballads*, possibly for a purpose like finding out in detail about or checking the story of *Goody Blake and Harry Gill* (see esp. Moorman I, 389). Another reasonably safe conjecture is that when DW's note to Cottle of c 13 Mar (*STCL* I, 399n) thanks Cottle for "the books," which "have already completely answered the purpose for which William wrote for them," she is speaking of the *Zoönomia*. The Coleridges' having been at Alfoxden "for a few days" [since the 9th] implies that the best guess for the date of W's letter, headed "Wednesday Morning," is Wednesday 7 Mar. In any case, the letter almost certainly dates about the time of W's composition of the bulk of the other short-stanza poems for *LB*.

1300—included cannot be known precisely. PREL xlvi suggests the "Prospectus" (probably over seventy-five lines) plus, from contents of the Alfoxden Nb evidently of this date, work on *OCB* and the Discharged Soldier, and other work descriptive of the Pedlar, plus the 900 lines mentioned by DW as belonging to the RC (*EL* 176). A considerable portion of the *OCB* work in the Alfoxden Nb is rather sarcastic and topical (see *PW* IV, 236 *app crit*; lines 173–80 are drafted here also), and seems unlikely to be meant for *The Recluse*. Moorman I, 364–65, and John Finch's forthcoming article on the early development of *RC* make further conjectures on the contents of the 1300 lines; Finch's is the most advanced comment yet made on the subject.

"Nicias Erythræus." [It seems possible that this poem draws on work of W's which has not survived.] (See Woof *SB* 167–69; Smyser *PMLA* 422; GCL 34; 1798:105.)

65. Mar 9 (–Mar 18)

[W,] DW go meet STC and Sara C, who come [probably with Hartley] to Alfoxden for a visit. (They depart 18 Mar.) (*DWJ* I, 12. See entries below through 1798:76; 1798:8n; 1798:53.)

66. Mar 10

W, DW, STC, Sara C pass the morning in "sauntering about the park and gardens" watching the children play; see "the old man at the top of the hill gathering furze." W, DW, STC walk to the top of the hill in the evening. (*DWJ* I, 12.)

67. Mar 11

The children go down toward the sea. W, DW walk to the top of the hill above Holford. (*DWJ* I, 12.)

68. [1798] Mar 11

W writes to James Losh from Alfoxden: The Wedgwood annuity for STC. They are to leave Alfoxden at midsummer. W, DW, STC, Sara C have decided to pass two years in Germany, acquiring the language and learning natural science, probably at a university town near Hamburg; Losh and [his former fiancée, but now, unknown to W, his wife,] Cecilia Baldwin to join them. Suggests that Losh have [John?] Tweddell send him information on Germany.

W has been industrious during past few weeks. Has done 1300 lines of a poem, *The Recluse; or, Views of Nature, Man and Society.* (*EL* 189–90; Losh Diary.)[14]

---

[14] Mrs. Moorman at one point dates this letter 6 Mar (I, 378), but elsewhere (I, 363) has the correct date. This is the first mention of the plan for a trip to Germany; the project was probably evolved in definite form after W's letter to Tobin of 6 Mar in which he speaks of his uncertainty as to future plans.

69. Mar 12

Poole "returns to dinner" at Alfoxden with STC, [who has apparently walked to Nether Stowey. The others] do not walk. (*DWJ* I, 12.)

70. [Probably c 1798 Mar 13]

DW writes a note in a letter from STC to Joseph Cottle from Alfoxden: They have sent Cottle's *Malvern Hill[s]* on to Bristol; will send "the great Coat and the waistcoat" next week. STC, Sara C have been visiting here a few days. Thanks Cottle for the books [see 1798:62], which have already answered their purpose; will send them at the appointed time, or explain to their owner Pinney. (*STCL* I, 399n. See 1798:62.)[15]

W and STC offer their tragedies for sale. W offers *SP*, "Tale of a Woman" [*RC*], and a few other poems for a volume. (*STCL* I, 400. See Appendix XII.)

71. Mar 13

Poole dines at Alfoxden; W, DW stroll in the wood until called in by STC. (*DWJ* I, 12.)

72. [Mar 14]

[No record exists of this day, DW either having failed to make an entry for it, or Knight to copy the entry. (See 1798:8n; 1798:73.)]

73. Mar 15

DW, [having failed to note in her journal the events of this week as they occurred,] forgets how this day was spent. (*DWJ* I, 12.)

[15] This message can be dated only on the basis of the time of the Coleridges' visit; my date follows the suggestion of Griggs. A remote possibility remains (see 1798:62n) that the note was written a day or so later. The "great Coat and the waistcoat" are unexplained; it would be pleasant to think that they pointed to a visit by Cottle in early Feb (see 1798:25n), but even if they did, there seems no reason why the W's should have waited so long to forward clothing left behind. Cf Lamb *Letters* I, 112, 117.

74. Mar 16

W, DW, STC walk in the park a short time. DW writes a letter (addressee unknown). W ill, but better in the evening; [W,] DW, [STC?, Sara C?] "call round by P[u]tsham." (*DWJ* I, 12.)

75. Mar 17

DW forgets this day. (*DWJ* I, 12. See 1798:72; 1798:73.)

76. Mar 18

[The Coleridges return to Nether Stowey; W,] DW walk halfway with them. The W's shelter "under the hollies" during a hail shower on their return. [W perhaps writes "A Whirl-blast from behind the Hill" today; but see 1798:78.] (*DWJ* I, 12–13.)

77. Mar 19

W, DW, little Basil walk to the hilltop; meet a hailstorm on their return. Probably at this time, on Quantock Hill, W resolves to memorialize a thorn he notices there along with [a small hillock] resembling a child's grave. (*DWJ* I, 13. See 1798:78.)

78. [Probably Mar 19–almost certainly by c May 16]

[Probably on 19 Mar W writes probably the first two stanzas of *The Thorn*, which is probably finished very shortly after, almost certainly by c 16 May, and also "A Whirl-blast from behind the Hill" or at least a version of it. (*DWJ* I, 13; *The Thorn* IF note; [J. R. Dix,] *Pen and Ink Sketches of Poets, Preachers and Politicians*, London, 1846, 123. See 1798:112.)][16]

---

[16] *DWJ* plainly indicates that W wrote "A Whirl-blast" on the 18th and the lines describing the thorn on the 19th. What must be W's first efforts to describe the thorn, drafts for *The Thorn* 1–22, appear in the Alfoxden Nb, and a draft of the entire poem of "A Whirl-blast" appears immediately below (it begins on the same page and continues on the next). The MS indicates that all this work was very likely done at the same sitting, and that the "Whirl-blast" draft did not precede the *Thorn* draft. W could have done other work on "A Whirl-blast" the day before, of course, but DW could equally easily have been writing up the entries for these days at a later time (see,

79. [Probably between Mar 19 and c May 16]

W writes the fragments quoted *PW* V, 341, *II, v, vii.* (See Appendix IX.)

80. Mar 20

STC comes to dinner. W, DW walk more than halfway home with him in the evening. (*DWJ* I, 13.)

81. Mar 21

W, DW drink tea at STC's. (*DWJ* I, 13.)

82. Mar 22

DW spends the morning starching, hanging out linen. [W,] DW walk through the wood in the evening. (*DWJ* I, 13. See 1798:8n.)

83. Mar 23

STC comes to dinner, bringing [*AM*] finished. W, DW walk with him to the miner's house. (*DWJ* I, 13.)

84. Mar 24

STC, the Chesters, Ellen Cruikshank call. [W,] DW walk with them through the wood. [They] go in the evening to the combe to get eggs; return through the wood, walk in the park. (*DWJ* I, 13. See 1798:8n.)

85. Mar 25

[W,] DW walk to STC's after tea; return home at 1. (*DWJ* I, 13. See 1798:8n.)

---

for example, her entry for 15 Mar) and have gotten her facts slightly confused. This draft may at least be W's first written work on "A Whirl-blast." W's IF note date, Alfoxden "in the spring of 1799" (the poem is assigned to that same year in editions from 1836 through 1850), is obviously a year off.

86. Mar 26

[W,] DW go to meet [Tom] Wedgwood at STC's after dinner; return home at 12:30. (*DWJ* I, 13. See 1798:8n.)

James Losh receives a letter from W. (Losh Diary.)

87. Mar 27

[W,] DW dine at Poole's. Arrive home a little after 12. (*DWJ* I, 14. See 1798:8n.)

88. Mar 28

DW hangs out the linen. (*DWJ* I, 14. See 1798:8n.)

89. Mar 29

STC dines at Alfoxden. (*DWJ* I, 14.)

90. Mar 20

[W,] DW walk. (*DWJ* I, 14. See 1798:8n.)[17]

91. Mar 31

[W,] DW walk. (*DWJ* I, 14. See 1798:8n.)

92. Apr 1

[W,] DW walk by moonlight. (*DWJ* I, 14. See 1798:8n.)

93. Apr 2 (–Apr 3)

STC comes to Alfoxden to escape the smoke [at his cottage]; he spends the night. They [all] walk in the wood and sit under the trees. (*DWJ* I, 14.)

---

[17] DW says [they] walked "she knows not where"—presumably an indication that she had forgotten by the time of making her entry (see 1798:72; 1798:73).

94. Apr 3

W, DW, STC walk to [Crowcombe] "to make the appeal." DW, STC leave W there; STC parts from DW at the top of the hill. (*DWJ* I, 14.)

Robert Southey repeats a "singular but fine little poem" of W's to James Losh. (Losh Diary.)[18]

95. Apr 4

[W,] DW walk to the seaside in the afternoon. Caught by a shower in returning, they shelter under some fir trees at P[u]tsham. (*DWJ* I, 14. See 1798:8n.)

96. Apr 5

W, DW walk in the woods in the morning; DW fetches eggs from the combe. STC comes to dinner [and perhaps spends the night]. (*DWJ* I, 14. See 1798:8n; 1798:97; 1798:99.)

97. Apr 6

[W,] DW walk part of the way home with STC [who calls, or has perhaps spent the night,] in the morning; walk up the lesser combe, intending to reach the source of the brook, but dark and cold prevent them. (*DWJ* I, 14. See 1798:8n; 1798:96; 1798:99.)

98. Apr 7

[W,] DW walk in the morning up the [lesser] combe to the source of the brook (see 1798:97), and home by the tops of the hills. (*DWJ* I, 14. See 1798:8n.)

99. Apr 8

[W,] DW walk in the morning in the wood; afterwards, walk halfway to Nether Stowey. (*DWJ* I, 14. See 1798:8n.) [STC's *The*

---

[18] The "appeal" perhaps had to do with taxes (see *EL* 193). I know no really convincing identification of the "singular but fine little poem." Most of W's short poems written since early Mar would be likely possibilities.

Three Graves 468–500, 505–17 possibly refer to activities, feelings, and conversation of this day; but there is no evidence of STC's having been with the W's. (See Moorman I, 389–90.)][19]

100. Apr 9

[W,] DW walk to Nether Stowey; they meet STC as they return. (*DWJ* I, 15. See 1798:8n.)

101. [Between Apr 9 and Apr 15 (–Apr 18)]

STC departs for a short visit to Ottery St. Mary. (He returns 18 Apr.) (See *STCL* I, 398n; 1798:100; 1798:110.)

102. Apr 10

DW hangs out linen in the evening. W, DW walk to Holford. DW turns off to the baker's, walks beyond Woodlands, meets W on the hill. (*DWJ* I, 15.)

103. Apr 11

[W,] DW walk in the wood in the morning; walk to the top of the hill. DW then goes down into the wood. (*DWJ* I, 15. See 1798:8n.)

Lines Imitated from Catullus (*Lesbia*) appears in *MP*, signed "Mortimer." [It was undoubtedly sent in by STC.] (See Woof *SB* 169–70; Smyser *PMLA* 421.)

104. Apr 12

[W,] DW walk in the wood in the morning, and in the evening up the combe. (*DWJ* I, 15. See 1798:8n.)

W writes to Joseph Cottle from Alfoxden (a fragment of the letter survives): W is adding rapidly to his stock of poetry. Invites Cottle to visit. (*EL* 190–91.)

---

[19] If STC was speaking accurately in describing a "Sunday," there can be little question, in view of the weather (*DWJ*, *EL* 190–91), that this was the Sunday concerned; STC was probably away the next Sunday (*STCL* I, 398n; 1798:101). But *DWJ* in no way indicates that STC was with the W's any time during this day. If STC was thinking of some other day of the week (Sunday would be the day of the week poetically most appropriate for the scene described), 5, 6, and 9 Apr look like the best choices.

105. Apr 13

[W,] DW walk in the wood in the morning. They go to Nether Stowey in the evening. W goes to Poole's; DW stays and sups with [Sara C?]. (*DWJ* I, 15. See 1798:8n.)[20]

Lewti, STC's revised version of [*Beauty and Moonlight*], appears in *MP* over the signature "Nicias Erythrœus." (See Woof *SB* 170; Smyser *PMLA* 421; 1798:64.)

106. Apr 14

[W,] DW walk in the wood in the morning. Stay indoors in the (stormy) evening. [William Godwin's *Memoirs of the Author of a Vindication of the Rights of Woman* and other books sent by James Tobin, probably including books of travel, arrive.] (*DWJ* I, 15. See 1798:8n; *EL* 188–89.)

107. Apr 15

[W,] DW walk to [Crowcombe] after breakfast; they walk about "the squire's grounds." Return to dinner about 3. (*DWJ* I, 15. See 1798:8n.)

108. Apr 16

W walks in the wood in the morning. W, DW walk in the park in the evening. (*DWJ* I, 15.)

109. Apr 17

[W,] DW walk in the wood in the morning; walk on the hill in the evening. (*DWJ* I, 15. See 1798:8n.)

---

[20] DW says she "staid with Mr. Coleridge" and "supped with Mr. Coleridge." DW only once elsewhere uses "Mr." with STC's name in the Alfoxden Journal, and that in specifying STC and his wife as a couple (9 Mar). I suspect that Knight here misread "Mrs." as "Mr." It seems not unlikely that STC had left to visit his brother by now (see *STCL* I, 398n; 1798:101). Mrs. Moorman (I, 391) suggests that the W's spent the night with Sara C, but *DWJ* seems to offer insufficient evidence for such a conclusion.

110. Apr 18

[W,] DW walk in the wood in the morning; they meet STC returning from his brother's. [He had departed between 9 and 15 Apr.] He dines with them and drinks tea with them. They walk with him nearly to Stowey. (*DWJ* I, 15–16. See 1798:101; 1798:8n.)

111. [Apr 19]

[DW or Knight omits a journal entry for this date. (See 1798:8n; 1798:72; 1798:73.)]

112. Apr 20

W spends the morning in "wearisome composition." [W,] DW walk in the evening up the hill dividing the combes, come home the [Crowcombe] way, by the thorn and "the little muddy pond." They reach home at 9. [*Peter Bell* is probably begun this day. *The Thorn* is probably complete by this time.] (*DWJ* I, 16. See GCL 72; 1798:8n.)[21]

113. [Probably between Apr 20 and c May 16]

W composes first version of *Peter Bell* and MS 1 (if the two are not the same). (See 1798:112; 1798:131; GCL 72n; *PW* II, 527–28.)[22]

114. [Perhaps between Apr 20 and c May 16 or shortly after]

W writes:

"Away, Away, It Is the Air" (*PW* IV, 357–58). (See Appendix IX.)

Fragments quoted *PW* V, 341, *vi*, *viii*; 341–42, *ix*; 342, *III*, 1–11 (a draft). (See Appendix IX.)

115. [Apr 21, 22, 23]

[DW or Knight omits all journal entries for these days. (See 1798:8n.)]

---

[21] DW's record of the moon's being crescent, just preceding the note on the start of *PB*, suggests that the poem was possibly begun after their return from their evening walk. While most of the short poems composed for *LB* about this time probably were composed before *PB* was well under way, DW's quotation from *The Thorn* seems to make the completion of that poem by now especially likely. (Also see 1798:113n.)

[22] *PW* II (1944), 527, misdates the beginning of *PB* 12 Apr.

116. Apr 24

[W,] DW walk a considerable time in the woods, sit under the trees. In the evening they walk on top of the hill; find STC on their return; walk with him toward Nether Stowey. DW sends off shirts to RW [on this day]. (*DWJ* I, 16; *EL* 191; *LY* 1339. See 1798:8n.)

117. Apr 25

STC [calls,] drinks tea at Alfoxden; [W,] DW walk with him to Nether Stowey. (*DWJ* I, 16. See 1798:8n.)

118. Apr 26

W goes to have his picture "taken" [by W. Shuter]; DW walks with him. They dine at home; W and STC drink tea. [STC possibly spends the night.] (*DWJ* I, 16; 1798:119; Blanshard 42; Cottle *Recollections* I, 317. See 1798:124.)

119. Apr 27

STC breakfasts and drinks tea at Alfoxden. [W, DW, STC] stroll in the wood in the morning; [W, DW accompany STC] through the wood in the evening, then walk on the hills. (*DWJ* I, 16. See 1798:8n.)

120. Apr 28

[DW's only comment for this day concerns the weather.] A fair morning. (*DWJ* I, 16.)

121. [Apr 29–May 5]

[DW or Knight omits all journal entries for this period. (See 1798:8n.)]

122. [1798] Apr 30

DW writes to RW from Alfoxden: DW has sent ten shirts [including the five left by Montagu at Stowey—see 1798:4; 1798:116] and a parcel for Miss Nicholson to RW. Their impending departure from Alfoxden and plans for two years in Germany. W is about to publish some poems, for which he is to receive 20 guineas for one volume; and he expects twice that for another nearly ready for publishing. They expect to see RW in London before departing. (*EL* 191.)[23]

123. [1798] May 5

W writes to RW from Alfoxden: Sends RW release of Calvert legacy; gives account of sums received in payment of legacy. Problems connected with the legacy; W's wishes concerning funds. The current state of his affairs with Montagu. W's wishes concerning Calvert money yet owing him. (*LY* 1338–39. See 1798:140; 1798:148; 1798:167.)

124. May 6

[W,] DW "expect the painter" [no doubt W. Shuter] and STC. Meet STC as they are walking out; go with him to Stowey; hear a nightingale, see a glow worm. (*DWJ* I, 16. See 1798:8n; 1798:118; Blanshard 41–42, 140–41.)[24]

125. May 7

[W,] DW walk in the wood in the morning. STC calls. They walk to Nether Stowey in the evening with him. (*DWJ* I, 16. See 1798:8n.)

126. May 8

STC dines at Alfoxden; [W,] DW go to tea at Nether Stowey in the afternoon. (*DWJ* I, 16. See 1798:8n.)

[23] The two volumes of poems which DW mentions, and the 20 guineas which W is to have for one, must represent some arrangement with Cottle which was not carried out; the plan probably concerned the projected volume of *SP* and [*RC*] mentioned *STCL* I, 400 (see *LY* 1339; plans to publish *The Borderers* had fallen through by the end of Apr—*STCL* I, 402–03) and a volume corresponding to *LB*. For the volume which became *LB* Cottle eventually agreed to pay W 30 guineas (see *STCL* I, 402; *EL* 199, 225).

[24] The painter presumably did come.

127. May 9

W writes to Joseph Cottle from Alfoxden: Thanks Cottle for Charles Lloyd's works, three volumes of Massinger, and £13/6/6. Has not read "the novel" [perhaps Lloyd's *Edmund Oliver*] yet. They expect a visit from Cottle soon. W is determined to finish *SP*, and that Cottle will publish it; has been very busy with another plan lately. (*LY* 1339–40. See *DWJ* I, 16; *EKC* 101.)[25]

128. [May 10–15]

[DW or Knight omits all journal entries for this period. (See 1798:8n.)]

129. May 10

"The Hour Bell Sounds and I Must Go" appears in *MP* with prefatory note and without title, signed "Mortimer." [It was undoubtedly sent in by STC.] (See Landon *RES* 392n; Woof *SB* 170–72; Moorman I, 352; Appendix XVI.)

130. May 14

Berkeley Coleridge, second son of STC and Sara C, born at [Nether] Stowey. (See *STCL* I, 407–09.)

131. May 16 [–probably May 18, probably May 22 or perhaps a day or so after]

W, DW, STC depart, [probably in the afternoon or evening,] for a visit to the Chedd[a]r Rocks. They spend the night at Bridgewater. W's object is to bring back Lloyd [from Bristol to Nether Stowey. (DW, STC return probably 18 May, W returns probably 22 May or perhaps a day or so after.)] (*DWJ* I, 16; *STCL* I, 410. See Margoliouth *N & Q* 352; 1798:133; 1798:136.)

---

[25] There cannot be much doubt of the accuracy of the suggestion of EKC 101 that the *DWJ* entry "Wrote to Coleridge" was a misreading by Knight for "wrote to Cottle" (Cot read as Col), and that this is the letter referred to. The "plan" is probably that which produced the bulk of W's part of *LB* (see Reed *UTQ*).

132. [May 17]

[W,] DW, [STC complete their] walk to Cheddar; they spend the night at Cross. (*DWJ* I, 16; *STCL* I, 410.) [This day's entry is the last recorded as surviving in DW's Alfoxden Journal.][26]

133. [Probably May 18 (–probably May 22 or perhaps a day or so after)]

W, despite the fact that it has been learned that Lloyd has left Bristol for Birmingham (see 1798:131), departs from [DW] and STC at Cross, carrying a letter from STC to J. P. Estlin in Bristol. [W remains in Bristol until probably 22 May or perhaps a day or so after; DW, STC return, probably this same day, to Alfoxden and Nether Stowey.] (*STCL* I, 410–11. See 1798:136.)[27]

134. [Probably May 20, or perhaps a day or so after (–probably June 10)]

William Hazlitt arrives at Nether Stowey. Hazlitt and STC spend the night at Alfoxden and read MSS of W's. [Hazlitt departs from the neighborhood probably 10 June.] (*STCL* I, 413; *First Acquaintance* 122. See Appendix VIII.)

135. [Probably May 21, or perhaps a day or so after (the day following that described in 1798:134)]

Hazlitt, STC read [*The Idiot Boy*], *The Thorn*, *The Mad Mother*, *The Complaint . . . Indian Woman* at Alfoxden; return to [Nether Stowey] in the evening. (See *First Acquaintance* 116–17; 1798:134; Appendix VIII.)

[26] Margoliouth *N&Q* 352 suggests the possibility that they spent the night at the home of the dissenting minister John Howell. The correct interpretation of the date of DW's entry for "May 22nd, Thursday" (a day which did not exist) is without question that of Griggs: DW meant (and probably wrote) 17 May.

[27] STC was at Nether Stowey all day on the 19th, and had probably walked home on the 18th. He was pretty surely accompanied by DW. W most likely met Estlin now for the first time; STC's letter appears partly one of introduction. *LY* 349 possibly refers in part to this visit of W's to Bristol (W passes time under the roof of Cottle's father and mother); see 1798:142.

136. [Probably May 22, or perhaps a day or so after (the day following that described in 1798:135)–probably May 30]

W returns from Bristol, [probably with Joseph Cottle, who, if not with W, arrives about this time. He departs probably 30 May.] W [or they] stop first at Nether Stowey, where W meets William Hazlitt; W is there at sunset; eats cheese; [probably goes on to Alfoxden this evening. This evening probably offers the best choice for the occasion of the dinner of bread and lettuce described by Cottle.] (See Appendix VIII.)

During his stay, Cottle visits at Alfoxden. W, STC, and he visit Linton, Linmouth, Valley of Stones; make plans for the publication of *LB* on the terms stipulated "in a former letter," [probably 30 guineas]. They read MS poems. (Cottle *Recollections* I, 314–24; *STCL* I, 402–03, 411–12; *First Acquaintance* 117–18; Appendix VIII. See W. C. Hazlitt, *Four Generations of a Literary Family*, London, 1897, I, 233; *LY* 511.)

137. [Probably May 23, or perhaps a day or so after (the day following that described in 1798:136)–June 12]

[Hazlitt, STC, and perhaps others walk over to Alfoxden; W reads *PB*. W, Hazlitt walk to Nether Stowey together, engaging in metaphysical argument; STC walks with DW, tries to explain the notes of the nightingale to her. W composes *Expostulation and Reply* and *Tables Turned* on or shortly after this date, the poems having grown out of the conversation with Hazlitt. The verses are almost certainly composed by 12 June. (*First Acquaintance* 118–19; *Expostulation and Reply* IF note; *Advertisement* to *LB* 1798. See 1798:136; 1798:142; Appendix VIII.)]

138. [Probably May 30 (ff)]

[Probably on 30 May] Cottle departs for Bristol, probably taking with him MSS for *LB*, including *AM*. [It is unlikely that W added many poems to *LB* 1798 from this point.] (Appendix VIII; Cottle *Recollections* I, 315; *EL* 192.)

139. [Probably May 31–probably June 2]

[Probably on 31 May] STC [perhaps alone or with unknown companions, possibly with Chester, Hazlitt,] walks to Linton. He returns to Nether Stowey [probably 2 June. If this trip is made without Hazlitt and Chester, a trip with them is probably begun c 5 or 6 June (see 1798:143). (See Appendix VIII.)]

140. [1798] May 31

DW writes to RW from Alfoxden: W supposes the remainder of the Calvert legacy paid; wants £30 of it. W has some poems in the Bristol press now; has sold them advantageously. (*EL* 192. See esp. 1798:123; 1798:136; 1798:137; 1798:138.)

141. [June 4]

[W, STC are together during this day.] STC writes to Cottle of his and W's mature considerations concerning *LB* 1798. W interjects a sentence concerning type size. [It is not until after this time that the plan of the general nature and authorship of the contents of *LB* 1798 are finally settled in the minds of both publisher and authors.] (*STCL* I, 411–13.)

142. [Probably between June 4 and June 12–probably between c Aug 10 and Aug 25]

[Probably between 4 and 12 June W travels to Bristol. (See 1798:141; 1798:145.) He departs finally probably between c 10 Aug and 25 Aug. (See 1798:166.) W probably takes *Expostulation and Reply* and *The Tables Turned* with him, if they were not composed before Cottle's departure. (See 1798:136; 1798:138.) Probably during this visit or that beginning 2 July Cottle has a portrait drawing made of W by Robert Hancock. (Cottle *Recollections* I, xxxi; Blanshard 141–42 and plate 2.) W perhaps now passes some time under the roof of Cottle's father and mother. (See *LY* 349; 1798:133.)]

143. [Perhaps between c June 5 or 6 and c June 8 or 9 (three days)]

[Perhaps c 5 or 6 June] STC, Hazlitt, Chester begin a walking trip to Linton; they talk about *LB* and other subjects on the second day; return to Nether Stowey the third day, [c 8 or 9 June]. (See Appendix VIII; 1798:139.)

144. [Probably June 10]

STC, Hazlitt depart from Stowey. (See Appendix VIII.)

145. June 12

W, Amos Cottle eat supper with James Losh [in Shirehampton]. (Losh Diary. See Moorman I, 400.)

146. June 13 [–probably June 16]

W eats supper with James Losh, spends the night. [W visits Losh and his wife probably until 16 June.] (Losh Diary. See Moorman I, 400; entries below through 1798:150.)

147. June 14

W and Losh converse and walk. (Losh Diary. See 1798:146.)

148. [1798 June 14 (–July 3)]

DW writes to RW [from Alfoxden]: They expect to vacate Alfoxden 23 June; repetition of W's request [first made 5 May] for £30. (EL 192–93. See 1798:140; 1798:167.)

RW records remission of £30 in Bank of England notes to Alfoxden under this date. (RW, draft account with W and DW, 1816, DCP.)

DW begins a letter to her "Aunt" Rawson on this day (she is to finish it 3 July): Their impending departure from Alfoxden; plans for their trip to Germany; they must leave little Basil behind. Descriptions of little Basil and his progress while living with the W's. (EL 193–95. See 1798:153.)[28]

149. June 15

W and Losh converse; Losh hears W's poems. (Losh Diary. See 1797:14n.)

---

[28] RW's note is crossed off the accounts because of its duplication of a £30 remission, used in the final account, to Stowey in "July." I have used this date in view of the detailed character of RW's entry and the fact of W's departure from Stowey in early July (see 1798:153).

DW dates the letter to RW "Thursday 13th June." That Thursday was, however, the 14th. The letter to Mrs. Rawson was also dated the 13th, but I am assuming that DW was consistent in her dating error.

150. June 16

W and Losh converse; [W almost certainly ends his visit to Losh on this day]. (Losh Diary. See Moorman I, 400.)[29]

151. [Probably between June 16 and 24]

[W returns to Alfoxden. (See 1798:152; Moorman I, 400; *Mem* I, 116, *Mem*, R, I, 118.)]

152. [Probably June 25 (–probably July 2)]

[Probably on the morning of 25 June W,] DW depart from Alfoxden and travel to Nether Stowey, taking many belongings to store at STC's. [They depart from Nether Stowey probably 2 July.] (*Mem* I, 116, *Mem*, R, I, 118; *EL* 195, 197, 201. See Moorman I, 400n.)[30]

153. [Probably July 2–July 7; probably between c Aug 10 and Aug 25]

[Probably on 2 July W, DW depart from Nether Stowey on foot for Bristol. (Whether they walk all the way is not clear.) They arrive that night. They perhaps remain with Cottle through 7 July; they depart from Bristol finally probably between c 10 Aug and 25 Aug. (*Mem* I, 116, *Mem*, R, I, 118; *EL* 195, 197. See 1798:155; 1798:166.)

STC probably has not returned from his trip begun 10 June before the W's depart from Stowey. (See *STCL* I, 413–14.)

[29] Losh's entry is written curiously:

John & T. Taylor   who left us
conversation with   Wordsworth

It seems fairly certain, however, that Losh's characteristic method of noting at the top of each entry the addressees of letters he has written that day is being followed here, and that "who left us" refers to W.

[30] The *Mem* quotation describing the departure from Alfoxden and the July tour in Wales has, from its exactness, the look of being from a contemporary letter of W's or DW's, and not from anything written late in W's life (cf Moorman I, 401); it is probably a more accurate guide to the date of their departure than DW's statement of their plans on 14 June (*EL* 193). The passage in question states that the departure took place on "Monday morning, the 26th of June"; if the departure was on Monday, as is likely, the date would have been the 25th.

In Bristol. W possibly gives a copy of *The Borderers* to (Josiah) Wade for transmission to Poole (but see 1798:195). W probably draws on Wade for £2/16/–. (*EL* 200; RW, accounts with W and DW, 1816, DCP. See 1798:195.) The W's see Henry Gardiner (*EL* 201–02). A portrait of W is made by Robert Hancock (if it was not made in June) (see 1798:142). James Tobin sees *We Are Seven* and advises W to cancel it from *LB*; W refuses (*We Are Seven* IF note). W, DW probably visit (for how long is unclear) with the John Wedgwoods at Cote House, sharing the company of Miss Allen. (*LY* 852. See *DWJ* II, 117.)][31]

154. July 3

DW, in Bristol, finishes her letter to her "Aunt" Rawson (begun 14 June): Their departure from Alfoxden; visit at STC's, trip to Bristol; plan to go into lodgings at Shirehampton [see 1798:161]. Southey described. Bristol is hateful after Alfoxden. General plans about trip to Germany; mail problems in Germany. Income, expenses at Alfoxden and on German trip. (*EL* 195–97.)

155. July 8

W, DW [visit] James Losh [probably at Shirehampton], have dinner, tea, and supper with him, along with Warner; spend the night with him [probably tonight]. (Miss Warner and Johnson are also at tea.) (Losh Diary. See 1798:156n.)

156. July 9

W, DW breakfast with Losh; Losh walks with them. They dine at Mr. Warner's along with a Mrs. Fielder. [The W's perhaps spend the night at Cottle's.] (Losh Diary. See 1798:153.)[32]

[31] DW says in 1820 that it has been twenty-one years since W saw John Wedgwood, but it is unlikely that they met in 1799.

When the W's parted from little Basil is unknown. It might have been as late as after their arrival in London—that is, after 27 Aug.

[32] The entry in Losh's Diary for the 9th, that the W's visited "all night and at Breakfast," suggests that the W's breakfasted with Losh after having spent the previous night there. He concludes his description of his day's activities with the remark "returned to Shirehampton in the evening."

157. [Probably July 10 (–probably July 13)]

[Probably on 10 July W, DW depart from Bristol for a ramble of four days. (They return probably 13 July.)] They cross the Severn Ferry, walk to Tintern Abbey; spend the night [at Tintern. W possibly begins *TA* this evening.] (*Mem* I, 116–17, *Mem*, R, I, 118–19; *TA* IF note. See also 1798:156; 1798:152n. On the tour generally see esp. J. B. McNulty, "Wordsworth's Tour of the Wye: 1798," *MLN* LX, 1945, 291–95.)[33]

158. [Probably July 11 (–July 13)]

W, DW walk along the Wye through Monmouth to Go[o]drich Castle, where they spend the night. W probably begins composing *TA* upon his departure from Tintern. [The poem is completed probably 13 July.] (*Mem* I, 117, *Mem*, R, I, 118; *PW* II, 517. See 1798:157.)

159. [Probably July 12]

W, DW return to Tintern, go thence to Chepstow, thence back by boat to Tintern, where they spend the night. (*Mem*, I, 117, *Mem*, R, I, 118–19. See 1798:157.)

160. [Probably July 13 and shortly after]

W, DW return by boat to Bristol. W finishes *TA*, the last twenty lines or so as he walks down the hill from Clifton to Bristol in the evening. [Probably this evening in Bristol] W writes down *TA*. [Probably this same day or shortly after W gives the poem to Cottle for inclusion in *LB*. Probably shortly after W or DW writes an unknown correspondent] a letter including a description of their trip. (*Mem* I, 116–17, *Mem*, R, I, 118–19; *TA*, title, IF note. See 1798:157; 1798:152n.)[34]

[33] *TA* IF note says that W began his poem as he left Tintern; but elsewhere W said also that he had taken four days to compose it (*PW* II, 517). The "soft inland murmur" of the fourth line definitely places the scene above the abbey, where he would have been on the second day of his tour, but one might wonder whether he did not begin giving thought to such a poem before the first day was ended.

[34] The "July 13" in the title of *TA* probably refers to the date of the poem's completion.

161. [c July 14]

[W, DW perhaps enter lodgings in Shirehampton. (*EL* I, 195.)][35]

162. July 18

DW writes [to an unknown correspondent from Bristol]: W's poems are in the press; will be published in six weeks. (*EL* 198.)[36]

163. July 20

James Losh receives a letter from W. (Losh Diary.)

164. [Perhaps shortly before Aug 3; probably Aug 3 or very shortly after]

[STC sees W, DW in Bristol or Shirehampton perhaps shortly before 3 Aug; probably on 3 Aug or very soon after W, DW meet STC in Bristol or Shirehampton. That evening STC proposes that W, DW accompany him on a short tour in Wales. (*STCL* I, 414; *EL* I, 201.)][37]

---

[35] DW's statement of their plans to take up lodgings in Shirehampton, made on 3 July, seems (although its tone is rather definite) the only basis for assuming that they did. They probably did not do so before 10 July, and there is, likewise, no positive evidence to show that they made such a move afterwards. Losh's Diary indicates, however, that Losh, who was living in Bath at the time, wrote to W on 19 July and received a letter from him on the 20th, and other letters from him on 20 and 25 Aug. Moorman I, 408, states that Shirehampton was their headquarters for the next five weeks.

[36] One wonders—but can only wonder—whether this fragment and the apparent quotation from a letter cited 1798:160 might have come from the same source. MH seems the most likely recipient for the letter or letters, but no certainty is possible (see *EL* 167–68nn).

[37] STC does not mention to Poole, as one would expect if such plans had been formed before his writing, that W and DW are to accompany him to Wales. On the other hand, he speaks of his departure on his tour as imminent. He also says that he has seen W and DW since his arrival in Bristol. (He had left Stowey 10 June and visited Bristol, Brentford, and the Wedgwoods at Stoke d'Abernon (and probably London itself) in the meantime. (*STCL* I, 413–14; EKC 98). Probably STC saw the W's in Bristol before 3 Aug, as the letter to Poole was written on that date. He evidently proposed the journey to W and DW only the night before they set out.

165. [Probably Aug 4 or very shortly after–c Aug 10 or shortly after]

W, DW, STC depart from Bristol for a short tour in Wales at 6 AM [4 Aug or very shortly after]. During this tour they travel along the banks of the Usk and Wye. They proceed into Brecknockshire and visit John Thelwall at Liswyn Farm on the banks of the Wye near Brecon. They return to Bristol [and possibly Shirehampton c 10 Aug or shortly after]. (*EL* 201; *LY* 959; *STCL* I, 414. See *STCNB* 304; 1798:161; 1798:164.)[38]

166. [Probably between c Aug 10 and Aug 25–Aug 27 (and Sept 14)]

[Probably between c 10 Aug and 25 Aug] W, DW, [possibly STC or little Basil Montagu or both] depart from Bristol for London. They travel to London on foot, wagon, coach, post chaise, via Blenheim and Oxford. They are admitted to the presence chamber at Blenheim and see Oxford University. They arrive in London on the evening of [27 Aug]. (They depart 14 Sept.) (Losh Diary; *EL* 198. See 1798:165; 1798:176; *DWJ* I, 397.)[39]

167. Aug 13

RW records a credit of £367 to W under this date: "To bill of exchange & Bank of England Notes recd from Mr Wm Calvert

---

[38] Liswyn Farm contributes its name to *Anecdote for Fathers*, but the poem itself was probably composed in Apr. The travelers probably began their tour by going up along one river, and ended it, after their visit with Thelwall, by going down along the other. STC remarked to Poole on 3 Aug that he was to be absent a week. If they walked most or all the distance except when on the water, and if they paid more than the briefest of visits to Thelwall, a week would be a very short time for their trip—the more so if anything of STC's original plan of returning "per viam Swansea usque ad Bridgewater sive Cummage [Combwich]" was carried out. They may have spent somewhat more than a week. STC's movements from the end of the tour till mid-Sept are virtually unknown; see below and EKC 99.

[39] In view of the travelers' route and varied means of transport, their trip must have begun by the 25th (and see 1798:168; 1798:169). W's speaking of the expenses "per passenger" (£1/18/6) suggests that more people than W and DW made the trip. STC and little Basil are obvious choices (although the elder Montagu was not in town when they arrived—*EL* 198). John Chester is possibly another.

for your use." [This sum completes payment of the legacy of Raisley Calvert to W.] (RW, accounts with W and DW, 1816, DCP.)[40]

168. [Aug 20]

[James Losh probably receives a letter from, writes a letter to, W. (Losh Diary.)][41]

169. [Aug 25]

[James Losh probably receives a letter from W. (Losh Diary; 1798:168n.)]

170. [Between Aug 27 and Sept 14]

[W perhaps pays a visit to Josiah Wedgwood at Stoke Cobham (if so he is probably accompanied by STC). He arranges transmission of a MS of *The Borderers* to Wedgwood, probably through RW. (*EL* 199–201; Sandford I, 278–79; Woof *UTQ* 44. See 1798: 195n.)]

171. Aug 28

W writes to Joseph Cottle [from London]: The trip to London from Bristol [see 1798:170]. Their box has not arrived; financial matters; W wishes to sell his copies of Gilpin's *Tours* [see 1796:24]; can Cottle help him? W wants a letter of introduction to Longman from Cottle. (*EL* 198.)

RW records payment of £7/10/6, [premium on £300 policy on Basil Montagu's life,] under this date. (RW, accounts with W and DW, 1816, DCP. See esp. 1796:54.)

---

[40] This sum represents the £315 of the legacy that had been owing W since 25 July 1797, plus interest on this and the earlier sums that were paid after the legacy became due, less a £16 legacy stamp. (RW, correspondence with William Calvert, 1798, DCP; see *LY* 1339.) There is no indication that the £30 which RW sent W 14 June came from Calvert (see 1798:148; *LY* 1339; *EL* 192–93).

[41] In his entries for 20 and 25 Aug Losh writes the name "Wordsworth" in the position (at the bottom of the entry) normally given names of people from whom Losh has received letters on a given day. On 20 Aug and 1 Sept he writes "Wordsworth" in the position (at the top of the entry) normally given names of people to whom he has written letters.

172. [Between early Sept and Sept 14]

[STC, in London, visits (and dines with) Mrs. Barbauld; meets with Joseph Johnson the bookseller at least three times. During dinner at Mrs. Barbauld's, John Pinkerton, not knowing the authorship of *LB*, complains about the book to STC. STC perhaps pretends to agree to collaborate with Pinkerton in writing a review damning the volume. (*STCL* I, 420; T. C. Grattan, *Beaten Paths*, London, 1865, II, 133–34. See 1798:173; 1798:176.)]

173. [Probably c early Sept, by Sept 5, by Sept 14]

[Probably c early Sept, by 5 Sept, *Lyrical Ballads* is printed by Cottle, and at least some copies have been given out. News of the volume and its contents is fairly well spread, at least in London literary circles, by 14 Sept. Actual publication of *LB* has probably not yet taken place, unless on 13 or 14 Sept in Bristol. (Daniel *MLR*, esp. 408–10; T. C. Grattan, *Beaten Paths*, London, 1865, II, 133–34; *EL* 199. See 1798:172; 1798:174; 1798:176; 1798:196.)][42]

174. [Between Sept 13 and Sept 17]

[If *LB* is published at all in Bristol (which is not likely), it is probably published at this time. Probably during this period Cottle concludes an agreement making over his interest in *LB* to J. Arch of London. (Daniel *MLR*, esp. 408–09. See 1798:181; 1798:196.)]

175. Sept 13

DW writes [to an unknown correspondent from London]: [*LB*] printed but not published. Cottle has given 30 guineas for W's share of the volume. (*EL* 199.)

---

[42] STC remarks, in Grattan's story, that his conversation with Pinkerton took place at Mrs. Barbauld's "a few days after [the *LB*] were published," but DW's statement on 13 Sept (*EL* 199) that the poems were "printed, but not published" and the implications of W's letter of the 15th (see *EL* 224) must be taken as more definitive than casual comments by STC many years afterwards. There cannot, however, be much possibility that STC fabricated all the basic elements of his anecdote about Pinkerton, and the story at least offers sufficient indication that *LB* was relatively well known in London before STC's departure for Germany—Mrs. Barbauld, for example, evidently had a copy. The *LB* must have been that of 1798 since Pinkerton's faux pas resulted from the book's anonymity.

176. Sept 14

[Before leaving London] W writes to Joseph Johnson: Instructs Johnson to deliver six copies of *LB* to RW. (*EY*, letter no. 98.)

[W, DW, STC, John Chester] leave London for Yarmouth. (*DWJ* I, 19.)

RW records an advance of £13 cash to W previous to his setting off for Yarmouth. (RW, accounts with W and DW, 1816, DCP.) W leaves instructions for RW: RW to pay £20 into hands of Josiah Wedgwood on W's account; honor draft of Cottle for £9/11 [see 1798:177]; Douglas to pay £110 c 25 Dec to be disposed of to best advantage; Montagu's £100 to go to an annuity redeemable at end of three years (and assign insurance policy); receive [any money due W] from Johnson [the bookseller]; inquire about a receipt for Calvert legacy. (Memorandum, 14 Sept 1798, DCP.)[43]

177. [Sept 15]

[W, DW, STC, Chester] arrive at Yarmouth at noon. (*DWJ* I, 19.)

W writes to Joseph Cottle [from Yarmouth] (letter not surviving): W requests Cottle to make over his interest in *LB* to Joseph Johnson in London. (Cottle *Recollections* II, 23; *EL* 224. See 1798:174.) [Cottle has paid W, before his departure, only £9/11 of the 30 guineas W was to receive for *LB*. (See 1798:176; *EL* 224, 225.)][44]

178. [Sept 16–Sept 18, 1799 probably late Apr, esp. after c Apr 26, or very early May, esp. c May 1]

[At 11 AM on 16 Sept W, DW, STC, Chester sail from Yarmouth. DW is confined to her cabin before the anchor is weighed; extremely sick, she does not leave it until the ship arrives at the mouth of the Elbe, 18 Sept. W likewise retreats before long (and is quite ill, probably also until 18 Sept); Chester is also ill. STC is not ill. (*DWJ* I, 19; *STCL* I, 416; *BL* II, 132–41. On this day generally see esp. *STCL* I, 420–25.)

[43] On the state of W's English finances during the German visit see below, esp. 1799:33n.

[44] W later remembered the amount Cottle had paid him as £10 (*EL* 225), but RW's memorandum notes that Cottle was to be paid, in event of making over his interest in *LB* to Johnson, £9/11, almost surely the sum W had received from Cottle.

The Wordsworths return to England probably late Apr, esp. after c 26 Apr, or very early May, esp. c 1 May, 1799. (See 1799:27. On the German trip generally see esp. Moorman I, 409–36.)][45]

179. [Sept 17]

[W, DW remain ill. On this day generally see *STCL* I, 425–26; *STCNB* I, 335; *BL* II, 141–42.]

180. Sept 18

At 10 AM the ship reaches still water at the mouth of the Elbe. DW leaves her cabin for the first time since departing from England. The boat proceeds to Cuxhaven and thence up the Elbe, dropping anchor between 6 and 7 PM. [W, DW, STC, Chester] drink tea, retire between 10 and 11. (*DWJ* I, 19; *STCL* I, 426–27. See *STCNB* I, 335; *BL* II, 142–43.)

181. [Sept 19 and shortly after]

[The ship proceeds up the Elbe at 10 AM after a delay from fog. W, DW, STC, Chester transfer to a boat at Altona, and are rowed to the Baum-House at Hamburg. By this time W has become closely acquainted with M. de Loutre. W and De Loutre hunt lodgings; STC makes calls; DW, Chester, and perhaps De Loutre's servant guard the luggage. After an hour W returns and they proceed to the inn (where everyone but W is to stay), Der Wilde Mann; they find the inn dirty and expensive. They eat a makeshift dinner. W has procured a room at The Duke of York's Hotel, the lodging of his acquaintance John Baldwin. He probably moves to the inn the next day or very shortly after. STC joins the party at Der Wilde Mann; finds W and De Loutre drinking claret. (*DWJ* I, 20–22; *STCL* I, 416–17, 424, 427–28, 431–34; *STCL* II, 705; *STCNB* I, 336; *BL* II, 144–46, 148–55.)

Some copies of *LB* are surely in the hands of people in the Bristol area by this date. (Losh Diary. See Moorman I, 409.)][46]

[45] STC says DW retired to her cabin at once after sailing; DW's own less dramatic description is probably the more correct.

[46] Moorman I, 409, says they reached Hamburg on the 18th. *STCL* I, 431, 433, and *BL* II, 148–55, make clear that there is no significance for present purposes in the cancellation in *STCNB* I, 336, in which STC has first stated that W sought lodgings

182. Sept 20

DW looks at the market. [W, DW, STC, Chester] breakfast with De Loutre. DW walks with Chester for two hours. STC takes W to see Klopstock's brother Victor, who takes them to see Professor Ebeling (Professor of Greek and History at the Akademisches Gymnasium); they discuss the Greeks, the Turks, and other topics. [The travelers] dine (and are cheated) at the Saxe hotel; go to the French theater in the evening; dislike it and come home early. (*DWJ* I, 22–23; *STCL* I, 436–40; *STCNB* I, 337; *BL* II, 155–58. See 1798:181. On V. Klopstock see *EL* 199.)

183. Sept 21 (and Sept 26)

[The travelers] dine at the ordinary at Der Wilde Mann. W, STC, call with Victor Klopstock on G. F. Klopstock at 4. G. F. Klopstock talks with W in French for over an hour, largely about poetry (esp. on versification and English blank verse, the power of concentrating meaning in German, the English prose translation of Klopstock's *Messiah*). W, STC walk to the ramparts. [Probably on this day or 26 Sept Klopstock gives W a copy of (at least the second part of) J. A. Ebert's *Episteln und vermischte Gedichte* (Hamburg, 1795)]. (*DWJ* I, 23; *STCL* I, 438–40; *STCNB* I, 339; *BL* II, 169–74; note in copy of second part of Ebert's *Episteln*, DCP. See esp. 1798:188. See also *The Life and Correspondence of Robert Southey*, ed. C. C. Southey, London, 1850, III, 258.)

DW writes [to an unknown correspondent] from Hamburg: The landing at Hamburg. (*EL* 199.)

"with the agreeable French Em.," but later marked out the first four words. They also make clear that M. de Loutre, whose company the group shared in Hamburg (*DWJ* I, 21, 22, 24, 26, 28), is the French emigrant mentioned in *STCL* I, 416, 424, 431, as among their fellow passengers on the voyage. De Loutre's plan of residing near Hamburg had evidently already been put into effect before the W's' departure for Goslar (see 1798:190; 1798:192); previous to that he was probably of the party at most meals when the others dined together and much of the rest of the time.

[John] Baldwin was the brother of Cecilia Baldwin, wife of James Losh (see Venn; Moorman I, 257, 400). *STCL* I, 433, says that W found a bed at "Sea Man's Hotel," which must be the same as "The Duke of York's hotel, kept by Seaman" mentioned *STCL* II, 705. James Losh notes in his diary under 19 Sept: "Coleridge and Wordsworth's poems aloud."

184. Sept 22

W, STC, [and no doubt DW and Chester] ponder their eventual destination and the possible expense of a journey to Weimar. Victor Klopstock recommends Ratzeburg, offering a letter of introduction [to Amtmann Bruner] which they accept. [STC is selected to go there and investigate.] (*STCL* I, 446; *STCNB* I, 340, 342.)

185. Sept 23 (–Sept 24, 27)

DW unwell in the morning. [The party] dine at the ordinary at 12. W departs for Harburg at 3:30 (he returns next day); [W, DW, probably STC and Chester] look into a church on the way to the boat. STC leaves in the diligence at 5 for Ratzeburg (he arrives 24 Sept; returns 27 Sept). Chester accompanies DW towards Altona; they return by the ramparts. (*DWJ* I, 23–24; *STCL* I, 443–44, 446–48; *STCNB* I, 341; *BL* II, 165.)[47]

186. [Sept 24]

W returns from Harburg. (*DWJ* I, 24.)

187. [Sept 25]

[W,] DW see some French pictures with De Loutre. (*DWJ* I, 24.)

188. Sept 26; [probably between Sept 26 and 1799 Feb 23]

On 26 Sept W calls on G. F. Klopstock. He takes him a copy of *The Analytical Review* with a review of Cumberland's *Calvary* and some specimens of a blank verse translation of the *Messiah*. Their conversation covers a wide range of literary topics. W, DW dine with Victor Klopstock (see 1798:182–184), his wife, his child, a young German, a niece of Klopstock's, the poet Klopstock and his wife; they spend the afternoon there. W and G. F. Klopstock carry on a conversation during the whole afternoon, covering a wide range of literary and philosophical topics. W, DW return home a little after 7.

---

[47] W's trip to Harburg seems to have concerned the hiring (or purchase) of a carriage—no doubt for their projected trip to Weimar, Ratzeburg, or wherever they should decide to go.

[Probably today or shortly after] W makes notes of his conversations with Klopstock in MS Journal 5. (The first conversation is referred to in W's *Essay, Supplementary to the Preface*—see *PW* II, 422.) (*DWJ* I, 24–25; *STCL* I, 443–45; *EL* 432, 482; *Mem* I, 128–31, *Mem*, R, I, 130–33; *BL* II, 175–79. See the last four references for additional details of W's visits and conversations with Klopstock.)

STC makes an agreement for board and lodging for himself and Chester in Ratzeburg. (*STCNB* I, 344.)

[Probably between 26 Sept and 23 Feb 1799] W writes a fragment of a Moral Essay in MS Journal 5. (See GCL 77.)

189. Sept 27

W, DW set out at noon, walk a mile and a half beyond Altona. On their return they meet a drunken man and the first beggar they have seen in Hamburg. [On this day] they see a man beating a woman. They get cakes and bread, [and probably today] W is cheated by a baker. DW lies down till STC's return. STC arrives at the inn, having walked from Empfield; informs W, DW that Ratzeburg is beautiful but very expensive. (*DWJ* I, 25–27; *EL* 199–200; *STCNB* I, 345–47; *BL* II, 168.)[48]

190. Sept 28

[Probably on this day] W indicates a determination to seek lodgings toward the South. [On or by this day] the landlord cheats the party of 4 guineas on their bill. [W, DW] settle accounts with De Loutre, [who evidently departs for other lodgings; see 1798:181n]; seek STC at the bookseller's; go to the promenade. The party dines at the Ordinary. After dinner W, STC walk to Altona; observe the prostitutes all in one street; walk on the ramparts; see a splendid sunset. (*DWJ* I, 26–27; *STCL* I, 456; *STCNB* I, 346.)[49]

[48] The stories of the beaten woman and the baker occur in the *DWJ* entry for 28 Sept, but are preceded by the word "yesterday," apparently meant to apply to both items.

[49] *STCL* would imply that STC returned from Ratzeburg to find W determined on seeking residence in the South; but W probably did not reach this decision before he had heard from STC about Ratzeburg (see 1798:189).

191. Sept 29

[W,] DW visit St. Christopher's Church in the morning; take places in the [Braunschweig] coach for the following Wednesday [3 Oct]; W carries two trunks to the post in the rain. W, DW, STC, Chester walk on the promenade; dine at the ordinary at 12:30. The party is disappointed by the lack of celebration for St. Michael's Day. (*DWJ* I, 27–28; *STCL* I, 456; *STCNB* I, 347; *BL* II, 174.)

RW records payment of "Mr. J. Wade's Draft of Bristol by [W's] order" of £2/16/– under this date. (RW, accounts with W and DW, 1816, DCP. See 1798:153.)

192. Sept 30

STC, Chester depart for Ratzeburg at 7 AM; [W, DW see them off]; W calls on De Loutre, discusses the price of bread. W, DW set out at 11:30 on a walk to Blankenese and a pretty village half a league further. They see a Jew mistreated; see Klopstock in a carriage; dine by the river; walk along the river to Altona; reach home between 5 and 6. W sleeps; they sup at the ordinary. (*DWJ* I, 28–31; *STCL* I, 456.)

STC, Chester arrive in Ratzeburg this evening; enter their lodgings. (*STCL* I, 457.)

193. Oct 1

DW breakfasts in her room. W calls on [Victor] Klopstock to inquire about the road into Saxony. [W, DW] buy [Bürger's] Poems, Percy's *Reliques of Ancient English Poetry*; sit an hour at the shop of Remnant the bookseller. [W, DW] walk on the ramparts; dine at the ordinary, drink tea in the afternoon. (*DWJ* I, 31. See also *HCR & W Circle* 871.)

CW is elected fellow of Trinity College, Cambridge. (*Mem* I, 31.)

194. Oct 2

W draws on the Wedgwoods for £32/7/3 through the Von Axens, who act as the Wedgwoods' Hamburg bankers. (Wedgwood accounts, Wedgwood Museum, Barlaston. See Eliza Meteyard, *A Group of Englishmen*, London, 1871, 99.)

195. Oct 3

W writes to Thomas Poole from Hamburg: The town; Victor Klopstock; the infamous baker [see 1798:189]; scenic observations. Their projected trip to Brunswick. STC is at Ratzeburg. Klopstock the poet. W has sent a copy of [*The Borderers*] to Poole through Wade. Ward is to transcribe it and Poole is to transmit the original to Wade. The belongings of the W's at STC's need a dry place, airing; W would like Alfoxden back. (*EL* 199–201.)[50]

W writes to Henry Gardiner from Hamburg: The trip to Hamburg. Regrets missing Gardiner in Bristol; they had gone off unexpectedly to Wales [see 1798:165]. Hamburg. W is ignorant of who is publishing *LB*. (*EL* 201–02.)

W, DW depart from Hamburg at 5 PM in the diligence for [Braunschweig]. DW quickly becomes ill. (*DWJ* I, 31–32; *EL* 202.)

196. [Oct 4]

The diligence party stop for coffee at 1 AM; cross the Elbe; stop at another public house, arrive at next station at 5:30. W, DW breakfast at Luneburg; dine about 4 in a pretty little town. (*DWJ* I, 32–33; *EL* 202.)

[50] DW writes of the copy of *The Borderers* early the following year in terms that can leave little doubt that it is the only copy W left behind him in England (*EL* 214). Evidence about what was done with it at W's departure is ambiguous. W here writes Poole, 3 Oct 1798, that he had sent "a copy" of his tragedy by Wade; and W could easily have left it with Wade in Bristol for transmission to Poole at his convenience. But Poole, who had been wanting the copy in early Sept (BM Add MS 35, 343; see also *STCL* I, 415) wrote STC on 8 Oct (probably before receiving W's letter of the 3rd) that he was to receive the play "from the Wedgwoods" (Sandford I, 278–79), and DW's reference to the copy on 3 Feb 1799 speaks of it as left originally with RW to be sent to Josiah Wedgwood, Wedgwood having been supposed to sent it to CW (Poole is not mentioned). Miss Nicholson was to receive MSS (see *EL* 216) from RW, but whether *The Borderers* was to be included is uncertain. The evidence seems to point to Wedgwood's having virtual charge of the MS for at least a time (see also Woof *UTQ* 44–46), with responsibility for sending it on to CW and Poole both. It was in CW's hands before 28 Dec. Thomas Manning had read it in Cambridge before that date, and CW and Charles Lloyd carried it to Birmingham, where Lloyd wrote on that date of having it, and having read it "again" (Lloyd to Manning, 28 Dec 1798, Cornell Collection; see Lamb *Letters* I, 210). But DW had received no word that it had reached Poole by 3 Feb. It is perhaps just possible that W was referring in his letter of 3 Oct to *A Somersetshire Tragedy*, but the chance is remote.

The second issue of *Lyrical Ballads* is published in London on this day. (*Morning Chronicle*, *Times*, *Morning Herald*. See Daniel *MLR* 407.)

197. [Oct 5]

W, DW arrive at [Braunschweig] between 3 and 4 PM; take places in the Goslar diligence; dine at The English Arms or King of England. (The party of six eats well, consumes two bottles of wine, a bottle of beer.) They walk about after, sleep at the inn where they ate. (*DWJ* I, 33; *EL* 202.)

198. Oct 6–[1799 probably Feb 23]

On 6 Oct W, DW rise shortly after 7 AM; leave their inn; probably breakfast on apples and bread. They set off at 8 in the diligence for Goslar. They arrive at Goslar [between 5 and 8] PM. On this day or shortly after they take lodgings in the home of Frau [Deppermann] at 86 Breitestrasse. [They depart from Goslar probably 23 Feb 1799.] (*DWJ* I, 34; Harper, R, 282; EdS *DW* 99; *EL* 202, 216–17. See 1799:12.)

[On the W's stay at Goslar generally see esp. Moorman I, 413–33.

W refers to Goslar: *Prel* VIII.324–53; *Prel*₂ VIII.185–215 (pastoral tract seen in his walks); *Written in Germany* and IF note (the extremely cold winter; a kingfisher). (See also *DWJ* I, 222.)][51]

199. [Probably between 1798 Oct 6 and 1800 c June 5]

W composes early version of what is now *Prel* I. (See 1798:201; also esp. *GCL* 63.)

200. [Probably between Oct 6 and 1799 Feb 23 or, almost certainly, 1799 late Apr]

[Probably at Goslar, almost certainly before leaving Germany,] W composes:
  The Danish Boy. (See *Danish Boy* IF note; W's note 1827.)[52]
  Ruth. (*Ruth* IF note.)
  To a Sexton. (*To a Sexton* IF note.)

---

[51] DW's account of their trip to Goslar was probably written up shortly after their arrival.

[52] A few lines of draft for *Danish Boy* appear in the Christabel Nb, and could have been entered any time up to 15 Oct 1800, when the poem was copied in final MS

The Matthew Poems (see GCL 79): *Matthew; The Fountain; The Two April Mornings;* "Could I the Priest's Consent Have Gained" (*PW* IV, 452–53); "Remembering How Thou Didst Beguile" (*PW* IV, 453–55); *Address to the Scholars of the Village School* (IF note. See also Appendix IX.)

[W probably does not compose "I Travelled among Unknown Men" here. See *PW* II, 472.][53]

201. [Probably between Oct 6 and 1799 Feb 23]

[Probably at Goslar] W composes:
Lucy Gray. (*Lucy Gray* IF note.)[54]
Written in Germany on One of the Coldest Days of the Century. (*Written in Germany* and IF note.)[55]
A Poet's Epitaph. (*Written in Germany* IF note.)

---

[53] All the Matthew Poems published in W's lifetime were, when dated by him, dated 1799, except the *Address*, which is dated 1798. The IF note to the *Address* states that it was written in Goslar. Probably all were composed within a short period of one another. It would be easy to imagine that the relatively crude "Remembering How" (which clearly bears a close relation to the *Address*, esp. its "Dirge") and "Could I," along with the *Address* itself, were the earliest of the Matthew Poems, but I do not think that W's slightly different date for *Address* offers safe grounds for concluding more than that there is a small chance that *Matthew, The Fountain,* and *Two April Mornings* were of 1799 as opposed to *Address*'s 1798. It is probably fair to suppose, in view of common subject matter and the fact that most of W's Goslar work was based on his childhood, that *Address* was a Goslar poem, and the other five were probably Goslar poems, or at least German. EdS states that "Remembering How" and "Could I" appear in a Nb in use at Alfoxden; they appear in Nb 18A, which cannot be shown on the basis of present evidence to have been in use until after the Alfoxden period (see Appendix IX). I should guess that W's final prepublication work on the poems, including the full title of the *Address*, was not completed until after his visit to Hawkshead of 2 Nov 1799. (See Appendix IX.)

[54] As in cases cited above (see 1798:200n), I have not felt quite confident of W's accuracy in his "1799," but have counted his "Goslar" as probably correct.

[55] DW states that Christmas day was the coldest day of the century (*EL* 212). W's title might refer to that day, but of course no definite conclusion is possible. W dated the poem 1798 from 1815 through 1824, 1799 from 1836 through 1850.

---

form (see Appendix VIII); but as the last line of the draft is "And happy &c" (line 50), more of the poem probably already existed. There is no reason to doubt W's statement that it was "written in Germany." That his "1799" is correct seems less certain.

W composes autobiographical and meditative materials including *Prel* MS JJ (PREL 633–42). [These materials may be regarded as the beginning of *The Prelude*, although W probably has not yet formed a plan of writing an autobiographical poem addressed to STC. They include drafts of materials used in the Preamble (*Prel* I.1–54, *Prel₂* I.1–45). For materials in MS JJ which can be dated within narrower limits of time see esp. 1798:203; 1798:204.]

[Probably here] W composes *Ellen Irwin* [composition possibly any time up to 29 July 1800. (See *Ellen Irwin* IF note; *EL* 221–22; Moorman I, 429; Hale White 6–9.)][56]

202. [Probably between Oct 6 and Dec, possibly 1799 Jan]

W composes:
"How Sweet When Crimson Colours Dart" (*PW* II 465). (See *EL* 222.)
"One Day the Darling of My Heart" (possibly an unknown variant of a surviving poem; probably a poem which has not survived). (See *EL* 222.)
"A Slumber Did My Spirit Seal." (See *STCL* I, 479–80.)[57]

203. [Probably between Oct 6 and possibly Dec 14, probably Dec 21 or 28]

W composes:
First versions of "She Dwelt among the Untrodden Ways" and "Strange Fits of Passion I Have Known." (*EL* 204–06. See 1798: 210.)
The Stolen Boat (*Prel* I.372–427, *Prel₂* I.357–400) and at least lines 25–63 of *Influence of Natural Objects* (*Prel* I.452–89, *Prel₂* I.425–63). (*EL*

---

[56] Bürger (see *Ellen Irwin* IF note) is most likely to have influenced W at and shortly after the time he was engaged in his most extensive reading of that poet—that is, at Goslar; but the evidence is not conclusive. *Ellen Irwin* was sent to Biggs and Cottle 29 July 1800 for *LB* 1800.

[57] "How Sweet" and "One Day" seem, like "A Slumber," to have been composed as part of the "Lucy" poems—probably around the same time as "She Dwelt" or "Strange Fits"—in Dec or before. They had, in any case, pretty surely been sent to STC before the end of Jan 1799. (See *EL* 216, 222; *STCL* I, 479–80; 1798:210.)

208–09. See MS JJ, Prel 633–42; 1798:210.)

Nutting. (See Appendix XI.)[58]

204. [Probably between Oct 6 and late Nov or early Dec]

W composes "There Was a Boy" (*Prel* V.389–422, *Prel*$_2$ V.364–97). (*STCL* I, 452; *EL* 211. See MS JJ, *Prel* 639–40; 1798:208.)

205. [Probably late Oct or Nov, and possibly between c Nov and 1799 early Feb]

DW writes [to MH?] from Goslar: The trip from Hamburg to Goslar; STC at Ratzeburg; (dull) life at Goslar; their good progress in German; W is very industrious—too much so (he has pain and weakness in his side). [The second paragraph possibly belongs to a second letter, of between c Nov and 1799 early Feb.] (*EL* 202–03.)[59]

206. [Probably early or mid-Nov (and at least two months thereafter)]

W, DW write to STC from Goslar, their first letter to him since their arrival there: [Apologies for delay in writing; Goslar described; their intention of leaving in late Nov because of lack of society or opportunity to learn German. DW remarks that "William works hard, but not very much at the German." (*STCL* I, 445.)

[Probably W, DW, and STC correspond frequently for at least two months hereafter. (See esp. *STCL* I, 459.)]

207. [Probably c Nov 1]

A review of *LB* [by Robert Southey] appears in *The Critical*

---

[58] Lines corresponding to *Influence of Natural Objects* lines 8–14 are drafted in JJ, and it is possible that the entire "poem," as *Prel* I.428–89, had been completed by this time. (W dated *Influence* 1799 in editions from 1836 through 1850.)

[59] If both paragraphs belong to one letter they imply that the arrival at Goslar had not yet become a matter of the distant past, but that W and DW had had time to settle into a regular style of living and evaluate the advantages and disadvantages of their situation. Topics in the second paragraph (on the confused history of which see *EL* 202n) so resemble the Dec letter to STC (*EL* 204) and the letter to CW of 5 Feb 1799 as to suggest the possibility of the paragraph's having come from a later, otherwise lost letter dating any time through early Feb, but present evidence allows no final conclusion.

Review (XXIV, Oct 1798) over the signature "Aristarchus." (See Smith 30–32; 1787:7n; Daniel *MLR* 407; *EL* 229–30.)

208. [Probably late Nov or very early Dec]

[W sends STC "There Was a Boy" apparently very much in its present form. (See *STCL* I, 452; *EL* 211.)][60]

209. Dec 4

RW records purchase of £500 stock in 3 percent consols in his own name (the purchase is for W) under this date:

£300	at 53⅛	159/7/6
£200	at 53⅞	107/15/- : £267/2/6

(RW, accounts with W and DW, 1816, DCP.)

210. [Possibly Dec 14, probably Dec 21 or Dec 28]

W, DW write to STC from Goslar: Inquiries about early German poets, esp. a 13th-century anthology mentioned in Ramond's translation of Coxe's *Travels*. STC's hexameters [see *STCL* I, 451–52]. Inquiries about Wieland, Klopstock, Goethe's [*Hermann und Dorothea*]. W would be writing more were it not for the "uneasiness and heat" in his side. STC's skating at Ratzeburg [see *STCL* I, 449]; STC could skate in the Lake District; intentions of visiting the North at end of summer 1799. STC's eyes. Request advice on books to be purchased on their journey; STC is asked to preserve any MS of W's that he has (for fear of W's losing his while traveling). Copies of early versions of: "She Dwelt," "Strange Fits," *Nutting* (described as "the conclusion of a poem of which the beginning is not written"); *Prel* I.452–89, *Prel*₂ I.425–63 (Skating); *Prel* I.372–427, *Prel*₂ I.357–400 (The Stolen Boat). (*EL* 203–11.)[61]

[60] W and STC were probably corresponding rapidly by this time (see *STCL* I, 459), but mails were wretchedly slow (*EL* 211). STC's letter of 10 Dec, on these lines, was probably written very shortly after their receipt—but W had probably not sent them off after the very first days of Dec.

[61] Problems in dating this letter are complex, but at least three points look clear: One is that at this general time of the autumn and winter W did not write STC, nor STC write W, without having first received a letter from the other (*STCL* I, 459; *EL* 211). The next is that the letter was written—certainly completed—on a Friday (*EL* 211). The third is that STC had an eye ailment in advanced condition on 2–3 Dec (*STCL* I, 449–52), but that he expected it to be gone in a few days—and that in fact nothing more is heard of it in what survives of letters which can be dated after early Dec. STC would probably have mentioned the ailment to Poole in his letter of 4 Jan

W walks by moonlight. (*EL* 211.)

211. [Probably between late Dec and 1799 Feb 23]

W writes two letters to STC [probably from Goslar, of which only two fragments survive]:

(1) W, DW have read *Leonora* and a few other poems of Bürger; they think, esp. in *Leonora*, that several passages are inferior to William Taylor's English translation. (*STCL* I, 565.)

(2) More about Bürger, esp. his versification, absence of character in his personages, his liveliness and genius, his lack of the qualities of a great poet. *Susan's Dream.* (*STCL* I, 565–66.)][62]

[62] STC's comments and quotations indicate that these fragments represent early, probably the first, stages of their discussion of Bürger, and that the second fragment was written in reply to STC's answer to the first. STC's comments further imply that once the discussion was started, it was probably kept up in each exchange of correspondence. The W letter of 21 or 28 Dec 1798 does not mention Bürger; so that they had either finished or else had not started on the subject then. W was still dealing with Bürger in his letter of 27 Feb; his comments are in reply to STC's comments on the last letter of W's to which he has responded; and he and STC had not yet reached the point (although it looks like the point is imminent) of the "metaphysical disquisitions on the nature of character" which developed from their discussion (*STCL* I, 566). So it seems likely that the exchanges on Bürger began after the 21 or 28 Dec letter. W's comments on 27 Feb assume some previous discussion of character but appear to introduce manners as a new topic. The later fragment would not postdate the departure of W and DW from Goslar on 23 Feb.

1799 or to his wife in his letter of 14 Jan (see *STCL* I, 449, 453–64) had it lasted on through the month. DW's thoughtfulness about STC's eyes (*EL* 211) would probably, then, not date from any time appreciably after the beginning of Jan.

A fragment of a letter written by STC to W on 10 Dec survives (*STCL* I, 452–53); the letter was written in answer to a letter of W's which has not survived. There would almost certainly not have been time between 26 Nov, when STC was quite well (see *STCL* I, 448, last line), and 10 Dec for a complete exchange of letters, including news from STC of an illness which had begun to trouble him only after 26 Nov (and probably not until about 2 Dec), then a response from W, then a letter to W on 10 Dec, unless the mail had been incredibly rapid (see *STCL* I, 459; *EL* 211). Anyhow, it appears that W was writing STC around the end of Nov. It is thus most probable that the W's learned of STC's illness in STC's letter of 10 Dec; probably STC's hexameters, in view of the recentness of the illness described in them, were part of the same letter. It would have been miraculous had STC's letter of 10 Dec reached Goslar by 14 Dec (*EL* 211); so that a date of 21 Dec or 28 Dec, becomes probable. In view of the frequency of the correspondence (*STCL* I, 459) 21 Dec is perhaps the more likely choice.

1799

1. [During this year]

[On writings of W possibly of this year see below and GCL 32, 33, 45, 52–53, 57, 60–63, 72, 78–81, 83–87.]

DW writes [to an unknown correspondent]: Racedown the place dearest to her recollections [in England]. (*Mem* I, 94.)

2. [Possibly during this year; probably 1804]

[Possibly during 1799] W composes *The Simplon Pass* (*Prel* VI.553–72, *Prel*₂ VI.621–40). [More likely the passage was composed in 1804.] (See *PW* II, 506.)[1]

3. [Early this year]

W works two days on *SP*; resolves "to discard Robert Walford and invent a new story for the woman." [He does not appear to have implemented this decision any time very soon.] (*EL* 222–23; Appendix XII.)

W employs himself in cutting down *PB*. [No MS work on the poem known to date from this time has survived.] (*EL* 222.)

4. [Perhaps c early this year, by c Mar 14–21 or Apr 20 or 21; probably between Apr 20 or 21 and Sept]

W evolves a plan for an autobiographical poem addressed to STC; this plan resulted in *The Prelude*. [W had commenced the actual work on *Prel*, without this plan fully in mind, at Goslar.] (See Appendix XII; PREL xlvii; *STCL* I, 538.)

5. Jan

RW records under this general date receipt of £10 cash for W's use [from Douglas] and £7/10/–, interest for a half year on W's 3 percent consols, due [5 Jan]. (See 1798:209; 1799:33n; *EL* 215–16.)

6. [Probably c Jan 1, c Jan 12]

[Probably c 1 Jan] A review of *LB* appears in *The Analytical*

---

[1] W's statement about the date of the passage (editions of 1845 and after) differs so widely from other available evidence (see esp. PREL l–li) that suggestion of the possibility of a date of 1799 seems justified. As noted elsewhere, "compose," with W, need not mean "write."

Review (XXVIII, Dec 1798). (See Smith 33–34; 1787:7n.)

[Probably c 12 Jan] a review of *LB* [probably by Dr. Aikin] appears in *The Monthly Magazine* (VI, 1798, Supplement). (See Smith 32–33; *Monthly Magazine* VI, 405.)

7. Feb 3–Feb 5

DW writes to CW from Goslar 3 Feb: Inquiries about CW. Their long delay in leaving Goslar; the cold. Their plans for travel to Nordhausen, thence to other, undecided places. Their merely moderate progress in German, a result of social difficulties. More about climate; they walk an hour a day; Goslar inhabitants; their landlady; STC. Their probable return to England in the spring. Inquiries about the copy of *The Borderers* [see 1798:195n]. Life in Goslar. (*EL* 211–15.)

[DW writes to her Aunt Cookson (letter not surviving). (*EL* 215.) Between 3 and 5 Feb W and DW write at least eight letters, seven of them long. (*EL* 216. See 1799:8.)]

8. Feb 5

W, DW write to RW from Goslar: Information about financial arrangements to be made, including those about his debt to Wedgwood. Has drawn on Wedgwood for £72 and some odd shillings in Germany, [£40 recently]. Their projected tour into Saxony. RW to pay Wedgwood as much as possible. Hopes RW forwarded MSS to Miss Nicholson and Wedgwood [see 1798:195n]. They expect to be in Hamburg in two months. (*EL* 215–16.)[2]

W writes to Josiah Wedgwood from Goslar: Financial information. Has drawn on the Wedgwoods for £40—his last expected need for funds. He has perhaps overdrawn himself by £15 [see 1798:176]—will remain Wedgwood's debtor. Their projected tour in Saxony. Goslar; their slow progress in German; an old man among their friends; probable early return to England if no opportunity for improved learning of German is presented. (MS, Wedgwood Museum, Barlaston.)[3]

---

[2] EdS appears to have misread the date of this letter as 6 Feb.

[3] Moorman I, 414n, dates the letter 6 Feb; but the figure on the MS looks like a 5.

9. [Between Feb 5 and Apr 20 or 21]

[W probably draws on the Wedgwoods for £10/2/9 (or there-abouts). (See 1799:25n.)]

10. Feb 6–12

On 6 Feb STC departs from Ratzeburg for Göttingen. He arrives in Göttingen 12 Feb. (*STCL* I, 471–74.)

11. Feb 10

Berkeley Coleridge, second son of STC and Sara C, dies in Bristol. (EKC 110.)

12. [Probably Feb 23]

W, DW put together their last parcel, take it to the post office, and depart from Goslar on foot at 1. They walk into the Hartz forest. They arrive at Cl[a]usthal at dusk; spend the night there. (*EL* 216–17.)

[The departure from Goslar perhaps contributes to *Prel* I.1–54, *Prel*₂ I.1–45 (see also *Prel* VII.1–9, *Prel*₂ VII.1–8). (See *Mem* I, 142–44, *Mem*, R, I, 143–45; 1795:34. On the Hartz forest see *DWJ* I, 197n.)]

13. [Probably between Feb 23 and Feb 27]

[In the Hartz forest] W composes "Three Years She Grew in Sun and Shower." ("Three Years" IF note. See Moorman I, 422.)

14. [Probably Feb 24]

W, DW depart from Cl[a]usthal in the morning; see a gibbet; hear larks; see a village in the bottom of a valley. They arrive at Osterode at 4. People coming out of church stare DW "out of countenance." They find no room at an inn on the far side of town; are told they need a passport before leaving; an officer takes W to the Burgomaster; DW waits at a guardhouse. On W's return they are admitted to the inn, where they spend the night. (*EL* 217–19.)

15. [Probably Feb 25]

W, DW arise at 7, and, their passport arranged (see 1799:14), depart from Osterode after 10. They pass H[e]rtzburg; are overtaken by darkness; but a wagon takes them to Schazefeld, where they spend the night. (*EL* 219.)

16. [Probably Feb 26]

W, DW depart from Schazefeld, walk till 4, when they stop for
the night at [a country] inn, with a varied group. (*EL* 219–20.)

17. [Feb 27]

W, DW travel by post wagon ten miles; arrive at the posthouse,
[Nordhausen,] in the afternoon. They find [two] letters from STC;
find an inn. (*EL* 216, 220.)

18. [1799] Feb 27

W, DW write to STC from Nordhausen: (DW:) Description of
the journey from Goslar to Nordhausen [see entries from 1799:12].
(W:) Their plans, esp. to wander about for two or three weeks, then to
come to Göttingen. His poor progress in German, incapacity for translation work. STC's two letters, esp. one on German poets, Lessing,
Wieland, Goethe. Enduring values (or lack of them) in B[ü]rger,
Theocritus, Aristophanes, Congreve, Vanbrugh, Farquhar, Burns (esp.
Ode to Despondency). STC's criticisms of poems W has sent him; W
does not care for "How Sweet When Crimson Colours" or "One
Day the Darling of My Heart." He has lately been cutting down *PB*;
worked two days on *SP*; his plans for *SP* [see Appendix XII]. They
intend to stay at Nordhausen two or three days. They have a plan for
"a new invention for washing" to import to England. (*EL* 216–23.)

19. [Feb 28–Apr 20 or 21; esp. c Mar 14–Mar 21]

[The movements of W and DW during this period are unknown.
They evidently wander about, esp. in Saxony and toward the South.
W and no doubt DW keep a journal which has not survived. Probably
they visit STC for an undetermined period c 14–21 Mar, and W and
STC (perhaps also DW) go for a ramble of about two days' duration;
possibly one night during this ramble they are mistreated by a landlord
and obtain lodgings only with difficulty. (*EL* 212, 221; *STCL* I, 654–55;
Clement Carlyon, *Early Years and Late Reflections*, London, 1836, I, 16,
186–97; William Howitt, *Homes and Haunts of the Most Eminent British
Poets*, London, 1847, II, 257–58. See EdS *DW* 106.)][4]

[4] Carlyon's story of the Wordsworths' visit and the ramble, of which he was
informed by "one, well acquainted with the fact," can neither be confirmed nor denied.

20. [Between possibly c Mar 14–21, probably Apr 20 or 21, and 1800 c June 5]

W writes an abortive start on *Prel* II, and drafts toward *Prel* II quoted PREL 525. *Prel* MSS RV, U, V are written. (See Appendix XII.)

21. [Between possibly c Mar 14–21, more certainly very late Apr, and 1800 perhaps c June 5, fairly certainly c July]

RC MS D is written. (See Appendices IX, XIII.)

W and DW had planned to be (though not for long) in Göttingen "a fortnight or three weeks" after 27 Feb—a month, that is, before the only visit they are known definitely to have paid there. Their travels must have been far different from what was originally projected if their only visit was that of late April. Something like a "fortnight" or a little beyond would also have allowed them to visit and depart before Carlyon's arrival at Göttingen on 22 Mar, after which Carlyon would almost surely have had firsthand knowledge of the visit. Margoliouth 48 (see also 58) states that W and DW met STC at Göttingen "only . . . twice, for a matter of hours"; if they did meet twice—and I incline to believe that they did—the first visit was more than a matter of hours. Moorman I, 434, suggests that the visit of 20 or 21 Apr was the only one paid; EdS (*DW* 106) likewise says that there was one visit, for "a day of two"; L. A. Willoughby in "Wordsworth and Germany," *German Studies Presented to Professor H. G. Fiedler* (Oxford, 1936) 436, states that the late Apr visit was for "some few days." It is interesting to note that the MS of W's letter of 13 May to Josiah Wedgwood (Wedgwood Museum, Barlaston), in which he informs Wedgwood that he and DW "left Coleridge at Göttingen a month ago," shows that W's amanuensis, DW, originally wrote "tw" instead of "a" before "month."

If W did not visit STC for a longer period, it is difficult to imagine when an incident occurred that Howitt reports as heard from W himself—that, arriving late at a hamlet in Hesse Cassel, W and STC were set upon by a landlord with a cudgel, and were able to gain lodgings for the night only after much persuasion. Howitt says that STC describes the same incident in *BL*, but he must have been thinking of Carlyon I, 35–38, an incident in which Carlyon participated, and at which W was definitely not present. Both incidents took place in Hesse Cassel, but it does not seem very likely that Howitt would have presumed to claim to have heard a story from W's mouth when he had not, especially since W was alive when he wrote, or that Carlyon was essentially inaccurate on the points that show his story had nothing to do with W. The best solution appears to be that while Howitt may have erred slightly in his recollection of W's anecdote, some incident of the sort really took place (in Hesse Cassel or elsewhere); the only possible time for it seems to be the presumed longer visit with STC. Howitt reports that DW was with W and STC on this trip, and Carlyon reports that DW stayed behind when W and STC walked from Göttingen. If the trip was the same, Carlyon is more likely right, but further speculation is futile.

22. Apr 18

RW records payment to Richard Hilton of £3 for W (and £2 for DW) under this date. (RW, accounts with W and DW, 1816, DCP. See 1795:44n.)

23. [Probably Apr 20 or 21 (ff)]

[Probably on 20 or 21 Apr] W, DW pass through Gottingen; STC spends the day with them, walks on with them five miles. The W's are melancholy; they discuss the possibilities of living near STC on their return to England; W's desire to live near the Lakes and near a large library. STC's unwillingness to move from Nether Stowey. STC gives W 3 guineas, to be considered as advanced from the Wedgwoods. (*STCL* I, 484, 490–91; letters of W to Josiah Wedgwood 13 May 1799, 23 May 1799, 13 July 1800, Wedgwood Museum, Barlaston. See *EL* 224, 228; 1799:32; 1799:34.)

24. [Probably between Apr 20 or 21 and c Apr 25]

W, DW travel from Göttingen to Hamburg, [most of the way] in a diligence, arriving in Hamburg c 25 Apr. (*EL* 228. See 1799:23.)[5]

25. [Probably c Apr 25]

In Hamburg W draws on Josiah Wedgwood for £25 from the Von Axens. This sum probably represents W's last draft on Wedgwood, bringing the total advanced to W by Wedgwood to £110/13/–. (Letters of W to Josiah Wedgwood 13 May 1799, 13 July 1800, Wedgwood Museum, Barlaston. See 1799:32.)[6]

---

[5] The diligence trip down to Goslar from Hamburg (3–6 Oct) would have proceeded at an average of something like fifty miles per day. The trip from Göttingen to Hamburg has been calculated at that rate. (See also *STCL* I, 459.)

[6] The Von Axens in Hamburg paid out a total of £106/10/– to STC and W between 29 Mar and 8 July (Wedgwood accounts, Wedgwood Museum, Barlaston; see Eliza Meteyard, *A Group of Englishmen*, London, 1871, 99). There is no direct evidence that more than £25 of the amount was drawn by W, but surviving records of W's drafts on Wedgwood appear to indicate a debt by W of only £100/10/3 (see 1798:194; 1799:8; 1799:23; 1799:25); and W said in 1800 that he owed Wedgwood £110/13/–. He also said on 13 May that he had drawn for only £25 in Hamburg.

26. [Probably c Apr 26]

W, DW, proceeding to England with as little delay as possible, take a boat down to Cuxhaven, where they rest for refreshment. (*EL* 228. See 1799:24.)

27. [Probably late Apr, esp. after c Apr 26, or fairly early May, esp c May 1]

W, DW sail to Yarmouth from Cuxhaven in two days and nights. (*EL* 228. See 1799:24.)

28. [Probably late Apr or very early May–Dec 17]

[W, DW proceed immediately from Yarmouth to Sockburn-on-Tees. They depart from Sockburn 17 Dec. (*EL* 223, 228. See 1799:27; 1799:90.) (On this visit at Sockburn see *Incident Characteristic of a Favorite Dog* IF note.)][7]

29. [Probably between very late Apr and 1800 Oct 10]

W composes the version of *OCB* that is finally published. (See Appendix XV.)

30. [Probably between very late Apr and 1800 c June 5]

SP MS 2 is written. (See Appendix XII.)
The Borderers MS B is written. (See Appendix X.)

31. [Probably c very early May]

[Probably shortly after arriving in England W, DW write to, or possibly see, CW. (*EL* 223.)]

---

[7] No evidence exists to confirm D. H. Bishop's conjecture (*Stud Phil* XXXII, 1935, 445) that W paid a visit to London while at Sockburn.

The extra sum of slightly over £10 was thus probably withdrawn between 5 Feb and 20 or 21 Apr (see 1799:8, 1799:25). Meteyard notes no record of the £40 withdrawal made by W before his letter of 5 Feb; the £10 was perhaps included in the sum paid out between 29 Mar and 8 July.

32. [1799] May 13

W writes to RW from Sockburn: Their safe arrival in England. Requests immediate information on his general financial condition. Fears mismanagement in case of *LB*; has not heard from Cottle. (*EL* 223–24.)[8]

W writes to Josiah Wedgwood from Sockburn: His draft on Wedgwood for £25 in Hamburg [see 1799:25]; his ignorance of his general financial condition now; hopes to hear from RW in a few days and to repay Wedgwood in a short time. His visit with STC at Göttingen [20 or 21 Apr]; STC proposes staying two months longer. (MS, Wedgwood Museum, Barlaston.)

33. [1799 probably c May 13]

W writes to Joseph Cottle from Sockburn: W's request of [15 Sept 1798] that Cottle transfer his rights in *LB* to Johnson; how has *LB* in fact been disposed of? Their visit with STC at Göttingen. (*EL* 224.)[9]

---

[8] RW's reply (DCP; see Moorman I, 438–39) informs W: Only £10 of the £100 Douglas debt is paid; a note from Montagu for £21/5/- (23 Jan) was not honored; RW has advanced about £50. He sends W copies of the letters from Cottle to Johnson and from Cottle to Tobin concerning *LB*. Has laid out £267/2/6 for W in 3 percent consols (see 1798:209); has £7/10 dividend (see 1799:5); that and Douglas's £10 is all W's money. Wants his two volumes of Blackstone which W left at Windy Brow. Includes an account of advances to Montagu totaling £49/18/6.

It may be briefly noted here that W's summer correspondence included two letters to James Losh, who received them 17 July and 13 Aug (Losh Diary); but nothing further is known of them.

[9] This letter inaccurately dates the time since they left STC as "a month," just as does the letter to Wedgwood of 13 May. W speaks of "not having heard from Cottle" about his business concerns in the letter to RW of 13 May, and he tells Wedgwood on the same day that he "has not heard from [RW]" about similar subjects. As the letter to RW is plainly the first he has written him since his return from Germany, his telling Wedgwood that he has not heard from RW does not indicate that he has written RW earlier; his use of a similar phrase to RW in regard to Cottle need not imply an earlier letter to Cottle. Probably the letters to RW, Wedgwood, and Cottle all date from the same day. In any event, the letter to Cottle must date from almost the same time.

34. [1799] May 23

W writes to Basil Montagu about their financial arrangements (letter not surviving). (*LY* 1341.)

W, DW write to RW [from Sockburn]: (W:) Thanks RW for his letter [see 1799:31. Cottle's procedures concerning *LB* rights; fears sales may have been hurt or his connection with Johnson broken. His resolution to have his finances dealing with Montagu straightened out; has written Montagu today, also Wedgwood [perhaps today], also Cottle [c 13 May]. Douglas. Requests account of all money paid by RW on W's account set off against receipts from Calvert. (DW:) The books [see 1799:32n] are in a box at Windy Brow. (*LY* 1340–42.)

W writes to Josiah Wedgwood from Sockburn: The letter from RW [see 1799:32n]; W has only received £17/10/– instead of the £85 he ought to have received. Requests Wedgwood to wait until he has inquired further among his debtors; hopes after hearing from them to discharge entire debt to Wedgwood, including 3 guineas borrowed from STC at Göttingen. (MS, Wedgwood Museum, Barlaston.)

35. [1799] June 2

W writes to Joseph Cottle [from Sockburn]: W sees that it would have been impossible for Cottle to have transferred *LB* to Johnson, in view of his arrangements with Arch; still regrets loss of possible connection with Johnson. Cottle owes W £21/10/–; W owes Cottle for paper purchased long ago. Cottle should send the remainder; failing that, should send £5 and the rest to RW. Inquiries about sale of *LB* and what is to be done about the copyright [see esp. 1799:61]; *AM* to be replaced by other poems if *LB* should sell. W would like three copies of *LB* for friends; will he have to buy them? (*EL* 225–26.)

36. [1799] June 24

W writes to Joseph Cottle from Sockburn: Thanks Cottle for £5 [see 1799:35]; asks him to send remaining £15 to him and not to RW after all. Would like exact information on number of copies of *LB* sold; *AM* appears to have injured their sale (by its archaisms and its strangeness)—would put shorter poems in its place if a second edition is called for. Send three copies of *LB* to Charles Lloyd; W can easily get them from Penrith. Their plans for residence are unsettled. They seek news of STC. (*EL* 226–27.)

37. July

RW records under this general date receipt of £7/10/–, half-year dividend on W's 3 percent consols, due 5 July. (RW, accounts with W and DW, 1816, DCP.)

38. [c July 1]

A review of *LB* [by Dr. Charles Burney] appears in *The Monthly Review* (ser. 2, XXIX, June 1799). (See Smith 34–37; EKC 115. See 1787:7n.)

39. [1799] July 4

DW writes to Thomas Poole from Sockburn: Apologizes for delay in writing since their return. Germany, their departure from it and from STC; their trip to Sockburn. They are anxious to hear from STC. Their uncertainty about their future plans for a residence. (*EL* 227–29.)

40. [Probably between July 4 and Sept 10]

[W and DW determine to settle in the North. (See 1799:39; *STCL* I, 527; Moorman I, 446.)][10]

41. [Probably c mid-July, certainly by July 29]

STC returns to England from Germany. (Wedgwood accounts, Wedgwood Museum, Barlaston. See Eliza Meteyard, *A Group of Englishmen*, London, 1871, 99; *STCL* I, 523.)[11]

---

[10] There seems little question that if W had "renounced Alfoxden altogether" by 10 Sept, he had given up the idea of living in the South; having given up that idea, he could only have been thinking of the Lakes (see 1799:23; *STCL* I, 490–91). Cf Margoliouth 65.

[11] The accounts of sums advanced by the Von Axens (Hamburg) to W and STC close on 8 July; STC probably drew his last sum on that date. See also Clement Carlyon, *Early Years and Late Reflections* (London, 1836) I, 170–86.

42. [1799] July 27

W writes to Joseph Cottle from Sockburn: Thanks Cottle for his draft [probably for £15; see 1799:36]; refuses interest; thanks Cottle for favorable news of *LB* sale, fears overoptimism in Cottle's remarks. Has heard of a review in *The Monthly Review*, but does not know its contents. His aversion to publication. (*EL* 229. See 1799:43.)

43. [Probably July 27; otherwise between July 27 and shortly before Oct 25 or 26]

[The letter to Cottle of 27 July probably also contains] remarks of W's published separately by Knight, as a fragmentary letter from W to Cottle, Sockburn, 1799: Southey's (not altogether favorable) review of *LB* [see 1798:207]; Southey knew the sale was important to them financially and should have reviewed favorably or not at all; W cares little for the praise of critics except as a financial aid. (*EL* 229–30. See 1799:55.)[12]

44. [By July 29]

STC reaches Nether Stowey on his return from Germany. (*STCL* I, 523. See 1799:41.)

45. Aug 1

The *Duke of Montrose* (JW second mate) reaches moorings in England. (It had sailed 22 Sept 1797.) (Hardy 187.)

---

[12] The subject of this fragment (a review) and its sentiments (publication "for money and money alone") closely parallel topics dealt with in the fragmentary letter of 27 July. Both letters are quoted incompletely, and I suspect that both fragments in fact belong to the same letter. The contents of W's earlier letters to Cottle from Sockburn make clear that no such letter is missing; the letter of 27 July is the first not published from MS. This fragment thus probably belongs to 27 July or after. Its remarks would hardly be appropriate for a time in 1799 after W had seen Cottle— that is, after 25 or 26 Oct (see 1799:55). The only other Sockburn letter to Cottle that survives is the fragment of 2 Sept, urging the publisher to visit the North of England.

46. [1799] Aug 20

W gives John Hutchinson of Stockton a bill for £15/18/6 to cash at the Stockton bank. (Hutchinson is to send £10 to RW; £5/18/6 is to be returned to W.) (*EL* 230–31.)

W, DW write to RW from Sockburn: (W:) W's inability to get matters settled with Montagu; hopes to hear something decisive from him. Encloses a bill for £10 to deposit with [Josiah] Wedgwood's bankers along with what RW has received on W's account since his departure for Germany. W would like a full statement of all RW's dealings for and with him, all sums received and paid, and the like; had hoped there would be £300 to buy into the stocks with; has received 30 guineas from Cottle as "part of payment" for *LB*. (DW:) They want news of JW's arrival as soon as RW knows of it [see 1799:45]. (*EL* 230–31.)

47. [Aug 21]

W, DW hear of JW's arrival in England (see: 1799:45; 1799:46). (*EL* 231–32.)

48. Aug 23

RW records a credit of £10 to W by draft received from W at Sockburn under this date. (RW, accounts with W and DW, 1816, DCP. See 1799:46.)

49. Aug 31

RW records payment of £7/10/6, [premium on £300 policy on Basil Montagu's life,] under this date. (Receipt, DCP; RW, accounts with W and DW, 1816, DCP. See esp. 1796:54.)

50. Sept 2

W writes to Joseph Cottle from Sockburn (a fragment of the letter survives): [W urges Cottle to visit the North of England; W will accompany him on a tour;] suggests plans. (*EL* 231.)

51. [1799] Sept 3

DW writes to RW from Sockburn: The financial arrangements made [on 20 Aug; see 1799:46]; please send the accounts which W then requested. Requests information on JW. W has been unwell lately—pain in his side. [CW is probably in Birmingham with the Lloyds.] (*EL* 231–32.)

52. [Probably c but by Sept 8]

W writes to STC [from Sockburn] (letter not surviving): Informs STC that he is quite unwell. (*STCL* I, 525–27.)[13]

53. [Probably c Oct 15]

Christopher Crackanthorpe Crackanthorpe (formerly Cookson) dies [at Newbiggin]. (See 1799:54.) His will leaves DW £100. (See 1799:61.)

54. Oct 17

CCC is buried at Newbiggin. (*Parish Registers of Newbiggin, Westmorland*, comp. J. F. Haswell, CWAA Soc, 1927.)

55. [Probably Oct 25 or 26–Oct 27, 30]

[Probably on 25 or 26 Oct STC, Joseph Cottle arrive at Sockburn-on-Tees, STC having been brought partly or largely by concern over W's apparent bad health (see 1799:52). Probably W or Cottle asks MH something like: "What do you think of Mr. Coleridge's first appearance?" The visitors depart from Sockburn 27 Oct (see 1799:58). Cottle leaves W and STC probably 30 Oct (see 1799:61).

While Cottle is present *LB* is mentioned only briefly: W attributes its failure to *AM* and unfavorable reviews. (*STCNB* I, 490–91, 493, 571, 1537, 1575, 1583, 1587; Cottle *Recollections* II, 26.)][14]

---

[13] STC received W's letter 10 Sept. Distances and coach speeds (Paterson; Joyce 290, 399-400) imply that W's letter would probably have been sent off by some time on 8 Sept.

[14] *STCNB* does not confirm an arrival on 26 Oct, the date given by Moorman I, 447, and others; it seems to indicate simply that they had not yet arrived by sometime

56. [Probably 1799 Oct 25 or 26]

Evening. W, DW go out to walk; STC reads parts of the introduction of Bartram's *Travels* to Sara Hutchinson. (See *STCNB* I, 218n.)

57. [Oct 26 or 27]

[Morning. STC, probably W and others evidently visit Mr. Ward
of Neesham Bank. (*STCNB* I, 494, 1588.)]

58. Oct 27–[between Nov 17 and Nov 20 or 21; Nov 26]

On the afternoon of 27 Oct W, STC, and Cottle (mounted on the
mare "Lily") depart from Sockburn on a walking tour. They proceed
by Neesham Bank to Herworth, where they observe the churchyard,
and Croft. [They spend the night in Piercebridge, at the George Inn.]
(*STCNB* I, 494, 1588; Hanson 368.)

W, STC tour together until [between 17 and 20 or 21 Nov (see
1799:82). W returns to Sockburn 26 Nov (see 1799:85). (On the tour
generally see *EL* 236–37; *STCNB* I, 494–563 *passim*, 1588–89; these
entries include what must be many references to conversations which
cannot be given specific dates.)][15]

59. Oct 28

W, STC, Cottle arrive at 9:30 AM at Gainford, where they observe
the churchyard. They proceed to Egglestone Abbey, which they reach
at 4:30. [They probably spend the night at Barnard Castle.] (*STCNB*
I, 495; *EL* 287. See 1799:60.)

---

[15] STC's reference to "Pierce Bridge," followed by "Landlady & Alfred," with
the next entry beginning "Oct. 28th," indicates where they passed the night.

on the 25th. An entry dated the 25th precedes a note on Easingwold, which is some
twenty-five miles south of Sockburn; the next entry but one plainly refers to STC's
meeting with MH; the next beyond that refers to the start of the walking trip, 27
Oct. *STCNB* I, 1575, mentions being on the road in a postchaise with "poor Cottle"
on "Oct. 22. 23. 24th"; 1583 says that STC was in a postchaise with Cottle at
Easingwold on the 25th. It seems at least as likely as not that they arrived at Sockburn
on 25 Oct. *STCNB* I, 562, 1579, refer to the Sockburn area.

60. [Probably Oct 29]

W, STC, Cottle spend this day in the Barnard Castle–Greta Bridge area; [they probably visit Brignall Church. They probably spend the night at Greta Bridge.] (*STCNB* 496, 1589; *STCL* I, 543. See *EL* 232; 1799:61; *To the River Greta* n.)[16]

61. [Probably Oct 30 and shortly after]

[Probably on 30 Oct] W, STC part from Cottle at Greta Bridge; [Cottle sets off for London, perhaps via Sockburn; on the same day] W, STC take the mail coach over [Stainmore] to Temple Sowerby, where W learns that CW has gone to Cambridge and that JW is at Newbiggin; W sends a note; JW comes. W learns from JW that CCC has left DW £100 (see 1799:53) and no one else anything. JW agrees to join W and STC for a few days' travel. (Cottle *Recollections* II, 26; *STCL* I, 543–44. Cf *EL* 232–33. See also *EL* 250.)

Cottle, giving up publishing, sells his copyrights except Fox's *Achmed* and *LB* to Longman; presents *LB* copyright to W. (Cottle *Recollections* II, 26–27. See Moorman I, 487.)[17]

62. [Probably Oct 31]

[W, JW, STC set off together; see the Hartshorn Oak, Mayborough; perhaps also see the Giant's Cave on the banks of the

---

[16] Moorman I, 448, indicates that W and STC traveled to Temple Sowerby (and thus would have parted from Cottle) on 29 Oct, but *STCL* I, 543, shows they left Cottle at Greta Bridge the morning of 30 Oct. If they slept at Greta Bridge, it would, of course, have been the 29th that they did so. (See 1799:61.) *EL* 287, however, confirms that they also spent a night at Barnard Castle. J. B. S. Morritt, mentioned *STCNB* I, 497, was the proprietor of Rokeby, near Greta Bridge, in 1799 (Paterson). The date of W's encounter with the landlady who explained the origin of the name of the River Greta by calling attention to the shape of the bridge (*To the River Greta* n) is unknown, but might well be now.

[17] Margoliouth 66 says that Cottle took the coach to Bristol; but even leaving aside the question of what happened to the mare "Lily" (or "Lilly") (see 1799:58; *EL* 238), there seems no reason to doubt Cottle's own statement that he proceeded to London (Cottle *Recollections* II, 26). Regardless of the publisher's route, STC and W would have had to be at Greta Bridge to catch their coach for Temple Sowerby (Paterson). *STCNB* I, 572, 1571, refer to Temple Sowerby.

Eamont; they dine with the Rev. Thomas Myers at Barton; proceed to Bampton, where they spend the night. Perhaps on the way to Bampton they see and laugh at a "backside"-shaped hill near Pooley Bridge. (*STCL* I, 544; *STCNB* I, 496, 560, 798 fol. 32. See Moorman I, 449. Cf *EL* 233.) (W refers to the Hartshorn Oak, although not necessarily this visit, in *Harts-Horn Tree, near Penrith—PW* III, 277, 534–35.)]

63. [Probably c Nov 1]

A review of *LB* [probably by Wrangham] appears in *The British Critic* (XIV, Oct 1799). (See Smith 37–41; 1787:7n.)

64. Nov 1

W, JW, STC walk along Haweswater, over Long Sleddale to Kentmere, [where they spend the night]. (*STCL* I, 544; *EL* 233; *STCNB* I, 510; *Mem* II, 304, *Mem*, R, II, 314; Moorman I, 449.)[18]

65. [Probably Nov 2]

W, JW, STC walk to Troutbeck, Rayrigg, Bowness, thence across Windermere and on to Hawkshead, [where they probably spend the night, although Hawkshead contains no horses or lodgings. W, JW] find a great change among the people since they were last there. (*STCL* I, 544. Cf *EL* 233. See 1799:64. Cf Moorman I, 449.) [W refers to this visit: "'Beloved Vale,' I Said, 'When I Shall Con'"; *Prel* II.33–41, *Prel*₂ II.33–40.]

66. Nov 2

RW notes payment for "postage of a French letter for" [W] under this date. (Accounts of RW with W, DCP.)

---

[18] Mrs. Moorman's interpretation of W's remarks as implying that they slept at Kentmere seems quite likely. The only readily apparent alternative would have them going all the way to Hawkshead on this day—a very long walk indeed—and would confuse the chronology, since 1 Nov was a Friday and W says they departed from Hawkshead "next day Sunday" (as *STCNB* 511 also indicates). *STCNB* I, 510–11n, has evidently fallen into such a mixup in speaking of a trip from Bampton to Hawkshead "Friday 1 Nov" and from Hawkshead to Grasmere "Sunday 2 Nov."

67. [Probably Nov 3–Nov 8]

[Probably on 3 Nov] W, JW, STC walk via Blelham Tarn, head of Windermere, and Rydal to Grasmere, where they stay at Robert Newton's Inn. [They remain there until 8 Nov. On their way] a servant admonishes them for passing in front of Sir Daniel le Fleming's house at Rydal. (*STCL* I, 544; *EL* 233; *STCNB* I, 511–14; *DWJ* I, 67n, 104. See 1799:72.)

[Probably during this visit at Grasmere W forms plans for building beside Grasmere; W also discovers "a small house" (Dove Cottage) at Grasmere which he and DW might take. (*STCL* I, 544; *EL* 233.)]

68. [Probably Nov 4]

[W, JW, STC remain at Grasmere. (See 1799:67; 1799:72.)]

69. [Probably Nov 5]

W, STC accompany JW over [Grisedale Hause]; bid him farewell at [Grisedale] Tarn. [Probably on this day, before or after departing from JW,] W and STC ascend Helvellyn. (*STCL* I, 543–44; *EL* 233; *STCNB* 515, 1589. See 1799:72; Moorman I, 451.)

70. [Probably Nov 6]

W, STC remain at Grasmere. They walk to the upper fall at Rydal [this evening]. (*STCL* I, 544; *EL* 233. See 1799:67; 1799:72.)

71. [Probably Nov 7]

W, STC remain at Grasmere. They start for Dungeon Ghyll; are turned back by bad weather. (*STCL* I, 544. See 1799:67; 1799:72.)

72. [Nov 8–10; probably Nov 8]

[On 8 Nov W, STC walk from Grasmere to Keswick, where they remain until 10 Nov. (See 1799:74.) While in Keswick they perhaps see, or even stay with, William Calvert. (See *STCNB* I, 564.)]

[Probably on 8 Nov] W, STC write to DW [from Keswick]: Their trip, itinerary. Various events. The meeting with JW. W discusses the possibility of building or at least residing at Grasmere. (*STCL* I, 543–45; *STCNB* I, 535.)[19]

73. [Nov 9]

[W, STC probably remain at Keswick. (*STCL* I, 545.)]

74. [Nov 10]

[Probably not early in the morning, as STC dates a letter to Southey from Keswick on this day,] W, STC depart from Keswick, [walk] to Ouse Bridge, [where they spend the night]. (*STCL* I, 545; *STCNB* I, 536.)[20]

---

[19] The comments of *STCNB* I, 535, on things seen "Friday" (see 535n) leave little doubt that the poets walked to Keswick over Dunmail Raise and along Thirlmere Friday 8 Nov. W says they have remained at Grasmere "till to day." Any implication in this phrasing that they were still there when W wrote his part of the letter seems balanced by W's later remark that STC "was much struck with Grasmere"—an unlikely comment (inasmuch as it plainly does not refer to their arrival there) if they had not already left. It is possible that W began his remarks on 7 Nov, but since STC describes his approach to Derwent Water (and hence Keswick) "this evening" at the conclusion of the letter as quoted, 8 Nov is probably the soundest guess for the date of the letter as a whole.

[20] Determination of resting places of W and STC the nights of 10, 11, and 12 Nov offers difficulty, although their route is fairly clear (as described below in the text). STC makes a journal entry about the view from the Inn at Ouse Bridge dated, at the end, the 11th, but whether in the evening or the morning is unclear. The next three entries, describing sights between Ouse Bridge and Buttermere, are undated. The next entry is dated the 12th, and describes the trip from Buttermere to Ennerdale. The next after that begins by describing Ennerdale, but changes to the Wastdale area, and remarks that they left T. Tyson's (at Wastdale Head—see, for example, *STCNB* I, 1214) Thursday morning [the 14th]. Thus they were at Wastdale Head the night of the 13th. It may be regarded as reasonably plain that they walked from Buttermere to Ennerdale on the 12th (*STCNB* I, 540). Beyond that all becomes conjecture. The following suggestions can be made: (a) The *STCNB* entry dated 12 Nov records activities from the beginning of that day, and thus the poets probably spent the previous night at Buttermere. (b) They did not walk all the way from Keswick to Buttermere in a single day, twenty-three or twenty-four miles (and if W went to Cockermouth, some five or so more miles for him), but they probably spent a night at Ouse Bridge, as *STCNB* I, 536, suggests. They thus appear to have spent the night at Ouse Bridge on 10 Nov and at Buttermere on 11 Nov. (c) Although the walk

75. [Nov 11]

W, STC walk from Ouse Bridge to Buttermere, via Lorton, Crummock Water. [W possibly reaches Lorton via Cockermouth, meeting STC on the way; STC at least reaches Lorton, via, probably, Embleton]. They spend the night at Buttermere, where they see Mary (Robinson) of Buttermere, [of whom W speaks in *Prel* VII.310–59, esp. 326–33, *Prel₂* VII.288–399, esp. 302–08.] (*STCNB* I, 535n, 537–39; 1799:74n.)[21]

76. [Nov 12]

W, STC walk from Buttermere to Ennerdale Water, [and probably spend the night there. (They possibly, however, continue on to Wastdale Head and spend the night there.)] At Ennerdale they learn the story of the death of James Bowman, which forms the basis of the story of the death of James Ewbank in *The Brothers*. (*STCNB* I, 540; *The Brothers* IF note; 1799:74n.)

77. [Nov 13]

W, STC [walk from Ennerdale Water, almost certainly via Black Sail, to Wastdale,] where they spend the night at Thomas Tyson's. (*STCNB* 541, 1214; 1799:74n; 1799:76.)

[21] There is no evidence that W visited Cockermouth now, but one doubts that he would have come within two miles of it after an absence of over five years without some attempt to do so. This trip is the only known occasion before the events of 1802–03, which brought Mary to public notice, when the poets are likely to have seen her at the same time (see PREL 563–64).

from Buttermere to Ennerdale via Floutern Tarn is only about six miles and the distance by that way to Wastdale Head some fifteen to seventeen miles depending on the route followed, the walk all the way to Wastdale Head would have been a rather demanding one; they probably did not make it, but spent the night near Ennerdale Water. They could, nevertheless, conceivably have gone on to Wastdale Head on the 12th and spent two nights at Tyson's, as suggested *STCNB* 540n. G. H. B. Coleridge, whose authority is cited as the basis for the *STCNB* statement—see *Wordsworth and Coleridge*, ed. E. L. Griggs, Princeton, 1939, 136, 144n—in fact expresses uncertainty on this point.

78. [Nov 14]

W, STC walk from Wastdale to Borrowdale, see a huge yew tree, spend the night (north of) the Yew Tree Rocks. (*STCNB* I, 541, 544.)[22]

79. [Nov 15]

W, STC walk via Grange, Lodore, Derwent Water, "King Pocky Estate" (see *STCNB* I, 541–42n) to Keswick; thence they walk to Threlkeld, where they spend the night. [If W does not already know the traditional story of Lord Clifford, which is employed in *Song at the Feast of Brougham Castle*, he possibly hears it at Threlkeld.] (*STCNB* I, 541–43, 549, 559; *Song at the Feast of Brougham Castle* n.)

80. [Nov 16]

W, STC walk via Matterdale, [Aira Force,] and the west shore of Ullswater [to Patterdale, where they spend the night]. (*STCNB* I, 549, 552, 554.)[23]

81. [Nov 17]

W, STC walk down the eastern shore of Ullswater [to Eusmere Hill, near Pooley Bridge, home of the Thomas Clarksons. They visit the Clarksons, and probably spend the night there.] (*STCNB* I, 551–53, 555.)[24]

---

[22] I do not know the evidence that they spent the night at Rosthwaite (as stated in *STCNB* I, 541n; G. H. B. Coleridge, "Samuel Taylor Coleridge Discovers the Lake Country," in *Wordsworth and Coleridge*, ed. E. L. Griggs, Princeton, 1939, 136, 144n; Hanson 372) rather than, say, Longthwaite or Seatoller.

[23] That they spent the night at Patterdale is not a certainty, but they did reach Patterdale, and they appear to have started directly down the eastern shore of the lake next morning as if from Patterdale. Probably the comment of *STCNB* I, 552, on "Clark's Niagra" is a reference to Aira Force, which James Clarke's *Survey of the Lakes* describes grandly, and not to Clarkson (cf *STCNB* I, 552n).

[24] *STCNB* records STC's sitting on a stump beside the lake by Clarksons' on Monday morning [18 Nov]. This is not conclusive indication of where they had slept, but the chance that they spent the night at the Clarksons' is perhaps increased by remarks in an unpublished letter from Catherine Clarkson to Priscilla Lloyd, 12 Jan 1800, which make it clear that W and STC paid the Clarksons a visit that amounted to more than a brief call. The following passage is quoted by permission of the owner of the letter, Mr. Jonathan Wordsworth: "I must tell you that we [had] a Visit from Coleridge and W. Wordsworth who spent a whole day with us. C was in high

82. [Probably between Nov 17 and Nov 20 or 21–early 1800]

[Probably between 17 and 20 or 21 Nov W and STC part. STC returns to Sockburn by 20 or 21 Nov. (*STCNB* I, 563, 1568, 1575.)

Possibly between the date of this parting and early 1800 W composes the Preamble, *Prel* I.1–54, *Prel*₂ I.1–45. (See GCL 63d3; 1795:34.)][25]

83. [Nov 18–25; almost certainly by Dec 14]

[W's activities and movements during this period are unknown; it is likely that he makes further investigation about possible places of residence in the Lake District for himself and DW; quite possibly he concludes basic arrangements for the rental of Dove Cottage. These arrangements are almost certainly completed by 14 Dec. (See 1799:82; 1799:88; Moorman I, 452–53; *EL* 558.)][26]

84. Nov 25 [and probably shortly after]

Afternoon. STC departs from Sockburn for London. (*STCNB* 590, 1575.)

[DW, Sara Hutchinson depart from Sockburn, perhaps to visit John Hutchinson at Stockton-on-Tees. (They probably return shortly after.) (See 1799:85; Moorman I, 453.)]

[25] I do not know the evidence on which *STCNB* I, 563n, bases its statement that W and STC parted at the Clarksons' on 18 Nov: All that is clear is that STC was at Scotch Corner on the 20th. Scotch Corner is only nine miles from Sockburn as the crow flies; so that STC could have completed the journey on the 20th. But the treatment of his foot at Scotch Corner suggests that he perhaps spent a night there. He must have arrived at the Hutchinsons' by the 21st.

[26] Although W had planned at first to talk with DW about Dove Cottage, he had also meant on 8 Nov to "write again when he knew more on this subject" (*STCL* I, 544; *EL* 233). This would have been the first time on the tour that he could have found out more about the house firsthand, or rented it, as in *Mem* I, 16–17 (*Mem*, R, I, 17) W says that he did. (W also says that the tour with STC took place "some months" previous to late Dec, but the present tour is W's only possible referent.)

Spirits & talk'd a great deal. W. was more reserved but there was neither hauteur nor moroseness in his Reserve He has a fine commanding figure is rather handsome & looks as if he was born to be a great Prince or a great General. He seems very fond of C. laughing at all his Jokes & taking all opportunities of shewing him off & to crown all he has the manners of a Gentleman."

85. [Nov 26 and probably shortly after]

[On 26 Nov] W returns to Sockburn, finds MH keeping house alone. [DW, Sara Hutchinson probably return to Sockburn shortly.] (*EL* 235. See 1799:84.)

86. Dec 11

W draws on RW for £15/17/– payable to Richard Dixon two months after date and £30 payable to John Hutchinson forty days after date. (*EL* 234; bill, DCP.)[27]

87. [Possibly c Dec 14]

W receives £5 from "Pinney" [probably JFP Jr.], who hopes to offer further assistance soon. (*EL* 234, 237.)[28]

88. [By Dec 14]

[Arrangements are almost certainly completed for W's renting DC for £8 per year. (*EL* 234, 558; *Excursion* IF note—*PW* V, 457.)]

89. Dec 14

DW writes to RW from Sockburn: W's drafts on RW [11 Dec]; W has written Pinney [probably JFP Jr.] for help in making Montagu repay W's loan. Plans for traveling to Grasmere. (*EL* 234.)

90. [Dec 17–20]

[On 17 Dec] W, DW depart from Sockburn and set out on horseback, accompanied by George Hutchinson, for Grasmere, [which they reach 20 Dec]. They cross the Tees by moonlight; before entering Richmond they meet a little girl who describes a mansion as "old Bules"; they see Hart-leap Well, near which a peasant tells them its story; they dine at Leyburn. [In or near Wensley] W, DW part with

---

[27] The bill was made out to John Hutchinson, not "Messrs Hutchinson" as DW indicates.

[28] W's remarks do not make it clear whether Pinney's gift came before or after W sought his help in straightening out affairs with Montagu, as he had done by 14 Dec.

George and proceed up Wensleydale on foot. They see a waterfall; lose themselves nearby. They reach Askrigg about 6 PM; spend the night there. (*EL* 234, 238, 239; *DWJ* I, 179–81; Moorman I, 453–54.) [On Hart-leap Well see *Hart-leap Well*, esp. 97–180, its note and IF note (and *app crit*). On their trip up Wensleydale see *DWJ* I, 180.

W writes of this trip generally in "Bleak Season Was It, Turbulent and Wild"; see *The Recluse*, esp. 152–78. The trip probably also contributes to *Prel* I.1–115, *Prel*₂ I.1–107 (see 1795:34).][29]

91. [Dec 18]

W, DW leave Askrigg, turn aside to visit the waterfall there; obtain a ride about one and a half miles from Askrigg to Hardraw, where they warm themselves. They walk up a brook to see [Hardraw Force], which impresses W deeply. They walk on, rest at an inn near Garsdale Chapel, drink a pint of ale, walk on to Sedbergh, [where they spend the night]. (*EL* 238–42; *DWJ* I, 182. See Moorman I, 456–57.) ["Bleak Season Was It, Turbulent and Wild" refers especially to this day. (See 1799:90; *EL* 239–42; Moorman I, 457.)]

92. [Dec 19]

W, DW walk from Sedbergh to Kendal, where they buy and order furniture. [They spend the night at Kendal.] (*EL* 242; *DWJ* I, 182. See 1799:91.)

93. [Probably Dec 20–1813 May 1]

[Probably on 20 Dec W, DW proceed to Grasmere from Kendal in a post chaise, arriving at Dove Cottage probably c 4:30. They are greeted by Molly Fisher; find no preparation for them except beds and a spark of fire. They find two letters from STC. (*EL* 234–42; *MY* 687. See 1799:92.) They reside in Grasmere until 1 May 1813. (See *MY* 559.)

---

[29] W says on [27 Dec] that they left Sockburn "tuesday before last." *Hart-leap Well* IF note and the lines quoted *PW* II, 515, possibly imply that W and DW were alone; but George's having dined with them at Leyburn (beyond the well) proves that he had not yet left them. The speaker of *Hart-leap Well*, also, is on horseback, as W would have been, although proceeding in a direction just the opposite of W's (from "Hawes to Richmond").

They reside at DC until c end May 1808. (EdS *DW* 237. See esp. *MY* 228–29.)

(DW refers to their arrival, and to a walk which she takes possibly on the evening of 20 Dec, more probably shortly after 24 Dec, in *Grasmere: A Fragment—West Country Magazine* III, 1947, 176–78. See also 1799:95n; 1799:98.)

W speaks of his return to his native mountains in his 1814 Preface to *The Excursion*. *Prel* I.1–271, *Prel₂* I.1–269 perhaps draw on emotions felt as the result of taking up residence here; but see esp. 1795:34n; PREL 512.

W refers to the early days at Grasmere: *The Recluse*; "When to the Attractions of the Busy World" 1–7; *PW* II, 118–19 *app crit*. On the early residence at Grasmere generally see esp. Moorman I, 459–615.]³⁰

94. [Shortly after Dec 20]

Early days after arrival at DC. W, DW occupy themselves in necessary labors of repair and improvement about the house. They agree with [Molly Fisher] for her to help them two or three hours a day for two shillings a week. (*EL* 234–36.)

95. [Probably between Dec 20 and Dec 23, esp. Dec 23; by Dec 28]

On one evening [probably between 20 and 23 Dec] W tempts DW out for a walk. They see Jupiter; DW returns with a toothache. They perhaps walk to Rydal Upper Park; [if not, such a walk takes place

---

³⁰ Mrs. Moorman (I, 457) adds a day to the trip in having them arrive at Kendal on the 20th, thus implying arrival at DC on the 21st. Other evidence also appears to point to the 21st or even 22nd: *Mem* I, 16–17, 149 (*Mem*, R, I, 16–17, 150), states that they arrived on St. Thomas's Day, which falls on the 21st; *Mem* II, 439 (*Mem*, R, II, 449), however, implies the 22nd (in Lady Richardson's reminiscence, dated 22 Dec 1843, of W's remarking that he and DW arrived "this day forty-four years ago"). But in view of (1) W's statement on Christmas eve that they arrived "last Friday" and have been at DC "four days" and (2) his description of the trip, there is no doubt that they arrived Friday 20 Dec. The hour of the arrival is variously reported, but again W's recollection on 27 Dec is almost certainly correct.

The name Dove Cottage is employed throughout the Chronology to refer to W's residence at Town End, although the term was not actually used at this time (see Moorman I, 459–60).

shortly after 24 Dec]. They [perhaps instead] walk into Easedale, [which becomes a favorite haunt; if this is their walk, 23 Dec is possibly its date. Only one of these walks can take place before 24 Dec; both take place by 28 Dec.] (*EL* 234–36; *To M.H.* and IF note; *PW* II, 448; *Mem* II, 439, *Mem*, R, II, 449. See 1799:93; 1799:101.)[31]

96. [Probably shortly before, certainly by, Dec 24–probably early 1800]

[Probably shortly before, certainly by, 24 Dec W begins *The Brothers*. The poem is probably completed in early 1800. He has possibly by the time when he commences the poem developed the idea of having it the conclusion of one of a series of "pastorals." (*EL* 237. See 1799:97; 1799:75; *The Brothers* n in edns 1800–32; *STCL* I, 611.)]

97. [Dec 24 (–Dec 27)]

[On 24 Dec W begins a letter to STC from Grasmere; he is to finish it 27 Dec]: Cooke's affair; W's return to Sockburn from the Lakes; early impressions and descriptions of DC and their activities there; financial aid from Pinney [see 1799:87]. STC in London. W has begun [*The Brothers*]; DW will [copy] PB, *The Borderers* soon. (*EL* 234–38. See 1799:100.)

98. [Probably shortly after Dec 24]

[DW walks out alone; discovers a lovely sheltered spot. (DW refers to this event: *Grasmere: A Fragment*.) (See *West Country Magazine* III, 1947, 176–78; 1799:93.)]

99. [Dec 25]

[W possibly goes skating. (See *EL* 236.)]

[31] W writes on 24 Dec that DW has scarcely been out since their arrival—only once, in fact, when they saw Jupiter and DW caught her toothache. *Mem* indicates that they discovered Easedale 23 Dec or very shortly after ("three days" following their arrival at Grasmere); but it is not probable that an early walk of this kind would have taken them both to Rydal Upper Park and Easedale, and there had only been one walk together before the 24th.

100. [Dec 27]

W finishes his letter to STC from Grasmere [begun 24 Dec]: Their journey from Sockburn to Grasmere. (*EL* 238–42.)[32]

101. [On or shortly before Dec 28 (certainly between Dec 20 and Dec 28)]

W composes *To M.H.* (*To M.H.* and IF note; MS Journal 4, DCP; *PW* II, 488. See 1799:95.)

---

[32] The letter was finished "Friday Evg"; the Friday must have been the first one following Christmas Eve, when the letter was begun.

APPENDIX I

References in Wordsworth's Writings to the Years before He Enters Hawkshead School

W makes frequent references in his writings to the years before he entered Hawkshead School. When these references can be dated more or less specifically, mention of their substance is made in the text or its notes. The following passages also have a clear or probable bearing on these years, but their dates seem to me incapable of precise determination. IF notes are treated as writings of W's.

A. Probable references to W's early infancy (but with an application altogether hypothetical)
  1. *Prel* I.271–85, *Prel₂* I.269–81. (Composition of his thoughts to "more than infant softness" by the river Derwent.)
  2. *Prel* II.237–87, *Prel₂* I.232–72. (Development of the child's mind begins as he is nursed in his mother's arms.)

B. Probable references to only the years before he entered Hawkshead School
  1. *In Sight of the Town of Cockermouth.* (General reference.)
  2. *Address from the Spirit of Cockermouth Castle.* (His young thoughts made "acquainted with the grave" as he plays in Cockermouth Castle.)
  3. *Prel* V.246–90, *Prel₂* V.246–93. (W's mother.)
  4. *Prel* XIII.211–18, *Prel₂* XIV.232–39. (Reference to DW; her early aid in W's perceptions of nature.)
  5. *To a Butterfly* ("Stay near me"). (See also *DWJ* I, 123. Reference to DW. Chasing butterflies.)
  6. *The Sparrow's Nest* and IF note. (The garden of W's house at Cockermouth.)
  7. *On a High Part of the Coast of Cumberland* IF note. (Reference to DW. Early visit to the sea at Whitehaven.)
  8. *Composed by the Seashore* IF note. (Early experiences with the sea.)

9. *The Childless Father* IF note. (Funerals and hunting.)
10. *The Old Cumberland Beggar* and IF note. (Observes original of the beggar.)
11. *Catechizing.* See *Mem* I, 8. (Catechism.)

C. Probable references to the years before he entered Hawkshead School, but bearing both on these and later years, esp. those spent at Hawkshead. (The possibility that the reference is only to later years cannot be excluded in every case.)

1. *Tintern Abbey* 73–74. ("The coarser pleasures of my boyish days.")
2. *The River Duddon* IF note. (Early angling, including angling on the banks of the Derwent.)
3. *Nunnery* IF note. (Penrith, esp. on summer holidays. Visits to the Nunnery.)
4. *Prel* I.305–06, *Prel₂* I.301–02. (W fostered by beauty and fear.)
5. *Prel* I.351–71 and *app crit*, *Prel₂* I.340–56. (The ministry of nature to favored beings from their infancy.)
6. *Prel* V.166–79, *Prel₂* V.166–80. (W's early love of story and verse.)
7. *Prel* VIII.69–101, and *app crit.* (W's early love of man; sight of shepherd.)
8. *Prel* VIII.101–19 and *EW* 165–68. (Another early sight of a shepherd.)[1]
9. *Prel* VIII.119–220, *Prel₂* VIII.70–172. (The paradise where he was reared. Growth of his human love in his native regions.)
10. *Prel* IX.217–25, 236–41; *Prel₂* IX.215–22, 233–38. (Early knowledge of the falsity of artificial inequalities between men.)
11. *Prel* XIII.211–26, *Prel₂* XIV.232–46. (Probably applicable until at least c 1795–97. His predilection for beauty with terror in it.)
12. *To the Daisy* ("In youth"). ("Most pleased when most uneasy.")
13. *To the Rev. Dr. Wordsworth* 25–30. (Christmas minstrels.)

[1] This experience took place, according to *Prel* VIII.103, at "as early age" as the experience just cited—that is, "while yet a very Child" (*Prel* VIII.82). But since the IF note to *EW* indicates that he saw this sight while crossing Dunmail Raise, the occasion may belong to the Hawkshead years. W implies (although he does not state) that the sight of Grasmere described in *The Recluse* 1–14 was his first, and it seems fairly certain that this event took place while W was at Hawkshead. It would hardly have been possible to cross Dunmail Raise without seeing Grasmere. On the other hand, such a ramble by W while a schoolboy in Cockermouth or Penrith would have been impossibly long; it is eighteen miles from Cockermouth and sixteen from Penrith to Dunmail Raise as the crow flies, and W had only just reached his ninth birthday before his departure for Hawkshead. The poet may thus have seen this sight after discovering Grasmere from Hawkshead. See Appendix II, note 9.

14. *Excursion* IV.109–22. (Visionary powers of eye and soul; he watches sunrises and sunsets.)
15. *Recluse* 703–20. (Love of daring feats as a child.)
16. *Mem* I, 8–13, Autobiog Mem. (Various early experiences at Cocker-mouth and Penrith.)[2]

D. Probable references both to years before W entered Hawkshead School and the rest of W's life up to the time of the composition of the given passage.

1. *Prel* X.1007–09, *Prel*₂ XI.424–26. (W's love of dreaming of Sicily from "earliest school-day time.")
2. *Prel* XII.145–219, *Prel*₂ XIII.142–220. (W's love of a public road from the "dawn of childhood"; see PREL 616.)
3. *The Egyptian Maid* IF note. (His delight in the water lily.)
4. *Excursion* I (and *RC*). (Much of the growth of the Pedlar's mind from childhood can be taken as the poet's description of the growth of his own mind.)
5. Worth note here also are:

   a. The only direct indication of the character of W's earliest known literary training (*Mem* I, 34), his being required to memorize long passages of Shakespeare, Spenser, and Milton.

   b. The remark made by STC to Richard Sharp in a letter of 15 Jan 1804 (see *STCL* II, 1032), noting W's tendency to melancholy from childhood.

---

[2] Moorman I, 19, dates the contemplated suicide and attack on the portrait in 1778 or after.

APPENDIX II

References in Wordsworth's Writings to Hawkshead and His Years in School There

References in W's writings to Hawkshead and the years he spent in school there are quite numerous. For references, many of them important, which appear to refer to both these and earlier years, or to either period, see Appendix I. When references can be dated more or less specifically, mention of their substance is made in the text or its notes. The following passages also have a clear or probable bearing on the Hawkshead years, but the dates to which they refer seem incapable of precise determination. IF notes are treated as writings of W's.

A. Passages which seem to refer to times primarily within the earlier Hawkshead years.

1. *Nutting* and IF note. (See also *PW* III, 504–06. Nutting. See also section D below.)
2. *Prel* I.309–50, *Prel₂* I.306–39. (Trapping birds; birds'-nesting. Noted by W esp. in connection with first autumn and spring at Hawkshead, but probably recurrent for some years. See 1782:5.)
3. *Prel* I.372–427, *Prel₂* I.357–400. (During a vacation, probably before the death of his father, W steals a boat [for a few minutes] on Ullswater. See PREL 517.)[3]
4. *Prel* V.501–15, *Prel₂* V.477–90. (Before death of W's father. Reading on vacations at Cockermouth. On this subject see also *Mem* I, 10.)
5. Worth note here also are:
   a. TWT *Hawkshead Church* 5: W told Miss Mary Hodgson of Hawkshead (d. 1915, aged 92) of going up to the churchyard on summer evenings during his early years at the school. W would some-

---

[3] Moorman I, 39, states that W was on his way to Penrith when this incident occurred. While Ullswater is out of the way for a journey to Cockermouth, W says in the *app crit* that he was "in travel to [his] father's house," that is, Cockermouth. This statement can be used as the basis for a conjectural dating.

times talk to the old men sitting there, and be invited to share their seat.

b. TWT *Hawkshead Church* 19: W also told Miss Hodgson of his pleasure "as a new boy" in watching the parish clerk in Hawkshead Chapel give the parish singers their keynotes. See 1779:1. Also, during his first year at Hawkshead, W saw a decrepit pew collapse as a result of the deliberate efforts of four or five larger boys sitting on it.

B. Passages which seem to refer to times primarily within the later Hawkshead years.

    1. *LLSYT* and IF note. (A local misanthrope. The site of the yew tree a favorite walk of W's in "the latter part of [his] school-time." W leads a boy to look at the view from the spot.)[4]

    2. Worth note here also is Edward Whatley, "Personal Recollections of the Lake Poets," *The Leisure Hour* XIX (1870), 653 (noted by Bateson 65). An older boy of the school asks W: "How is it, Bill, thee doest write such good verses? Doest thee invoke Muses?" As Bateson remarks, *PW* (Knight, 1882–89) IX, 38, reports the same story (less amusingly) as told by W to the Rev. Mr. Hill.

C. Passages which seem to refer to times (with qualifications as noted or as indicated in cross-references) that can be dated no more specifically than as falling within the Hawkshead years.

    1. *Written in Very Early Youth.* (Possibly refers to an evening scene at Hawkshead. See Appendix IV; GCL 32.)

    2. *Anacreon.* (Perhaps refers to youthful feelings for MH. See 1786:14; GCL 11.)

    3. [*Beauty and Moonlight, an Ode,*] *Fragment.* (Perhaps refers to youthful feelings for MH. See GCL 10.)

    4. *Sonnet Written by Mr. _____ Immediately after the Death of His Wife.* (Perhaps refers to an actual death at Hawkshead, Penrith, Whitehaven, or elsewhere. See 1787:4; GCL 17.)

---

[4] TWT *W's Hawkshead* II, 14, 16, date W's leading the boy to see the view in early 1787, but unless further evidence becomes available the date should be left more general. The boy is identified by the same source as one of the grandsons of Bartholomew Purcell of Near Sawrey (but cf W's remark that the boy was "Irish" and the servant of an "itinerant conjurer"). The yew tree is stated to have been situated on a piece of common land between Smooth Beck Bridge and Water Side. The misanthrope himself is identified (see also Moorman I, 312) as the Rev. William Braithwaite of Satter How.

5. *A Ballad*. (Perhaps refers to a love affair well known in the Hawkshead area.)[5]
6. *Dirge, Sung by a Minstrel*. (Perhaps refers to an actual death at Hawkshead or elsewhere. See below, note 12.)
7. *V of E*. (Heavy use made of observation of natural and other scenes in Hawkshead area. Some lines capable of closer dating are noted elsewhere. Many scenes here are duplicated in *EW*. See esp. Fink 20, which suggests that the castle mentioned in the poem has its origin in Calgarth Hall on Windermere—but cf "Dear Native Regions" IF note. See Moorman I, 47–74, on relation of *V of E* to W's life and reading. Also see GCL 13.)
8. *EW* and IF note. (Heavy use made of observation of natural and other scenes in Hawkshead area. Some lines capable of closer dating are noted elsewhere. See GCL 28.)[6]
9. *To Lucca Giordano*, 11–14. (Love of moon. For an early working of this passage see *PW* V, 340, *II, i*.)
10. *The Two Thieves* and IF note. (Observes originals of the two thieves at Hawkshead.)[7]
11. *PB* 881–915 and IF note. (Knows Benoni at Hawkshead. See above, entry 5.)
12. *Ode. Intimations of Immortality* and IF note. (Occasional convictions of ideality of material universe and related early attitudes.)
13. *Ode to Lycoris* IF note. (Reading of classics at school, esp. his admiration for Ovid.)
14. "Grief, Thou Hast an Ever Ready Friend" IF note. (Watches spinning in Westmorland cottages.)
15. *Composed in One of the Valleys of Westmorland, on Easter Sunday.* (Easters.)

---

[5] TWT *W's Hawkshead* II, 16, offers evidence that the poem refers to the death of Mary Rigg of Greenend after and apparently as a consequence of being forsaken by her lover, David Kirkby of Thwaite. David Kirkby was the supposed father (Hawkshead PR, TWT) of Mary's child Benoni, on whom see *PB* 886–915 and IF note.

[6] *EW* 71–84, which refers to Rydal Falls (in the vale of Grasmere), must have its origin in the time following W's discovery of Grasmere. See entry 22 below and Appendix I, note 1.

[7] TWT (*W's Hawkshead* I, 12) identifies "the two thieves" as Daniel Mackereth, an aged shoemaker, and his grandson Dan Mackereth, of Hawkshead. TWT dates the scene in which the two are mentioned in the early summer 1780 (old Daniel is said to be then about 90), but W's observations probably occurred over a period of time.

16. The Matthew poems, and *Matthew* IF note. (Concerning references in these works to William Taylor see 1781:1. TWT, *W's Hawkshead*, I, 8, and information in letter to Mrs. J. P. Hogan, suggests that John Harrison, the Hawkshead schoolmaster and W's fishing companion— see 1779:4—contributed also to the character of Matthew. Other references to Hawkshead and its inhabitants appear to be contained in the following works.)

    a. Esp. *Matthew*, *The Fountain*, *PW* IV, 452–55, *The Two April Mornings*: TWT *W's Hawkshead* I, 19, and TWT *Hawkshead Church* 45–56 explain that Thomas Cowperthwaite, ironmonger, of Hawkshead, who died 6 July 1782, aged seventy-two, is commemorated on a memorial stone at Hawkshead for "his facetious disposition" and "other good qualities." Furthermore, he seems to have had few surviving relatives in old age, and no son or daughter. TWT *Hawkshead Church* 45–46 quotes some of his "witty rhymes" which have survived at Hawkshead.

    b. Esp. *Matthew*, *The Fountain*, *PW* IV, 452–55: TWT *W's Hawkshead* I, 20, and II, 16, indicate that the primary model for the Wanderer in *The Excursion*, and thus *RC*, David Moore, sang and made up verses. (See *PW* V, 405–09, and entry 17 below.)

    c. "The Fountain" 71–72 (the "crazy old church-clock" and "bewildered chimes"): TWT *W's Hawkshead* II, 1, and TWT *Hawkshead Church* 46 show that the Hawkshead Church clock in W's day was old and often needed fixing. Thomas Cowperthwaite (on whom see just above) possibly celebrated the clock's irregularities.

17. *The Excursion*, esp. I (notably I.52–76), and IF note; also *RC*. (Many aspects of the Wanderer probably first noted by W in his friendship with the packman David Moore—see above, 16b—during these years; TWT *W's Hawkshead* I, 20 and II, 16. For additional details see *PW* V, 405–09, which probably, like the *Excursion* itself, draws on Thomas Cowperthwaite—see above, 16a—in its portrait of the Wanderer.)[8]

18. *Excursion* V.150–53. ("Admonitory texts" perhaps seen at Hawkshead Church. TWT *Hawkshead Church* 22–23.)

---

[8] PREL 515 states that one Drummond was the original of the Wanderer. W gives the name Drummond to the character fitting this role in MS E of the *Excursion* (see *PW* V, 405–09), but such was not the name of the packman "who told [W] stories as a boy." It is interesting to note that on 24 Sept 1833 (*LY* 668) W was reminded of the poet "Drummond, an Author with whom I became acquainted in my Youth," and that "the Jacobite" (see *Excursion* VI.404–521 and IF note) was named Drummond.

19. *Excursion* VI.95–211 and IF note (see *PW* V, 456–57). (The disappointed lover once a schoolfellow of W's. Another schoolmate [William Pearson].)

20. *Excursion* VI.404–521 and IF note. (The Whig and the Jacobite. See below, entry 29.)

21. *Excursion* IX.483–88. (Rowing on Windermere.)

22. *The Recluse* 1–45. (Perhaps refers to W's first sight of Grasmere. See Appendix I, note 1.)[9]

23. *The Waggoner* III.110–29. (See below, entry 30.)

24. *PW* III, 159 *app crit.* (Passage originally intended for *Ode. The Morning of the Day Appointed for a General Thanksgiving.* Reads of chivalry; hears old ballads.)

25. *PW* V, 342, III. (Listens to wind. Hawkshead date highly conjectural.)

26. *Prel* I.442–570, *Prel₂* I.415–543. (Scenes and sports through the Hawkshead years. November, winter skating, nutting, angling, kite flying, local cottages, card playing.)

27. *Prel* II.7–18, *Prel₂* II.7–18. (The boys' "round of tumult.")

28. *Prel* II.33–47 and *app crit, Prel₂* II.33–46. (The market place and its stone in Hawkshead.)[10]

29. *Prel* II.48–202, *Prel₂* II.47–197. (Activities, esp. summer excursions on horse to Furness Abbey. On these excursions see also *Prel* X.559–67, *Prel₂* X.595–603. The inn at Windermere was "The White Lion," Bowness, notable also as a haunt of the Whig and the Jacobite; *TWT W's Hawkshead* II, 10. See also section D below.)

30. *Prel* II.291–434, *Prel₂* II.276–418; and PREL 525 (*Prel* II.434/435). (Growth of mind from early youth to "seventeenth year," esp. interaction of nature and his mind. Observations of nature.)[11]

---

[9] One may reasonably guess that W's mention of "Grasmere's stream" in *Anacreon* points toward his having seen Grasmere at least before 7 Aug 1786, when he probably completed a fair copy of the poem. But he had no doubt heard the attractive name of Grasmere before seeing the object to which it applied.

[10] While W says that the stone was named after "the old Dame" who watches her table there, and the *app crit* gives it the name of "Stone of Rowe," TWT *W's Hawkshead* I, 14–17, states that the stone was known widely as the "Rocking Stone," and was kept by "Nannie" [Mrs. Ann] Holme.

[11] *Prel* II.294–96, *Prel₂* II.279–81 perhaps refers to the death of W's parents (see 1778:1; 1783:11). As his companion on his morning walks (*Prel* II.348–353, *Prel₂* II.329–34) was John Fleming (see PREL 524; *V of E* 542–45), who went up to Cambridge in 1785, W's reference in these lines must be to that year or before.

31. *Prel* V.389–449, *Prel₂* V.364–425; ("There Was a Boy"—see poem
    of that title and IF note—and general reflections on Hawkshead life.
    On the owls on Windermere see also *The Waggoner* III.110–29.)¹²
32. *Prel* V.483–500, *Prel₂* V.460–76. (Saves to buy *Arabian Nights*.)
33. *Prel* VII.81–135, *Prel₂* VII.77–141. (Early beliefs about London; the
    schoolmate who visits it.)
34. *Prel* VII.480–87, *Prel₂* VII.448–57. (Visits country playhouse. Hawks-
    head date highly conjectural.)
35. *Prel* VII.600–02, *Prel₂* VII.632–34; PREL 533 (from a MS of *PB*). (Sees
    dreamlike shapes while lying in bed. See GCL 14.)
36. *Prel* VIII.119–311, *Prel₂* VIII.73–172. (Nature and man in his youth.
    Story of shepherd told him by Ann Tyson. See section D below.)
37. *Prel* VIII.353–471, *Prel₂* VIII.215–339. (Man ennobled for him through
    sights of shepherds and other dwellers and workers in the Lake
    area.)
38. *Prel* VIII.472–97, *Prel₂* VIII.340–64. (Nature still secondary to W's
    own pursuits.)
39. *Prel* VIII.624–40, *Prel₂* VIII.476–94. (Man rises in his opinion to crown
    of "visible natures." See *Prel* VIII.482–85, *Prel₂* VIII.346–56.)
40. *Prel* VIII.761–96, *Prel₂* VIII.632–38. (Early feelings nursed by natural
    scenes.)
41. *Prel* IX.217–25, *Prel₂* IX.215–22. (See Appendix I, C10.)
42. *Prel* X.382–86, *Prel₂* X.416–20. (Begins to yield self to nature.)
43. *Prel* X.559–67, *Prel₂* X.595–603. (See above, entry 29.)
44. *Prel* XI.199–240, *Prel₂* XII.151–90. (Dating conjectural—perhaps refers
    to a later time. Description of MH. W's love for his native hills.)
45. *Prel* XIII.313–31, *Prel₂* XIV.329–47. (Training in sturdy independence
    at Hawkshead.)

¹² Various suggestions have been made as to the identity of the "boy" who hooted
at the owls. See esp. Robertson 67–68; Moorman I, 37n. Probably he was not simply
W, as the latter source states, but a composite of at least W and William Raincock
(see "There Was a Boy" IF note). In addition TWT *Hawkshead Church* 42–43 explains
that when speaking of the "boy's" early death and grave, W was thinking of a
school friend, John Tyson. (W himself informed a daughter of his cousin Richard,
no doubt RW of Branthwaite, of this fact; she, before her death in 1890, told it to
TWT's informant.) TWT quotes an entry of 1782 from the Hawkshead PR: "John
Son of Willm Tyson Gallobarrow Taylor Died Aug. ye 25th Buried ye 27th in the
Ch yard Aged 12." Tyson attended Joseph Varty's writing class (on Varty see also
1784:10n) and sold the Grammar School students birds' eggs obtained by his brother
William (on whom see also 1782:5n).

46. PREL 623–34. (Storm on Coniston Lake; horse silhouetted against moonlit sky.)
47. *Mem* I, 9–13. (Autobiog Mem. Recollections of Hawkshead years.)
48. *A Guide through the District of the Lakes*, ed. W. M. Merchant (London, 1951), 157. (Sees ravens suspended beside Hawkshead Church.)[13]
49. *EL* 233. (W to DW, 7 Nov 1799. The "great change amongst the People" at Hawkshead since "we [JW, W] were last there." See 1799:65.)
50. *EL* 269. (W to Miss Taylor, 9 Apr 1801. General reference.)
51. *HCR & W Circle* 624. (W to HCR, 20 May 1846. Over a hundred boys were playing and roaming the vale in W's day.)
52. Worth note here also are:

a. The recollection by Mrs. Davy of Ambleside (*Mem* II, 463–64; *Mem*, R, II, 472–73) of W's remarks to her about the only times he had felt envy. One of these cases, when he tripped up his brother's heels in a race, was possibly a Hawkshead incident, but such a date is quite conjectural.

b. W's comment in a letter to Mrs. Fisher, probably 1837 or 1838 (*Fortnightly Review* N.S. LXXXVIII, 1910, 880): "One of my School-masters, whom I most respected and loved, was, unfortunately for me, a passionate admirer of Dr. Johnson's prose, and having not been much exercised in prose myself, I have not got over the ill-effects of that injudicious [word illegible], upon my own way of expressing myself." The schoolmaster was probably Taylor, but certainty is not possible.

c. "Memoir of William Wordsworth, Esq.," *The New Monthly Magazine* XI (1819), 48–50. The unidentified author of this memoir appears to have received some of his information about W's school-days from at least one of W's Hawkshead contemporaries. Among the facts noted are the following: That once when W or CW was attacked by a larger boy, the other brother rushed to the defense of the first and helped drive off the aggressor [CW entered Hawkshead 1785]; that W's writings frequently were praised by Taylor; that W "before the morning hour of repairing to school . . . has been often seen and heard in the sequestered lane, either alone, or with a favorite companion, repeating aloud beautiful passages from Thomson's Seasons, and some-times comparing, as they chanced to occur, the actual phenomena of nature with the descriptions given of them by the poet." (See above,

[13] TWT *Hawkshead Church* 45 reports that a bounty of 4d per raven was paid at that time.

entry 30n.) For the comment of this source on W's earliest poetic composition see Appendix III.

    d. *MY* 246. (W to Francis Wrangham, 2 Oct 1808. W reads White's *Natural History of Selborne*.)

D. Passages which seem to refer in particular to Ann Tyson.
1. *Nutting* 9–11. (She provides clothes for nutting expeditions.)
2. *Composed in One of the Valleys of Westmorland, on Easter Sunday*. (Her new clothes at Easter.)
3. *Excursion* VI.404–521 and IF note. (W learns of the Whig and Jacobite from her.)
4. *Prel* IV.16–28, *Prel*₂ IV.27–39. (W's grateful memories of her.)
5. *Prel* IV.208–21, *Prel*₂ IV.217–30. (Her "smooth domestic life.")
6. *Prel* VIII.216–311, *Prel*₂ VIII.168–72; see also PREL 578 and *PW* II, 478–84. (Her tales, esp. one which W originally intended for *Michael*.)
7. See also *DWJ* I, 309. (She tells W long stories of Bonawe, Argyll, where she worked in her youth.)

APPENDIX III

Wordsworth's Earliest Poetic Composition

Available evidence on the time and place of W's first composition is somewhat confusing. The following references are those with the most direct bearing on the case.

1. *Mem* I, 10: "The first verses which I wrote were a task imposed by my master; the subject, 'The Summer Vacation'; and of my own accord I added other verses upon 'Return to School.'"

2. *Prel* X.514–15, *Prel*₂ X.551–52; W first begins to compose his "toilsome Songs" at William Taylor's command.

3. *Mem* II, 304 (Justice Coleridge's Personal Reminiscences): "He told me . . . that his first verses were a Popian [*sic*] copy written at school on the 'Pleasure of Change'; then he wrote another on the 'Second Centenary of the School's Foundation'; that he had written these verses on the holidays, and on the return to school; that he was rather the poet of the school."

4. *The New Monthly Magazine* XI (1819), 48: "At the age of thirteen his genius was indicated in verses on the vacation, which procured him the praise of the master; but it would seem that this incipient effort did not quite satisfy himself, since we are told that at the next returning season of welcome relaxation from scholastic discipline, he composed another poem on the same subject, which was also applauded by those to whom it was shown." [The parts of the memoir of Wordsworth from which this quotation is taken (see also Appendix II, C 52) appear to have used information directly from at least one unidentified contemporary of W's at Hawkshead.]

5. *Lines Written as a School Exercise at Hawkshead, anno aetatis* 14: Composed "upon the completion of the second centenary from the foundation of the school in 1585" (*Mem* I, 10, Autobiog Mem). CW Jr. remarks (*Mem* I, 10n) that "such is the title, but he must have been at least in his fifteenth year, if the year of the foundation is stated correctly."

6. Moorman I, 56–57: "In 1785, when Wordsworth was fifteen, Hawks-

head school celebrated its bicentenary ... Wordsworth produced over a hundred lines of heroic couplet ... [These lines] led directly to his beginning to compose verse 'from the impulse of [his] own mind.' Before that he had written some lines on 'The Summer Vacation,' ... a subject set by his master: he added of his own accord some more on 'Return to School.' [A statement of Wordsworth's recorded in the Diary of Miss Serle, in the possession of Miss Bell, Ambleside, that a walk home from a dance in Egremont occasioned his 'first voluntary verses' suggests that the 'Return' lines] were probably written during the Christmas holidays of 1784-85 ... From the summer of 1785 onwards he wrote fairly constantly. About this time he was given [the MS book mentioned by Aubrey de Vere]." (See entry 8 below.)

7. *Mem* I, 10-13: The assigned lines on the bicentenary of Hawkshead School "put it into [W's] head to compose verses from the impulse of [his] own mind, and [he] wrote [*V of E*]."

8. *PW* I, 366 (Aubrey de Vere to W. R. Hamilton, Jan 1843, in R. P. Graves, *The Life of Sir W. R. Hamilton*, Dublin and London, 1882-89, II, 402): "Did W. ever tell you that the accident of his being given a manuscript book was the first *occasion* (I do not say *cause*) of his writing poetry? He thought it a pity, after filling up a few pages, to leave the remainder 'white and unwritten still,' and so got into the habit of reducing to shape the thoughts which had before been vaguely haunting his brain, like to body-waiting souls, which wandered by the Lethean pools." [This Nb was undoubtedly DCP MS Verse 4.]

9. *The Idiot Boy* (1798) 337-38: "I to the Muses have been bound/ These fourteen years by strong indentures."

10. *EW* IF note: W states that he could not have been above fourteen years of age when he resolved to supply the deficiency in natural imagery in all previous poetry—so far as he knew it. (W would not have reached this determination before he had done some writing.)

11. Moorman I, 53: "It was not until his sixteenth year that [W] began to attempt to write verse."

12. See 1784:10: TWT indicates that W may have written verses on the Castlehow arrest, which evidently took place early Sept 1784.

Consideration of these various statements and relevant facts tends to establish a few points as reasonably probable. Plainly the bicentenary lines would hardly have been written before 1785 (see 1785:4). The skill shown in this poem (see, for example, M. L. Barstow Greenbie, *Wordsworth's Theory of Poetic Diction*, New Haven, 1917, 73-75) presupposes some previous practice in composition. The first verses which W wrote, as he himself clearly states, were probably assigned to him by William Taylor (this fact is confirmed by *Prel* X.514–15, *Prel*₂ X.551–52), and their subject was the summer vacation; to these W added verses of his own accord on the subject of the return to school. Mrs. Moorman's conjecture (I, 57) that the Return to School verses were written during Christmas holidays is given confirmation by the passage from *The New Monthly Magazine*. And it can be concluded that Justice Coleridge pretty certainly misunderstood W's comments on his earliest composition, and confused statements by the poet on his early subjects with chronological data in saying that W wrote *The Pleasure of Change* and the bicentenary lines "on the holidays and on the return to school." It is almost certain that W could not have been going to a dance at Egremont before the Christmas vacation of 1784–85 (see entries and notes for that and following Christmas vacations in the Chronology). Inasmuch as the bicentenary lines probably date from 1785, it can be concluded that W's first voluntary composition took place during Christmas vacation, 1784–85 (perhaps c 20 Dec–perhaps c 20 Jan), and that his first composition, the verses assigned by Taylor, took place upon his return from summer holidays in 1784. The title "The Pleasure of Change" would appear well suited for the Egremont lines, but might have served for the assigned lines on the vacation. Apropos of the dance at Egremont, the only record of W's having received formal instruction in dancing refers to 1785 (see 1785:7), but this fact scarcely precludes his having known enough of the art to have attended a dance the preceding winter. (One wonders whether any of this experience was fused with his memory of his imaginative "dedication" some years, evidently, later, and also after a dance.)

W clearly did not consider, however, that the determination, implied by the bicentenary lines, "to compose verses from the impulse of his own mind" was equivalent to his having added verses on the "return to school" "of his own accord": He mentions both circumstances within four sentences of each other. Nor need either remark necessarily be supposed to concern his "first voluntary verses." The first technically voluntary verses he wrote, the lines on the "return to school," had been strongly suggested by the assigned lines on the summer vacation, and were thus not voluntary in the sense that they would have been had the occasion, subject, and execution been all the result of his own thinking. Likewise, "to compose verses from the impulse of his own mind" implies an extended poetic intention (W thinks of the long poem *V of E*, which ran well over a thousand lines, as its first principal result) which a number of casual original compositions, and certainly the Egremont lines, could easily have preceded.

W's statement in *The Idiot Boy* that he had in the spring of 1798 been bound to the muses fourteen years (a figure obviously not chosen at random) "by strong indentures," W's earliest comment on this subject, is open to varying interpretations. Its most likely reference is to the time when he reached an enduring determination to write verses. "Fourteen years" would put this event in 1784, in W's fourteenth or fifteenth year; the event probably did not occur, however, until after the writing of the bicentenary lines, pretty certainly in his sixteenth year.

If the supposition that W's first composition dates from the end of summer 1784 is correct, then his determination to supply the defects of previous poets in natural imagery, if it occurred at all before he was fifteen (as he said), must have come before 7 Apr of the following year. But such a determination would seem necessarily corollary to an enduring determination to write poetry—and therefore also more likely to have occurred when W was in fact fully fifteen.

The chief remaining problem concerns the possibility of W's having written verses in celebration of the Castlehow incident of early Sept 1784. As remarked above, the basis for the dating of that incident is not indicated. The statement of TWT would normally be sufficient warrant for the accuracy of the date, but there seems reason to doubt that W was at Hawkshead in early Sept. He could, of course, have written all his first verses, plus the Castlehow verses, sometime after 20 Sept (the date after which he probably returned to school). The Castlehow verses could in addition have been short, casual, and soon forgotten. Finally, there seem no very good grounds for certainty that he ever wrote them at all.

To summarize: It appears likely that W's first verses, on "The Summer Vacation" (assigned by William Taylor), were composed after his return to school from summer vacation 1784, after 20 Sept and perhaps in early Oct. He possibly composed lines on the Castlehow incident about this time or later, but the first verses W later remembered writing of his own accord were added during the following Christmas vacation, their subject, The Return to School. These were written "after walking six miles to attend a dance at Egremont." Either these lines or the lines written after the summer vacation probably had the formal title *The Pleasure of Change*. The following spring, doubtless near the end of the school year, he composed his earliest surviving work, *Lines Written as a School Exercise at Hawkshead*. Probably during the summer of 1785, after the latter work and partly as a result of its stimulus, he determined to make a continued effort to compose original verse. The gift of a manuscript book about or not long after this time proved a strong inducement toward this goal. Objections to these conclusions are possible, but alternative conclusions seem subject to even greater doubts.

APPENDIX IV

The Dates of Several Early Translations and Drafts in the Racedown and Windy Brow Notebooks

EdS has given conjectural dates in *PW* I for several of W's translations or adaptations on the basis of the dates of main usage of the Nbs in which the MSS appear. These poems include: (1) *Septimi Gades*, (2) *The Birth of Love*, (3) *From the Greek*, (4) *Lesbia*, (5) *Septimius and Acme*, (6) "If Grief Dismiss Me Not to Them That Rest." He has also dated the earliest surviving work toward *Written in Very Early Youth* by this method: these lines and items 4, 5, and 6 are dated 1795–97 on the basis of their presence in the Racedown Nb; items 1, 2, and 3 are dated 1794 on the basis of their appearance in the Windy Brow Nb. The following remarks explain, with one exception, the dates that are given to these works in the chronology. On *The Birth of Love* see esp. GCL 41.

Items 1, 2, and 3 follow immediately upon one another, on verso pages, in the Windy Brow Nb and face MS work on *SP* that fairly surely was entered earlier than they were; despite a few corrections and gaps, they have clearly been copied into the Nb from another source. *From the Greek* follows so closely upon the end of *The Birth of Love* (here called *From the French*) that its title has had to be stuck in somewhat inconveniently between the last line of the one and the first of the other, a fact implying what the autograph tends to confirm, that all the copying probably took place at once—possibly from a common source and perhaps not without absentmindedness. The question of how W could by the time of writing *Septimi Gades* have forgotten Annette Vallon to such an extent that he would use the poem to ask "Mary" to share a cottage with him in a valley above the Rhone or in Grasmere (see, for instance, *PW* I, 371; Margoliouth 56–57; EdS, *Wordsworthian and Other Studies*, London, 1947, 21–25) may be dismissed if the poem from which the Windy Brow copy is made is assigned to late 1790 (after the walking trip) or 1791 before W became acquainted with Annette. There appears no reason why the poem should not be so dated. *The Birth of Love* was probably translated between 1792 and 23 May 1794 (see GCL 41). The Greek original of *From the Greek* is a simple and quite well-known poem (see Armandus Gasté, *De Scoliis sive de Convivalibus Carminibus apud Graecos*, Caen, 1873, 23–29), and this fact along with the character of its emotions make it a poem which a schoolboy would have been likely to meet and wish to translate. Woof *SB* 165 seems almost certainly correct in concluding that W's verses date from his school days. (See also 1794:7n.)

Of the three translations and the other poem mentioned above from the Racedown Nb (principal use of which was in fact in 1795–97), one of the translations, *Lesbia*, has been described above (see GCL 10) as quite surely schoolboy work (see Woof *SB* 169); it is copied fairly into this Nb. Despite the fact that a few lines of draft for *Septimius and Acme* appear in the Racedown Nb as well as the poem in its entirety, the poem is also plainly copied into this Nb from elsewhere. As Woof *SB* and Miss Landon indicate, it was clearly adjacent to the copy of *Lesbia* before W used the intervening pages for drafts toward *Inscription for a Seat by a Road Side, Half Way up a Steep Hill, Facing the South*; it, *Lesbia*, and *The Starling* are W's only known translations from Catullus. The tone of the poem has nothing in common with any composition in which W is definitely known to have been engaged during 1795–97. I suspect that the work dates from W's schoolboy period, or, at latest, his college days. It may be added that *Juvenal* and "The Hour Bell Sounds" are the only works of translation or adaptation from foreign languages in which W is definitely known to have been engaged at any time during the few years after 1794.

"If Grief Dismiss Me Not," a translation from Petrarch (see Landon *RES* 393; Woof *SB* 166–67), appears complete in the Racedown Nb along with some six lines of another copy. Whether any of these materials represent W's original work on the poem it is impossible to say with certainty, but one cannot assume that even if the earliest surviving work on the poem does appear in the Racedown Nb, the poem must date from the Racedown period. The earliest date at which the Nb was used is in fact not clear. The question of whether such an assumption would preclude the possibility of any early work on the sonnet having taken place in W's college days brings up the related problem of the dates of two other sonnets, both incomplete, in the same Nb—lines that formed the basis of *Written in Very Early Youth* and *Written on the Thames near Richmond*—and the yet larger problem of the time of W's first use of the Racedown Nb.

A translation of one stanza from Ariosto appears in the Nb; W possibly knew enough Italian to read Ariosto as early as late 1788, and was definitely

Appendix IV

reading Ariosto during the summer of 1790 (notes in W's pocket copy of *Orlando Furioso*, DCP), and the Nb contains an itinerary of the 1790 walking trip. On the other hand, W and DW almost certainly read Ariosto at Racedown (see GCL 34n), and the fact that the itinerary was plainly entered all at once with a few omissions of the names of towns suggests that the itinerary was later than the trip itself—although how much later, and whether from another written source, cannot be told. "Tour" is written grandly across the back of the Nb, as if the whole book had been intended for a journal of a trip (European or other), but only a stub or two even remotely resemble such a record; another stub in an autograph quite similar to the stubs mentioned contains materials toward a probable revision of *SP* in the direction of MS II (see Appendix XII), and thus probably dates from after 1793. Likewise draft lines containing materials employed in *DS* 626–31 appear on a torn page; but some of the same lines are written by W into a published copy of *DS* now at the Huntington Library (and see *PW* I, 79 *app crit*), and while the lines in the Nb might have been a casual draft overlooked in working up the published version, but written into the Huntington *DS* after W had come across them later, it seems as probable that they are simply later than the published poem (that is, after 29 Jan 1793). Other entries, however, seem fairly certainly to represent work of summer 1793: the fragment "How Sweet to Walk along the Woody Steep" (see GCL 43), the sonnet fragment "In Vain Did Time and Nature Toil to Throw," the elegaic quatrains "The Western Clouds a Deepening Gloom Display" (GCL 44). If W was not using the Racedown Nb before the Racedown period, the number of copies of earlier work and the amount of draft toward enlargement of that work must be regarded as an extraordinary phenomenon, indicating a large and hitherto unnoticed area of W's poetic endeavor during the Racedown period. The only really reasonable question appears to be simply how long before Racedown W used the Nb. Since a clear answer appears impossible to determine, one is, I think, obliged to depend a good deal on what W himself has indicated about the dates of the poems and on the implications of their styles and tones.

To speak in more detail of the sonnet fragments: Both Thomas Hutchinson (in his edition of *Poems in Two Volumes*, London, 1897, 199) and *PW* (Smith) I, 481, state that in the 1837 edition of his poems (the reference is clearly to the collected edition of 1836–37) W gave *Written in Very Early Youth* a date of 1786; and EdS must refer to that same edition when he states (*PW* I, 318; *The Early Wordsworth*, London, 1936, that W gave the poem that date in 1836. Miss Darbishire also records that W dated the poem 1786 (*Poems in Two Volumes*, Oxford, 1914, 393). I have been unable to find a copy of this edition in which the poem is given a date; nor have I been able to discover any edition of W's poems published within his lifetime in which it is dated. The authorities mentioned may in fact refer to a source with which I am unfamiliar; or copies of the 1836–37 edition may exist in which the date is present. Other editors, notably Knight, Dowden, Smith, and Hutchinson (*PW* Oxford) have generally given the poem a conjectural date of 1786, although Knight in one instance (*PW*, Knight, 1895, I, 3n) states that "the date of this fragment is quite unknown." Beatty (*RP* xxvi, 9) dates the poem both 1787 and 1795–97; he probably came to the conclusion of EdS, that the first shaping of the poem "into anything like its present form" must have taken place in 1795–97. The unmistakable fact of W's title, nevertheless, remains: If "very early youth" does not mean 1786, it can hardly mean a great many years later.

W gave the poems developed from *Written on the Thames* a date of 1789 in editions from 1836 through 1850. As noted elsewhere, this poem probably did not reach its final form as a single set of verses until early 1797. On the other hand, the contents of the poem strongly suggest that the basic work on it was done at college, as the IF note to the two resultant poems and W's dates for them indicate. The work in the Racedown Nb which forms the source of *Written on the Thames* is clearly a very early draft; it consists of twelve lines apparently toward an Italian sonnet. The lines toward *Written in Very Early Youth* (*PW*, I, 3, "MS" variants) appear on the Nb page facing these twelve lines and are quite similar in ink and autograph. It seems at least possible that the two drafts were composed at much the same time. The remarkable gap between W's date of 1786 for *Written in Very Early Youth* (if he did give it such a date) and EdS's (and Beatty's) later date may be considerably reduced if these lines are considered the work—or a copy of work—of W's college period. And though *Written in Very Early Youth* could be based on a scene at Hawkshead, both it and the draft of *Written on the Thames* share the sentimentally gentle and melancholy tone and twilight setting that are more typical of *EW* (mostly 1788–89) or "Sweet Was the Walk" than W's schoolboy verse. I am inclined to believe that both *Written in Very Early Youth* and *Written on the Thames* were in fact poems of W's college days, and suggest that both entries in the Nb represent work or copies of work that can be dated roughly between c late 1788 and 1791 inclusive. It is just possible that they had their inspiration in William Lisle Bowles's *Fourteen Sonnets*, which they resemble closely in subject, tone, and phrasing, and which W almost certainly read for the first time during Christmas holidays 1789–90; but, as already implied, nothing in Bowles's sonnets—however much their twilights, castles, and melancholy musings may have appealed to W—would be essentially new to the poet who had long been at work on *EW* (except perhaps, their concentration in a series of sonnets), and W's familiarity with Bowles's predecessors (and sources) had been amply demonstrated as early as *V of E*.

Whatever the case as regards Bowles, the appearance of work on "If Grief Dismiss Me Not" in the Racedown Nb does not, it seems, contradict at all what in any case (see Woof *SB* 167) would be a reasonable assumption, that the poem was a college translation, and that it need not certainly fall much later than whatever time W had obtained sufficient mastery of Italian to read Petrarch—possibly late 1788, more probably 1789–91. It seems not beyond the realm of possibility (although clear proof is of course not available) that it, the composition toward *Written in Very Early Youth*, and the composition toward *Written on the Thames* may have been entered in the Racedown Nb during W's college years.

APPENDIX V

Four Notebooks: Their Use in Dating
An Evening Walk
and Other Early Composition

Examination of MSS Verse 4, 5, 6, and 7 suggests that these Nbs were probably in use within a short period of each other, in some cases simultaneously, and allows various inferences regarding the development of W's conception of *EW*. Verse 4 and Verse 5 contain extensive work on *V of E*; where the Nbs contain parallel passages capable of being given relative dates, Verse 5 can be seen to contain the later work on the poem. Verse 5, Verse 6, and Verse 7 all contain much translation, most of it from the *Georgics*. Translated work in Verse 5 is in heroic couplets and includes *Orpheus and Eurydice*; that in Verse 6 is in blank verse and includes lines of *Moschus*[14] and lines on the beehive society (see Schneider 166); that in Verse 7 is in blank verse, and includes *The Horse*. Verse 4, Verse 5, and Verse 6 all contain composition on the subject of the "shipwreck of a soul." The lines of this kind in Verse 5 are in tetrameter and are clearly intended for *V of E*; those in Verse 4 and Verse 6 are evidently in prose or very loose blank verse, and are developed much more extensively (Verse 4 also contains an extended heroic fragment—apparently closely related—describing a warrior). Verse 4 also contains a proselike description of a storm on which fragmentary work, probably earlier, appears in Verse 5, and which is developed extensively in blank verse in Verse 6.

To speak in more detail of a few passages: W works in Verse 4 on blank verse describing a freezing mother and her children, also on a closely related passage about a castle (the latter forms the basis of *Gothic Tale* 17–23);

[14] Miss Landon, whose dissertation summarizes in detail the *Georgics* translations in this Nb, identifies the source of these lines, corresponding to *Moschus* 11–15, as *Georgics* III.66–68. In Nb Verse 7 W copied these lines beneath the lines now preceding them in the version of *Moschus* published by EdS in *PW*; whether W actually meant them to form part of the same poem is unclear.

extensive work on these subjects appears also in blank verse in Verse 6, in one case apparently combined with the description of a storm, mentioned above, on which W works in Verse 4, Verse 5, and elsewhere in Verse 6. Verse 7, however, contains extensive draft work on the freezing family in iambic pentameter couplets; and these lines form the basis of the couplets of *EW* 257–300. Several passages of blank verse devoted to natural description appear in the later pages of Verse 4. Verse 6, likewise, contains efforts at recasting the lines on Madness, *V of E* 395–97, into blank verse. It can be noted also that Verse 7, which includes much couplet composition contributive to *EW* (it is the Nb described *PW*, I, 319), contains no blank verse work except in translations; that Verse 4 (in entries of this time) and Verse 5 contain almost no couplets at all except in translations, while the other passages are in tetrameter, blank verse, or prose (or something like prose); and that Verse 6 contains virtually nothing but blank verse or work toward blank verse.

One might suspect—although the evidence will support no unshakable conclusion—that W first turned from *V of E* toward efforts to develop a blank verse poem on roughly the same lines, and then turned to heroic couplets for a descriptive and meditative poem, free of Gothicism, which may definitely be described (whether or not W had thought of the name) as *An Evening Walk*. Verse 7 includes lines, corresponding to *EW* 413–22, concerning the cottage that the speaker hopes to share with his sister, a fact which implies strongly that W had arrived at a conception of *EW* along its present lines while Verse 7 was still in use.

The shift from couplets in Verse 5 to blank verse in Verse 6 and Verse 7 for translations, the fact that Verse 5 contains many *V of E* materials but nothing developed from them (unlike Verse 6 and Verse 7), and the passages of blank verse in Verse 6 developed from *V of E* or Verse 5 all suggest that most of the contents of Verse 6 were written after those of Verse 5, although the similarity of the materials in the Nbs and their identical sixteen-leaf formats indicate that the times at which they were principally used were not far apart. The obviously close relationship of certain of the contents of Verse 4 to contents of Verse 5 and Verse 6 also strongly suggests that W used that Nb in close connection with the other two. The relevant drafts in Verse 4 seem generally closer, however, to Verse 6 than Verse 5.

A relatively certain date can, as it happens, be given Verse 6. The *Cambridge to Hawkshead* fragment, probably of 8 June 1788 (see 1788:17) appears on the first page, and was evidently intended as the first entry of a journal never continued; W had probably planned to use the Nb for a journal, and the other writing in it is likely to be later than the fragment. Proximity of material is shaky evidence for chronological order, but the Nb is small (sixteen leaves), and W surely had it with him in the summer of 1788. One may justifiably assume that most of the work dates from that summer. Thus most of the contents of Verse 5, including any *V of E* materials, may be conjectured to date from early 1788, perhaps by late spring. Most of the contents of Verse 7 probably date from late summer or autumn 1788, with some work possibly slightly later.[15] The relevant materials in Verse 4 probably date from about the same time as Verse 6.

W said in the IF note to *EW* that he composed the poem "at school, and during [his] two first College vacations," and in all editions of the poem published in W's lifetime it is given the date "1787, 88, 89." EdS remarked in *The Early Wordsworth* (London, 1936) 27 that W probably used the date of 1787 for *EW* because he worked up several passages from *V of E* in it: "*An Evening Walk* is really the work of his first two long vacations, 1788 and 1789." Clearly such exactness is unjustified, and EdS apparently retreats from this position in *PW* I, 319, where he remarks that W was engaged on *V of E* "up to the end of his school-days and after" and concludes only that it is "extremely unlikely that [*V of E* and *EW*] were actually contemporaneous." From the evidence cited above, it appears nonetheless probable that W worked out his conception of *EW* during the summer of 1788 or shortly thereafter, and that he began work on it no earlier than late summer, possibly in the autumn or after. But he may indeed have brought his main efforts to an end by the close of the following summer. As there is no evidence to contradict the assumption that the bulk of the work was in fact composed by that time, and as such an assumption would be reasonable, I have chosen out of deference to W to date the poem accordingly—noting, however, that additional composition may have taken place at any time up to the publication of the poem. The general advance in stylistic complexity in *DS* over *EW* suggests that most work on *DS* took place months, or even a year or more, after most work on *EW*.

The remarks above allow assignment of rough dates to various passages:

[15] Two passages in Verse 7, as Miss Landon notes, may be the work of 1790 or later, after the walking trip in France. One is a few lines mentioning a figure whose eyes glow with "fearful light" as he gazes into the chasm of the "Infant Rhine." The description possibly draws on W's visit to Via Mala in the summer of 1790, but it is clearly related to the description of suicide in *V of E* (391–94), and could well date earlier (cf *PW* I, 324n). Miss Landon suggests that W may have drawn on a traveler's account. Some lines on the cock, contributive to *EW* 125–38, with their origin in Rosset, may likewise date later than 1788. One explanation for either passage might be that W wrote it in the Nb as he was working up the poem for publication.

Appendix V

1. Probably early or summer 1788:
   a. Drafts, developed into blank verse, of an elaborate description of a storm, comparing the storm to an eagle or condor (Verse 5, 6).
   b. Drafts describing someone's madness as the "shipwreck of a soul" (Verse 4, 5, 6).

2. Probably early 1788—possibly as late as summer (couplets).
   Probably summer and/or autumn 1788, with some composition slightly later (blank verse):
   a. Various translations from Vergil (Verse 5, 6, 7).

3. Probably early 1788—perhaps by late spring:
   a. *Orpheus and Eurydice* (translation from *Georgics* IV.464–77, 485–527) (Verse 5).
   b. Short prose fragment forming basis for *EW* 37–42 (Verse 5; see Moorman I, 115n).
   c. Simile describing the terror of a shepherd (Verse 5).

4. Probably c summer and autumn 1788, with some composition possibly slightly later:
   a. *In Part from Moschus—Lament for Bion* (Verse 6, 7).
   b. Development, from blank verse to heroic couplets, of a passage describing a female vagrant freezing with her two children; the passage forms the basis of *EW* 257–300 (Verse 6, 7).
   c. Development into heroic couplets of a description of pity, *V of E* 125–30, 139–52; the passage forms the basis of *EW* 379–88.

5. Probably c summer 1788:
   a. Description of a warrior moving (apparently) to battle (Verse 4).
   b. Description of a castle, in blank verse; the passage forms the basis of *Gothic Tale* 17–23 (Verse 4, 6).
   c. Several fragments of natural description, in blank verse (Verse 4).

6. Probably late summer or autumn 1788—possibly slightly later (the last two on the list less certainly of this date, and at least the last possibly of any date up to late Jan 1793—see 1793:4):
   a. *The Horse* (Verse 7).
   b. *Ode to Apollo* (Verse 7).
   c. Draft of a few lines mentioning a figure whose eyes glow as he gazes into the chasm of the "Infant Rhine" (Verse 7).
   d. Draft of lines forming basis for *EW* 125–38 (including lines on the cock based on Rosset) (Verse 7).

Appendix V

The simile describing the terror of a shepherd (entry 3c) is discussed in an unpublished article by Miss Landon. The lines are short, but whether intended as tetrameter is unclear. They are perhaps intended as draft work for *V of E*, of which the last surviving work appears in this same Nb. The fragment is, however, similar in phrasing to, and obviously connected closely with, the fragments, all similes or involving similes, quoted Fink 76, 80, 86, 88, and 95, and to which Fink gives a possible date of 1784–85. The simile on Fink 86 also mentions a shepherd, and possibly precedes the fragment in Verse 5. Most of the Fink fragments are related to some sort of heroic tale. The fragments quoted Fink 76, 80, 86 seem parts of elaborate descriptions of warriors, their armor and attitudes, all evidently as related to an approaching battle. The other Fink fragments are clearly of the same time and almost certainly are connected with them in purpose. It seems probable, as remarked above, that the draft work in Verse 4 apparently describing a warrior moving into battle is very closely related to these fragments, and equally probable that the work in Verse 4 toward a grandiose description of someone's madness as the "shipwreck of a soul," with various personifications on the deck clinging about their parent Reason, is similarly related. It thus seems not improbable, inasmuch as Verse 4, Verse 5, and Verse 6 all contain "shipwreck of a soul" materials, that all these heroic fragments may date from sometime around summer 1788. (It is not impossible that the castle fragments were at one point connected with the fragments under discussion, although, as has been noted, the castle appears in Verse 6 in conjunction with the vagrant mother. The elaborate description of the storm may also have been connected.)

Fink 6–7 suggests that the fragmentary simile concerning an ash tree, Fink 6, may well form a source for *V of E* 95–102 and *EW* 193–94 and the *EW* IF note (all of which deal with a description of an oak in similar terms), but the evidence is not conclusive, and even if Fink is correct, the simile need not, I think, date before 1787. There is likewise, it should be added, no conclusive proof that the simile describing the terror of the shepherd, the storm fragments, the warrior passage, the "shipwreck of a soul" passage—or even the translations from Vergil—in Verse 4 and Verse 5 were not there before the *V of E* copies. But Verse 5 and Verse 6 are identical in format and were almost surely obtained or made (they are probably homemade) at the same time. Most use was probably made of Verse 6 in summer of 1788, and W would probably not have kept it clean for a year or more while using only Verse 5 in the meantime; and Verse 4 and Verse 6 were, as already noted, used closely together. If the Fink fragments do bear some close relationship to the fragments in Verse 4 or Verse 5 or Verse 6, as seems to me fairly certain, it is unlikely that any such length of time would have elapsed between them as between 1784–85 and 1788. While the Fink fragments possibly could precede anything of their sort in Verse 4, 5, or 6, they may well be regarded, in absence of evidence to the contrary, as close to them in time, and thus as belonging to 1787 or 1788. But none of the evidence cited can absolutely refute Fink's suggestion.

APPENDIX VI

The Dates of Certain Early Passages
in MS Verse 4

For the dating of the following passages little or no evidence can be cited other than their general position in Nb Verse 4 and their general appearance —autograph, ink, and the like. Such criteria are ordinarily not very safe in dating works of W's. But reason and the little evidence available suggest that they were probably not composed later than 1789.

1. *A Tale*. (Prose fragment, unpublished, cited Moorman I, 17n, and there assigned to a time when W was "about sixteen"; elsewhere it is assigned by the same authority—I, 57—to "Hawkshead days.") The fragment describes the speaker's meeting with a woman "above the average size" with eyes of "a certain wild brightness" (see Moorman I, 17n) who seems clearly not "in her true and perfect mind." *A Tale* is the next obviously early material following the second copy of the second version of *A Dirge* (see 1788:7) in the Nb. The incident in the fragment occurs as the speaker is passing the churchyard from which the congregation was issuing as Gray passed "twenty years ago." The speaker may be taken to be W, and he must be referring to Gray's Journal of his Tour of the Lakes for 8 Oct 1769: "Past by the little Chapel of Wiborn [Wythburn], out of wch the Sunday congregation were then issuing" (*The Poems of Mr. Gray*, ed. William Mason, York, 1778, IV, 181). The "twenty years ago" may be based on calculation from the meeting or from W's writing of this passage; in any event there is no reason to suppose that W was aiming at more than a general indication of the span of years since Gray's visit.

The *V of E* "Extracts" were probably copied into the Nb not earlier than late summer or autumn 1787 (see 1787:5), and they are the next early materials in the Nb; but they follow a number of then blank pages, and whether they were entered there before *A Tale* cannot be known. Whether *A Tale* was entered before or after either version of *Dirge* cannot be determined either; four then blank pages as well as stubs of torn out leaves which contained the second copy of the second version of *Dirge* separate it from what still survives of *Dirge*. A date as early as summer 1787 need not be considered out of the question, although a difference of two years from the "twenty years" since Oct 1769 would suggest that a date of 1788 or 1789 is more likely. A date of 1790 or after, at the same general time as the fragment describing the events in the Valley of Lauterbrunnen (see GCL 38)—the latter is the only other extended passage of prose in Verse 4—can certainly not be rejected either. W could have met the woman any time he was traveling north or south through Dunmail Raise and Grasmere, a likely route between Hawkshead and Penrith. The incident must have occurred late in his school days at the earliest, for he was evidently traveling alone; c summer of 1788 or 1789 would appear the most likely dates.

2. Two "Epitaphs" (in prose, unpublished): One epitaph is for a "maid," the other for "M____" or "M. ____," the latter of whom "lived a patriarch's days." These are the first early items following the *V of E* extracts and drafts, and the autograph suggests that they were done about the same time as the early 1788 work on *Dirge*. One of these is perhaps the referent of *DWJ* I, 103, as suggested by Miss Landon; it is doubtful that either, however, is the one composed (if one was composed) by W on 28 Jan 1802.

3. "When Slow from Pensive Twilight's Latest Gleams" (unpublished Italian sonnet; mentioned Bateson 212, where it is dated 1788–89). This sonnet is copied into the Nb fairly from another source; and it is less surely, in my opinion, work of 1788 or 1789 than the items mentioned above. But in tone and subject, as Miss Landon points out, it shares much with *EW*; it is likewise close in these respects to the sonnet fragments for *Written in Very Early Youth* and *Written on the Thames near Richmond* (see Appendix IV) and "Sweet Was the Walk" (see GCL 33). I have given it a conjectural date corresponding to those given the latter poems. As any of these sonnets, it could have been inspired by Bowles's *Fourteen Sonnets*, which W first read Christmas vacation 1789–90. The autograph does not tend to confirm that it is contemporary with other works more definitely of 1788–89 in Verse 4. The date must be left quite vague on the basis of present evidence—probably between c 1789 and 1791 inclusive, but possibly later.

APPENDIX VII

Wordsworth's Early Travels in Wales

W makes no clear distinctions in his writings between his two early trips to Wales, from late May to mid-Sept 1791 and from sometime by 27 Aug until perhaps as late as c 15 Sept 1793. Some uncertainty thus exists about what W saw and did in Wales at either time. It is difficult to arrive at final conclusions even concerning the itinerary of the 1791 walking tour, when he and Jones "visited the greater part of North Wales." Available evidence suggests at least the following. (1) W speaks in 1824 of a "midnight ascent" of Snowdon "almost thirty years ago" from Beddgelert (*LY* 154). He almost surely made only one midnight climb of Snowdon. If he had been thinking accurately, he would not have said "almost" thirty years ago, since the second of the two Welsh trips to which he could refer took place in 1793, or over thirty years before; and no evidence of any sort points to his having made an extended walking tour in North Wales in 1793. While Lloyd 340 doubts whether the date of the Snowdon climb can be determined, and EdS (PREL, EdS, 599) dates the climb 1793, it is reasonable to suppose, since Snowdon and Beddgelert are among the places which W names in the Dedication of *DS* as being already visited by him and Jones, that *Mem* I, 71, T. H. Bowen (*English* VIII, 1950, 18), and Moorman I, 161–62, are correct in their assumption that the Snowdon climb took place in 1791.[16] (2) W visited in 1791, in addition to Snowdon, the other places or areas mentioned by him in the dedication of *DS*, namely the vale of Clwyd, Cader Idris, Menai, the "Alpine steeps of the Conway, and the still more interesting windings of the wizard stream of the Dee." *DS* was, of course, published before the 1793 Welsh visit. (3) Much of W's route north from Salisbury Plain to Jones's house, Plas-yn-Llan, Llangynhafal, in summer of 1793 can be fairly well determined: He went from Salisbury Plain to Bath, thence to

---

[16] *LY* 154 also notes that W and Jones took refreshment in a public house in Beddgelert before their climb (see *Prel* XIII.3, *Prel*$_2$ XIV.4), and *Prel* likewise shows that the climb took place as part of a tour with Jones. Some aspects of the description of the mist-filled valley, *DS* 492–509 (see Moorman I, 162n), perhaps draw on the memory of this climb (see also 1790:77).

315

Bristol, and thence (by water) to the "banks of the Wye" (*G & S* IF note); thence he proceeded past Tintern Abbey (see *TA*) to Goodrich Castle (*We Are Seven* IF note), Hay, and probably Builth Wells (*PB* IF note) before proceeding to Plas-yn-Llan.

One point of difficulty in determining his route in the walking trip of 1791 and part of his trip north in 1793 emerges from the fact that *LY* 154–55 (W to Sir George Beaumont, 20 Sept 1824) states that W saw, "in his youth," Machynlleth, Aberystwyth, and Devil's Bridge. There is no doubt that the visits occurred in either 1791 or 1793; but the IF note to *PB* states that W met the rover who formed a chief model for Peter Bell at Builth and walked *downward* with him nearly as far as Hay. Did W reverse his steps at Builth Wells and return back down the Wye, up which he had just come, to the vicinity of Hay before proceeding north? W's memory in the *PB* IF note seems so clear that one is inclined to believe that such must have been the case. On the other hand, in 1836 W advised HCR (*HCR & W Circle* 308–09) to plan a trip up the Wye, proceeding on past Rhayader to the upper Wye, crossing thence to Devil's Bridge. It would have been simple for W to have traveled along that route himself in 1793; and Cader Idris, the southernmost point mentioned by W in his dedication of *DS*, while in relatively easy reach of Machynlleth, would have lain a walk of some forty miles (the distance about twenty-five miles as the crow flies) north of Devil's Bridge. It is hardly possible that W could have gone as far as Devil's Bridge in 1793 and then returned toward Hay. The time of W's visit to the Aberystwyth–Devil's Bridge area must be left in some doubt, but in view of W's distinctness about his 1793 route in the *PB* IF note, it seems more probable that W made his trip here in 1791 than 1793.

Two short personal visits made by W while in Wales also seem incapable of precise dating. One was to Thomas Pennant at Downing (near Whitford, Flints), and the other, of several days' duration, to Llechweddgarth, the home of Pennant's friend Thomas Thomas, located in the small valley which contains the church of Pennant Melangell, near Llangynog, Montgomeryshire. Thomas' house was the scene of an altercation between W and a Welsh priest that was climaxed by the priest's threatening the poet with a carving knife. (See esp. *Some Letters* 19–20; Thomas Pennant, *Tours in Wales*, ed. John Rhys, Caernarvon, 1883, III, 165; T. W. Hancock, "Pennant Melangell: Its Parochial History and Antiquities," *Collections Historical and Archaeological Relating to Montgomeryshire and Its Borders* XII, London, 1879, 83; *STCNB* 502, 1586.) W could no doubt have called upon Pennant when near "the wizard stream of the Dee" in 1791, but he would have observed more spectacular reaches of the river when proceeding southwest from

Plas-yn-Llan (as he would have if on the way toward the home of Thomas Thomas) or when proceeding northeast toward Plas-yn-Llan from the Cader Idris or Devil's Bridge area, a route that would also easily have allowed a visit to Thomas Thomas. A special trip to Pennant would have been easy any time during W's 1791 or 1793 Welsh visit, however; Pennant lived only some fifteen miles from Plas-yn-Llan. (W might likewise, indeed, have visited Thomas directly from Plas-yn-Llan either year, although the distance would have been over thirty miles.)

W twice (1826, 1836) suggests that HCR visit Conway Castle, and also, specifically, that HCR take the road from Capel Kerig to Bangor (*HCR & W Circle* 169, 309). In 1826 he speaks of the Llangollen–Bangor road in its entirety, and also advises HCR to proceed from Llanberris to Snowdon, to descend to Dolbarden Inn; thence to Cwnyngloed and on to Bangor. In 1836 he suggests that HCR proceed up the Conway to Llanrswstr, thence to Capel Kerig—W had seen almost all of these places in 1824 (except the full length of the Llangollen–Bangor road; see *LY* 150–55), but it is hardly possible that he could have visited Menai, Snowdon, and Beddgelert in 1791 without having seen most of the same places. W's mention of the "Alpine steeps of the Conway" in the *DS* dedication suggests the upper Conway, but his references to Conway Castle (see above) and Penmaenmawr (*Excursion* VII. 8) raise the possibility that he also reached the area near the mouth of the river: certainly an excursion covering the "greater part of North Wales" would scarcely have been complete without a visit to Conway Castle.

A tour which left out the lower stretches of the Dee (and the nearby home of Thomas Pennant), but included Conway Castle and the Penmaenmawr area, the Aberystwyth–Devil's Bridge area, the upper portions of the river Dee (and possibly a visit to Thomas Thomas) would have a vaguely oval shape, and would be an easily imaginable route for the walkers in 1791.

APPENDIX VIII

The Visits of Hazlitt and Cottle, Spring 1798

The dates of the spring 1798 visits of Hazlitt and Cottle have been a matter of minor vexation to scholars for some time.[17] Some points resolve themselves more clearly than others. First of all, Hazlitt's distinct recollection of leaving the Nether Stowey–Alfoxden area with STC on a Sunday can be placed beside STC's letter of Saturday 16 June, which refers to his arrival in Bristol the previous Monday, to make it certain that both authors departed on Sunday 10 June (*My First Acquaintance* 122; *STCL* I, 413). Hazlitt indicates that his visit lasted three weeks (*My First Acquaintance* 122). This statement was made from a distance of thirty years, but his memory in this noted essay usually rings true, and the recollection can be taken as at least roughly accurate. Three weeks *qua* twenty-one days before 10 June would be 20 May. Hazlitt recalls that W's arrival on return from Bristol, fresh from a viewing of Monk Lewis's *The Castle Spectre*, occurred two days after his own. Bristol was treated to Lewis's drama the theater week of 21 May, but not the week before or the week after. Thus Hazlitt can be supposed to have arrived either on 20 May or very shortly after, and W to have arrived at Stowey two days later (and to have met Hazlitt), probably 22 May or very shortly after.

The dating of the visit which Cottle paid to Alfoxden during this period is made difficult by the publisher's own ambiguous comments. He several times mentions visits to Alfoxden, but the number of the visits is left unclear. Twice he remarks (*Reminiscences* 174, 182) that "a visit to Mr. Coleridge" at Stowey "had been the means of my introduction to Mr. Wordsworth," although it is hard to believe that W and Cottle could have escaped meeting somehow during the poet's visit in Bristol Aug–Sept 1795, and the two were certainly acquainted by Jan 1796 (*EL* 149; see Moorman I, 271). The publisher states in one instance that this visit occasioned W's reading of his

[17] See esp. G. W. Whiting, "The Date of Hazlitt's First Visit to Coleridge," *MLN* XLII (1927), 504–06; A. F. Potts, "The Date of Wordsworth's First Meeting with Hazlitt," *MLN* XLIV (1929), 296–99; P. P. Howe, *The Life of William Hazlitt* (London, 1947), 37; Margoliouth *N & Q*; Moorman I, 373, 397; H. C. Baker, *William Hazlitt* (Cambridge, Mass., 1962), 126.

"Lyrical Pieces," and that he departed leaving W still objecting to Cottle's urgings that the poet publish. Cottle elsewhere (*Reminiscences* 175–78) mentions invitations for "another visit," and quotes three letters of spring 1798 from W and STC in which such invitations occur. "In consequence of these conjoint invitations," he reports, "I spent a week . . . at Allfoxden house"; it was during this visit that final plans were made for *LB*. Lastly, Cottle mentions (*Reminiscences* 182) an occasion when "soon after our acquaintance had commenced, Mr. W. happened to be in Bristol, and asked me to spend a day or two with him at Allfoxden." The publisher "consented, and drove him down in a gig." This was the visit that was the occasion of the *débacle* of the bread and lettuce dinner.

Sorting out the various confusions in these remarks would require rather more space than the matters justify, but it can be noted that, without constituting a remarkably unusual example of Cottle's unreliability, all the remarks could refer to a single visit. In any case, the Cottle visit of May 1798 can have been the only occasion when plans were laid for *LB*, and even Cottle is unlikely to have erred basically about a related trip to Linton and elsewhere. Nor can there be much doubt that the May visit was describable at least in general terms as having been one of "a week" in length. Only one other occasion is known when W may have "happened to be in Bristol" and invited Cottle down for "a day or two" when STC was at Nether Stowey, W at Alfoxden, and lettuce in good fettle—late Sept–early Oct 1797; but even in this case the only clue is W's comment that he *planned* to be in Bristol within three weeks (see *EL* 172; *STCL* I, 345–46). The only remote hint of a visit by Cottle other than that of May is the unlikely one of the enigmatic entries in *DWJ* for 3, 4, 5 Feb 1798 (see 1798:25n).

STC wrote Cottle on a Monday which must have been, as Griggs shows, either 28 May or 4 June, that he had walked to Linton the day after Cottle left and returned on "Saturday" (*STCL* I, 411, 413). Even had STC not lingered a day in Linton—and the evidence implies that he did (see below and Margoliouth *N & Q* 353)—Cottle would have had to depart 24 May if STC were to write to the publisher on 28 May after having made such a trip. There is certainly no information that implies—indeed, since W was in Bristol, it is most unlikely—that Cottle came before W's return, much less that so many events involving the author of *The Malvern Hills* and later remembered by him as parts of a week's visit could in reality have been compressed into two days' time, no matter how foggy his later recollections tended to be. Thus STC's letter was probably written 4 June, and Margoliouth's conjecture that Cottle's departure took place on 30 May is probably correct. It seems quite possible that Cottle drove W down in his gig on

22 May, and came as a result of personal urgings from W, while the latter was in Bristol, which supplemented earlier written invitations from him and STC. If Cottle did not come with W, he probably arrived soon after him.

STC's trip to Linton just after Cottle's departure would almost certainly date, of course, 31 May–2 June. Hazlitt, however, recalls in *My First Acquaintance* that his departure from Nether Stowey, on 10 June, was a "day or two" after his return from his tour to Linton with STC and Chester. One is faced with the need to decide whether Hazlitt erred by over a week about the time of his own walking tour, or whether STC in fact made three separate trips to Linton and back between 22 May and 9 June—two, perhaps all three, walking trips of not less than three days' duration—the first with W and Cottle and the last with Hazlitt and Chester. Certainly Hazlitt's description (as well as Cottle's) quite precludes any possibility that the Hazlitt and Cottle walking trips were one and the same; it is hard also to believe that STC would have gone off on such excursions, the first time with Cottle, the second time perhaps alone, leaving Hazlitt behind twice, or that Hazlitt would have neglected reporting two walking tours had he taken two. The matter cannot be settled on the basis of present evidence. If one assumes that Hazlitt would not have used the phrase "a day or two" to describe a period of over a week, even when remembering the events many years after, one is obliged to infer that STC did in fact make three trips, and that the three-day tour with Hazlitt began about 5 or 6 June and ended about 8 or 9 June.

The date of the famous and ridiculous dinner of bread and lettuce likewise remains impossible to establish with certainty. Mrs. Moorman's supposition (Moorman I, 396) that the fiasco took place this May is probably the best that can be made; but it is curious that neither Hazlitt nor Cottle ever mentions the other in connection with any part of his narrative. There is, however, no case in which any of their statements are finally in conflict.

APPENDIX IX

Three Notebooks:
Alfoxden, Christabel, 18A

To arrive at exact dates for the materials in the Alfoxden Nb, Christabel Nb, and Nb 18A is often quite difficult. Where exactly parallel passages appear among the MSS the order of composition is that of the Nbs as just listed.[18] Further comment will require somewhat more detailed discussion, although exhaustive descriptions cannot be offered within the limits of the present study.

(1) The Alfoxden Nb starts at one end with a few draft lines for, and a stub of a leaf that once contained some version of, *A Night-Piece*; these materials probably date from or very slightly after 25 Jan 1798 (*DWJ* I, 4; *A Night-Piece* IF note). Next is work mostly on *OCB*, The Discharged Soldier (see *Prel* IV.450–67 with Alfoxden variants; Prel 536–37), and *RC*. The *RC* work (including lines corresponding to MS B 31 [full line]–32, rejected lines, and some of the fragments on *PW* V, 413, and originally including, as stubs show, drafts for ?633–?643, ?656–?665, ?667–?673, ?30–61, ?301–?309, 333–?343)[19] precedes the readings of DW's letter of 5, [6] Mar 1798 (see *PW* V, 413); so that this and the other materials mentioned probably, in absence of further evidence, fall between 25 Jan and 5 Mar 1798. A few other draft materials in this part of the Nb all appear to be of much the same time; all precede drafts for *The Thorn* 1–22 (*PW* II, 240, "MS") and "A Whirl-blast" (*PW* II, 127–28, with "MS" variants), which probably date from 19 Mar 1798: fragments quoted *PW* V, 340–41, *II, i, ii, iii, iv*, and some lines on the Pedlar, including materials used *Prel* II.321–41 (which was also contributed to by *PW* V, 340, *II, i*); quotations from these lines appear *PW* V, 413.

[18] In one instance draft work on *RC* in Christabel appears to precede other work on that poem in Alfoxden, but the passages are not parallel. See below.

[19] The lines (318–25, 342–61, 681–96) said by *PW* V, 389, 398, to appear in Alfoxden are actually in Christabel. Information from Dr. Finch has aided in determining the identity of the lines from which only stubs survive. Some work on The Discharged Soldier also stood on the stubs.

After *The Thorn* and "A Whirl-blast" appear the fragments *PW* V, 341, *v*, *vii* (*vi* is later in the Nb); these can be conjectured to fall between probably 19 Mar and c 16 May, since they are followed by a draft (which eventually became *Andrew Jones*) for *PB* (probably completed by c 16 May). Following materials also seem to be of about the same time: "Away, Away" (*PW* IV, 357–58); fragments *PW* V, 341, *vi*, *viii*, and 342, *ix*; and a draft for *PW* V, 342, *III*, 1–11. The rest of the work in this end of the Nb appears to be of later date: It consists of a German alphabet and translation of *The Two April Mornings*, *Die Zwey Aprilmorgens*, first called attention to by Miss J. Wisely (Miss Wisely's notes, DCP), in a copybook hand which, like the translator himself, I cannot identify. The translation must date from Goslar or after (see 1798:200; GCL 79). The other materials consist of drafts toward the lines on the Pedlar *PW* V, 405–08, lines 5–82 (see 406n) omitting lines parallel to 25–38 and 56–78 (after "his" in 82 comes "Among the hills" as if work like 57–78 were to follow, and four pages are torn out). These drafts can be dated between W's arrival at Goslar and early 1802, probably near early 1802 (see *PW* V, 405–08, 408n).

Inverting the book and starting from the other end, one finds on the inside cover a draft of the opening of "There Is a Little Unpretending Rill," probably work of 1802 (*PW* III, 419). The pages of the book begin with an abortive start on *DWJ* for 20 Jan 1798; a snatch of blank verse contributive to The Discharged Soldier, including lines on a dog's howling to the village stream (see *DWJ* I, 4–5, entry for 27 Jan 1798); and a pair of quotations, one from Boswell. In default of evidence to the contrary, these materials on the pages of the Nb may be supposed to date from late Jan 1798.

(2) Work also proceeds inward from both ends of the Christabel Nb, but only that of one end appears to date before 1800 (on the other end, which includes *PW* V, 342–45, *i–viii*; see *PW* V, 369). The end with earlier work begins with *A Night-Piece* (as *PW* II, 208, with "MS" variants), some version of which once began one end of Alfoxden also; this copy must date on or after 25 Jan 1798 (see *DWJ*; *A Night-Piece* IF note). Christabel continues with work on *OCB* (see Appendix XV) and *RC*; the relative order of entry is not perfectly clear but *OCB* seems fairly surely the later. The *RC* work includes passages corresponding to MS B 318–21, 338–41, 322–25, 342–56, 359–61, 353–58 (see *app crit*), 681–96 and stubs on which appeared lines 697–728 (through "frost"; 696 ends "Five tedious years"). The *RC* work surely precedes DW's letter of 5, [6] Mar 1798, and looks probably earlier than the *RC* work of the Alfoxden Nb; no extensive work on the Pedlar himself, in any case, appears here. Since, as noted in Appendix XIII, there appears no direct indication that W worked on *RC* between mid-1797 and early 1798,

this work possibly dates as early as between c Mar and early summer 1797. It was almost surely in existence by, and, in view of the other work in the Nb, was more probably written in, early 1798. The *OCB* work is later than that of Alfoxden.

A draft of The Discharged Soldier, *Prel* IV.363–502, comes next, and with it problems of relatively specific dating in these Nbs become even greater. The work is later than that of the Alfoxden Nb, as shown by its completeness and comparative readings, but there is on the other hand no basis for certain conclusion that it dates appreciably before the time by which the (yet later) version of the episode was copied into 18A—not necessarily long before late Oct 1800 (see below)—and the same observation applies to the extended *OCB* work which comes next; stubs show that this *OCB* work once included at least 109 lines of rather fair copy, plus drafts for lines 124–32 (including the lines quoted *PW* IV, 446–47). If some significant quantity of work below in this Nb could be shown to date certainly before 1800, it would leave open the possibility of an earlier date for these materials, but little can be definitely dated either before the beginning of that year or after.

A number of stubs follow, revealing that *A Character*, *The Farmer of Tilsbury Vale*, and *The Reverie of Poor Susan* were among the poems copied here. The final version of *A Character* probably dates from Sept or Oct 1800, as EdS suggests, but the bulk of it need not do so. Professor Griggs' conclusion ("A Note on Wordsworth's *A Character*," *RES* IV, 1953, 57–63)[20] that parts of it refer to STC is confirmed by draft work as well as by STC (*STCL II*, 784). Such lines as these, for example, from a draft toward this or a similar poem in the other end of the Nb (seemingly of the time that *Michael* was being written, but not yet in the stanza pattern finally adopted) almost certainly speak of STC:

> On himself is so fond of bestowing advice
> And of puzzling through what may befall
> So intent upon making his bread without leaven
> And of giving to earth the perfection of heaven
> That he thinks and does nothing at all.

Most of W's poem could date earlier than Jones's visit (no stubs indicate materials that necessarily point to Jones) and have been worked up finally with Jones and STC both in mind. The version indicated by stubs here, with many variants from the published version, would be most safely

[20] See also *Wordsworth. Centenary Studies*, ed. G. T. Dunklin (Princeton, 1951), 60–61.

placed during whatever general time the copies of the other anapestic poems with which it shares stubs can be dated.

The version of *The Farmer* here seems to have had many variants from that published in the *MP* 21 July 1800, and must date before that time. *Poor Susan* resembles *The Farmer* closely in style and content (see *The Farmer* IF note), and was likely composed about the same time. W heard the story of *The Farmer* from Poole, doubtless sometime between 29 Mar 1797 and mid-1798. W dated *Poor Susan* 1797 in editions from 1836, but in its IF note dated it 1801 or 1802. Mrs. Moorman suggests a date not before winter 1798–99 (Moorman I, 428), since the title is a translation of Bürger's *Das Arme Süsschen's Traum*, which the poet came to know at Goslar (*STCL* I, 566). The fact that in 1800 the poem is entitled only *Poor Susan* does not detract a great deal from this supposition, but the English and German verses have little in common, and W's poem could certainly have been written without knowledge of Bürger's. STC possibly recited some version or part of it c Jan or Feb 1800 (*STCNB* 647). Stubs give grounds, indeed, for a guess that *Poor Susan* may have developed directly out of *The Farmer*.[21] The two poems as they stood here and the version of *A Character* already mentioned can be dated in any case probably between 29 Mar 1797 and 18 July 1800. Work standing before these stubs may, other evidence failing, be supposed to precede 18 July 1800.

Next in the Nb follows an incomplete copy of *Excursion* VIII.324–27, and *A Character* (as *PW* IV, 58–59, with "MS" variants), including lines which refer to Jones, and thus date not before Sept 1800, and probably by 15 Oct (see Hale White 25–26; *STCL* I, 637); but the latter follows two blank pages and could have been written in after much of the rest of the book was filled. Stubs following indicate possible work on *The Oak and the Broom* (surely 1800, by probably 4 Aug; see IF note and Hale White 10) and *The Two April Mornings* (probably a Goslar poem, this copy almost surely written by 13 Aug 1800; see Hale White 12–13). *The Childless Father* (probably 1800, and surely by 15 Sept 1800; see IF note and Hale White 14) fairly certainly stood here.[22] After the stubs appears a copy of *Prel* I.271–304, 310–14 (see PREL xxvii), and more stubs which show that some version of *Prel* I itself once stood here. Identifiable are lines corresponding to *Prel* I.331–45 (close to the JJ version), 407–11, 419–27, 485–88, and 567–70. This version of Book I probably dates between sometime at Goslar (after 6 Oct 1798) but after MS

---

[21] Readings here apparently belonging to *The Farmer*: A/Th/O/In/Tis/A/B; readings apparently belonging to *Poor Susan*: As/The/Poo/In///Tis a/A no/Br.

[22] Possible stubs of *Oak and Broom* 61–64: Di/W/An/W; possible stubs of *Two April Mornings* 21–23: "Yo/B/A; stubs of *Childless Father* 13–20: Now [canceled]/The /Ol/W///Pe/The/B/An.

JJ, and Oct 1800, the latest likely date for any materials in this Nb. Chances are not good, in view of W's work on *LB* 1800, that this copy was made after July 1800; and since the earlier versions among parallel materials in Christabel and 18A (see below) seem to be those of Christabel, and since 18A's *Prel* I probably comes before c 5 June 1800 (see Appendix XII), this MS may also be conjectured to fall before that date. Next stands a rather fair copy of *Excursion* IX.128–40 (see *PW* V, 290, "MS" variants for lines 132–40) and a perhaps closely related passage *PW* V, 344, *ix* (possibly contributive to *Prel* XII.194–201). Following is extensive work toward *Nutting* (discussed in Appendix XI); it probably dates between 14 Dec 1798 and c 5 June 1800. Next come six lines corresponding to PREL 612 lines 17–22, then four stubs which indicate that an early version of PREL 612–14 ("I would not strike a flower") once was copied here. A small amount of messy draft possibly based on Ariosto and a few lines of draft toward *The Danish Boy* (before 15 Oct 1800; see Hale White 25–26; *STCL* I, 637) conclude the book. Any work mentioned in this paragraph for which no other evidence of an earliest possible date exists may be regarded as coming after 6 Oct 1798, when W arrived at Goslar; and no work here can, apparently, be placed after Oct 1800. Other work on much of the composition in this Nb appears also in Nb 18A.

(3) Study of 18A is facilitated by MS notes which Miss Darbishire has left with the MS at Dove Cottage. Inside the front cover of the Nb are entries probably made after 1799: some draft lines on the Pedlar closely related to *Excursion* I c line 406, and pencil drafts, some probably related to *Excursion* I.441–43, and others toward the beginning of *Prel* III; drafts toward *Prel* III are continued inside the rear cover. The Nb proper begins with quotations from Marlowe's *Edward II* and from John Newton's *Authentic Narrative . . . to the Rev. T. Haweis* (1764).[23] Next follows one imperfect Spenserian stanza referring to "Robert" and his aimless wife, which Jonathan Wordsworth has rightly identified to me as surviving lines from W's lost *Somersetshire Tragedy*; in view of the probable dates of the other work in this Nb one is inclined to suspect that the lines were written in here about the time that W was preparing the version of the poem that was copied in the Nb of MSS made up for Poole in 1800 (DCP), although no certain date is possible (see also GCL 72n). Next appears work on several Matthew poems, including *The Two April Mornings*, the rejected elegies quoted *PW* IV, 451–55, "Carved, Matthew, with a Master's Skill" (later contributive to *Address to the Scholars*), *Address to the Scholars*, and *The Fountain*. Then comes a considerably

[23] Professor Havens identified the *Narrative* as W's source for *Prel* VI.160–74, *Prel*₂ VI.142–54 (*ELH* I, 1934, 120–21; see also EdS, *RES* XIX, 1943, 71–72).

corrected copy of *A Character*; comparative readings prove it later than Christabel's last copy but before 15 Oct 1800 (Hale White 25–26; *STCL* I, 637). Stubs follow; poems which can be distinguished as having once stood here include *The Farmer of Tilsbury Vale*, "'Tis Said, That Some Have Died for Love," and *Song for the Wandering Jew*. The date of *The Farmer* has been discussed above. "'Tis Said" and the *Song* were sent off for *LB* 1800 by 13 Aug in a letter postmarked 16 Aug 1800 (see Hale White 11); "'Tis Said," from its contents, is plainly a Grasmere poem, and both it and (in default of other evidence) the *Song* can probably be dated before 13 Aug 1800. Thus *A Character* must have been copied in after the other poems—perhaps, indeed, after they were cut out of the Nb.

Part I of *SP* MS 2 appears next, followed by draft work on a passage corresponding to *Prel* V.370–88 (see PREL 545–46), and "There was a Boy," readings as *Prel* V.389–415 with 18A variants—both passages certainly work of Goslar or after. Then come four stubs revealing, as Miss Darbishire notes, work leading up to the end of *Prel* I, the end itself of *Prel* I, and an abortive beginning for *Prel* II (called "2nd Part"—see PREL xxvii). Next follows Part II of the *SP* MS; its position makes it almost certainly later than the *Prel* work. For reasons outlined in Appendix XII the *Prel* work appears to have been finished between possibly c 14–21 Mar, probably 20 or 21 Apr 1799 and c 5 June 1800, and was probably not begun before early 1799; the *SP* MS was probably also written by c 5 June 1800. EdS's *RC* MS D (see *PW* V, 404) follows next. A "Fragment," drawing on Alfoxden drafts, corresponding to *Prel* II.322–41 with a few additional verses, follows MS D. The lines had probably been used in *Prel* II by c 5 June 1800, and MS D may precede that date. It would hardly date after c July, when W's thoughts were turned to *LB* 1800; nor, probably, would it antedate the *Prel* and *SP* work. Copies such as *SP* and *RC* MS D are, however, more likely to have been made after than before W and DW were settled at Sockburn, after very late Apr 1799. Scattered additional *SP* drafts here and there in the Nb up to this point can also be considered to fall within this period.

A series of fragments follows (several are so called), some partly descriptive of W or the Pedlar (or both), some purely philosophical and meditative: the fragments relating to *RC* are described in the list of Addenda corresponding to the lines omitted from MS D of *RC* (MS B 41–303) on *PW* V, 404–08. The set of lines quoted *PW* V, 405–08, like the shorter corresponding passage in the Alfoxden Nb (see *PW* V, 408n), were probably added to the book around late 1801 or early 1802. The next fragment is *A Night-Piece*; then come four stubs, part of which must have contained "There was a Boy," since the last four lines of the poem appear on the first page following.

Thereupon appear a version of The Discharged Soldier (*Prel* IV.363–502); a fragment corresponding to *Excursion* IX.1–26, 124–52 (see *PW* V, 286–91 and *app crit*; *PW* V, 369); a fragment corresponding to *Excursion* VIII.276–334 (see *PW* V, 274–76 and *app crit*; *PW* V, 369); a fragment containing the skating description, *Prel* I.452–89; a fragment, *Redundance*, quoted *PW* V, 346; a fragment of a few lines corresponding to *Prel* I.565–70; and a fragment, quoted *PW* V, 344–45, eventually contributive to *Prel* XII.194–201. Next is found *Nutting* in the version quoted *PW* II, 504–06, with the last part cut away (see also Appendix XI). After four stubs appears the last stanza of the story of *Andrew Jones*; since the last stanza of the poem as published is not present, this copy probably dates not after 13 Aug 1800 (see Hale White 11). The next verses are "I Love upon a Stormy Night" (*PW* II, 464–65; probably also rejected work for *PB* and to be dated like *PB* or *Andrew Jones*—see *PW* II, 531); next, "I Would Not Strike a Flower" (PREL 612–14; see Appendix XI). A single line closely related to *To M.H.* 23–24 stands at the top of a page preceding a draft toward the *RC* MS D version of *Excursion* I.463–68; the gathering is defective—other verses may have preceded this—but it appears impossible to be certain whether the line precedes or follows the related lines in *To M.H.* itself.[24]

The only works in this Nb that can be regarded as fairly surely later than 15 Sept 1800 are *A Character* (not likely completed before 15 Sept in view of its reference to Jones—see above) and the lines on the Pedlar, *PW* V, 405–07, clearly added to the Nb well after the entries around it (*PW* V, 405). *The Childless Father*, ready for forwarding to the printer by 15 Sept 1800, and *The Danish Boy*, probably completed by 15 Oct 1800 (Hale White 14, 25–26; *STCL* I, 637; see *EL* 225) are the only other poems in either Christabel or 18A with definite terminal dates later than 13 Aug 1800. Therefore, when other evidence of a more specific nature is lacking, the date by which all these works not dated above were written can be taken as late Oct 1800. *A Night-Piece* and *Andrew Jones* (as part of *PB*) seem the only two poems in 18A that look fairly certain to have existed before W's visit to Goslar. Both

[24] Inverting the Nb and reading in from the other end, one finds: a fragmentary quotation from *Address to Silence* (see *PW* II, 532–34); quotations from Massinger and Donne; a note in the hand of MH, "Mary Hutchinson late of Sockburn now of Gallow Hill," probably written in before the end of W's spring 1800 visit to Gallow Hill, c 5 June 1800; some lines of draft for *SP* in the hand of MH. Why the excerpts from *Address to Silence* (in *The Weekly Entertainer* of 6 Mar 1797, which they almost surely read at Racedown) would appear in a Nb otherwise of so much later date is something of a puzzle. Could *The Weekly Entertainer* have been among the "Somersetshire goods" which DW was unpacking on 25 July 1800 (*DWJ* I, 51–52)?

appear (or did appear) among the fragments described above, and of those fragments a number could not have existed before Goslar on account of their origin in W's earliest work on his autobiographical poem. *A Night-Piece* and *Andrew Jones* were almost surely not entered in this Nb before the entries surrounding them here, and none of these materials gives any indication of having been entered earlier than any materials elsewhere in the Nb—that is, than early 1799. This date, when other evidence is wanting, may be taken as the earliest probable date for the materials in this Nb. I am not aware of the basis on which EdS concluded that the Nb was in use by summer 1798 (see *PW* II, 504) or at Alfoxden (*PW* IV, 452).

While no firm conclusions can be reached from the fact, it is worth noting that no short poem of W's in these Nbs can be decisively attributed to his visit at Sockburn (between very late Apr or very early May 1799 and 17 Dec 1799), and no long poems to the period between July and Oct 1800.

APPENDIX X

The Date of The Borderers

W was "ardent" in the composition of [*The Borderers*] on 24 Oct 1796 (*Mem* I, 96). His false starts on a poem of some length—notably *Fragment of a Gothic Tale* and *XVI a, b*—probably since late Mar of the same year (see Appendix XVI) suggest that W could not have evolved his conceptions of the play a great many months before DW's remark of 24 Oct, almost surely not before the latter half of the year. W was "nearly finished" with a first draft probably c but by 25 Feb 1797 (*EL* 161; JRM, "The Date of Composition of *The Borderers*," *MLN* XLIX, 1934, 104–11). The bulk of composition was thus pretty much complete by late Feb, and EdS's MS A, the fragments in which represent two stages of the play's development, may be assumed to date from the same period.

In the 1842 note to *The Borderers* W states that he "at first" wrote the play without view to its exhibition on the stage. Whether the fact that W had still only "nearly finished" his tragedy on 28 May 1797, but now had hopes of Sheridan's seeing it (*EL* 166), points toward a new and shortened version aimed at the stage as the work presently being brought to completion (as suggested Moorman I, 310–11) is uncertain. Whether the play was even finished early in the year is also unclear. STC's remarks of 8 June 1797 (*STCL* I, 325) imply strongly that he has heard a complete work, and "Wordsworth's tragedy" was supposed to be read "under the trees" on [23 July] (*STCL* I, 332). A remark of Lloyd's, probably 15 Sept 1797 (*STCL* I, 345–46), that he has not heard the last two and one-half acts of the play may bear on the problem; one can hardly conclude from his statement that these acts were necessarily incomplete when he heard what he did hear. On the other hand there is Lamb's remark of 6 Aug 1800 (Lamb *Letters* I, 199) that he has "seen so little" of the play—"only what I saw at Stowey" (see 1797:37); but his having seen so little could again be simple accident. DW states on 20 Nov 1797 that W's "play is finished." Her phrasing is suggestive of W's having been lately engaged in work on the drama (although most of W's time after 12 Nov was spent on walking trips). I doubt that W would have made two revisions after the first draft, and suspect that what revision he did make at Alfoxden dates mostly or all from weeks not long before 12 Nov. Further revisions were undoubtedly made in London late in the year, probably sometime between 20 Nov and 8 Dec. The stage revision which was made as the result of a suggestion by [Thomas] Knight (see IF note), can, then, be dated probably between c Sept and 12 Nov 1797 and between 20 Nov and 8 Dec 1797. How long it took W to complete the first version of the play in its entirety—if he ever did—and the time at which he began to give his thoughts to revision are problems which remain unsolved.

The exact relationship of the work just described to MS B is not finally certain either, although it is unlikely that MS B represents a state of the play much different from the latest revised version of 1797. The MS is mostly in the hand of MH, and probably dates from the Sockburn visit of 1799 (*PW* I, 344; see 1799:31) or MH's visit to Grasmere c end of Feb–c 4 Apr 1800; it is not impossible that MH worked on it also during W's visit to her between c 16 May and c 5 June 1800 (see also *EL* 237). W is in any case hardly likely to have worked much on the drama after c July, when he became heavily concerned with *LB* 1800.

W's remarks (IF note) imply that his preface to the play was composed at the same time that he was composing the first draft of the play itself. The MS, a fair copy, is, as EdS states, prefixed to MS B of the play, and clearly contemporary with it.

APPENDIX XI

The Date of Nutting

Nutting MSS are found in *Prel* MS JJ, the Christabel Nb, Nb 18A, a fragment on a loose sheet measuring 22.2 by 13.8 cm. (DCP), and DW's letter to STC of [probably 21 or 28 Dec, possibly 14 Dec 1798] (*EL* 206–08). Where parallel or closely related readings of the poem or its "overflow" exist, the JJ lines precede those of the Christabel Nb, and those of the Christabel Nb precede the more integrated readings of 18A. The copy on the loose leaf contains work later than that of 18A. No sure conclusion seems possible about the chronological relationship of the MS of the letter to other MS work, except that the loose fragment, in the hand of Sara Hutchinson, is most unlikely to have been written during the winter in Germany. One might well guess that the work in JJ (see PREL 641) formed the germ of the poem, and that W's reference there to the "dearest maiden" provided the basis for the conclusion of the work as presently known (the full passage in JJ was used with a variant version of *PW* II, 505, lines 28–33, in Christabel for an unpublished draft of meditative verse). It is fairly certain that the copy of *Nutting* in the letter precedes the introductory work quoted *PW* II, 504–06, from 18A, which in turn carefully organizes draft work in the Christabel MS; the work both in 18A and on the later loose sheet includes an extended beginning for the poem, and DW's copy in the letter is described as the "conclusion of a poem of which the beginning is not written." This copy is plainly unsuitable for the conclusion of a poem corresponding to *Prel*, or even such parts of it as the draft work of JJ, if organized and unified, might represent; the "dearest maiden" of *Nutting* is hardly an appropriate object for the rhetorical tones of most of JJ.

It seems evident, then, that W began very early to consider *Nutting* a work independent from the rest of the "mass" of what he was then writing, although it no doubt had its origin in those autobiographical materials (see MS JJ [PREL 633–42] and *Nutting* IF note). The work copied in 18A (part of the last of it is cut away) and on the loose sheet has the title *Nutting* in both MSS. The work on the loose sheet may be regarded as the latest surviving state of the poem in its long form. (It commences as *PW* II, 504–05, lines 1–5,

331

followed by an eight-line expanded version of lines 15–17 of the same passage, then continuing as those verses, with minor variants, to their conclusion, then as line 3 of the published poem, then as *EL* 206–07, with variants mentioned *PW* II, 506, through line 10.) The loose sheet copy was probably written by c 5 June 1800 (when W set out from Gallow Hill to Grasmere). The MSS offer no grounds for concluding with EdS that the poem was composed in the summer of 1798, or any basis for contradicting W's statement that it was composed in Germany; it is improbable that W would have sent STC a copy of pre-German work, with explanation, during the German winter. *Nutting* as published may, practically speaking, be said (since the copy in the letter includes most of it) to date between W's arrival at Goslar (6 Oct) and the letter to STC.

The object of the full projected poem, as Miss Darbishire remarks, was to state and describe "the spiritual sympathy between man and nature." Drafts in Christabel seem to imply that at one point the materials intended to precede the "conclusion" (the present *Nutting*) were to commence as *PW* II, 504–05, lines 1–24 (with considerable but not fundamental variants); then, line 24 (reading "The driving storm. I would not strike a flower") continuing with certain variants as PREL 612, lines 1–12; then continuing as *PW* II, 505, lines 28–33 (the original surviving draft of which is in MS JJ, PREL 641); then closing as PREL 641 (JJ) "Then dearest maiden . . . idle sympathies." The long passage quoted from 18A on PREL 612–14, "I would not strike a flower," draws on materials in the Christabel drafts just mentioned, which in turn draw on JJ. That passage implies a different conception of the maiden from *PW* II, 504–06, and can definitely be regarded as separate from *Nutting* by this time, and probably intended as an independent poem. It eventually contributed to *Prel* XI.214–21, *Prel$_2$* XII.165–71; it can be dated between early 1799 and late Oct 1800 (see Appendix IX). As EdS remarks, *PW* II, 505, lines 15–19, were finally used in the sequel to *Lycoris* 42–45; *PW* II, 505–06, lines 34–52 (see also PREL 610) were used in *Prel* XI.15–22, *Prel$_2$* XII.24–31.

APPENDIX XII

The Dates of Salisbury Plain *and Some Early Work on* The Prelude

On the early MSS of *SP* see esp. *PW* I, 330–33. It seems possible that something corresponding to the Female Vagrant's story was composed by sometime in 1791 (see *G & S* IF note and *EL* 270); but nothing is known of this early stage, if it did indeed exist. The earliest surviving part of the story is embodied in *SP*. W indicates that he began the latter work on his "lonesome journey" from Salisbury Plain to northern Wales in the summer of 1793 (see *Prel* XII.357–59, *Prel₂* XIII.352–54), perhaps before leaving Salisbury Plain itself. He had probably composed something corresponding to or identical with *SP* MS I by the end of that summer (*EL* 117); and MS I was copied into the Windy Brow Nb by DW in the spring of 1794. When W considered the poem "ready for the press" on 23 May 1794 (*EL* 117; see also *EL* 128), MS I was probably complete.

Some drafts, at least, in the Windy Brow Nb were very likely written at the time of W's extensive revision of *SP* in the autumn of 1795 at Racedown, when, as his comments to Wrangham of 20 Nov show, he must have added much or all of the character and story of the sailor (*EL* 145). (At least one stub at the beginning of the Racedown Nb contains brief prose notes toward a version of the story in which the traveler has been changed to a sailor, and in which the woman still tells a story.) Had he removed the story of the Female Vagrant now, however, he could hardly have referred to the poem as the same he had read Wrangham in London, and it seems certain that the work of which he planned on or after 7 Jan 1796 to send Cottle the MS "in a few days" included the stories both of the Female Vagrant and the sailor. W finally sent the MS to Cottle with Aza Pinney in early Mar 1796, and probably did not get it back before visiting London, sometime between 1 June and 9 July. EdS, in concluding that MS 2 represents *SP* as it stood at this time, is, in view of the emotional and political attitudes expressed here, and the relatively crude presentation of character, very probably right insofar as the MS itself is concerned. His assumption that the story of the woman, which MS 2 introduces but does not include, would have been, if included, that of the Female Vagrant, seems open to some question. The state of the poem between Jan 1796 and 1799 must, I think, be regarded as something of a puzzle: There cannot be much doubt that the fragments edited by EdS as *XVI* among W's Juvenilia were designed as part of a narrative which would have included a tale similar to that of the Female Vagrant (see *PW* I, 370). As indicated in Appendix XVI these fragments probably date sometime about mid-1796 (and see Landon *BNYPL*). W later remembered that he wished to improve on the mariner's story before publishing (*G & S* IF note). The *XVI* fragments look much (although the first especially is not long enough for absolute certainty) like false starts toward a rewriting, in a new verse form, of the Female Vagrant's story apart from the context of *SP*. W's troubles with *SP* during the next few years appear to have stemmed from his inability to draw the poem into final state from this point.

It would be difficult to guess his thinking in the matter between 1796 and early 1799, when he resolved to "invent a new story for the woman." His use of the name "Robert Walford," which he mentions at the same time (*EL* 222–23), must have occurred after the beginning of his acquaintance with Poole (see 1797:17; 1797:19), but the fact tells nothing of whether the Old Soldier himself was introduced before this time (it does not even make certain that the Old Soldier was Robert Walford—see *PW* I, 332–33). Likewise unclear is whether W continued through these years to assume the exclusion of the Female Vagrant or whether he was ever in fact resolved to eliminate any and all stories for the "woman." The *FV* was, of course, published separately in *LB*. The "Tale of a Woman" offered Cottle c 13 Mar 1798 (*STCL* I, 400) along with *SP* was probably, as Moorman suggests (I, 371), *RC*, not *FV*: it is likely that he would offer Cottle in a formal proposal of this kind something that he considered a fully integrated and independent poem; *RC* then fitted such a description, while the *FV*, even when published, retained the appearance of a makeshift, without graceful introduction or conclusion. W's phrasing in his letter to STC in early 1799 could be read as an implication that he had meant to keep the Female Vagrant in the poem. Certainly at the time he wrote MS 2 of *SP* he did not intend, as the MS shows, that the woman go without *some* story. Does MS 2, then, date before or after W's letter of 27 Feb 1799, when he expressed an intention of inventing a new tale for her?

The answer to this question requires investigation of a yet more important subject, the date of some early work on *Prel* which is present in the same Nb (18A) as *SP* MS 2. Working partly with evidence from stubs, Miss

Darbishire has been able to determine that work on the end of *Prel* I and a brief start—surely the first draft, headed "2nd Part"—on Book II were written consecutively into this Nb. The "2nd Part," speaking of the "small green island" where the poet rested (from the poem to his friend), in need of the encouragement of STC's "cheering voice" before continuing (see PREL 42, *app crit*), stood between the two parts of DW's copy of the *SP* MS (see also Appendix IX). The *SP* copy was plainly completed after the entry of the *Prel* work; the latter plainly postdates the conception and early stages of execution of a poem, in parts, to STC. W had not worked out anything like a First Part of *Prel* before he had resided in Goslar for some time (see PREL xxvi). As he heard not infrequently from STC by letter during that time, his reference to the stimulus of STC's "voice" at the start of the Second Part must refer to personal contact after long separation or correspondence after a long lapse, and not after such expected delays as the miserable German postal service would have produced between Nov 1798 and Feb 1799. Thus, while there is a remote chance that the silence was one terminated by the letters of STC which W received on 27 Feb 1799, it is not at all probable that this event took place before W and STC met in Göttingen, possibly in mid-Mar, not certainly until 20 or 21 Apr. The actual idea of addressing STC, however, while possibly occurring to W c early 1799, was more likely not evolved until after the April visit in Göttingen: W would hardly have kept quiet about his decision had it been reached earlier, and STC's manner of speaking on the subject 12 Oct 1799 (*STCL* I, 538) seems to me to imply that he had not known the news for any great length of time. The encouragement of STC's cheering voice may have been attendant on a resumption of correspondence after STC's return from Germany.

The "2nd Part" of *Prel* in 18A, then, can in any case be regarded as after possibly c 14–21 Mar, probably 20 or 21 Apr, 1799. The First Part probably did not long precede the "2nd." The second part of *SP* MS 2 must, then, also date after this time; and both parts (along with the stanzas quoted *PW* I, 337, 341) can probably be supposed to have been copied in not earlier than the commencement of the visit to Sockburn in very late Apr or early May 1799 (there is no appearance of delay between the copying of the two parts). Unless the brief drafts concerning the old soldier represent part of what was accomplished in W's "two days" of work on the poem at Goslar (*EL* 222–23), none of that work has survived at all (cf *PW* I, 330–41).

Only a tiny amount of work in Nb 18A appears to date after late Oct 1800 (see Appendix IX). The abortive beginning of *Prel* II pretty certainly dates before c 5 June 1800 (when W set out for Grasmere after seeing MH for the last time before late Oct), by which time the Second Book had reached an early finished state (see PREL xxviii–ix; Appendix XV); the spring visit to Gallow Hill probably represents the last occasion MH had to copy *Prel* MS U. (*Prel* MS RV and the contents, if not necessarily DW's writing out, of V can be taken as preceding this date also—see PREL xxviii–ix.) Since many corrections to *SP* are also in the hand of MH, and the *SP* copy would not date after c July 1800 anyhow (when W became heavily concerned with *LB* 1800), MS 2 of *SP* can reasonably be supposed to date before c 5 June 1800. It seems unlikely that W engaged in further efforts on *SP* after this time, aside from *FV* (see *EL* 270–72), until working up *G & S* for its 1842 publication.

APPENDIX XIII

The Date of The Ruined Cottage

Early MSS of *RC* appear in the Racedown Nb, Verse 32 (MS A), the letter of STC to Estlin of [10 June] 1797 (*STCL* I, 327–28), the Alfoxden Nb, Christabel Nb, Nb 18A, *RC* MS B, and DW's letter of 5, [6] Mar 1798. It can be regarded as certain that the story of Margaret postdates *XVI a, b* and the Baker's Cart fragment on the recto of Verse 31 (*PW* I, 315–16), both of which deal with poor women: the nameless woman and five children of Verse 31 could hardly have been created after W had started the story of Margaret and her two children. *XVI a, b* (from mid-1796)—perhaps abortive efforts at a recasting of the story of the Female Vagrant—are apparently designed as works of social protest, with no psychological analysis of the person telling the story. Social protest is an obvious purpose of the Baker's Cart fragment as well, but W is also as clearly interested in the woman's "sick and extravagant mind" and her rebellious heart which "fashions the laws of nature" to its "own will." She is both a victim of an imperfect social order and also a near mental relative of the misanthrope of the yew-tree (about whom W probably wrote in early 1797) or the speaker of *Incipient Madness*. The fragment appears to occupy a place transitional between the XVI fragments and *RC*. *RC* not only omits any strong note of direct social purpose, but displays distinct advances over the Baker's Cart fragment in conception of character and subtlety of psychology.

W would not have engaged in extended work on anything like the *RC* during the time he was most busy on the first draft of *The Borderers*, in late 1796 and very early 1797. On the other hand, I feel fairly certain that when DW refers to W's "new poem," the *RC*, as having been read to STC in early June 1797, she means a real new poem—that is, something reasonably complete and unified, and largely done recently. And while Lamb's recollection of "Margaret's story" in Aug 1814 (Lamb *Letters* II, 126–27) is an old memory, probably from 7–14 July 1797, it is unlikely that Lamb would have remembered the "story" so definitely had W read him only a few lines and simply outlined the rest. Lamb's visit was, however, a month after DW's letter, and W might have worked extensively on the poem in the meantime.

337

W later stated (*Excursion* IF note) that lines 871–916 were the first part written of the poem (although his date of Racedown, 1795, has often been noted as impossible—see, for example, G. W. Meyer, *Wordsworth's Formative Years*, Ann Arbor, 1943, 221; T. M. Raysor, "Wordsworth's Early Drafts of *The Ruined Cottage* in 1797–98," *JEGP* LV, 1956, 1–7); lines 880–916 were quoted to Estlin on 10 June 1797. W would not have written these closing lines without a clear conception of the progress of the heroine's story (so that these lines probably date after the Baker's Cart); and stubs in the Racedown Nb make it plain that some early copy of the closing lines was there, along with some later (from its position surrounding the stubs) work on Margaret's discovery of the gold. No entries in the Racedown Nb are known to—or seem likely to—date after MH's departure from Racedown on 4 June. This indication of work on Margaret's story before MH's departure is not contradicted by anything in DW's letter to MH of Mar 1798. For DW to say at the start of her letter that "the Pedlar's character now makes a very, certainly the *most* considerable part of the poem" plainly implies, in fact, that MH has known of the presence of such a figure in the poem previously; and such knowledge would indicate that she knew more of the poem than just the closing lines. I should think that the "new poem" STC heard must have included the essentials of Margaret's story and almost as certainly the Pedlar as narrator.

The description of the decline of the prosperity of Margaret's family followed by the decay of her husband (Verse 32) and of Margaret's discovery of the gold left by her husband upon his desertion (Racedown Nb) concern events so fundamental that the MSS containing such work almost surely date before the completion of the story of Margaret that STC heard. It appears safe to say that W was too greatly occupied with *The Borderers* until about Mar 1797 (see Appendix X) to work much on *RC*. I should thus date Verse 32 and the Racedown Nb fragments probably between c Mar and 4–7 June 1797. Raysor's argument in *JEGP* (cited above) that *Incipient Madness* was developed *from* Verse 32 appears to be confirmed by MS evidence, although *Incipient Madness* is plainly, in itself, poetry much inferior to *RC*. The two MSS must be regarded as dating from about the same time (see also Appendix XVII). The Baker's Cart, as verse transitional between *XVI* (mid-1796) and work of the first half of 1797, including *RC*,I should give a very general date of perhaps late 1796, more certainly between the latter half of 1796 and c Mar 1797. Out of deference to W (and since no evidence contradicts the assumption) I should date the closing lines of *RC* (*Excursion* I, 871–916) first among composition on the poem in anything like its present form: a fair estimate is probably c Mar–Apr 1797.

Appendix XIII

Descriptions and reasons for the dating of the RC work in the Alfoxden Nb, Christabel Nb, and Nb 18A are given in Appendix IX. No direct indication exists that W engaged in any extensive work on RC between mid-1797 and early 1798, although more work is possible between the time that STC first heard the poem and Lamb's visit, or even later. Comparative readings show that RC work in both the Alfoxden and Christabel Nbs must precede MS B, and that MS B precedes DW's letter of 5, [6] Mar, MS B$_2$. No surviving work in the Alfoxden Nb appears to precede 25 Jan 1798; thus the materials in that Nb and MS B can be dated between 25 Jan and 5 Mar 1798. The "Addendum" to B (*PW* V, 400–04) contains the lines which W later indicated were written next after the passages describing Margaret in her affliction, corresponding to *Excursion* IV.958–68, 1207–75; since STC quotes from "Addendum" c 10 Mar 1798 (*STCL* I, 397–98), the passage can be given the date of MS B as a whole or, more probably, shortly after, esp. 6 Mar–c 10 Mar, inasmuch as DW's letter gives no sign that lines like the "Addendum" were intended to conclude the poem. Work in the Christabel Nb very likely precedes that in Alfoxden; it possibly dates from as early as between c Mar and early summer 1797; it was more probably written in early 1798, and was certainly in existence by then (see Appendix IX). In general it appears that W worked with great energy on the RC between Jan and c 10 Mar 1798, and his letters confirm that much work— in particular on *The Recluse*, to which he must now have regarded the RC as belonging—was just what he had been doing.

APPENDIX XIV

The Date of Juvenal

W and Wrangham very likely worked out an imitation of a large part of Juvenal VIII.1–86 while W was in London in 1795. These lines are never dealt with or mentioned in W's and Wrangham's correspondence on the poem (and see *EL* 143). An adaptation of lines 85–86 (*Juvenal* 163–73) appears in the Racedown Nb, evidently entered about the same time as the other Juvenal work in that Nb—and thus, as will be seen, it is probably after 7 Mar 1796; the lines could be a copy of, or further work on, a passage composed in London or elsewhere. No lines parallel to Juvenal VIII.1–84 have, however, survived.

W composed an "extremely periphrastic" imitation (which also has not survived) of Juvenal VIII.87–124 soon after leaving Wrangham—probably in Bristol; and *Juvenal* 1–28, which have no parallel in Juvenal VIII, pretty surely were done in Bristol, as Southey contributed to them (lines 9–10) (*EL* 143–45; see 1795:25). W was heavily concerned with *SP* right after coming to Racedown on 26 Sept 1795 (*EL* 145); and there is no evidence, and no reason to suppose, that W did any work on *Juvenal* between his departure from Bristol and 7 Mar 1796. His comments of that day imply that he has not worked on the poem for a long time. On that day he "sketched out ideas to run parallel" with VIII.231–75 (the end), and announced his intention to turn them into verse at once (*EL* 153). I suspect that W produced in the near future most or all of his subsequent work on the poem. He had not done lines 235–53 by c 25 Feb 1797, despite his "sketch" of ideas, and had "lost or mislaid" his Juvenal by then, evidently not within the last few days (*EL* 160–61); so that his verses imitating VIII.163–230, 254–75 (*Juvenal* 29–162) were not written immediately before c 25 Feb 1797. His interest in the poem was plainly low at this point (see *EL* 162); and he had been hard at work recently on *The Borderers*. These facts added to W's statement (*EL* 153) that he means to bring the scheme to a speedy conclusion suggest that the verses parallel to VIII.254–75 should be dated shortly after 7 Mar 1796. Drafts for this material appear in the Racedown Nb, along with drafts for virtually all the lines parallel to VIII.163–230 (and, as remarked above, VIII.

85–86); all these drafts are grouped rather closely together in the Nb, and were surely done about the same time. W informs Mathews on 21 Mar 1796 that he is presently only attempting satires. His opinion of the value of this work is indicated by a remark elsewhere in the same letter—"As to writing, it is out of the question"—a poor augury for long-continued application to *Juvenal* should he feel himself able to write more satisfying types of verse. A date of 7 Mar–Apr 1796 would probably include virtually all W's work on *Juvenal* 29–162. The consecutive, still mostly fair, copy of *Juvenal* 29–136 in Verse 4 (part of a page cut out doubtless contained lines beyond 136) could date any time between 7 Mar 1796 and c 25 Feb 1797; it is reasonable to assume that it was entered not long before—perhaps in preparation for— the c 25 Feb letter to Wrangham.

No lines by W parallel to Juvenal VIII.125–62, the only portion of VIII not hitherto mentioned, are known to have survived. W's intended part in the plan had perhaps been completed by c 25 Feb 1797 (see *EL* 162). In any event, he seems certain to have done no more work on it after that time.

APPENDIX XV

The Dates of The Old Cumberland Beggar *and* Old Man Travelling

On the MSS of *OCB* and *OMT* see *PW* IV, 446, 448 (EdS's MS 1 of *OCB* and his "Dove Cottage" MS of *OMT* evidently both refer to MS Verse 44). The Pierpont Morgan sheet is the first surviving MS from which anything can be told of the progress of the poem. It shows a poem intended simply as the description of a beggar. It corresponds closely to *OCB* 44–66 (55–66 were worked out only after a number of attempts). All but a few words of what became *OMT* appear after what corresponds to *OCB* 66 (work parallel to *OMT* 3–5, 8–12); in the margin appear lines parallel to *OMT* 3–13. Thus W's description of *OMT* as "an overflowing" from *OCB* is quite accurate, if the name *OCB* can be applied to what was then only a descriptive poem. *OMT* with its additional title *Animal Tranquillity and Decay* appears in Verse 44, which was originally part of the same Nb as the Pierpont Morgan sheet, and the MS was probably copied in about the same time. As remarked in Appendix XVII, both the *Description of a Beggar* and *OMT* can be dated between the latter half of 1796 and early June 1797 inclusive.

Surviving work on *OCB* in the Alfoxden Nb shows that the full conception of the *OCB*, as an overtly exhortatory poem much in its present form, had been evolved by the time of these entries, which fall in the Nb between work on *A Night-Piece* (including a stub of closely written work on that poem) and work on *RC* which, by corrections to the form of the same lines in the letter of 5, [6] Mar 1798, can reasonably be dated before that time. Thus the *OCB* itself can best be dated between 25 Jan and 5 Mar 1798. (All dated editions of the poem within W's life describe it as work of 1798.)

Work on the poem in the Christabel Nb, where comparisons between the Alfoxden Nb and the Christabel are indicative (these include materials not used in the published poem), show that the Christabel version is the later, but how much so is uncertain. Stubs show that the Christabel Nb also contained what was apparently a fair copy of the work at least through line

109, possibly much further. Draft work for later portions survives in both the Alfoxden and Christabel Nbs; in the latter several final readings are developed. The stubs of the Christabel Nb show that its version was earlier than the other surviving MS of *OCB*, that in the Nb containing *Prel* MS U. It there follows directly upon MSS written by MH, and probably falls between the Sockburn visit (beginning very late Apr or early May 1799) and 10 Oct 1800 (see PREL xxviii). The final reading of the poem cannot be dated definitely at any particular time before 10 Oct 1800 (see *DWJ* I, 65; *EL* 259), although it must come after the MS in the *Prel* MS U Nb.

APPENDIX XVI

The Dates of Several Minor or Incomplete Poems of the Racedown Period

The similar autograph and manner of entry into Nb Verse 4 of the MSS of *Gothic Tale*, *The Convict*, and *XVI a, b* strongly suggest that all this work was written in the Nb about the same time. Landon *BNYPL* convincingly establishes a date of 1796 for *XVI a, b*. *The Convict* (on this MS see Woof *SB* 160–64) can probably not be dated before W's long visit in London of 1795, when W was in close and frequent contact with Godwin, whose sentiments are so richly reflected in the poem. W's *The Borderers* plainly draws on *Gothic Tale*, but greatly complicates its moral and psychological explorations, and almost certainly represents work of a later date. Since W was "ardent" in the composition of his play on 24 Oct 1796 (*Mem* I, 96), *Gothic Tale* probably was set aside before that date. On the other hand, W evidently engaged in little serious composition between his efforts on *SP* in autumn and perhaps early winter 1795 and late Mar 1796 (see *EL* 145, 149, 153, 155), and hitherto undated work, especially on nonsatiric poems clearly intended to have been of some length, like *XVI* or *Gothic Tale*, is probably more safely dated after than before 21 Mar 1796, when W was complaining that "writing" was "out of the question."

In his 21 Mar letter W asks Mathews to have his books at Montagu's, including Gilpin's [*Observations . . . Highlands of Scotland*] and [*Observations . . . Cumberland and Westmorland*], nailed up in a box, and it is possible that Mathews sent them on to W. In "The Genesis of *The Borderers*," *PMLA* XLIX (1934), 922–30, J. H. Smith makes a persuasive argument for W's indebtedness to Gilpin's *Observations* in the play. Several of the gothic analogies drawn by Smith between Gilpin and *The Borderers*, especially concerning the castle scene of Act II—which is certainly indebted to *Gothic Tale*—apply also to the poem. If the books were in fact not sent on (see *EL* 198), W, as remarked by Woof, could have looked at them during his June–early July visit to London. A chance remains that W's memory supplied all the Gilpin echoes in both the poem and the play, but the circumstances cited can be regarded as offering at least possible further evidence of a date after 21 Mar for *Gothic Tale*.

As already remarked, *The Convict* and *XVI a, b* appear to have been entered in Verse 4 about the same time as *Gothic Tale*. Since *XVI* also represents the beginning of a poem of some length, one may conclude that it too was quite possibly begun after 21 Mar 1796 and probably abandoned before *The Borderers* was under way. I would give it the same date as *Gothic Tale*, except that there is a somewhat greater chance that it was begun before late May, since it does not seem at all likely to have depended upon W's London books. The same qualification would apply also to *The Convict*, and an additional one, that the date before which work on this shorter poem ceased must be regarded as less certain.

Two other poems in Verse 4 have been dated by Miss Landon. Drafts for *Address to the Ocean* probably represent work of after mid-Apr 1796, when W appears to have received STC's *Poems on Various Subjects* (see *STCL* I, 203–04), with *The Complaint of Ninathoma*, the source of the first line of W's poem. W's verses were published 21 Nov (JRM *RES*). Landon *BNYPL* points out that "The Hour Bell Sounds," in fair copy in Verse 4, is based closely on a poem in Helen Maria Williams' *Letters Containing a Sketch of the Politics of France*, 1795. Aza P wrote W on 26 Nov 1795 that he was to bring "Miss Williams Letters" with him when he came to Racedown (PP)—and he arrived, evidently, only on 2 Jan 1796. Miss Landon observes that earlier editions of other H. M. Williams *Letters* might possibly have been Pinney's referent, but that the rhyme pattern and mood of W's poem closely resemble those of the *Address to the Ocean*. One may reasonably assume that "The Hour Bell" belongs to 1796.

APPENDIX XVII

A Dismantled Early Notebook

Comparison and fitting together of the sheets containing MSS Verse 31, 32, 44, and 46, and use of photographs and information kindly sent by Herbert Cahoon concerning the *OCB* MS sheet owned by the Pierpont Morgan Library, have shown, especially by size, tears, and stains, that all belonged originally to a single gathering, or notebook.[25] All have the watermark W ELGAR 1795 or a crown over a shield containing a fleur-de-lys. Leaving aside a translation from Ariosto and work on *The Cuckoo and the Nightingale*, *The Prioress's Tale*, and *The Manciple's Tale*, which are of later date, the materials on these sheets are written mostly in narrow columns and in rather similar autograph as compared to random examples of W's hand. They are probably all of about the same general date. The style and ironic tone of *Argument for Suicide* (Verse 44) probably indicate, as EdS remarks, that this fragment bears a close relationship to *The Borderers*. The dates of most of the rest of this work depend on what can be gathered about the chronology of the *RC*, particularly Verse 32, MS A. Appendix XIII suggests that Verse 32 is likely to date between c Mar and 4–7 June 1797, and *Incipient Madness* (Verse 31) probably from about the same time. The Baker's Cart fragment (also Verse 31), as noted in the same appendix, precedes Verse 32, although not immediately, and can be dated between the latter half, probably late, 1796 and c Mar 1797. *Argument for Suicide* may reasonably be given a date loosely contemporary with main composition of *The Borderers*, between the latter half, probably late, 1796 and early 1797. A date as late as summer is not impossible, but the period between the latter half of 1796 and the early June 1797 reading of *The Borderers* to STC may be taken as a reasonable date for the other materials in the Nb, namely the *Description of a Beggar* and the "Yet Once Again" fragment (referring to the Derwent; see *PW* V, 340) on the Pierpont Morgan sheet, and *OMT* (Verse 44), which developed out of the *Description of a Beggar*.

[25] I am further indebted to Dr. John Finch for confirming and expanding my information on this subject.

Index to Writings

Abbreviations:

c composition or writing
p publication
r review
e events, persons, or circumstances prompting or referred to in the work

Subject Index